Kill All the Lawyers?

SHAKESPEARE'S LEGAL APPEAL

Daniel J. Kornstein

UNIVERSITY OF NEBRASKA PRESS

LINCOLN AND LONDON

© 1994 by Princeton University Press
All rights reserved
Manufactured in the United States of America

∞

First Nebraska paperback printing: 2005

Library of Congress Cataloging-in-Publication Data
Kornstein, Daniel.
Kill all the lawyers?: Shakespeare's legal appeal / Daniel Kornstein.
p. cm.
Originally published: Princeton, N.J.: Princeton University Press, c1994.
Includes bibliographical references and index.
ISBN 978-0-8032-7821-9
1. Shakespeare, William, 1564–1616—Knowledge—Law. 2. Law—Great
Britain—History—16th century. 3. Law—Great Britain—History—17th
century. 4. Law and literature—History—16th century. 5. Law and litera-
ture—History—17th century. 6. Lawyers in literature. 7. Law in literature.
I. Title.
PR3028.K67 2005
822.3'3—dc22 2004025305

For my mother

                              Nay, mother,
Where is your ancient courage? You were used
To say extremities was the trier of spirits,
That common chances common men could bear,
That when the sea was calm all boats alike
Showed mastership in floating; fortune's blows
When most struck home, being gentle wounded craves
A noble cunning. You were used to load me
With precepts that would make me invincible
The heart that conned them.

                    —*Coriolanus*, 4.1.2–11

Why might not that be
the skull of a lawyer?

—*Hamlet*, 5.1.95–96

CONTENTS

Prologue   xi

CHAPTER ONE
Shakespeare and the Law   3

CHAPTER TWO
The First Thing We Do
  Henry VI, Part 2   22

CHAPTER THREE
A Scarecrow of the Law
  Measure for Measure   35

CHAPTER FOUR
Fie upon Your Law!
  The Merchant of Venice   65

CHAPTER FIVE
Skull of a Lawyer
  Hamlet   90

CHAPTER SIX
Liberty! Freedom! Tyranny Is Dead!
  Julius Caesar   107

CHAPTER SEVEN
The Lunatic, the Lover, the Poet—and the Lawyer?
  A Midsummer Night's Dream   125

CHAPTER EIGHT
Old Father Antic the Law
  Henry IV, Parts 1 and 2   135

CHAPTER NINE
Final Verdict on *Richard III*   143

CHAPTER TEN
Much Ado about Slander
  Othello and *Much Ado about Nothing*   156

CHAPTER ELEVEN
A Just and Open Trial?
   The Winter's Tale   176

CHAPTER TWELVE
To Break Our Country's Laws
   Richard II   193

CHAPTER THIRTEEN
Breath of an Unfee'd Lawyer
   King Lear   210

CHAPTER FOURTEEN
Shakespeare the Scrivener?   227

EPILOGUE
Unacknowledged Lawgiver   239

Notes   247

Works Cited   259

Index   265

PROLOGUE

WHEN THE TIME comes to talk about the glories of our era, surely someone will say a few kind words about free Shakespeare in New York's Central Park. Each summer I marvel at the New York Shakespeare Festival, brainchild of the late Joseph Papp. A producer and director with a mission, Papp loved Shakespeare and brought the Bard's plays to the people, for whom they were intended. He believed in Shakespeare for a mass urban audience. He helped keep Shakespeare alive.

Shakespeare is always a treat; Shakespeare under the stars in Central Park, a special one. At the outdoor Delacorte Theater next to a lake in the park, with little Belvedere Castle as a backdrop, accomplished actors tread the boards in a scene that often looks eerily like one in the shadows of Hamlet's Elsinore or any of several other royal castles found in Shakespeare. Even the weather can add special effects: wind, lightning, thunder, or drizzle (not dreaded rain) can, at the right moment, almost seem as if they were called up at the director's command.

I remember seeing my first Shakespeare play in Central Park in 1963, in between my junior and senior years of high school, and ever since have looked forward to summer in New York with special anticipation. Summer in New York without Shakespeare in the park is like winter in Vermont without snow on the ski slopes.

With so much excellent Shakespeare available, it has over the years been easy to see the plays and to think about how they bear on lawyering, for lawyering is what I have chosen to do with my life. I am a full-time, practicing, shirtsleeve lawyer in a small Manhattan firm that concentrates on litigation. During the summer of 1985, the New York Shakespeare Festival production of *Measure for Measure* was a reward—a short respite—for a tired and frazzled attorney trying to relax after a week of writing legal briefs and preparing cases for trial. It turned out to be one of those experiences in the realm of art that remain forever associated in my mind with the time and place where I thought the art was first fully revealed to me.

Viewing the play that night changed my ideas about Shakespeare. I had spent the day rereading the play and remembering the fine performance of it I had seen in Central Park in 1966, but none of that fully prepared me for my reaction that night. Sitting in the Delacorte Theater, I watched the actors, heard them speak their lines, and rather than being relaxed (or perhaps because I was so relaxed), felt myself tensing with excitement as the large number of legal issues in *Measure for Measure* began to strike me for the first time. I was stunned, surprised, and amazed at how many basic problems that still face judges and lawyers and everyone else were raised four centuries ago by the play. From that 1985 performance of *Measure for Measure*, which took on some aspects of an epiphany for me, I date my concern with Shakespeare and the law.

I do not know why it had taken me so long (I was thirty-seven years old, and had been practicing law for twelve years) to realize this connection, and I cannot really explain why I had failed to see what to others may seem obvious. Of course, to borrow from our subject, "The fault, dear Brutus, is not in our stars, / But in ourselves" (*Julius Caesar*, 1.2.141–42). Or as Dr. Johnson once said, "Ignorance, madam, pure ignorance."

Later experience may augment my knowledge, alter my perspective, and deepen my understanding, but it can never quite eradicate the impression made on me by the quality of that initial encounter. At that moment, something central to the spirit of Shakespeare was revealed. Thereafter, all the plays seemed to carry the spirit of that revelation. To try to understand that revelation, I started to write about Shakespeare and the law—first some short, exploratory essays for the *New York Law Journal*, and then this book. I have found that I often do not know what I really think about something until I attempt to write about it, that writing brings clarity and precision to thought.

As I reread more of the plays, and read some for the first time, I found that *Measure for Measure* was no anomaly in its use of legal themes. Shakespeare's plays, I naively thought I was discovering for the first time, constantly refer to the law. Some of them, like *The Merchant of Venice* and *Measure for Measure*, have their basic action turn on the outcome of a legal proceeding. Two-thirds (that is, more than twenty) of Shakespeare's plays have trial scenes, which vary from posing serious problems of justice and mercy to mere burlesque. Several other plays have many comments on the problems of law, lawyers, revenge, equity, government, the nature of the state, the nature and transfer of power, inheritance, and contracts.

Taken together, the plays reflect much knowledge of legal intricacies. Legal themes of one kind or another run throughout. And woven all through, like barbed wire sewn into a tapestry, are deftly cutting observations about law and lawyers, each glinting shard designed to draw just a little blood from the legal profession. Even where there are no legal terms and allusions, the plays have a style of philosophical debate and discourse aimed at lawyers. Law is essential to our understanding and interpretation of Shakespeare's works: great art is often inspired by a passion for justice.

So pervasive and varied is the use of law in Shakespeare that one could well employ the plays' texts to teach law. William Carlos Williams once wrote that "Shakespeare is the greatest university of them all." We could paraphrase that to read, "Shakespeare is the greatest law school of them all."

The number and intricacies of the legal references in Shakespeare have led to much speculation. Some commentators have thought the legal knowledge too detailed for anyone without formal legal training or experience. Thus was born the notion that lawyer Francis Bacon or some other attorney was the true author of the plays. Others, unwilling to concede that someone besides Shakespeare of Stratford was the author, have gone so far as to argue that Shakespeare must have acquired his impressive legal knowledge by working as a lawyer's clerk between 1585 and 1595, a decade for which almost nothing is known of Shakespeare's life. To still other critics (including me), these speculations seem idle or even farfetched, mainly because they ignore the possibility of acquiring legal knowledge by common reading, conversation, and life experience in legal London.

Weighing the speculations and debates of the commentators, and evaluating the evidence myself, I end up with a reasonable explanation of why there is so much law in Shakespeare. Shakespeare's environment—litigious London, the Inns of Court (small residential teaching communities of lawyers and law students), audiences full of lawyers and young law students—combined with legal disputes in Shakespeare's personal life to produce the Bard's abiding concern with the law. Faced with such evidence, I do not stretch the plays to find in them important legal themes. To do otherwise would be to ignore the clear and convincing evidence.

By stressing these legal themes, I hope I—as a lawyer—am not simply projecting or adopting a strained, partial, single-minded interpretation. To be sure, it is a common observation that whoever writes about Shakespeare no doubt writes about him or herself. Lawyers, Marxists, Freudians, feminists, and others often yield to the temptation to put the role of their special interest above all else, and end up sifting through Shakespeare's plays in search of echoes of their own preoccupation. In the process, such readers often ignore a great deal of contrary evidence supporting a different notion of Shakespeare. They make the mistake of seeing both in the plays and in Shakespeare's own attitudes only those elements that accord with their wishes.

Aware of that mistake, I have tried to avoid it. Yet even as we try to avoid personal projection, we strive to understand a work of art in light of our personal experience. At least one element in a literary judgment is the capacity of a text to reward sustained meditation and analysis. I find some considerations striking me more than others, if only because in phrasing them I begin to tap emotional and professional concerns within myself.

I practice law as a profession but when it comes to Shakespeare I am only an amateur. The Bard, however, belongs most of all to the educated amateur, and we need more amateurs. Richard Posner, an eminent federal appeals judge interested in law and literature, goes too far when he writes, "The biggest danger in any interdisciplinary field is amateurism. . . . The danger is particularly acute in the case of the lawyer who writes about literature."[1]

Culture has been delegated too much to the experts. It is no longer the property of whoever wants to partake of it for the good of his or her soul. The good things are no longer valuable for their direct effect on the head—and heart. Amateurism is about enthusiasm. It may even be about love.

As a lawyer, what I read I filter through my training, experience, and knowledge of the law. Surely a lawyer might have something useful to say about legal themes in Shakespeare. Just as the Reformation showed that ordinary people can interpret the Bible without expert intermediaries, so too can each of us read and interpret Shakespeare for ourselves. As A. C. Bradley, the renowned turn-of-the-century Shakespearean critic, wisely wrote, "Close familiarity with the plays, that native strength of perception, and that habit of reading with an eager mind . . . make many an unscholarly lover of Shakespeare a far better critic than many a Shakespeare scholar."[2] The result may be a spontaneous reaction, unburdened by too much academic tradition or learning, at the same time without, as controversial physicist Richard Feynman used to do, entirely ignoring the relevant literature so as to be "anti-intellectual" or "anti-culture." A lawyer can perhaps draw new connections, and open new perspectives, not only on the plays, but also on notions of law.

Reading is not enough, however. Obviously, Shakespeare is often a reading experience, allowing the imaginative reader to judge the potential of the drama. But Shakespearean drama, no matter how firmly rooted in the written word, is also something that must be seen in the theater. Plays are best grasped not by reading alone but by reading and viewing. Stage directions, scene settings, actors' gestures, intonations, and inflections all affect our reaction to Shakespeare's plays. They must be seen to be fully understood and experienced, else why use the dramatic medium?[3] We need to feel the power of the theatrical moment in our professional lives.

Mulling over the tension between the "stage-centered" and "text-centered" interpretation of Shakespeare, I thought about how to awaken interest in Shakespeare as I researched this book at the Folger Shakespeare Library in Washington, D.C., the shrine for Shakespeare studies in this country. The Folger is a depository of Shakespeare materials, with a main reading room lined with dark wood bookshelves, stained-glass windows, Renaissance tapestries, and portraits and a bust of Shakespeare. Working in such a Shakespeare atmosphere is inspiring—if not a little intimidating. On leaving the reading room one day, I browsed around the Folger's gift shop and saw for sale, in the lobby of the American Shakespeare temple, a new series of comic books based on Shakespeare's plays. Similarly, in November 1992, a series of thirty-minute cartoons called "Shakespeare, the Animated Tales" was broadcast on American television. Lucky is the child who gets such a lively comic book introduction to enjoying Shakespeare.

Even the geographic location of the Folger Shakespeare Library illustrates, in an unexpected way, the theme of Shakespeare and the law. The Folger is set catercorner to the Supreme Court building in Washington, D.C., just across East Capitol Street. There are those who would no doubt argue that the physical proximity of these two national temples of law and Shakespeare is mere coincidence. But even if such rationalists are right, the striking symbolism based on geographic nearness still highlights the links between Shakespeare and the law. That symbolism became even more enhanced for me when in June 1991 I saw Supreme Court Justice Sandra Day O'Connor in the Folger's gift shop. All I could think about then was this new facet of the symbiotic relationship between Shakespeare and the law.

In high school and college, we are exposed, unless we take a course devoted to Shakespeare, to only a few of Shakespeare's plays: *Hamlet*, *Macbeth*, *Romeo and Juliet*, *The Merchant of Venice*, *Julius Caesar* (maybe), *King Lear* (maybe), and *Twelfth Night* (maybe). But at that age, in our teens or barely out of them, we are usually too young to understand fully or appreciate the plays. We have not lived enough, we are too inexperienced. We bring too little to the encounter. We can perhaps memorize a few lines and parrot the narrative, but not much beyond that, and certainly not with real understanding.

As adults it is useful at some point to return to the most significant books we first read in our youth. Justice Oliver Wendell Holmes—one of the wisest and most cultured of judges—thought that to read a great book "as it should be read," with "intelligent appreciation," we must "come back to it in the fullness of knowledge and the ripeness of age."[4] Although the books may not have changed, we definitely have, and our reading will be entirely new. Writing this book is the kind of a venture that gives us—the reader and me—a chance to revisit Shakespeare.

The need to read is even greater if someone has never read the books, which unfortunately seems to be the case too often these days. Many current law students, even at the best law schools, are unfamiliar with the classics of Western literature. But to read a great book for the first time in one's maturity is an extraordinary pleasure. Then one is more likely to appreciate many more details and levels and meanings.

Jurists have always loved Shakespeare, and Shakespearean scholars have come to understand that there is law in Shakespeare. All this has happened despite some noted Shakespeareans asserting that the law in Shakespeare is not good or real and some significant jurists declaring that Shakespeare did not write the plays. There is a long tradition of lawyers commenting on Shakespeare. Lawyers have had a large role in Shakespeare scholarship, some ultimately finding law distasteful and abandoning it entirely for literature.

As early as 1709 a lawyer from Middle Temple, one of the English Inns of Court, published the first critical edition of Shakespeare's plays with a preface biography. During the eighteenth century four other English lawyers produced editions of Shakespeare. The tradition continued in the nineteenth century with a book by Lord John Campbell, the chief justice of England, in 1859. So too down to the twentieth century. In these works, lawyers have identified, explained, and critiqued the hundreds of legal terms, expressions, and allusions in Shakespeare. They have searched for meaning and significance and the legal qualifications of the author of these plays.

This book differs from other books about Shakespeare and the law. Most of those other books, which form a rich literature, fall into one of two distinguishable categories. Either they try to catalogue and explain, exhaustively and comprehensively, every technical legal reference in Shakespeare's works, or they speculate on the biography of the Bard. Neither is my goal here.

My purpose, rather, is to identify some major legal themes in Shakespeare, some not previously discussed, and their modern relevance and implications in an attempt to engage current moral and social issues. My objective is to find and to ponder in a number of Shakespeare's plays those theatrical moments that most affect our legal thoughts today, that establish that Shakespeare still speaks *to us* about some of the legal questions that matter most to us today—which on examination always prove variants of age-old human problems. I aim to make Shakespeare the theme of reflections on law, a source of serious study of our own contemporary legal problems and political philosophy, to show that there is a connection between literature and law, between the life of the mind and the life of the law. My approach is free of ideology and school of thought. New light, I hope, will be shed on law and on the dominant characteristics of our age by these meditations and essays on Shakespeare and law as joint fashioners of modern civilization.

I try to connect Shakespeare and law to *our* contemporary scene. Shakespeare's plays—taken individually and as a whole—supply lawyers with a rich source of commonsense material about their everyday practice. I update the significance of the Bard to many of today's most pressing legal issues: race relations, personal autonomy and privacy, natural law, free market versus regulation, censorship. At the same time I try not to lose sight of more technical areas of the law also illuminated by Shakespeare's prose and dramatic situations: libel, inheritance, sovereign immunity, conveyancing, and delegation, among many others. Shakespeare is an authority on such matters, and he allows each generation to produce fruitful perspectives on the law.

Not all of Shakespeare's plays are included. Partly for reasons of length, I chose only those that seemed most useful and fertile for the theme of Shakespeare and the law. Some might disagree with my choices, or insist that I wrongly omitted certain plays. Others might say I do not do enough about Shakespeare's life, or the law, or each play, or the theories of how we can make the connections. To that charge I plead no contest. But in mitigation I would say that each of us approaches Shakespeare idiosyncratically, with subjective likes and dislikes. Someday we will have a complete encyclopedia on the subject of Shakespeare and the law. This book is a beginning, an introduction to many issues.

Measured by the number of his plays currently being performed, our culture is in the midst of a Shakespeare renaissance. Shakespeare is enjoying one of his greatest periods of popularity. Everywhere we turn all over America there is a production of a Shakespeare play, often several going on simultaneously in a large city. Some years ago the New York Shakespeare Festival launched a marathon effort to perform all of Shakespeare. Other productions adorn Broadway, Lincoln Center, and Off-Broadway, and many theaters—especially outdoor theaters during summer—throughout the country. Whatever the reason, more Shakespeare is being produced now than ever before.

This abundance of Shakespeare creates a rare opportunity. Obviously, Shakespeare still holds us in thrall, but we must disenthrall ourselves. Rather than simply surrendering to the power, beauty, and wisdom of Shakespeare, we need to try to understand what his works mean for law without overstressing their relevance. Is Shakespeare as useful to lawyers as he has been to psychologists? Why and how is he as universal about law as he is about things of the heart and the id? Can William Shakespeare, poet and playwright, teach lawyers how to read and write better? Can we see how Shakespeare might speak to lawyers, at least those with ears to hear?

As Posner complains in his 1988 book *Law and Literature*, "Although some fine scholarship has appeared, the extent to which law and literature have been mutually illuminated is modest. . . . important opportunities for mutual illumination have been overlooked."[5] What follows is an effort not to overlook one such important opportunity.

Kill All the Lawyers?

———————————————

Chapter One

SHAKESPEARE AND THE LAW

IT WAS THE young judge's first trial, and it was a tough one, but the judge surprised them all.

The plaintiff thought he had an airtight case, one he could not lose. He had lent some money to a wealthy importer, who failed to repay on time. As other lenders have done before and since, this lender went to court to enforce a written loan agreement. Their unusual contract clearly stated that if the borrower missed his payment, then the lender was entitled to a penalty: a pound of flesh nearest the borrower's heart. Everything was as it should be—the law was the law, and the lender, sensing fatal victory in the courtroom, started to sharpen his knife.

For his part, the defendant thought he had a case he could not win. He generally agreed with the lender's view of the likely outcome. After all, the borrower knew he had defaulted, and he knew he had freely agreed to the extreme penalty for default. All he could do was throw himself on the mercy of the court. Considering the undisputed facts and the clear and ominous language of the contract, the borrower grew dejected and depressed as he contemplated how the judge would rule.

But the youthful judge did the unexpected. At first seeming to side with the plaintiff, the judge tried, with eloquence, to persuade the lender to show mercy. When the hardhearted plaintiff refused, even after being offered three times the amount of the debt, the judge took everyone unawares by finding a technicality to justify getting out of the contract. The loan agreement, ruled the judge, was illegal and therefore would not be enforced. To boot, not only was the borrower freed from his obligation, but the judge imposed a heavy punishment on the lender.

The judge's performance impressed everyone who witnessed it. Tension and fear had mounted with the suspense and uncertainty of awaiting the verdict; then all those feelings gave way to relief as the sudden judicial turnabout saved a life and produced apparent justice. Those in the courtroom remembered the judge's speech about mercy and her novel solution to a vexing legal problem. The judge became a folk heroine whose courtroom triumph has been retold from generation to generation.

LAW AND LITERATURE

This is not a story of a real legal case, although the law books do record actual cases with similar themes but lesser penalties. A fictional case, it captures the essence of one of the most memorable trial scenes in all of literature. The scene comes, of course, from William Shakespeare's *Merchant of Venice*, and ever since has rightfully become a stock part of our cultural heritage and education, helping to shape our view of law, what it is, and how it should work. The dramatic scene at least suggests, forcefully and indelibly, that two fields—law and literature—can work together to yield special results, insights, and effects.

"Work together" is one way to describe what happens when two fields or disciplines help each other, but there are better ways. We could say they "combine" or "mix," although those are not quite right either, because they do not truly convey the sense of something new, different, and better. "Blend," "harmonize," "fuse," and "weld" come closer to the idea of a product in which the components are no longer distinct. To get just the right notion, however, we have the term *synergy*, which refers to something whose total effect is greater than the sum of its parts. This concept of synergy, as the trial scene in *The Merchant of Venice* has demonstrated for centuries, aptly fits law and literature.

Law by its nature is often the stuff of literature. In its grandest sense, law deals with the great themes of relations with our fellow human beings: how we are governed or how we are to govern ourselves, how risk is allocated when loss occurs, how rules are formed and interpreted, how conflict is resolved. Since law deals with life, law has the variety and drama of life. The myriad permutations and combinations of the human condition, widely differing personalities, emotions and fact patterns, all sooner or later become entangled in the law. Strong emotions, like hate, envy, and revenge, run up against the curbs of the law. Any random volume of reported cases in any jurisdiction in any era could supply much raw material for literature.

It is not surprising then that law is a frequent literary subject. Literature that lasts must deal with things that do not change much over time, the continuing concerns of people, the general and permanent features of the human condition. Law is one of those perennial features of our experience. It is a universal aspect of culture whose basic aspects have changed little. Law deeply fascinates, and lawyers—heroes and villains alike—attract much attention.

Even the processes of the law, especially trials, are tailor-made for literature. Legal processes meet literature's structural needs. There is conflict and resolution, whether in a civil or criminal setting, in the adversary system. There is suspense and uncertainty, especially while the verdict is up in the air. There is occasional eloquence, when a gifted advocate speaks well during a withering cross-examination or a brilliant closing argument. There is drama, as hopes are dashed or fulfilled, as serious penalties are imposed or escaped, as evil wins or loses. And there is symbolism, as each party represents a larger idea in society. From such stuff can come good, even great literature.

Despite the role of law in literature, the correlative place of literature in law remains more controversial. Legal scholarship has been marked by ambivalence about what benefits literature promises the study of law. The two opposing views essentially reflect an ancient struggle within the legal profession between law as humanism and law as science. To one faction, which believes in the synergy of law and literature, law is romantic in ideology, more like poetry, an act of persuasion, a cultural practice of justification using language, ritual, drama, and legitimating ideology. The other group, which assumes that nothing could be more remote from law's theory and practice than poetry and literature, sees law as a science of reason and analysis, of coercive and imperative commands (expressed as clearly as possible), or organized coercion, a system operated by lawyers who, at best, resemble scientists and engineers.[1]

The scientific lawyers think the idea that literature has direct and immediate uses for lawyers and judges has been greatly oversold. Their champion is Richard Posner, who is, as most readers of books and law reviews know, more than a talented federal appellate judge. A founder and leading exponent of the University of Chicago interdisciplinary law and economics approach, Posner originally built his professional reputation as a conservative legal scholar with a pronounced economic bent. He has published numerous books on a wide variety of law-related subjects—law and economics, antitrust, jurisprudence, Benjamin Cardozo, Oliver Wendell Holmes, and even the regulation of sex.

But Posner is not merely prolific; he is the closest thing we have among judges to what used to be called a "man of letters." His written judicial opinions are marked by an elegance, clarity, style, and erudition unique among judges in America. Often in my legal research I have been reading an opinion and, on being struck by the high quality of the prose, have turned to the front to discover that Richard Posner was the author. No judge writing in America today has so many stimulating things to say about such a broad range of subjects. To acknowledge Posner's great productivity and the high level of his output, however, is not necessarily to agree with him.

Some years ago, Posner became interested in "law and literature" and in 1988 published a book with that title that seems, on balance, to take a decidedly negative view of such an interdisciplinary approach. He there argues that the true claims of law and literature should be modest and limited, that the literary should be a sphere apart from the legal. He thinks that the study of literature and the interpretation of statutes are very different activities and that one "has little to contribute" to the other. He chides what he calls the "misguided quest" for literary analo-

gies to problems of legal interpretation. He warns us to be careful not to
think that literature does more than reveal character, that legal details in
literature are necessarily anything more than peripheral to the action, that
law in literature is more than a metaphor. The "occupational hazard" of
lawyer-critics, writes Posner, is "putting literature to tendentious use."

But at times Posner seems to be at war with himself. For all his criticism
of law and literature, Posner himself recognizes its potential as a "valuable supplementary perspective, stimulating new insights and inquiries."
Shrinking from the prospect of a "stunted race of legal specialists,"
Posner acknowledges that the study of literature on legal themes can illuminate issues of justice and enrich an understanding of law. As an extremely well-read person who obviously loves books of all kinds, Posner
understands that literature enlarges a reader's imagination, expands cultural perspectives, and assists in reading difficult texts and expressing
complex thoughts.

Posner "commends" the "effort to mine literature for its nuggets of
insight into fundamental issues that lawyers should think about more
than they do—issues relating to the connection between the legal outlook
and the sense of justice, between legalism and civilization, and between
laws and other forms of institutionalized morality."[2] According to
Posner, "The insights as well as the rhetorical devices of literature can be
professional assets for lawyers." Inasmuch as professional training in law
and the professional experiences of lawyers are "narrowing," lawyers
ought to read the great works of literature that take law as their theme as
a "convenient, though not the only, point of entry to broaden thinking
about law."[3] Here Posner is obviously correct and sounds like a "literary
lawyer," a term he uses with derision.

As these differing views show, internal tension and perhaps cognitive
dissonance mark Posner's own views about "law and literature." But
even so, one detects a strong Posnerian tilt against this interdisciplinary
approach. Posner's criticisms strike a reader as more earnest and crucial
than the perfunctory and faint praise. The whole thesis of his book is to
reexamine and then scale back reliance on the new field of law and literature. Posner's overall thrust is to severely limit the impact of the law and
literature movement.[4]

One of Posner's chief intellectual antagonists on these issues, who uses
the term "literary lawyer" not as a criticism but as a badge of honor, is
Richard Weisberg, a professor of law at Cardozo Law School in New
York and one of the founders of the law and literature movement. Armed
with a Ph.D. in French and comparative literature as well as a degree in
law, Weisberg is well equipped to think and write about law and literature. In 1979 Weisberg organized the Law and Humanities Institute,
which over the years has sponsored conferences on various aspects of law

and the humanities. In 1989 he initiated a new law journal devoted to this field, *Cardozo Studies in Law and Literature.*

Weisberg's three books deal with law and literature. In *The Failure of the Word*, Weisberg explores the role of lawyers as protagonists in modern continental fiction, focusing on Flaubert, Dostoyevsky, and Camus. His second book, *When Lawyers Write*, is a writing guide that recommends lawyers read "great novels about law" on weekends. In 1992 he published *Poethics and Other Strategies of Law and Literature*, which heralds the arrival of law and literature into the realm of contemporary legal philosophy. Weisberg and Posner have clashed over their interpretations of the subject, but that is a vital sign of a living school of thought.

Unlike Posner, Weisberg rightly contends that literature has much to teach about law; it "provides unique insights into the underpinnings of law."[5] Stories such as *Bleak House* and *The Merchant of Venice* are sources of understanding about legal ideas that are more accessible than traditional sources of legal philosophy. Weisberg's literary jurisprudence has two distinct but related branches. First, literature teaches about ethics in law. Second, literature demonstrates the great extent to which law is intertwined with language. For Weisberg, these two aspects blend, so that form and substance become one. The substance of literary jurisprudence is its potential for "greater ethical awareness" in law. By careful reading of literature about law, Weisberg shows that we can learn much that is "either ignored, unstressed, or misperceived in traditional approaches to jurisprudence." Such examples are bound to affect the literary lawyer, unless the teaching of ethics itself is hopelessly futile.

Literature can make lawyers and judges more empathetic, more aware of cultural variety and nuances of individual motivation. The fully experienced literary masterpiece tends to liberate. Great literature is seldom repressive. Literature can help lawyers understand and empathize with people and human conflicts in ways that more scientific sources of knowledge cannot. Narratives of human action in problematic situations induce the reader to identify with varied characters and to assess ambiguous actions, and thereby to extend sympathies and refine moral sensibilities in a way that improves legal judgment.

As for the form of the new literary jurisprudence, it underscores the skills of writing and reading. Reading good literature teaches good writing. In Weisberg's words, the "poetic method provokes us, as customary learning does not, to highlight the linguistic, sensory aspects of every part of our craft." The reality is that law, for better or worse, is "utterly dependent on language." Literature heightens our understanding of language and symbols, and communication in general.

Law and literature may be separate spheres, but clearly "they are intertwining webs."[6] Literature can obviously help us understand the law, as both Posner and Weisberg agree. It can take the raw materials of an otherwise dull lawsuit and transform them into living literature. Many authors, past and present, have used that old standby, a trial at law, for the setting of their literary works. Filtered, refined, and seen through the eye of capable literary artists, the law can emerge more clearly, in all its glory or with all its flaws. A poem, a play, a novel, a short story can expose the harshness or intellectual bankruptcy of shopworn legal doctrine; or it can portray a legal character or legal issue with sympathy and understanding, using an individual to illustrate a grander theme. Drama can be seen as a method by which we can translate abstract concepts like law into concrete human terms or by which we can set up a situation and work out its consequences (for example, what would happen if, say, all extramarital love were to become a capital offense, as in Shakespeare's *Measure for Measure?*).

Popularity can make a point. With a wider audience than a law book has, literature about the law can often reach more people and move more hearts and minds. Most people would rather read a novel or view a play than pore over a thick legal tome. Millions more people have read, for example, John Grisham's *The Firm*, Scott Turow's *Presumed Innocent*, Harper Lee's *To Kill a Mockingbird*, or Herman Wouk's *Caine Mutiny* than have perused any volume of Supreme Court cases.

Not only do literary insights enhance a lawyer's understanding of law, but from the reverse point of view, a lawyer's knowledge and legal insights can enhance and enrich understanding of literature. Even Posner concedes that "the lawyer's perspective can assist the reader to a greater understanding and enjoyment of works of literature."[7] A thoughtful and sensitive lawyer should be able to say something useful about literature with legal themes, on the roles of judges, law, and truth. On this point, there is no dispute; the dispute arises over interpretive technique.

Like law, literature builds on texts that must be read, studied, and interpreted. The key to law is its interpretation. The techniques used to interpret literature may be useful in finding ways to interpret law. To Posner in his cynical phase, this is a "great false hope," but even he admits that the "well-educated lawyer should have some acquaintance with current controversies in literary theory and their potential bearing on legal interpretations." Literary scholars have long discussed and argued about whether an author's intent or a reader's response should control interpretation of, say, a poem. Their literary debates often resemble perennial debates in the law, such as whether the Constitution ought to be interpreted according to the framers' intent or as a living document for contemporary needs. Thus law and literature involve some similarity of intellectual tasks, although I share Posner's understandable skepticism about wholesale application of literary interpretation and academic literary critics' jargon to legal interpretation.

Despite their distinctness, law and literature have, nonetheless, several definite connections. Like the structure of DNA, law and literature form a double helix with many points of contact. Law is not a dry, mechanical tool but a body of living thought inseparably connected with, dependent on, and invaluable to other branches of our culture, like literature. Literary works about legal proceedings climaxing in a trial are legion, as are literary works about justice and revenge. How law gets interpreted in literature, and what literature means in light of law, are rich and deeply textured subjects. Together, law and literature make up a field worthy of study. There are many links to explore and examine.

The mother lode of these many links between law and literature remained mostly unmined until our own generation. For a long time there simply was not much commentary in the field beyond reminders that law is frequently a subject of literature or that judicial opinions can have a literary quality. But that situation—that failure to explore and examine the synergy of law and literature—is starting to change.

The links between law and literature have recently created a rapidly growing and distinct discipline. During the last twenty-five years, four major new schools of American legal philosophy have emerged. First came law and economics, urged on by Posner, with its analysis of legal questions in terms of market efficiencies. Then, as a counterbalance to the free market approach, critical legal studies weighed in as an updated version of legal realism (an early twentieth-century legal philosophy that taught that judges, despite the reasons they gave, ruled according to their political, economic, and emotional views) heavily tinged with Marxism and 1960s counterculture (and some might say nihilism). In the mid-1980s, around the bicentennial of the Constitution, new interest focused on classical republicanism as a fertile field. Most recently, feminist legal theory has made a bid to be the fourth school of contemporary jurisprudence. Now make room for a fifth: law and literature.

The current wave of new interest in law and literature began with the publication of an unusual book by a law professor more than twenty years ago. In 1973 James Boyd White, who teaches at the University of Michigan Law School, published his seminal volume, *The Legal Imagination*, which drew heavily on readings from literature "to establish a way of looking at the law from the outside, a way of comparing it with some other forms of literary and intellectual activity, a way of defining the legal imagination by comparing it with others."[8] White claimed that those who study law should also study literature, and went on to demonstrate the validity of his claim. It was White's book, itself an effective stimulus to the legal imagination about which he wrote so well, that signaled the emergence of a separate field of law and literature.

Since publication of White's book two decades ago, several other volumes devoted to the relationship between law and literature have appeared (including Posner's and Weisberg's and a number by White himself), and literary studies and critical techniques have increasingly become an explicit part of legal debate. Within the last few years, various law reviews have sponsored whole issues on the subject of law and literature. To meet growing demand and interest, new specialized professional journals, such as the *Yale Journal of Law and Humanities* and *Cardozo Studies of Law and Literature*, have recently started publishing. New organizations, such as the Law and Humanities Institute (of which Weisberg is co-chairman and Posner is on the Board of Governors), have come into being. Seminars at bar association meetings and judicial conferences have begun to discuss law and literature, with perhaps the most frequent topic being *Billy Budd*, Herman Melville's story about a court-martialed sailor. In early 1992 the Law and Humanities Institute (LHI) and the New York County Lawyers' Association sponsored a program on the meaning and significance of Shakespeare's famous line "The first thing we do, let's kill all the lawyers" (*2 Henry VI*, 4.2.78). Later that same year, LHI and the Association of the Bar of the City of New York co-sponsored another well-attended program on the legal aspects of *The Merchant of Venice*. A number of colleges and law schools now offer courses on law and literature.

This is not to say that the relationship of law and literature is exactly a new phenomenon. On the contrary, the nexus between law and literature was prominent early in American history. As Robert Ferguson points out in his brilliant 1984 book, *Law and Letters in American Culture*, a "now forgotten configuration of law and letters . . . dominated literary aspirations from the Revolution until the fourth decade of the nineteenth century." Critics of the time trained for law, and attorneys controlled many of the important journals. Lawyers also wrote many of the country's first important novels, plays, and poems. Washington Irving (*Rip Van Winkle*, *The Legend of Sleepy Hollow*, *A History of New York*), William Cullen Bryant ("Thanatopsis"), Richard Henry Dana, Jr. (*Two Years before the Mast*), and James Fenimore Cooper (thirty-two novels, including *The Last of the Mohicans*, *The Pioneers*, and *The Pathfinder*) are only a few of the most notable lawyer-authors. The lawyer as writer dominated the literature of the early Republic.

But it was a two-way street. The result was, in Ferguson's words, "a remarkable symbiosis between law and literary aspiration." Literature informed the antebellum American lawyer. Such a lawyer was, as Ferguson states, "professionally dependent upon a fusion of law and literature."[9] He committed himself to public service through the written word.

When Daniel Webster, Rufus Choate, and Abraham Lincoln argued cases in court, they spoke with the aid of a rich literary tradition. Is it pure coincidence that the first half of the nineteenth century was for a long time known as the "golden age" of American law? Does today's renewed interest in law and literature prefigure another "golden age" of American law? We can at least hope so.

The important link between law and literature existed outside America as well. In Great Britain it was quite common, especially during the eighteenth and nineteenth centuries, for literary figures to have started their careers by training for the law. Samuel Johnson, William Wordsworth, Walter Scott, William Makepeace Thackeray, and Robert Louis Stevenson are names that come readily to mind. On the Continent we can point to Gustave Flaubert, who studied law at his father's insistence, only to stop in disgust and to portray his bad feelings about law and lawyers in *Madame Bovary* and other books. Franz Kafka is a more recent example of a law-trained writer of fiction.

Even if its precise scope and limits are unclear, the synergy of law and literature is nonetheless real. Posner sees the interdisciplinary law and literature approach as insignificant; Weisberg and White—and I—see it as vital. Can law and literature, as an interdisciplinary analytical technique, illuminate some secrets about Shakespeare and the law?

SHAKESPEARE'S LAW

Although law and literature for the most part had to wait until recently to emerge as a distinct field, this generalization had one great exception: Shakespeare. Almost from the start, ordinary viewers, as well as professional Shakespearean scholars, saw that Shakespeare often referred to law in his work, and they reacted to it. They were acutely aware that, for all his legal allusions, Shakespeare makes almost no complimentary references to lawyers. Two of the plays—*The Merchant of Venice* and *Measure for Measure*—have long been known as explicitly "legal" plays.

But that knowledge took root in a different, earlier era, centuries ago, when books played a larger role in society. People then lived in constant face-to-face intimacy with great literature. In that long-ago time, Shakespeare, Milton, and the Bible had a far greater part in teaching those who spoke English. Even humble homes, inhabited by those without benefit of formal education, contained these works. People used to read for emotional and intellectual extension, for the exercise. Reading then formed taste and language, common understanding and first principles. Such books demonstrated what virtue was and what the proper aspirations of a noble life should be.

Today we do not rely on these books in the same way. Books in general and great books in particular have become less important to our inner lives. If they are read, they do not move. Classic authors do not seem to matter to modern young people. Great books are not usually part of the furniture of the mind today, and that lack means reflections on life and its goals are poorer.[10] When David Souter, a lover of good books—literature, philosophy, history, as well as law—was nominated in 1990 to be a justice of the United States Supreme Court, the media actually raised doubts about his fitness to serve because he read too much.

To start to correct such philistinism, we need to understand Shakespeare's plays as something more than merely literary productions. We need to see the dramas of Shakespeare as our own dramas, the ordeals and the triumphs ours. We have to see the plays as relevant to the important problems that agitate the lives of living persons. One way to do that is to examine the role of law in Shakespeare and to relate it to the political, social, and legal problems of our own time. Literature is not antithetical to law. Law, like art, civilizes and unifies, providing a common language and ideas of right and wrong.

It probably comes as no surprise that a great playwright such as Shakespeare would use trial scenes. A legal trial lends itself to theater. As Posner points out, law provides in the trial "a ready-made dramatic technique." Posner goes on to explain, with considerable insight, "Whether historically the trial is molded on the theater and offers the litigants and society (the audience) the type of catharsis that the theater does, or vice versa, . . . few social practices are so readily transferable to a literary setting as the trial or so well suited to the literary depiction of conflict."[11]

Not only are trials inherently dramatic, but they are something more: they are tests of a society, and the special way those tests are conducted can reveal a society's strengths and weaknesses.

Something extraordinary happens when people view a play or a legal trial. In the process of viewing, they live more truly, see more deeply, and function for a brief time on a higher level than in their daily lives. Both the courtroom and the stage provide the settings for central ceremonies, with speech their most visible ritual. Throughout history, courtroom litigation has been a community event, particularly before the advent of television and movies. People have seen trials as ceremonies that supply entertainment, theater, and drama. A trial, like a play, attracts audiences for good reason.

Today, cameras in the courtroom are causing what Steven Brill, gifted editor of the *American Lawyer* magazine and creator of Court TV, calls "a revolution of public awareness and participation that will strengthen the justice system and restore confidence in it. . . . Video cameras are about to make the legal process as accessible and visible in the 1990s as it was in the 1890s when the courthouse was our favorite town theater."[12] Television airwaves already filled with fictional law are increasingly going to get a lot of the real thing. Inevitably, more and more actual trials will be televised, which will bring riveting moments.

Shakespeare moves us with more compelling trial scenes than anything on television. He disturbs the souls of his viewers. The catharsis that Aristotle wrote of so long ago operates in Shakespeare's plays. The dramatist shows us extremes of personality and behavior, and we see what we might be. Having read and seen Shakespeare, we understand life better; and because Shakespeare uses law so much, we understand law better as well. Whatever else we may say of Shakespeare's plays, we do them little justice unless we see at least some of them—not wholly, but partly—as dramas about the law, or at least dramas about character in which the law has a role.

Law in Elizabethan Life

The pervasiveness of law in Shakespeare is perhaps to be expected in light of the role law played in English life in his time. Centuries of experience with the common law had molded English attitudes. Legal proceedings were popular both as a form of entertainment and as a way for the litigious English to assert their rights. In Shakespeare's day, there was great popular interest in the law.

At a time when there were few places of recreation in town, people found attending the courts and watching judicial procedure a dramatic and diverting pastime. They derived amusement from the technicalities of property lawsuits and were impressed by political trials and public executions. In Elizabethan times law was not, as now, remote from the experience of even educated people. Law for the Elizabethans took the place of politics and sports as a main interest. Cases in court furnished a mirror in which the whole of English life from high to low could be observed. As a result, the law courts at Westminster Hall in London were a great magnet during the four terms of court each year. When the courts were in session, lawyers, litigants, and observers swelled London's population.

In addition to the courts themselves, London was also home of the Inns of Court, where well-born, affluent, university-educated men in their early twenties lived and studied law. Law students, together with their friends and relatives, had the money, leisure, and inclination for play going. They supplied many of those younger and livelier viewers who made up Shakespeare's audiences. Lawyers and law students filled the theaters and applauded Shakespeare's tragedies, comedies, and histories.

At that time the Inns of Court were more than residential law schools. They were more like gentlemen's clubs composed of the liveliest, brightest group in England. They were centers of literary life as well, where intellectuals gathered for friendship, discussion, and debate. Several playwrights came from the Inns, and literary figures such as John Donne and Francis Bacon (and 20 percent of Shakespeare's contemporary playwrights) were members. The Inns were also special patrons of the theater; the jurists would call for plays to be performed for them, sometimes by the law students.

No doubt Shakespeare absorbed some of this literary-legal life of the Inns of Court. His first London address was near the Inns, where he had friends and relatives. He would go to the Inns to fill several artistic needs: to find patrons, audiences, places for production; to talk over literature; to find new material to write about from legal figures and their law cases. He addressed several of his sonnets, which use legal language and reflect legal learning, to lawyers, members of Gray's Inn. Shakespeare's coat of arms was prepared by two members of Gray's Inn in 1599.

Shakespeare was part of the court crowd, involved in the jurisprudence of his day. He had extensive contact with the London legal world, picking up legal mores and jargon from the Inns. He probably wrote from personal observation when he put in the mouth of Tranio in *The Taming of the Shrew*:

> Please ye we may contrive this afternoon,
> And do as adversaries do in law—
> Strive mightily, but eat and drink as friends.
>
> (1.2.276–78)

Shakespeare's plays were themselves performed at the Inns of Court and at private audiences of Inn members. Before the Globe Theater was built in 1599, and even after, Shakespeare's troupe, like other Elizabethan players, acted on a variety of stages, including the large dining halls of the Inns of Court. At the organized "revels," especially at Christmas, part of the foolishness at the Inns included plays. Viewers' notes from the Inns help us date the first known performances of certain plays.

In 1594 Gray's Inn—the largest of the Inns of Court—gave Shakespeare the high honor of picking one of his plays for the famous Christmas "law revels." Shakespeare, knowing who was to be his audience, revised *The Comedy of Errors* to include trial scenes and legal passages. On December 28, 1594, professional actors performed the play to a reception recorded in the official contemporary reports of the Inn. It was a lighthearted occasion, marked by "disordered tumult," "dancing and revelling with gentlewomen," and delightful "confusion."[13] The next night, Gray's Inn brought mock charges "against a sorcerer or conjurer that was supposed to be the cause of that confused inconvenience."

We also have a diary from one John Manningham, a barrister of the Middle Temple, another of the Inns of Court, referring to a different

Shakespeare play. This time, the date was February 2, 1602, and the play was another comedy, *Twelfth Night*. Judging from their taste in plays (and their behavior), those judges, lawyers, and law students at the Inns of Court enjoyed a hearty belly laugh and a rollicking good time, not unlike "revues" held today at Christmas at some American law schools.

Up to seven of Shakespeare's plays were put on at the Inns of Court. Others were performed to instruct—however gently through art—the new King James I, who came from Scotland on Queen Elizabeth's death in 1603, on how to govern under English law. And lawyers made up a large part of the Bard's audiences wherever his plays were actually performed. Shakespeare wrote them with lawyers in mind.

No wonder Shakespeare liberally sprinkled his plays with references to law, lawyers, and all sorts of legal ideas. Shakespeare would not have made so many legal allusions if he had not expected them to be understood. He was writing for his audiences, and he knew his audiences well. How better to bring down the house than to have a character in a play say in front of an audience filled with those in the legal profession, "The first thing we do, let's kill all the lawyers"? (2 *Henry VI*, 4.2.78) Nonlawyers might howl too, but the line takes on more meaning if delivered before the equivalent of a bar association meeting.

In making legal allusions, Shakespeare was not unusual. During Shakespeare's career, more than a third of the plays performed in London had one or more trial scenes. At the time of his death, nearly one-third of English plays had a trial scene. Law was a staple of Elizabethan playwriting.

Poets and playwrights, like trial lawyers, must understand their audience. They must know the truly permanent human problems and must speak to the most vital concerns of the audience. They must know how to touch the audience, how to play on it. They must appeal to each of the viewers and each of their different levels of meaning and understanding. Shakespeare's legal language was not just for adornment, but was integral and important to his dramatic action; he relied heavily on it for audience rapport.

SHAKESPEARE'S LEGAL EXPERIENCES

A dramatist's understandable motivation to play to the galleries is only one of the reasons for so many legal references in Shakespeare's plays. His personal experiences with the law help to explain the rest. Sparse as is the factual material of Shakespeare's life, the little we do know, particularly about Shakespeare and the law, aids in illuminating his works. Indeed, thanks to court records of a litigious fellow in a litigious age, we know more about Shakespeare's legal affairs than about those of his contemporaries. We see the extent to which Shakespeare's personal life is blended with his written work; we start to recognize how the concerns in his writings reflect the facts in his life.

One version of events, based on a biography written in 1709, explains that Shakespeare left his hometown of Stratford because of a legal problem. According to this version, a local justice of the peace found Shakespeare guilty of deer poaching, and as a result Shakespeare had to leave. But today Shakespeare's early run-in with the law seems to be more myth than truth. No proof exists of a local deer park, or of the judicial proceeding. Yet the story has the virtue of showing why Shakespeare left Stratford without accusing him of abandoning his family.

Regardless of whether Shakespeare quit Stratford because of a petty crime, he learned how to be litigious from his father, John. John Shakespeare, who was bailiff (that is, mayor) of Stratford in 1568, fell into the law's clutches on several occasions. In 1580, when William was sixteen years old, John was summoned to appear in court in Westminster and was fined twenty pounds for not complying. John also acted as surety for John Audley, who likewise failed to show up, which led to a second fine of twenty pounds. Forty pounds was a very large sum.

In 1599 John Shakespeare sued John Walford, a clothier, for a debt of twenty-one pounds arising from Walford's purchase of wool in 1568. Reputedly "a considerable dealer in wool," John Shakespeare had to face charges in 1572 in the Court of Exchequer for illegal wool dealing. Two years earlier, he was twice accused of breaking the usury laws by lending money at 20 percent interest. In 1573 John Shakespeare was sued on a debt.[14]

William became obsessed with one particular piece of litigation involving his father. When examined even slightly, this lawsuit, which lasted over twenty years, highlights several of Shakespeare's attitudes toward the law as shown in his plays. The lawsuit that so preoccupied Shakespeare grew out of a contract between his father and his uncle. In 1580 John Shakespeare borrowed forty pounds from his brother-in-law Edmund Lambert. As security for the loan, John Shakespeare mortgaged forty-four acres of land in Wilmcote owned by his wife, which William would have inherited in due course. When the date for repayment arrived, Lambert refused to accept John Shakespeare's forty pounds until John's other outstanding debts were paid. Having rejected John's tender, Lambert claimed that a default had occurred and that the lands that had belonged to Shakespeare's mother were Lambert's. Lambert had possession.

After years of fruitless settlement talks, John Shakespeare sued Lambert in 1588, when William was an impressionable twenty-four years of age. It was about this time that William, reaching maturity, left Stratford.

Shakespeare's father, in essence, asked the court to ignore legal formality and to apply substantial justice by returning the lands—Shakespeare's inheritance—to the Shakespeare family. The case went on through 1590, until the parties apparently reached an out-of-court settlement.

But the settlement fell apart. In 1597 William reopened the case by suing Lambert's son in the Court of Chancery, a tribunal of equity. Such a court supposedly administered justice according to fairness, as contrasted to a court of law, which applied the often harsh and strictly formulated rules of common law. In 1599 the case was once again settled, but not before the court, relying on its equivalent of modern rules for sanctions, rebuked Shakespeare for wasting time by bringing a frivolous suit. "The Shakespeares," stated the court, "do now trouble and molest this defendant by unjust suits in law." Shakespeare never did recover the lands lost by his father, though he at least did not have to pay interest, fines, costs, or attorneys' fees.

This long-running family litigation, together with John Shakespeare's several other lawsuits, must have had a profound effect on the whole Shakespeare family, including William. Consider the impact on a poor, struggling young man when he learned that he had lost his inheritance in such a legalistic way. Is it any surprise that inheritance bulks so large in Shakespeare's plays? Do we wonder that it is at the heart of *King Lear*? Need we search very far for the psychological source of Fortinbras's quest for lands left for him as inheritance but which "by a sealed compact, / Well ratified by law and heraldry" (*Hamlet*, 1.1.85–86) went instead to Prince Hamlet?

Equally obvious, once the biographical facts are known, is the effect of *Shakespeare v. Lambert* on the playwright's treatment of law. Possibly the legal theme of *The Merchant of Venice* has its origin in Shakespeare's own litigation and his father's twice being accused of violating usury laws. The conflict between law and equity that marks some of the plays is the same conflict that was at the core of Shakespeare's own lawsuit. His critical attitudes toward legal formalities reflect his own bitter personal experiences at the hands of the law. There is little distinction between *Shakespeare v. Lambert* and *Shylock v. Antonio*.

Quite apart from the long-running lawsuit against Lambert, Shakespeare was involved in a number of other litigations, some of which involved what seem like trifling amounts of money. In 1596 the Court of Queen's Bench cited Shakespeare to give surety to keep the peace and issued a writ of attachment to arrest him in connection with a dispute involving the suppression of theaters in London. It is unclear what ultimately happened or even if the writ was ever served.

In 1604 Shakespeare retained a lawyer to sue a neighbor, Philip Rogers, in the Court of Record for thirty-five shillings and ten pence as the balance due for twenty bushels of malt. The Court of Record was comparable to our small claims court, with jurisdiction over cases of debt up to thirty pounds. On top of the debt itself, plaintiff Shakespeare asked for ten shillings in damages. We do not know how the court ruled.

We do know, however, that Shakespeare obtained a jury verdict in his favor four years later in another case before the same court. That case also involved a small debt—six pounds—from one John Addenbrooke. From several records, we know that the case dragged on from August 17, 1608, to June 7, 1609. When the defendant failed to appear, the court asked the defendant's surety (a blacksmith named Thomas Horneby) to show cause why he should not pay six pounds plus twenty-four shillings in damages. Whether or not Shakespeare actually collected on his judgment is unknown.

Also in 1609 Shakespeare and some friends started a suit in chancery over the "Stratford tithes." These tithes, in which Shakespeare had invested, were a substantial source of income for Shakespeare. He and his co-plaintiffs sued to get certain people to pay their rightful share.

These three minor litigations reveal part of Shakespeare's attitude toward the law. He was persistent in asserting his rights, even over small sums. We may discern even a Shylock-like quality in his tenacity in legal matters. His experience with the slowness of the legal system and with lawyers generally may have contributed to his reference to the "law's delay" in *Hamlet* and his apparent criticism of the legal profession in *Henry VI, Part 2*.

Such attitudes may have hardened by the time he took part in two other pieces of litigation. In late spring 1612 Shakespeare traveled from Stratford to London to testify as a crucial witness in a case in the Court of Requests. That case, brought by a son-in-law against his father-in-law for breach of a dowry contract, had the makings of a domestic comedy fit for one of Shakespeare's plays.

Stephen Bellott, the plaintiff, was an apprentice to the defendant, a wigmaker named Mountjoy, who had a daughter Mary. Mountjoy asked Shakespeare to act as matchmaker in negotiating a dowry for Belott's marriage to Mary. After the couple were married in 1604, rumors started that Mountjoy planned to disinherit the young people, in violation of the dowry agreement. The court in *Belott v. Mountjoy* had to decide what financial settlement had been agreed to.

As the middleman, Shakespeare was the key witness. But at a court hearing on May 11, 1612, Shakespeare's memory, like that of so many witnesses before and since, failed him. He testified that he could not recall the terms of the contract. The court set a second hearing for June 19, 1612, but Shakespeare did not testify then. His name appears in the margin of the court records as a witness to whom interrogatories should be directed.

Ultimately, the Court of Requests, as was common for such marriage-related matters, referred the case for arbitration to the French Church in London. The arbitration resulted in a modest award of six pounds thirteen shillings four pence. Nonetheless, a year later Mountjoy, the disgruntled father-in-law, still had not paid.

In 1613 Shakespeare's older daughter, Susanna, was involved in a litigation of Shakespearean dimension. She sued in a church court for slander, charging a certain John Lane with defaming her by accusing her of adultery. When the defendant failed to show up at the trial, he was excommunicated, and Susanna triumphed. Here we have life imitating art, real events repeating the slanders of infidelity in *Othello, The Winter's Tale,* and *Much Ado about Nothing.*

In 1615 Shakespeare joined a friendly litigation. The suit concerned Blackfriar Gate-house, which he had bought and mortgaged in March 1613. He cooperated with several other property owners in the Blackfriars in petitioning the Court of Chancery to give a widow's son and her executor authority to surrender certain legal documents regarding the real estate.

Just before he died, Shakespeare's other daughter, Judith, found herself involved in a court proceeding. In February 1616 she had married Richard Quiney, who was accused by another woman of getting her pregnant. In March the woman and her baby died, and Quiney was charged. He confessed at his trial.

In April 1616, on his fifty-second birthday, Shakespeare died. His will, with its famous "second best bed" bequest to his wife, was a legal document he either drafted himself or had a lawyer prepare for him. No doubt he had worked with lawyers to draft several other legal documents during his life, such as the purchase of the Stratford tithes, conveyances of property, and other business deals.

Just think for a moment what these several brushes with the law mean. Shakespeare was more litigious than the average man of his time. Even today, most people never get involved in a lawsuit in their entire lives; most probably never even see a lawyer except to draw up a will or handle a house closing. Those who become litigants do so rarely, usually not more than once in a lifetime. Once is enough.

But not for Shakespeare. There is proof of a number of litigations he vigorously pursued, one in which he was a key witness with a faulty memory, and one collusive litigation. There may be other litigations involving Shakespeare for which records have not been found. Shakespeare was a lawyer's dream, a walking litigation factory. Such abundant litigation activity must reflect repeated contact with the law, lawyers, courts, legal intricacies, legal delays, and legal doctrines. Shakespeare may not have been professionally trained as a lawyer, but he surely had a long and expensive education in the law.

Based on his personal experience with the law, legal reform might have been one of Shakespeare's goals. Perhaps Shakespeare meant his plays to influence those members of the legal profession who saw them. Like Hamlet, Shakespeare, aware of his audience, may have said to himself, "The play's the thing / Wherein I'll catch the conscience" of the chancellor (*Hamlet*, 2.2.606–7). Some insist that Shakespeare actively and persistently pursued a program for effecting change in the English jurisprudence of equity, and that he had a "permanent impact upon English legal history."[15] These expansive conclusions seem to be based on slender evidence. Can we really say with any degree of assurance that an English equity case decided shortly after Shakespeare's plays were performed would have come out differently were it not for those plays? To answer is to speculate.

Shakespeare set his plays in different times and different places with different laws. This variety gives us a wide-angle lens. For laws define what is good or bad, what conduct is to be encouraged or discouraged by society. We have the right to ask what Shakespeare thought about a good regime, a good ruler, a good law.

Interpreting Shakespeare is in some ways like interpreting the Constitution. There are those who insist that the only proper way to read Shakespeare or the Constitution is to interpret it as the authors intended. But there are also those who think of judicial review as permitting a continuing constitutional convention, where each generation reinterprets the Constitution for itself. Similarly, there are those for whom each generation reinterprets Shakespeare for its own needs, spiritual, psychological, legal.

Interpreting the Constitution sometimes involves interpreting Shakespeare, as can be seen from a 1989 Supreme Court case. In that case, *Browning-Ferris Industries v. Kelco Disposal*, the Court rejected the argument that unlimited punitive damage awards in civil cases are the kind of "excessive fines" barred by the Eighth Amendment to the Constitution. In a dissenting opinion, Justice Sandra Day O'Connor, who frequents the Folger Shakespeare Library right across the street from the Supreme Court, cited Shakespeare, whom she described as "an astute observer of English law and politics."[16] She quoted the passage from *Romeo and Juliet* in which Prince Escalus of Verona warns the Montagues and Capulets to call off their warfare:

> But I'll amerce you with so strong a fine
> That you shall all repent the loss of mine.

(3.1.189–90)

Justice Harry Blackmun, writing for the majority, replied to Justice O'Connor in a footnote to his own opinion. "As to the dissent's reliance on the Bard," Justice Blackmun wrote:

> Though Shakespeare, of course
> Knew the Law of his time
> He was foremost a poet,
> In search of a rhyme.[17]

Justice Blackmun's opinion contained no hint of the source of this quatrain, and later inquiry produced the answer that the author was "anonymous."[18]

This unusual exchange between Justices O'Connor and Blackmun is instructive. First, it shows a high-level point of contact between Shakespeare and the law: how Supreme Court justices can draw on and disagree over lines from Shakespeare. Second, it underscores the role of interpretation in both law and Shakespeare: how the same text can yield different meanings to different people. Third, it suggests a plan for our venture: how we can see if Shakespeare, "foremost a poet in search of a rhyme," has any effect on the law of *our* time. To begin this venture, we turn to Shakespeare's most famous comment on lawyers and see if we can, at long last, figure out what he meant.

Chapter Two

THE FIRST THING WE DO

HENRY VI, PART 2

"THE FIRST THING we do, let's kill all the lawyers" (2 *Henry VI*, 4.2.78). These ten words are Shakespeare's most well-known and lasting popular legacy to the law. Is it one of those key lines that seem to give us a glimpse into Shakespeare's own mind, or is it merely a joke? From all of Shakespeare's thirty-seven plays, that one familiar line stands out more than any other as a stinging comment on the legal profession. Its pith and pungency have helped it survive. Shakespeare's antilawyer line, once heard, clings to the mind like a burr. It has been repeated so often that many who have never read any Shakespeare know the quotation. It has passed into common usage and become a cliché that even shows up on T-shirts popular among law students, on souvenir plates, coffee mugs, pillows, and as a title of a movie about a young man's decision to reject a legal career in favor of becoming a gardener.

To turn the familiar into the fresh, however, we need to look at it anew, always keeping in mind the role of popular culture. A society's attitudes are often reflected in its popular culture. Inasmuch as Shakespeare's plays were part of the popular culture of his time, they should tell us something about Elizabethan attitudes toward law and lawyers. Likewise our own contemporary popular culture should reveal some insights about our attitudes toward law and lawyers. Consider these current jokes:

Q. What's the difference between a dead skunk and a dead lawyer in the middle of a road?
A. There are skid marks in front of the skunk.

Q. How many lawyers does it take to screw in a lightbulb?
A. Depends. How many can you afford?

Q. Why don't sharks bite lawyers?
A. Professional courtesy.

Q. How can you tell if a lawyer is lying?
A. His lips are moving.

What are we saying in such jokes? Why are they funny? Why do nonlawyers love them?

A major element in the 1992 Republican presidential campaign was a sarcastic attack on lawyers, which even extended to what they wear. President George Bush—the leader of what used to be called the free world, the most powerful man on the planet—attacked a previously unheralded article of lawyers' wardrobes: their shoes. In his 1992 speech accepting his party's nomination, Bush talked about reform of the legal system and putting an end to "crazy lawsuits." He criticized "sharp lawyers" who are "running wild" and "every trial lawyer who ever wore a tasseled loafer."

Put aside the substance of this passage. Leave for another day the question of whether the president's proposed legal reforms were good or bad. Focus instead on the rhetorical device of making fun of what lawyers wear on their feet. Observe how the verbal assault builds up to lawyers wearing tasseled loafers.

Lawyer bashing through humor is an old social custom that continues vigorously. Lawyers have been satirized for centuries. Dickens and Daumier did it. Ambrose Bierce's *Devil's Dictionary* included many barbs at the expense of lawyers. In recent years, an increasing number of books have been devoted to collecting jokes about lawyers. We make lawyers the butt of many jokes with social bite.

"HOOKED" ON *HENRY VI*

Such antilawyer jokes punctuate another example of popular culture: Steven Spielberg's 1991 film *Hook*, an updated version of the Peter Pan story. Spielberg's movie is a good vehicle for thinking about Shakespeare and the law. If we understand *Hook*, we go a long way toward understanding Shakespeare's attitude toward lawyers, especially his famous line about killing all the lawyers.

At the start of the movie, Peter is an out-of-shape, cold, ambitious, middle-aged lawyer. He specializes in mergers and acquisitions and does not spend enough time with his family. His world comes apart when his children are kidnapped by his old foe Captain Hook, forcing Peter to return to never-never land, rediscover his former self, and save his children.

The film's dialogue is marked by an antilawyer cast. First, Peter makes a self-deprecating speech in which he trots out the tired joke about why laboratory scientists prefer using lawyers rather than rats. (Answer: "The scientists get less attached to lawyers, and there are some things even rats won't do.") Next, when Peter explains how he earns his living as a lawyer, Granny Wendy exclaims in surprise, "Why, Peter, you've become a pirate!" Then, as the half-naked, uneducated, almost savage Lost Boys challenge Peter as an interloper, their leader eggs them on to the attack by shouting, of all things, "Kill the lawyer!" The movie theater audience cheered loudly and clapped more at that line than at any other, just as Shakespeare's audience must have at his almost identical line.[1]

But for all its criticism of lawyers, *Hook* makes Peter the lawyer into the movie's noble hero. Peter shakes off his grown-up persona and fears, trains vigorously for his dangerous new challenge, organizes the Lost Boys into a tightly knit commando unit, and risks death and destruction in an all-out fight against the forces of darkness, symbolized by Captain Hook. Without Peter, the boys really would have been lost, and Hook would have triumphed. Peter was the savior of never-never land. As he lies dying, mortally wounded by Hook's sword, Rufio, the leader of the Lost Boys before Peter returned, who earlier shouted, "Kill the lawyer," now movingly tells Peter, "I wish I had a dad like you."

The attitudes toward lawyers in *Hook* and in *Henry VI, Part 2* are similar, if not almost identical. They spring from the same complex, ambivalent view of lawyers as both heros and villains. Despite the antilawyer veneer in both works—indeed, the near identity of the "kill the lawyer" comment—in fact it is the lawyer and what he represents that saves the two societies. Could Peter have rescued never-never land if he weren't a lawyer? Might Peter have chosen a different profession than the law? Would "kill the architect" or "kill the doctor" have gotten as much audience reaction? And yet Peter's offensive embodiment of the lawyer at the start of the film—which does merit criticism—evolved into a truer and more admirable concept as the movie went on.

Hook helps us understand Shakespeare's most famous comment about lawyers. What we know of Shakespeare's other plays will also inform our judgment on this question. But for all Shakespeare's use of legal terminology and imagery, for all his legal themes, he never comes right out and says what he truly thinks of lawyers and the law. So when we find what appears to be such a statement, it is worth pondering. Thus, in thinking about Shakespeare and the law, sooner or later one must confront that deathless line: "The first thing we do, let's kill all the lawyers" (2 *Henry VI*, 4.2.78).

For a lawyer, however, the resonance of that line disturbs and disquiets. The line reverberates enough to send even the most complacent attorney into a fit of self-doubt. On its face, the passage has an obvious antilawyer animus, making the line a shopworn favorite of newspaper editorial writers, iconoclastic bar association speakers, and indeed any critic of the legal profession who wants to seem learned by invoking an apparently apt, if trite, line from an unimpeachable source. A lawyer's puzzlement at the acerbity of Shakespeare's antilawyer line is, therefore, understandable.

But what does the oft-repeated passage *really* mean? The most probable answer is that Shakespeare intended his character's comment to have not one but three layers of meaning. We cannot necessarily assume that Shakespeare's characters speak his personal beliefs. An author may be using the character for another purpose. On its face, the line overflows with antilawyer feeling. But right below the surface lies a second meaning that compliments the role of lawyers in civilized society. A third, still deeper interpretation makes the controversial line a criticism not of all lawyers but only of those who pervert and distort law. All three readings are possible, though the third is the most sensitive.

THE SOURCE

A curious fact about the popular passage is that while many people can recite it, almost no one can tell you where it comes from. The line is famous; the play it comes from is not.

The famous—lawyers might say notorious—line occurs in *Henry VI, Part 2*, one of Shakespeare's most obscure, neglected, and rarely read or produced works. It is among Shakespeare's earliest plays, written while he was still a young man in his twenties, not up to the high artistic level of his more mature works, and for that reason consigned to near oblivion.

Henry VI, Part 2 is the second play in a trilogy about the troubled reign of a weak and ineffectual English king in the fifteenth century. Son of Henry V, the strong and glorious victor over the French at the Battle of Agincourt, Henry VI inherited the crown as a nine-month-old infant on his father's premature death in 1422. Henry VI is exactly the opposite of his dynamic and powerful father; he is one more Shakespearean example of a feeble central authority. The result is constant fighting, with humiliating losses to the French abroad and with civil disorder at home (including a popular revolt and the Wars of the Roses) for control of the kingdom.

In Shakespeare's play, the duke of York stirs up the common people and manipulates Jack Cade, a boorish, violent, and uneducated man, to lead the rebellion. Cade, with a sour disposition, assumes de facto command of the poor and ragged troops.

The line about lawyers comes out of the mouth of one of the rebels as they are about to invade London. A fellow with the distinctive name of Dick the Butcher utters the line after Jack Cade, the rebel leader, "vows" to his followers what his reforms will be when he becomes king.

"There shall be in England seven halfpenny loaves sold for a penny," Cade proclaims, as he describes the utopia he will usher in. "All the realm shall be in common"—that is, held communally. "There shall be no money. / All shall eat and drink on my score, and I will apparel / them all in one livery that they may agree like brothers, and worship me their lord" (4.2.70–77).

On hearing Cade's radical platform for redistributing wealth and abolishing private property, Dick the Butcher shouts, "The first thing we do, let's kill all the lawyers" (4.2.78).

Cade likes Dick's brilliant idea. "Nay, that I mean to do," answers Cade, and goes on to tell of his own unfortunate personal experience with contracts under seal drawn by crafty lawyers (4.2.79).

A messenger returning from Cade's rebels reports that they call all lawyers (as well as scholars, courtiers, and gentlemen) "false caterpillars," a phrase meaning parasites and commonly used for capitalistic oppressors, and that the rebels "intend their death" (4.4.36–37). Dick wants the rebels to "break open the jails and let out the prisoners" (4.3.14–15). Cade wants to destroy the Inns of Court and to burn all the records of the realm.

First Meaning: Criticism of Lawyers

Cade's and Dick's negative attitude toward lawyers must be understood in the context of a class revolt. The rebellion led by Cade in *Henry VI, Part 2* is an uprising by the commons, a popular revolt by lower classes—"infinite numbers" of peasants, "laboring men," and "handicraftsmen" such as clothiers, butchers, weavers, sawyers, tanners—against the power and luxury of the English upper classes. Cade tells his cohorts they were fighting to recover their "ancient freedom" so they would no longer have to "live in slavery to the nobility" (4.7.181–82).

Then as now lawyers were more available to the wealthy and powerful, who could afford to retain them, than to the poor and the weak, and were the very symbols of the inequities and oppression that provoke a revolution. As a result, the folk image of lawyers has often been bad. Common people have frequently seen lawyers in their roles as conservative defenders of property and the status quo, as unethical "hired guns" or "mouthpieces" available to the highest bidder, as a professional elite of technical wizards adept at using the law to cheat honest but poor people. Many upright citizens, wearied by what Hamlet called "the law's delay" or caught in the intricacies of legal red tape, must have bitterly echoed Dick the Butcher's sentiment through clenched teeth at one time or another.

How, then, can we be surprised that Cade's rebellion, seeking redistribution of property, puts lawyers, who protect existing property arrangements, at the top of its "enemies list"? Killing all the lawyers is not second or third on the revolutionists' agenda, but first. The primacy of that task tells us a lot about how lawyers were perceived.

Harold Laski, the English political scientist and friend of Justice Holmes, used to say that in every revolution the lawyers are liquidated first. One reason given for lawyers leading the lines to the guillotine or the firing squad is that, "while law is supposed to be a device to serve society, a civilized way of helping the wheels go round without too much friction, it is pretty hard to find a group less concerned with serving society and more concerned with serving themselves than the lawyers."[2]

The ill will of Jack Cade and his rebels toward lawyers in *Henry VI, Part 2* reminds us of a strikingly similar incident in our own constitutional history. The American incident was Shays' Rebellion, an agrarian protest in 1786 by debt-ridden farmers in western Massachusetts in favor of tax reforms, paper money, and "stay" laws to postpone mortgage foreclosures. Those farmers, led by a former captain in the Continental Army named Daniel Shays, seized local courthouses to stop court-ordered foreclosures. Although Shays' Rebellion was crushed after several months, the fears it raised of a violent insurrection by an unruly mob with extreme radical views catalyzed the calling of a constitutional convention to form a strong central government.

Like Cade and his followers, the Shaysites attacked the legal profession. The down-and-out farmers who followed Shays saw lawyers as savage beasts of prey who moved in swarms. One local legislator reported that lawyers had, "almost universally, been represented as the pests of society" by backcountry farmers.[3] Shays would whip up crowds with attacks on courts and lawyers, accusing them of being in league with eastern creditors. He would attack the rapacity of attorneys, pointing out—as we have heard in our own time—that at the ridiculously high fees they charged, only the rich could hire them.[4]

So alike is the rhetoric that sometimes it is hard to tell the difference between the antilawyer attitudes of Cade's rebellion and Shays' Rebellion. According to one newspaper writer in Massachusetts in 1786, farmers, feeling pressure from creditors, looked "with disgust and aversion" at the lawyers' "great appearances of wealth by their splendid tables, rich furniture, sitting up chariots, and the like," and blamed them for the ruin of "many good worthy families." Members of the bar, these American farmers believed, were "an altogether useless order," and they hoped "to crush or at least put a proper check or restraint on that order of gentlemen denominated lawyers."[5]

Both Cade's rebellion in *Henry VI, Part 2* and Shays' Rebellion can be interpreted as popular uprisings driven by the spirit of economic justice, responsive government, and law that is neither oppressive nor rigid nor beyond the reach of the common person. On this reading, we can infer that Dick the Butcher's most famous line was intended to mean what it plainly says. But there is more than one reading and one inference possible.

SECOND MEANING: COMPLIMENT TO LAWYERS

It is equally plausible to read the line as less of a criticism and more of a compliment to lawyers. Not surprisingly, many lawyers, including at least one sitting Supreme Court justice, have adopted the complimentary point of view. In a 1985 case, Justice John Paul Stevens, who has always followed his own lights on the Court, dissented because he rejected the majority's "apparent unawareness of the function of the independent lawyer as a guardian of our freedom." In a footnote cheering to lawyers he wrote, "That function was, however, well understood by Jack Cade and his followers, characters who are often forgotten and whose most famous line is often misunderstood." Stevens went on to point out that Dick the Butcher's statement about killing lawyers "was spoken by a rebel, not a friend of liberty." Winding up his Shakespearean reference, Stevens wrote, "As a careful reading of that text will reveal, Shakespeare insightfully realized that disposing of lawyers is a step in the direction of a totalitarian form of government."[6]

Justice Stevens reacted to Dick's line the way one might expect all thin-skinned, oversensitive, defensive lawyers to react to it. They bridle at the criticism in the line spoken by Dick the Butcher. They believe that the line "was not intended as a slur" because "analysis . . . shows *conclusively* that the legal profession . . . was regarded as a stabilizing force in society, complimentary to say the least." To such readers, it is "*clear* that Shakespeare never intended the line mouthed by Dick the Butcher as the fountainhead for the proposition that eliminating lawyers would be best for society's welfare."[7]

One irate lawyer-literary critic announced with authority in 1988 that "the butcher's line was intended by Shakespeare as a compliment to the legal profession." So sure was he that he went on, in a paroxysm of ad hominem argument, to dispose of his opponents by impugning their intelligence and good faith. Only "the ignorant or malevolent person," he trumpeted, "uses it—rather, misuses it—as written."[8]

Although evidence exists to support such an interpretation, countervailing evidence—such as the plain meaning of the line itself—undercuts such a reading. A fairer and less defensive view of the line by an open-minded lawyer—one neither ignorant nor malevolent—must leave genuine doubts. The evidence is anything but conclusive or clear, one way or the other. And that may be one secret of good literature: like Frank Stockton's open-ended story "The Lady or the Tiger," it allows readers latitude to supply their own meaning.

Undoubtedly, there is evidence for the "compliment-to-lawyer" meaning. Shakespeare had put an important event—the plucking of the red and white roses in the fourth scene of the second act of *Henry VI, Part 1*—in the garden of Middle Temple, one of the Inns of Court. Why choose a lawyers' haven if the Bard thought so little of lawyers? The precise dramatic context and the circumstances surrounding Dick's line yield insight, but not certainty. It is absolutely correct to look at who speaks the line: Dick the Butcher, an unschooled, buffoonish peasant who is part of a class rebellion to overthrow the king and his lawful government. He lacks credibility and is totally irrational. Dick the Butcher and his cohorts in Jack Cade's rebel tide represent the opposite of civilization. They stand for rampant ignorance, anarchy, chaos, and disorder, coupled with the blood lust of the mob.

Lawyers stand in the way of successful revolution. Conservative by nature and training, lawyers think in terms of respect for precedent, rather than sharp breaks with the past. Even when lawyers or judges are innovative, they strain to prove that no novelty—not the slightest departure from earlier law—has occurred. Lawyers generally support the status quo, not radical change. Lawyers tend to be a stable, lawful government's first line of defense. To have a successful revolution, you must get rid of the lawyers.

But we should not go overboard in praising lawyers for opposing revolutions. Lawyers have also had more than a little to do with leading revolutions. Several of the signers of our own Declaration of Independence were attorneys. Many of the leaders of the French Revolution, such as Robespierre and Danton, were lawyers. Fidel Castro was a lawyer. Yet the point holds: lawyers do have a reputation for opposing radical change.

Shakespeare may also have simply been reporting the facts as he understood them. He took many of his plots from the second edition of Holinshed's *Chronicles*, published in 1587. (The authorship and sources of *Henry VI, Part 2* are a scholarly tangle.) The text of *Henry VI, Part 2* is consistent with Holinshed's account of the 1381 revolt. Holinshed states that the rebels wanted "to destroy first the great lords of the realm, and after the judges and the lawyers."[9] If Shakespeare was thus plagiarizing, it is unfair to impute to him any independent intention behind the famous line.

We should also stress the speaker's name and trade. It is more than coincidence that the fellow who proclaims "let's kill all the lawyers" is named Dick the *Butcher*. His name itself personifies revolutionary violence and bloodshed, and Shakespeare meant it to do so. On no less than four separate occasions in the play, some having nothing to do with Cade's rebellion, Shakespeare expressly links "butcher" with "slaughter."

The irrational, mindless, and uncivilized ferocity of Cade, Dick, and their cohorts reveals itself right after they speak of killing lawyers. Within a few lines, Cade orders a clerk executed for no offense other than his ability to read and write, including the ability to write "courthand," that is, formal legal script. "Away with him, I say, hang him with his pen and / inkhorn about his neck" (4.2.108–9). Cade's irrational fear of those who can read and write and interpret laws might reasonably be seen as indicating that lawyers were perceived as stabilizing forces in society, who helped dispense justice and create social cohesiveness. Cade's killing of the clerk may dramatically symbolize all those things he fears most in an organized and stable society. But there is a deeper layer of meaning here too.

To punish a clerk for being able to read and write serves in dramatic fashion to expose a gross inequity in the legal system of the time, which punished people simply for the opposite offense, that is, for being illiterate. Under the doctrine of "benefit of clergy," the law then exempted from hanging and other penalties those offenders who could read Latin. The rebel leader refers to "benefit of clergy" later in the play as he charges one nobleman:

> Thou hast appointed justices of peace, to call poor men before them about matters they were not able to answer. Moreover, thou hast put them in prison, and because they could not read thou hast hanged them. (4.7.38–42)

The earlier incident in which Cade executes the clerk for being literate, rather than being mere mindless violence, suddenly mocks the mindless violence of the mirror-image legal doctrine in the prevailing system.

Another reason for suggesting that Shakespeare may not have meant anyone to take seriously what Dick the Butcher said about lawyers is comedy. Dick the Butcher is a comical character, and all the Cade scenes are humorous, ridiculous scenes. The pretension of the rebels, their dialogue and actions all seem like comic relief. They are the main audience attraction in an otherwise unremarkable play.

And Shakespeare, like any playwright, must have kept his audience very much in mind. Lawyers and law students made up a large part of Shakespeare's playgoing public. Shakespeare's plays were performed, among other places, at the Inns of Court.

To a lawyer-filled audience looking to be entertained, a line like "The first thing we do, let's kill all the lawyers" was bound, if not designed, to get a reaction. There might be snickers or laughter, but there would certainly be reaction, much as Oliver Stone's film *Wall Street* drew a strong audience response from the investment banking community. Perhaps, then, Shakespeare meant Dick's lawyer line as no more than a comic throwaway for the lawyer-filled stalls.

The play itself seems to corroborate this comic reading. For example, when Cade talks of himself as the embodiment of English law, and Dick the Butcher says "the laws of England may come out of your mouth," three stage-whisper asides underline the abomination of a fool on the throne. One rebel says, "T'will be sore law"; another says, "It will be stinking law"; and a third adds, "Then we are like to have biting statutes unless his teeth be pulled out" (4.7.7–16). These expressions make it seem unlikely that Shakespeare would have put a serious statement or his own view about law into the mouth of such unsympathetic and violent characters as Cade and Dick.

On the other hand, for all their comical attributes, the rebels may well have served another, more serious Shakespearean purpose. Even though Dick the Butcher and Jack Cade seem like bloodthirsty buffoons, Shakespeare may well have been using comedy to make serious social comment about law. How better to cloak a mildly subversive attitude than in funny garb? It is a technique as old as Aristophanes, as trenchant as George Bernard Shaw, as current as "Saturday Night Live."

Shakespeare's portrayal of Cade's rebellion is a great satire on communism and bolshevism. Shakespeare's attitude toward Cade resembles his attitude toward the rabble in *Julius Caesar* and *Coriolanus*. One might well conclude from this that Shakespeare believed in law and order and that he did not sympathize with Dick the Butcher. A famous speech by Ulysses in *Troilus and Cressida* is often cited to support this view.[10]

In Ulysses's speech, he exalts authority and order, which he calls "degree": "Take but degree away, untune that string, / And hark what discord follows" (*Troilus and Cressida*, 1.3.109–10). According to Knight, the views expressed here by Ulysses, with their horror of chaos, are "the backbone of all of Shakespeare's judicial concepts."[11] But once again we run up against the problem of imputing to an author the views expressed by one of his characters. Is Ulysses any more than Dick the real Shakespeare? And besides, as Knight himself somewhat inconsistently recognizes, there is much to indicate that Shakespeare was no mere defender of the status quo, but one who sought reform in the law and elsewhere.

Using comedy as a mask for serious social commentary may be the only way to make such criticism under a regime of censorship, such as existed for Shakespeare. A government functionary called the master of the revels and his staff strictly scrutinized and carefully reviewed the texts of Elizabethan plays to make sure they were in accord with law, order, and current government attitudes. When authorities act as censors, as they did in Shakespeare's time, a playwright with a critical bent will search for a way to get his message across without it being gelded by the bureaucrats; the creator will make an end run around the censors.

THIRD MEANING: CRITICISM OF PERVERTED LAW

The most important—and often overlooked—point about law in *Henry VI, Part 2* is the crucial role of another character in the play, Humphrey, duke of Gloucester. One simply cannot understand Dick the Butcher's controversial line without seeing how it relates to Gloucester. Significantly, the full original title of the play is *The Second Part of Henry the Sixth, with the Death of the Good Duke Humphrey.*

As lord protector, Gloucester in effect rules England during Henry's minority. A "virtuous prince" (2.2.74), Gloucester symbolizes the rule of law, its fair execution and administration, as well as the need—reminiscent of Socrates—to submit to it when it wrongly turns on him. In Gloucester, one finds the humane impulses that should animate the law. Other advisers to the king, ambitious for themselves and jealous of Gloucester's sway, unjustly accuse him, and while holding him for trial, kill him. All the time, everyone around the king—scrupulous or not—pays lip service to the law, its integrity and symbolism.

In the three acts before Jack Cade appears, law—especially law in the person of Gloucester—is a dominant theme. We begin truly to understand Dick the Butcher's quote only by knowing its context, by seeing what preceded it in the play. Early in the play, for example, the king asks Gloucester, "What shall we say to this in law?" (1.3.206). Gloucester passes judgment: "This is the law" (1.3.213). At another point, when his wife is banished "by sentence of law" for witchcraft, Gloucester shows the same emotional self-control and devotion to law as Brutus the Elder when his sons were convicted of treason, saying, "The law, thou seest, hath judgèd thee, / I cannot justify whom the law condemns" (2.3.15–16).

Law still dominates as other nobles intrigue against Gloucester. He then becomes a victim of perverted law. Buckingham falsely accuses Gloucester of imposing punishments that "exceeded law, / And left thee to the mercy of the law" (1.3.136–37). As to these accusations, Gloucester spits back, "Prove them, and I lie open to the law." Even as his enemies have him within their grasp, Gloucester still believes in the integrity of the law, and his enemies at last say, " 'Tis meet he be condemned by course of law" (3.1.237).

Perhaps the sequence of events culminating in Gloucester's death means the death of law and the triumph of chaos and disorder. It is at this

point, and not before, that the commons rise up in anger. By fairly administering the law, by acting as a tribune of the people, Gloucester had "won
the commons' hearts" (3.1.28). When he, their lord protector, became
imperiled by what passed for law, "the commons haply rise to save his
life" (3.1.240). When they hear of Gloucester's murder as he is in the
clutches of the law,

> The commons, like an angry hive of bees
> That want their leader, scatter up and down
> And care not who they sting in his revenge.
>
> (3.2.125–27)

Most important, Cade's mob emerges only at the moment of Gloucester's death. They did not criticize the law before then. The people are
compelled, through lack of a lawgiver, through the total breakdown of
the constitutional rule of order, to take the law into their own hands.
They do not protest all law, but only perverted, false law, such as accused
and killed the good duke of Gloucester. As symbols of the evil legal system, lawyers become the object of hatred. This is the third, the most pen-
etrating, and yet previously unexplored layer of meaning in Dick the
Butcher's line.

The original intent behind Dick's line is not illuminated by Shakespeare's own experiences, which point in both directions. His many dealings with lawyers and lawsuits could have made him sour or happy. His
work near the Inns of Court could have made him admire or detest lawyers. In such equivocal circumstances, and without more definitive biographical facts, it is impossible to say for sure what Shakespeare himself
thought about lawyers or what he personally intended by Dick the
Butcher's line.

Whatever its original meaning, however, the Butcher's remark has
come to reflect society's impatience with legalistic delays, injustices, and
longwindedness, with the oppression often associated with what the lawyer does for a living. In this sense, the famous passage in *Henry VI, Part
2* has become like those parts of our Constitution that take on a life of
their own, acquire a gloss, and evolve into a meaning more vital than
anything originally intended. Today, Dick the Butcher's line has become
emblematic of a widespread antilawyer attitude that views attorneys as
parasites and enemies of productivity and economic well being. In 1990
Marlin Fitzwater, President Bush's press secretary, said publicly, "Everyone ought to take every opportunity to blast lawyers."[12] All of this con-
tributes to the relatively low esteem in which the public holds lawyers.

Our culture's deep ambivalence toward lawyers emerges clearly from
the remarks addressed by a nonlawyer government official to a gathering
of the bar in 1981: "You wouldn't think law was the honorable profes-

sion that it is. You'd think the opposite." The government official went on to say that "lawyers are blamed for a whole Pandora's box of social ills: for the endless proliferation of governmental rules and regulations, for national litigiousness, for a lot of things—for crime itself." Then the speaker shifted gears. "But we ultimately are thankful for you, and look to you, because you, along with the government, are the standard-bearers of the Constitution." He told the lawyers that he knew they viewed their work as a "sacred trust."[13]

Those are words of George Bush, who, during his service as vice-president, addressed them to the opening session of the annual meeting of the American Bar Association on August 10, 1981. It is the same George Bush who in 1992 strongly criticized the "sharp lawyers" shod in "tasseled loafers" who are "running wild" within the legal system.

Everybody loves to hate lawyers. Witness the popularity of antilawyer jokes. And nobody loves to hate lawyers more than lawyers themselves. That is why so many lawyers love to quote Dick the Butcher's line and to use Daumier's antilawyer prints to decorate their offices.

Hyperbolic rhetoric about Shakespeare's famous lawyer line in *Henry VI, Part 2* obscures the emotional and political nuances of reality. To give lawyers a simple thumbs up or thumbs down flattens out the ambiguities of politics and history, turning the chiaroscuro of real life into a one-dimensional caricature in primary colors. Is it likely that Shakespeare, usually so subtle in his personality portraits, made legal characters into stick figures in a morality drama?

If we would truly understand Shakespeare's view of lawyers in *Henry VI, Part 2* and in general, we should study it from two perspectives, always taking into account the ambivalence lawyers generate. First we should consider it from Spielberg's ambivalent angle of vision in *Hook*, for *Hook* has essentially the same point of view of lawyers as *Henry VI, Part 2*. Four hundred years from now, other dramatists, screenwriters, and their future equivalents will no doubt write other words in which angry characters shout, "Kill the lawyer." The second way to test the correctness of our understanding of the Bard's complex attitude in *Henry VI, Part 2* is to look at Shakespeare's approach to law and lawyers in some of his other plays.

Chapter Three

A SCARECROW OF THE LAW

Measure for Measure

A GOOD PLACE to start a canvass of law in Shakespeare, to see what Shakespeare really meant by his famous "kill all the lawyers" comment, is *Measure for Measure* and *The Merchant of Venice*, Shakespeare's two "legal" plays. In these two plays, after all, Shakespeare did more than use law as a metaphor; he cemented law into their very foundations. To some, what Shakespeare wrote about law in these two plays is radically unsound. Still, as Posner notes, "Maybe a lawyer can say something new about these works and correct some misunderstandings about them."[1]

Although *The Merchant of Venice* has been the subject of more legal commentary than any other Shakespeare play, *Measure for Measure* better introduces Shakespeare's overall attitudes toward the law. Of all Shakespeare's plays, *Measure for Measure* has by far the most serviceable legal themes. By considering *Measure for Measure* first, we also set up the important similarities, contrasts, and transition between it and the more well-known *Merchant of Venice*. Besides, I have a personal reason for beginning with *Measure for Measure*: it was the play that opened my dim eyes to the link between Shakespeare and the law.

Measure for Measure is an ideal play for lawyers. It quivers with legal immediacy and raises fundamental questions of law and morality. Legal themes permeate the play and rivet the attention of both lawyers and nonlawyers alike. "Good counselors lack no / clients," one character announces in the first act (1.2.198–99), and we know near the start that we are watching a play about law.

The underlying legal themes in *Measure for Measure* are perennial and controversial; they were controversial four hundred years ago and they remain so today, perhaps even more so. Then, as now, people have wondered about law intersecting with morality, especially when such morality is considered in some sense private. Then, as now, we have thought about how much public support and respect law needs, whether or not to enforce dead-letter statutes, and if it is better to interpret laws strictly or equitably. Then, as now, all of us have considered the effect of power on human nature, how judges may be corrupt, and how important mercy is. All of these legal themes—and more—run throughout *Measure for Measure*.

The story line of *Measure for Measure* sets up legal themes from the outset. The duke of Vienna is worried that his subjects have no respect for the laws he has been lax in enforcing. He pretends to leave his city, and in his supposed absence, appoints Angelo, who he thinks is a real straight arrow, as his deputy. The result is a resurgence of law and order, but also a collapse of mercy-tempered justice. Angelo starts to enforce laws that the duke did not. One, imposing the death penalty for making love outside of marriage, has not been enforced in fourteen years.

Angelo invokes this harsh law against Claudio, who made his fiancée, Julietta, pregnant. Claudio's sister, Isabella, pleads with Angelo not to execute Claudio. Angelo, before now assumed to be a paragon of virtue, tells Isabella he will let her brother live only if she will go to bed with him, Angelo. The rest of the play revolves around this basic conflict.

One of the many ways to approach the legal themes in *Measure for Measure* is to consider them in light of the law in that time and place—Vienna in the Middle Ages. Another way is to invoke the law of Shakespeare's England as a vehicle to analyze the play's legal aspects. A third possibility involves looking at *Measure for Measure* from the perspective of American law today. One wonders if the duke's complaints have a modern, topical ring to them in America at the end of the twentieth century. The last of these potential windows offers the clearest view of how the issues in *Measure for Measure* still trouble our law.

Every period reinterprets the arts of the past, visual and literary, in terms congruent with the interests of the present. Our current experience of a work of art almost four hundred years old must be affected by what is happening in our contemporary world. It would not be difficult for some people to see parallels between the Vienna of *Measure for Measure* and the America of today. Law seems to be in disrepute, crime rampant, and old notions of morality disregarded. "Liberty plucks Justice by the nose," declares a character in *Measure for Measure*, "and quite athwart / Goes all decorum" (1.3.29–31). But the parallels hardly end there.

At the end of June 1986, just about a year after I had seen *Measure for Measure* for the second time, the Supreme Court handed down a highly controversial decision that greatly helped clarify for me the continuing legal significance of *Measure for Measure*. In *Bowers v. Hardwick* the high court upheld, by a bare five-to-four vote, a Georgia law making it a crime to engage in sodomy.[2] After being charged with violating that statute, Michael Hardwick sued in federal court to challenge the constitutionality of the law insofar as it criminalized consensual homosexual acts in private. The district attorney declined to present the criminal charge against Hardwick to a grand jury. A majority of the Supreme Court ruled that the law, which had not been applied in decades and which carried a possible twenty-year prison sentence for one homosexual act, was constitutional—that it did not violate any fundamental rights of homosexuals, even though it was applied to an adult male's conduct in his own home with a consenting adult male partner. The Supreme Court's decision has received widely differing responses, favorable and unfavorable.

The parallels between *Bowers v. Hardwick* and *Measure for Measure* are striking. Both turn on laws used to enforce morals and regulate private behavior. Both raise the issue of public respect for law and statutes that had not been enforced. Both put offenders at risk of extreme punishment for minor infractions. Both involve questions of power. And both stand for theories of mercy and legal interpretation.

With so many common factors, the 1986 case and the 1604 play braid well, helping us better understand both the Supreme Court's decision and Shakespeare's work, as well as glimpse some of the unresolved problems of law and humanity. *Bowers v. Hardwick* therefore offers an excellent vehicle for examining *Measure for Measure*, an effective prism refracting the white legal light of *Measure for Measure* into a rainbow of its separate and colorful legal components.

LAW AND MORALITY

At the core of *Measure for Measure* and *Bowers v. Hardwick* lives an old, vexing, and still unresolved question: how much should law be used to enforce morals? Or put another way: if conduct is immoral, should it be criminal? Does such a question confuse public and private morality and mix up the realm of law with the realm of morals? These are daunting and disputable issues, made more complex by strong emotions, and illustrated by the play, the Supreme Court case, and other developments.

Both Shakespeare's play and the *Bowers* case use law to enforce morals, to prohibit what a person does in private. In the play, it is a law prohibiting nonmarital sex. In the *Bowers* case, it is a law prohibiting homosexual acts (actually, the statute reaches more broadly). In both, abstract morals translated into law clash with sexual conduct by real people or imaginary characters. We feel pressing into our spirit "the manacles / Of the all-binding law" (2.4.93–94).

Criminal law should be drawn from public morality, or so it is frequently said. But what is public morality? Probably a blend of custom and conviction, of reason and feeling, of experience and prejudice. Certain behavior, often regarded as a violation of a sexual code, is viewed by many as immoral. Thus, in those seventeenth-century colonies in America where the Puritans were in control, law generally made little or no distinction between sin and crime. Hundreds were whipped, fined, put in the stocks or forced to marry, because of the "crime" of fornication.[3]

Laws against sexual behavior—premarital and extramarital sex, abortion, homosexuality, prostitution, pornography, availability of contraceptives, sex education in public schools—all raise an issue at the heart of *Measure for Measure*. Such laws as well as pressures for others like them from various groups in society are closely linked to the enforcement of morals.

Laws to enforce morals provoke controversy, even among Shakespeare's descendants. In 1957 in England, the celebrated *Report of the Committee on Homosexual Offenses and Prostitution*, generally known as the *Wolfenden Report*, recommended that homosexual practices between consenting adults no longer be criminal. The committee declared that the function of criminal law in this field

> is to preserve public order and decency, to protect the citizen from what is offensive or injurious, and to provide sufficient safeguards against exploitation and corruption of others, particularly those who are specially vulnerable because they are young, weak in body or mind, inexperienced, or in a state of special physical, official or economic dependence. It is not, in our view, the function of the law to intervene in the private lives of citizens, or to seek to enforce any particular pattern of behavior, further than is necessary to carry out the purposes we have outlined.

In concluding "that homosexual behavior between consenting adults in private should no longer be a criminal offense," the committee stated the argument that it found to be

> decisive, namely, the importance which society and the law ought to give to individual freedom of choice and action in matters of private morality. Unless a deliberate attempt is to be made by society, acting through the agency of the law, to equate the sphere of crime with that of sin, there must remain a realm of private morality and immorality which is, in brief and crude terms, not the law's business. To say this is not to condone or encourage private immorality.[4]

Public debate followed. A year later, in 1958, Patrick Devlin, an eminent English judge, delivered an important lecture to the British Academy called "The Enforcement of Morals." In his lecture, Devlin disagreed with the *Wolfenden Report* and concluded that society has the right to eradicate conduct if a society, after "looking at it calmly and dispassionately," genuinely regards it "as a vice so abominable that its mere presence is an offense."[5] According to Devlin, society apparently has a right to punish behavior that it intensely dislikes, even where such behavior does not injure others, on the ground that the state has a Platonic role to play as moral teacher through use of the criminal law. By pronouncing through law what is legal and illegal, the state—so goes the argument—tells its citizens what is good and bad, what is to be encouraged and discouraged. As Justice Louis Brandeis wrote in one of his most famous Supreme Court dissents, "Our Government is the potent, omnipresent teacher. For good or ill, it teaches the whole people by its example."[6]

But a closer look shows that Devlin's argument is more complex and is really composed of two separate though related points. The first point would be that society has a right to protect its own existence as follows: two kinds of moral principles exist in modern society, those adapted for our own guidance without attempting to impose them on others (for example, dictates of a particular religion), and those beyond toleration and imposed on all (for example, monogamy). Inasmuch as society cannot survive without some moral conformity essential to its life, society has the absolute right to insist on such conformity to preserve its existence. And if society has such a right, it can use the criminal law to enforce that right—to prevent the corruption of morality that ties society together. This right is restrained by "toleration of the maximum individual freedom that is consistent with the integrity of society." Thus, according to Devlin, not every act of immorality should be punished by the criminal law. It is only those that make public feeling rise to "intolerance, indignation and disgust," such as an "abominable vice."[7]

Devlin's first argument has serious weaknesses. If the theory is based on the very survival of society, how do we know when the danger of immorality is sufficiently clear and present? Is there a way to distinguish between an imminent actual threat and mere public disapproval?

Devlin's second argument is that society has a right, if it wants, to prevent the social environment from changing. But here we wonder if the threatened institutions are sufficiently valuable to protect at the cost of human freedom. And we may question whether a society is entitled to protect itself against a change in social institutions.

This debate still rages today. Victimless crimes is the current contoversial phrase we use for the category of offenses at the border of law and morals. The twenty years since *Roe v. Wade* have seen a huge increase in the level of violent anti-abortion protests. And the 1992 Republican National Convention showcased various spokespersons and groups that full-throatedly advocated the use of law to regulate morals. Shortly after the 1992 presidential election, the chairman of the Oregon Republican party complained, "We have simply got to take the party back from the mean-spirited, intolerant people who want to interject big government into people's personal lives."[8]

Advocates of government intervention in personal lives must have found solace in the majority opinion in *Bowers v. Hardwick*. The five-person majority, like Angelo in *Measure for Measure* and Lord Devlin in his notable speech, felt that law can be used to enforce morality. They faced the argument that there was no rational basis for the Georgia law, that the "presumed belief of a majority of the electorate in Georgia that homosexual sodomy is immoral and unacceptable" is "an inadequate rationale to support the law." To this argument, the majority retorted that the law "is constantly based on notions of morality, and if all laws representing essentially moral choices are to be invalidated . . . the courts will be very busy indeed." The majority did not agree that "majority sentiments about the morality of homosexuality should be declared inadequate" and was "unpersuaded that the sodomy laws of some 25 states should be invalidated on this basis."[9]

But the four dissenting justices in *Bowers*, who basically agreed with the *Wolfenden Report*, stated the opposing views forcefully. Two dissenting opinions, one by Justice Harry Blackmun and the other by Justice John Paul Stevens, strongly disagreed with the majority's notion that morality was always a sufficient basis for law. Justice Blackmun, in what may be the most powerful opinion he ever wrote, answered the argument that homosexuality has long been considered immoral by quoting a 1984 precedent that held, "Private biases may be outside the reach of the law, but the law cannot, directly or indirectly, give them effect."[10] Citing another precedent, Blackmun went on to say, "Mere public intolerance or animosity cannot constitutionally justify the deprivation of a person's liberty."

Blackmun saw the law in question as one of "those that enforce private morality." "Although reasonable people may differ about whether particular sexual acts are moral or immoral," he added, quoting British legal philosopher H.L.A. Hart, that "we have ample evidence for believing that people will not abandon morality, will not think any better of murder, cruelty, and dishonesty, merely because some private sexual practice which they abominate is not punished by the law." Summing up his position, Blackmun wrote, "The mere knowledge that other individuals do not adhere to one's value system cannot be a legally cognizable interest, . . . let alone an interest that can justify invading the houses, hearts, and minds of citizens who choose to live their lives differently."

Blackmun dealt with some of the key issues raised by Lord Devlin's speech, identifying the core of the majority's position in the supposed "right of the Nation and of the States to maintain a decent society." But he rejected the argument that "the acts made criminal by the statute may have serious consequences for 'the general public health and welfare,' such as spreading communicable diseases or fostering other criminal activity." At a time when the risk of AIDS had not yet been fully known, Blackmun found the record barren of any evidence that the activity was "physically dangerous, either to the persons engaged in it or to others." Nor could Blackmun find the statute "justified as a 'morally neutral' exercise of Georgia's power to 'protect the public environment.' " Although he conceded that "some private behavior may affect the fabric of society as a whole," Blackmun taxed the majority for failing "to see the difference between laws that protect public sensibilities and those that enforce private morality."[11]

Justice Stevens also wrote a dissent that dealt with the issue of using laws to enforce morals. According to Stevens, prior cases made it "abundantly clear" that "the fact that the governing majority in a State has traditionally viewed a particular practice as immoral is not a sufficient reason for upholding a law prohibiting the practice." To support his proposition, Stevens cited laws making miscegenation a crime, which "neither history nor tradition" could save "from constitutional attack" in 1967.[12]

The problem of law and morality, as all this amply shows, is complex and divisive. Law reflects and advances the prevailing moral values of society. All laws have a moral dimension, and judges are necessarily influenced by the spirit of the age. When a court's position is radically out of step with the existing moral climate, its credibility is strained and its authority undermined. As Justice Oliver Wendell Holmes, Jr., wrote in 1880 in *The Common Law*, "The first requirement of a sound body of law is that it should correspond with the actual feelings and demands of the community, whether right or wrong."[13]

Robert Bork, President Reagan's defeated nominee to the Supreme Court, sees the problem as a question of democracy. He rejects as "wholly fallacious" the notion that "you can't legislate morality." "Indeed," he adds, "we legislate little else." Bork, in his best seller *The Tempting of America*, argues that the majority has the right and the freedom to decide what kind of society it wants to live in. He asks whether the American people have given up something by failing to promote positive values for the law. Bork wonders: if communities are forbidden to regulate sexual conduct, pornography, and the like, do citizens feel further alienated from control over their own lives? If religion—which is linked with morality—is completely removed from all aspects of law and public life, Bork warns, "other transcendent principles, some of them very ugly indeed, may replace them."[14]

That being said, however, we still have to decide which moral convictions should be transformed into law, that is, which of various moral principles held by people in a pluralist society command (and should command) sufficient support to become enforceable through coercive power of the state. It helps to define terms a bit more clearly. When people speak of a crusade to legislate morality, they probably do not mean morality in the broad sense used by Bork. Rather, the debate over legislated morality tends to focus not on public morality, but on private morality, on that section of morality in which one's behavior is thought to affect only oneself, or, if other people, at least not to the extent that they suffer physical violence. It is the difference between, say, prohibiting couples from using condoms and prohibiting child abuse. The former is an example of legislated private morality; the latter is not.

Within the realm of such self-regarding or private actions, it is more difficult to accept Bork's statement that "knowledge that immorality is taking place" is a sufficient ground for prohibitory legislation. Such a statement invites dangerous and intrusive lawmaking and is a big step on a steep slippery slope much better left untrod. It is a path toward skewing the "Madisonian dilemma" (between the competing goals of self-government and limitations on majorities in order to protect minorities) in favor of majorities, without taking account of the qualitative difference between moral outrage and actual, real-world, physical harm to other persons. "Moral outrage"—the standard established by Devlin and Bork—is too subjective and amorphous a justification (and too threatening to individual liberty) to be the sole basis for law.

Measure for Measure is an important contribution to this old debate about law and morals. It comes down against laws seeking to enforce private morality. As applied to Claudio's relationship with Julietta in *Measure for Measure*, the antifornication law seems even more ridiculous than it might in the abstract.

Claudio and Julietta are engaged, their formal wedding delayed only due to a dispute over her dowry. In act 1, Claudio even refers to Julietta as his "wife" (1.2.150). Although the precise legal status is somewhat murky, such an engagement created a marriage contract giving rise to a marital relationship of sorts. If the church did not view them as married, civil law considered them as good as wed in that neither was free to marry anyone else. Under the circumstances, Claudio's "offense" hardly seems grave, if an offense at all.

Curiously, this issue of the status of a marriage contract has become the most discussed legal question in the play. Much has been written about whether Claudio, in light of his engagement to Julietta, violated the law. But one cannot help thinking that the status of marriage contracts, however interesting to legal antiquarians, is not of signal legal importance today, except as an extenuating circumstance in Claudio's case. *Measure for Measure* is legally important for other reasons, although it is perhaps relevant to point out that Shakespeare himself hurriedly married Anne Hathaway after she became pregnant.

One wonders if some overzealous guardian of public virtue, some misguided Comstock, ever thought of banning *Measure for Measure*, which itself has a bedroom trick, as obscene. After all, the duke persuades Isabella to yield to Angelo's proposition, with the plan to have Mariana, Angelo's ex-fiancée, whom Angelo had jilted because of a dowry problem, go in Isabella's place to Angelo's bed. In the dark, Angelo thinks he spent the night with Isabella without realizing it was Mariana instead. Was such a trick immoral? Or did Angelo's marriage contract with Mariana make everything proper? Is the duke correct in saying to Mariana, "He is your husband on a precontract / To bring you thus together, 'tis no sin" (4.1.70–71)? Should the play have been censored?

PRIVACY

Embedded in any discussion of using law to enforce morals are basic issues of privacy. This intertwining of issues is apparent from the major countervailing consideration, identified by both the *Wolfenden Report* and Lord Devlin as the maximum allowable freedom of choice and action to be given to individuals in matters of private morality. It is also obvious from the distinction between public and private interests drawn by Justice Blackmun in his dissent in *Bowers v. Hardwick*. Indeed the main argument against the antisodomy statute in *Bowers* was that it unconstitutionally violated the fundamental rights—including the right of privacy—of homosexuals.

In light of *Bowers*, it is a fascinating exercise to see if the antifornication law in *Measure for Measure* would be, under American law of today, an unconstitutional violation of Claudio's fundamental right of privacy. To be sure, it may be unfair to impose our own legal notions on an earlier epoch, but at the same time it may shed some light on how various doctrines interrelate and have developed.

Even though nothing in the express language of the U.S. Constitution specifically says so, the Supreme Court long has recognized certain individual rights beyond the power of the state to regulate, rights within "a certain private sphere of individual liberty [that] will be kept largely beyond the reach of government."[15] Finding a privacy interest regarding certain *decisions* that are properly for the individual to make and certain *places* where those decisions are made, the Supreme Court has called privacy the ability independently to define one's identity, which is central to any concept of liberty. "The concept of privacy," repeated Justice Blackmun in his *Bowers* dissent, "embodies the 'moral fact that a person belongs to himself and not others nor to society as a whole.' "

Among those privacy rights are several dealing with sexual conduct between consenting adults, including marriage, contraception, and abortion. In describing some of these cases, the Supreme Court has referred to them as conferring "a fundamental individual right to decide whether or not to beget or bear a child." The *Bowers* majority accepted these cases and this description of them.

But the Court in *Bowers* refused to say that those cases covered homosexual acts. "None of the rights announced in those cases bears any resemblance to the claimed constitutional right of homosexuals to engage in acts of sodomy. . . . No connection between family, marriage, or procreation on the one hand and homosexual activity on the other has been demonstrated." Going on, the majority stated that "any claim that these cases nevertheless stand for the proposition that any kind of private sexual conduct between consenting adults is constitutionally insulated from state proscription is insupportable," pointing to adultery, incest, and other "sexual crimes." The majority also declined to announce the discovery of what it disparagingly called a new fundamental right to engage in homosexual acts.

The Court's holding in *Bowers* in no way precludes a different ruling on the antifornication statute in *Measure for Measure*. Shakespeare's law involves intimate choices by an unmarried adult heterosexual couple to have sex and to have children. (Julietta is often portrayed in the play as obviously pregnant.) These choices surely seem to fall well within the perimeter of judicial authority cited by the *Bowers* majority. The Supreme Court has also held that constitutional protection for individual decisions by married persons concerning the intimacies of their physical relationship, even when not intended to produce offspring, extends as well to intimate choices by unmarried as well as married persons.

It would therefore seem likely that the antifornication law as applied to Claudio and Julietta would not pass constitutional muster in today's America. This conclusion is buttressed by public reaction to Robert Bork's views on privacy at his confirmation hearing in 1987. Bork took the view that a constitutional right to privacy is wholly manufactured and limitless. In large part, the Senate's ostensible reason for rejecting Bork was his position on privacy. Regardless of the absence of explicit constitutional language about a right of privacy, the American people and American law are not about to give up such fundamental protection, however unclear the constitutional source.

Public Respect for Law

If a society is going to use law to enforce morals, it had better be fairly sure it is gauging morals correctly. Both Shakespeare in the play and the Supreme Court in *Bowers v. Hardwick* know that law needs widespread public respect. Shakespeare underscores this in a comic sequence. Pompey, a comic character, points out that the law against illegal lovemaking tries to do the impossible: "to geld and spay all the / youth of the city" (2.1.220–21). If all the offenders are executed, Pompey predicts, in ten years there will not be anyone left in Vienna.

Pompey's prophecy calls to mind a similar comment in 1972 by a shore patrolman in the U.S. Navy. The Navy court-martialed a Navy chaplain for having illicit affairs with two Navy wives. According to a shore patrolman at the chaplain's trial, "If they ever started busting sailors for adultery they wouldn't have enough men left to run a destroyer."[16]

The Court in *Bowers* stressed how many states have antisodomy laws and how long such laws have been in existence. Early in its opinion, the majority stated, "This case does not require a judgment whether the laws against acts between consenting adults in general, or between homosexuals in particular, are wise or desirable." But then the Court went on to note that

> proscriptions against that conduct have ancient roots. . . . Sodomy was a criminal offense at common law and was forbidden by the laws of the original thirteen states when they ratified the Bill of Rights. In 1868, when the Fourteenth Amendment was ratified, all but 5 of the 37 states in the Union had criminal acts laws. In fact, until 1961, all 50 states outlawed acts, and today, 24 states and the District of Columbia continue to provide criminal penalties for acts performed in private and between consenting adults.[17]

The Court was trying to show as best it could that the laws at issue did have widespread public support. Especially in the field of morals, law should reflect what Justice Holmes once called the "felt necessities of the time"[18] and what Shakespeare elsewhere referred to as the "tide in the affairs of men" (*Julius Caesar*, 4.2.270). Sometimes the law misses, as it did with prohibition, as it might if it tried to ban the sale of cigarettes.

The risk of the law estimating wrongly is substantial. If laws lack public respect and are disobeyed, they become, as Angelo says, "more mocked than feared," so that "liberty plucks Justice by the nose" (1.3.27–29). Like the policeman Javert in the musical *Les Misérables*, the rigid and self-righteous Angelo thinks, "I am the law, and the law is not mocked." Again and again, Angelo repeats how strict enforcement of "the angry law" is the only way to engender respect for the law, to make the law something more than a "scarecrow" (2.1.1). That, if anything, is Angelo's signature theme.

Our view of Angelo's character tends to color our view of his ideas. We know that Angelo is a hypocrite; that he commits the same crime for which he sentences Claudio to death; and that he says he will bend the law if Isabella will sleep with him. We know that Angelo is both willing to violate the law himself and not enforce it against another, if his bribe is paid (although he treacherously breaks his promise after receiving the bribe). Angelo's hypocrisy (and perfidy) makes us look skeptically on his theory of respect for law.

But we should not flatten Angelo into an abject hypocrite. His position is more complex than that. What if Angelo were not a hypocrite? Might we have a different, more favorable reaction to Angelo's theory if Angelo would enforce the letter of the law without being hypocritical? It is in such light that we have to consider whether Angelo's point about respect for law is valid.

To highlight Angelo's notion of respect for law Shakespeare creates a marvelous image out of the mouths of two different speakers, neither of them Angelo. The duke, bemoaning his failure to enforce Vienna's "strict statutes and most biting laws," likens them to "an o'ergrown lion in a cave / That goes not out to prey" (1.3.19–23). A little later, Claudio's friend Lucio describes Angelo as seeking to stop disobedience and license, "which have for long run by the hideous law / As mice by lions" (1.4.62–63). The combination of these two leonine similes stamps itself memorably on the mind: we see lots of scampering, mocking mice running past a cave that is home to a tired, old, toothless lion of the law, who in younger, more energetic days crushed them with one swat of his mighty paw.

Angelo has a plan to energize the lion of the law. He "follows close the rigour of the statute, / To make him [Claudio] an example" (1.4.66–67). Going into his method of general deterrence, Angelo expounds:

> Those many had not dared to do that evil
> If the first that did th'edict infringe
> Had answered for his deed.
>
> (2.2.93–95)

And Angelo starts to put some teeth into the law as he enforces it, so that it hurts.

Is it so easy to say that Angelo is wrong as a matter of theory? Perhaps we do generate respect for law if it is enforced. But that would only seem to be true for law in accord with overall public sentiment. To enforce unpopular, harsh laws does not win public respect; it is not good statecraft. It is, rather, a form of tyranny. "The law," concedes Angelo, is "a tyrant" (2.4.115). We do not even know from the play if Angelo's strategy works, if his enforcement program cleans up the city.

We do know that the duke blames himself for creating disrespect for law. He laments, "T'was my fault to give the people scope, . . . When evil deeds have their permissive pass, / And not the punishment" (1.3.35–39).

DEAD-LETTER STATUTES

The problem of dead-letter statutes hangs over both *Measure for Measure* and *Bowers v. Hardwick*. For several years the duke had not enforced the "strict statutes and biting laws," including the antifornication law. The people had gotten used to ignoring the harsh laws. "So our decrees, / Dead to infliction, to themselves are dead" (1.3.27–28). The duke fears criticism of himself if he were now, after so long an interval, to revive those laws. "T'would be my tyranny to strike and gall them / For what I bid them do" (1.3.36–37).

To avoid such criticism the duke let Angelo become his stalking horse. Angelo had no qualms: "The law hath not been dead, though it hath slept," he says. "Now 'tis awake" (2.2.92–95).

Like the law in Shakespeare's play, the antisodomy law in *Bowers v. Hardwick* had not been enforced for a long time, apparently for decades. Asked at oral argument when there was a prosecution "where the activity took place in a private residence," the Georgia attorney general responded that "the last case I can recall was back in the 1930s or 40s."[19] To Justice Lewis Powell, "the history of non-enforcement suggests the moribund character today of laws criminalizing this type of private, consensual conduct."[20] Powell went on to note, "Some 26 states have repealed similar statutes." Justice Stevens in his dissent also focused on the "record of nonenforcement" but went further in detecting the potential for arbitrary and selective prosecution, thereby making "evenhanded enforcement of the law . . . a virtual impossibility."

In both situations, the play and the case, the question is whether a statute that has not been enforced and has not been obeyed for many years may suddenly be resurrected and applied. We see the difference between normal prosecutorial discretion and a consistent, total failure of prosecution over time, which allows a statute to fall into disuse, thus triggering the concept of desuetude. In his 1962 book *The Least Dangerous Branch*, Alexander Bickel, the noted legal scholar and Yale law professor who represented the *New York Times* in the *Pentagon Papers* case, gave perhaps the finest explanation of desuetude. Bickel wrote of desuetude in the context of an attempt to resurrect and apply Connecticut's 1879 anti-birth-control law, which had never been enforced or obeyed. He conceded that desuetude was "not an everyday, familiar doctrine of Anglo-American law."

Desuetude means that a law has been nullified through disuse. According to Roman law, statutes may be abrogated not only by a vote of the legislator, but also by desuetude with the tacit consent of all. A finding of desuetude neither strikes the statute off the books nor activates it; the finding means only that the prosecution fails on grounds of desuetude.

The doctrine of desuetude does not upset ordinary deference to the legislative and executive branches. Under conditions of normal law enforcement, the effects of a law are constantly being felt and there is a significant chance that such impact would permit reconsideration by the legislature if attitudes had changed. But as Bickel writes, "When the law is consistently not enforced, that chance is reduced to the vanishing point." Bickel continues: "The unenforced statute is not, in the normal way, a continuing reflection of the balance of political pressures. When it is resurrected and enforced, it represents the *ad hoc* decision of the prosecutor, and then of the judge and jury, unrelated to anything that may realistically be taken as present legislative policy."[21]

As Justice Stevens noted in his *Bowers* dissent, desuetude also depends on a lack of fair warning. The first offender prosecuted after the long period of nonenforcement had no fair warning, which is considered a prime requirement of the rule of law. Like statutes that are void for vagueness, a long-unused statute leads to irresponsible decisions. Even if future prosecutions would mark a return to a normal situation, the first prosecution has all the vices of an ad hoc official decision. Desuetude allows a court to decline to enforce a long-ignored criminal law resurrected and used against a defendant.

Desuetude accomplishes something else important too. There may be many dead-letter statutes on the books that the legislature will not repeal because of moral pressures. Legislators may find it difficult to accept the *Wolfenden Report*'s statement that repeal of, say, antisodomy laws "is not to condone or encourage private immorality." Rather, legislators may feel that repeal of such criminal laws, even though repeal is on its face neutral, effectively encourages those who wish to engage in immoral acts. That was the holding of the Supreme Court in *Reitman v. Mulkey*, a 1967 case in which California repealed antidiscrimination laws, so that racial discrimination was neither prohibited nor permitted by the state.[22] Despite such facial neutrality, the Court ruled that implementing a new policy of governmental neutrality had the effect of lending encouragement to those who wish to engage in discrimination. Desuetude allows the statute to stay on the books for whatever deterrent effect it might have without permitting it to be enforced at the expense of an unsuspecting defendant.

By means of its delicate balance, desuetude allows certain laws to operate as no more than aspirational goals. In such circumstances, as Justice Stevens wrote in his *Bowers* dissent, "it is, of course, possible that a statute has a purely symbolic role." The duke's fourteen-year failure to prosecute under the antifornication law is consistent with the argument that the purpose of the statute is merely symbolic.

This concept of desuetude is highly relevant to *Measure for Measure* and *Bowers v. Hardwick*. Shakespeare starts to enunciate the concept when he writes:

> Laws for all faults,
> But faults so countenanced that the strong statutes
> Stand like the forfeits in a barber's shop,
> As much in mock as mark.

(5.1.316–19)

Although the Supreme Court has never actually considered or canvassed the doctrine, desuetude was definitely lurking in the background of *Bowers*. But the issue in *Bowers* was only validity of the statute, not its enforceability; hence there was no call to apply the doctrine of desuetude where the prosecutor declined to present evidence to the grand jury. As for Shakespeare's play, a German lawyer named Josef Kohler in 1919 wrote a book in which he argued that the antifornication law should have been regarded as repealed by desuetude.[23] No doubt continental lawyers such as Kohler, with training in Roman law, were more familiar than Anglo-American lawyers with the doctrine of desuetude, which explains why he—and not one of the scores of English and American attorneys who have studied and written about Shakespeare—was apparently the first to see its importance to *Measure for Measure*.

In any event, revisiting *Measure for Measure* from this perspective reactivates the vital concept of desuetude, which itself has fallen into disuse.

CRUEL AND UNUSUAL PUNISHMENT

In both *Measure for Measure* and *Bowers v. Hardwick*, the appropriateness of punishment becomes an issue. Shakespeare's antifornication law carries a death penalty, although it is unclear whether death is mandatory or just a maximum punishment. Georgia's antisodomy statute authorizes a court to imprison a person for up to twenty years for a single, private consensual homosexual act. Such harsh penalties bring to mind the Eighth Amendment's ban on "cruel and unusual punishments."

One Supreme Court justice noted the Eighth Amendment issue in *Bowers*. Justice Lewis Powell wrote a separate opinion concurring with the majority that the Georgia statute did not deprive Hardwick of any fundamental right. "This is not to suggest, however," stated Justice Powell, "that respondent may not be protected by the Eighth Amendment of the Constitution." In Powell's view, "a prison sentence" for a single act of sodomy, even in the private setting of a home—"certainly a sentence of long duration—would create a serious Eighth Amendment issue." Powell chose not to decide this issue because it was not raised in the lower courts and because there had been no conviction rendered and no sentence imposed.

Unlike *Bowers*, the issue of punishment in *Measure for Measure* cannot be avoided. The penalty for Claudio's "crime" is death, and the sentence has been imposed. The condemned Claudio speaks eloquently about the psychological stress of death row. "Death is a fearful thing," he cries in despair (3.1.116). The horror of death presses Claudio to ask virtuous Isabella to succumb to Angelo's proposition.

The weariest and the most loathèd worldly life
That age, ache, penury, and imprisonment
Can lay on nature is a paradise
To what we fear of death.

(3.1.129–32)

Angelo, ever the proponent of law and order, sees the death penalty as a form of deterrence. Isabella anticipates modern arguments against the death penalty. "Good, good my lord," she says to Angelo,

Bethink you:
Who is it that hath died for his offence?
There's many have committed it.

(2.2.189–91)

And the provost says, "All sects, all ages smack of this vice; and he / To die for't" (2.2.5–6).

Analyzed under American constitutional law circa 1993, the death penalty imposed on Claudio would surely violate the Eighth Amendment as an impermissible cruel and unusual punishment. But it is an open question, even more so than usual, whether it is fair or proper to evaluate an old penalty by today's standards. For the Supreme Court has often stated that the definition of "cruel and unusual punishment" changes with time. The ban on cruel and unusual punishment, stated the Court, "is not static," nor is it "fastened to the obsolete but may acquire meaning as public opinion becomes enlightened by a humane justice." The Eighth Amendment, the Court held, "must draw its meaning from the evolving standards of decency that mark the progress of a maturing society."[24]

Centuries ago the death penalty was much more common even for trivial crimes. This was so for Shakespeare's England and for Vienna where *Measure for Measure* supposedly took place. But over time "evolving standards of decency" led to rarer and rarer use of capital punishment in Western countries. Although the death penalty was sometimes used for adultery, it was never used for fornication. In this country, the death penalty has always been controversial, and that controversy entered a new era in 1972.

In that year the Supreme Court held for the first time, in a five-to-four decision, that capital punishment as then practiced was cruel and unusual and therefore unconstitutional. Although the several separate opinions in that case, *Furman v. Georgia*,[25] make comment difficult, it is fair to say that the key feature of the ruling was that the lack of certainty and standards that marked imposition of the death penalty made it unconstitutional. Even so, the arguments made by some of the members of the Supreme Court embody certain of the points in *Measure for Measure*.

Claudio's expressed terror at being executed corresponds to a punishment being cruel and unusual if it is degrading to human beings. Angelo's reliance on the death penalty for its deterrent effect is reminiscent of the many pages written by the Supreme Court on whether such deterrence occurs. When Isabella points out that no offenders have actually been executed, she is underscoring exactly how arbitrary and unusual is the actual use of the death penalty. But most clear of all is the notion, referred to by the Supreme Court, of excessiveness in the sense that the penalty cannot be unnecessary, a pointless infliction of suffering measured against the seriousnes of that particular crime.

The cases since 1972 have clarified some of the points as they relate to the law in *Measure for Measure*. Although it is true that the Supreme Court has, over strong dissent, allowed the use of the death penalty in certain circumstances, it has defined more carefully what those circumstances are. The concept of excessiveness has evolved to the point where capital punishment will be deemed unconstitutionally excessive unless the crime for which it is imposed involves a victim's death. Even a violent rape will not justify, as a constitutional matter, the death penalty. To execute someone like Claudio for merely making love with his fiancée is obviously excessive and unnecessary, even if under some Puritan penal code the offense called for some lesser punishment.

Furman's progeny have also gone far to settle the constitutional status of mandatory death sentences. That issue was explicitly left open in 1972, although a number of justices noted that in America there was almost from the start a "rebellion against the common-law rule imposing a mandatory death sentence on all convicted murderers."[26] *Furman* turned on the standardless discretion that juries and judges had in administering the death penalty. Mandatory death sentences for certain crimes would at least eliminate the vice of too much discretion. But as it turned out the later cases, reflecting the deeply ingrained American distaste for mandatory death sentences, held such penalties—like the one that may apply in *Measure for Measure*—to be unconstitutional precisely because they failed to allow for some discretion.

As the Supreme Court stated in 1976, "In capital cases the fundamental respect for humanity underlying the Eighth Amendment . . . requires consideration of the character and record of the individual offender and the circumstances of the particular offense as a constitutionally indispensable part of the process of inflicting the penalty of death."[27] That is still the law today.

Mercy

The extreme nature of the penalty, death, for a minor offense, making love to one's fiancée, sets up a moving plea for mercy. Isabella, the condemned man's sister, beseeches Angelo:

> No ceremony that to great ones 'longs,
> Not the king's crown, nor the deputed sword,
> The marshal's truncheon, nor the judge's robe,
> Become them with one half so good a grace
> As mercy does.
>
> (2.2.61–65)

Isabella's eloquent plea closely resembles Portia's memorable "quality of mercy" speech in *The Merchant of Venice*.

But Angelo, like Shylock, remains unmoved. He refuses to relent even though he is often reminded throughout the play that he should show humility when measuring others. "Judge not, lest ye be judged" is a repeated theme. Even "the jury passing on the prisoner's life / May in the sworn twelve have a thief or two / Guiltier than him they try" (2.1.19–21). The duke says:

> He who the sword of heaven will bear
> Should be as holy as severe, . . .
> More nor less to others paying
> Than by self-offences weighing.
>
> (3.1.517–22)

Other characters hammer away at the hardhearted Angelo. Asks Isabella a little after lamenting the "just but severe law" (2.2.41):

> How would you be
> If He which is the top of judgement should
> But judge you as you are? O, think on that,
> And mercy then will breathe within your lips,
> Like man new made.
>
> (2.2.77–81)

Again, Escalus puts it to Angelo,

> Whether you had not sometime in your life
> Erred in this point which you now censure him
> And pulled the law upon you.
>
> (2.1.14–16)

Escalus, who had previously showed mercy by letting Pompey off with a warning against pimping, goes on: "Let us be keen, and cut a little / Than fall and bruise to death" (2.1.5–7).

In his complacent response, Angelo seals his own fate. He answers self-righteously, "When I that censure him, do so offend, / Let mine own judgement pattern out my death" (2.1.29–30). Of course, Angelo does "so offend" by sleeping with his ex-fiancée, Mariana, whom he is tricked into thinking is Isabella. At an informal trial arranged by the duke, Isabella charges Angelo with seeking a bribe and with sleeping with her. No longer talking of mercy, Isabella now vengefully demands "justice, justice, justice, justice!" (5.1.25).

Angelo eventually admits his guilt and, at least with the virtue of consistency, asks:

> But let my trial be mine own confession.
> Immediate sentence then, and sequent death,
> Is all the grace I beg.
>
> (5.1.369–71)

The duke appears to grant Angelo's request, apparently to permit revenge to balance violence with violence:

> The very mercy of the law cries out
> Most audible, even from his proper tongue,
> "An Angelo for Claudio, death for death."
> Haste still pays haste, and leisure answers leisure;
> Like doth quit like, and measure still for measure.
> Then, Angelo, thy fault's thus manifested,
> Which, though thou wouldst deny, denies thee vantage.
> We do condemn thee to the very block
> Where Claudio stooped to death, and with like haste.
>
> (5.1.404–12)

But of course the duke knows full well that Claudio has not been executed. His harsh sentence on Angelo sets the stage for Isabella to help her enemy Angelo escape the fate he in some sense deserves, for official corruption and treachery if not for breaking the law that had ensnared Claudio.

Isabella now launches into a second plea for mercy, but this time it is on behalf of the cold and beaten Angelo. Her passionate rhetoric gone, she speaks woodenly yet enunciates a vital principle:

> Look, if it please you, on this man condemned
> As if my brother lived. I partly think
> A due sincerity governed his deeds,
> Till he did look on me. Since it is so,
> Let him not die. My brother had but justice,
> In that he did the thing for which he died.

> For Angelo,
> His acts did not o'ertake his bad intent,
> And must be buried but as an intent,
> That perished by the way. Thoughts are no subjects,
> Intents but merely thoughts.
>
> (5.1.441–51)

Citing Isabella's lines about the difference between thoughts and actions, Justice William Rehnquist said for the Supreme Court in a 1980 case that they "express sound legal doctrine." For, as the Court reaffirmed in that case, "In the criminal law, both a culpable *mens rea* and a criminal *actus reus* are generally required for an offense to occur."[28] Here we have a second important limit on the law. The first was limiting the law to public, not private morality. The second is limiting the law to acts, not thoughts, mental reactions, and ideas.

Isabella's plea for Angelo differs sharply from her plea for Claudio. One is matter-of-fact, the other throbs with feeling and flies on the wings of rhetoric. This clear contrast shows how much easier it is to talk mercy than to practice it, but at least Isabella, unlike Portia in *The Merchant of Venice*, attempts to bridge the gap between thought and action.[29] She joins Mariana on her knees to make the plea; her passion for revenge has changed to mercy in deed.

But Shakespeare does not let the matter rest there. Near the beginning of the play, the Bard seems to question the practical effect of mercy in certain cases. When one character says the Lord Angelo is "severe," Escalus defends him on philosophical grounds:

> It is but needful
> Mercy is not itself that oft looks so.
> Pardon is still the nurse of second woe.
>
> (2.1.271–73)

Shakespeare appears to be calling for a discretionary approach to mercy also.

Abuse of Power

In many ways, *Measure for Measure* describes power, its nature, its effects on character, and what happens when it is delegated. For Angelo, who does not appear to be either an intentional villain or a tyrant, power has an intoxicating effect. His character, kept in rein when without absolute power, becomes hideous when he is in full control of the state. "Hence shall we see," anticipates the duke of the ascetic Angelo in the saddle, "if power change purpose, what our seemers be" (1.3.53–54).

Angelo ignores Isabella's insightful lines about power and its restrained use:

> O, it is excellent
> To have a giant's strength, but it is tyrannous
> To use it like a giant.
>
> (2.2.109–11)

These cautionary lines, with their simple but clear message, should be carved in every courtroom, right next to "In God We Trust." Every judge, every powerful government official, every business executive, every military officer—everyone who exercises power—should recite those lines before going to sleep each night.

Francis Biddle, who served as attorney general under President Franklin Roosevelt and as a judge at the Nuremberg War Crimes Tribunal after World War II, took the title of his memoirs, *In Brief Authority*, from one of Isabella's most famous speeches on the limits of power. "But man, proud man," says Isabella,

> Dressed in a little brief authority,
> Most ignorant of what he's most assured,
> His glassy essence, like an angry ape
> Plays such fantastic tricks before high heaven
> As makes the angels weep.
>
> (2.2.120–25)

The play also deals with the delegation of power. As in *King Lear* and *Richard II*, problems arise in *Measure for Measure* when there is no real authority, when there is a power void. The duke, the legitimate and recognized authority, pretends to leave and causes chaos by appointing Angelo as his stalking horse. Why does the duke leave, we may rightfully ask. By the duke's own testimony we have it that he did not want to incur the wrath of the people for suddenly enforcing strict laws long left unused.

Rather than risk losing popularity, he gives the difficult task to Angelo, who seems to carry out the duke's wishes with gusto. But when disorder and injustice eventually flow from the duke's delegated instructions, the duke steps in to take all the credit for correcting a situation—which he caused—that had gotten out of hand. For doing the duke's bidding, Angelo gets blamed and, in the end, humiliated. The duke, almost Machiavellian in this, is not an entirely attractive character.

When power is delegated, it had better be delegated to the right person. In *Measure for Measure*, we see what happens when power is delegated to the wrong person. Angelo's first spoken words in the play reveal to us something crucial about his personality, that he is not a leader, but a follower, a natural underling incapable of balanced decision making: "Always obedient to your grace's will, / I come to know your pleasure" (1.1.25–26). When the duke tells him he is in charge now, Angelo protests he is not ready. Rather than take responsibility for his decisions, he retreats behind the law; the law becomes his master in lieu of the absent duke. Thus, being a natural underling makes him prone to legalism.

Not only is Angelo excessively legalistic in the exercise of his temporary power, but he abuses that power as well. He becomes a corrupt judge in his sinister and hypocritical bedroom bargain with Isabella, which he compounds by not even honoring. His worst evil is ordering Claudio's execution even after he thinks he slept with Isabella. He becomes one of several crooked judges in Shakespeare, leading the duke to moan, "I have seen corruption boil and bubble / Till it o'errun the stew" (5.1.315–16).

Sexual Harassment

One controversial intersection of law and morality and the abuse of power beautifully illustrated by *Measure for Measure* is sexual harassment. Angelo uses his position of power over Isabella in a classic quid pro quo situation: her body for her brother's life. "Redeem thy brother / By yielding up thy body to my will" (2.4.163–64). It is that simple.

Today, an audience would likely react most strongly to the sexual harassment theme in *Measure for Measure*. The women's movement, greater sensitivity to individual rights, the Anita Hill–Clarence Thomas Senate hearings—all combine to alert this play's audiences to Angelo's harassment of Isabella. The emotional high point, when every head in the audience must nod knowingly, will come when Isabella warns Angelo to release her brother "or with an outstretched throat I'll tell the world aloud / What man thou art" (2.4.153–54).

Angelo's answer must still ring in Anita Hill's ears. "Who will believe thee, Isabel?" (2.4.154), he snaps, as all harassers have snapped before and since. Angelo speaks for them all as he goes on:

> My unsoiled name, th'austereness of my life,
> My vouch against you, and my place i'th' state,
> Will so your accusation overweigh
> That you shall stifle in your own report,
> And smell of calumny.
>
> (2.4.155–59)

A little later Isabella moans, "Did I tell this, who would believe me?" We moan with her, as we think of David Brock's book *The Real Anita Hill*, which savages Clarence Thomas's former assistant. It is unfortunate that during the Anita Hill–Clarence Thomas hearings none of the Shake-speare-spouting members of the Senate Judiciary Committee quoted these exquisitely apt passages from *Measure for Measure*.

SEXUAL REPRESSION

In light of the subject matter of *Measure for Measure*, it is perhaps not too far afield to suggest that the play involves the relationship between sexual repression and the law. As Northrop Frye has observed, authority without the understanding of equity leads to repressive legalism, which in turn can repress the sex impulse.[30] The enforcement of the antifornication law highlights this theme. But so do two of the main characters and their behavior. The result is a modern argument against sexual repression.

Angelo and Isabella resemble each other in this regard. Both are cold, priggish moral fanatics. Lucio says Angelo is

> a man whose blood
> Is very snow-broth; one who never feels
> The wanton stings and motions of the sense,
> But doth rebate and blunt his natural edge
> With profits of the mind, study, and fast.
>
> (1.4.56–60)

On the surface he appears to be the picture of virtue. To the duke, Angelo

> is precise,
> Stands at a guard with envy, scarce confesses
> That his blood flows, or that his appetite
> Is more to bread than stone.
>
> (1.3.50–53)

Likewise Isabella. When we meet her, she is about to enter a convent. She denies sex. She makes her sexually repressed attitude evident in pleading to Angelo for Claudio's life. "There is a vice that most I do abhor," she says to Angelo, referring to lovemaking (2.2.29). "And most desire," she goes on,

> should meet the blow of justice,
> For which I must not plead, that but I am
> At war 'twixt will and will not. ·
>
> (2.2.30–33)

To her condemned brother's pleas that she sleep with Angelo to save her brother's life, Isabella recoils in horror. As Lucio accurately tells her, "You are too cold" (2.2.45).

And yet both of these moralizing characters have strong sexual natures. Angelo wants so badly to sleep with Isabella that, to achieve his goal, he is willing to corrupt and debase his role as temporary leader of the city. Nothing is more important—none of his other virtues—than going to bed with Isabella. And Isabella, who for all her plans of chaste convent life is not a one-note prig, ends up as the unlikely wife of the duke.

When such sexually repressed people assume positions of power and interpret the law, difficulties arise. In this sense, *Measure for Measure* is a warning about the appropriate psychological makeup of people involved in the law. Interpretation of law must take account of "the nature of our people," as the duke tells Escalus at the start of the play (1.1.9). That "nature" includes the sexuality that Angelo and Isabella first deny. Then Angelo, a slave to passion, tramples on the law. As Posner wryly comments, "attempting to outlaw fornication would be as quixotic in the culture of the play as it would be in our own culture."[31]

LEGAL INTERPRETATION

All the individual themes in *Measure for Measure* seem important, yet they are subordinate to one all-encompassing legal theme that marks the play indelibly. That grand theme is a theory of legal interpretation. The enduring legal contribution of *Measure for Measure* is its sensible and balanced approach to the fundamental problems of law: how to control human behavior effectively by means of rules. By eschewing extremes, Shakespeare comes up with a theory of moderation that blends law and discretion, and all that those two concepts mean, into a workable system of legal interpretation.

Angelo stands for one concept of law. He embodies the notion of a government of laws, of formalism, rules, logic, of rigid enforcement and maximum punishment. Angelo separates law from human feeling; he thinks of law as an abstraction, as consisting of unbendable rules that must be enforced regardless of consequences. In administering the law, Angelo minimizes the human factor and discretion, and maximizes legalism and strict rules, quite apart from the specific circumstances of a case or the personalities of the people involved.

For Angelo, strict enforcement of the law without heed of the persons involved is the best way to govern. He is a law-and-order man; he is, in the duke's words, "precise." "We must not make a scarecrow of the law," Angelo says,

> Setting it up to fear the birds of prey,
> And let it keep one shape till custom make it
> Their perch, and not their terror.
>
> (2.1.1–4)

Angelo, the Draconian magistrate, symbolizes the notion of law as something apart from the people responsible for enforcing the law. When Isabella pleads for her brother's life, Angelo replies,

> It is the law, not I, condemn your brother.
> Were he my kinsman, brother, or my son,
> It should be thus with him.

(2.2.182–84)

This reply by Angelo reflects the hackneyed thinking of those who believe that judges find but never make the law, and to some degree it is a type of judicial restraint. But even as he says it, we find Angelo slightly disingenuous about his own role in interpreting the law.

Before the obvious weaknesses in Angelo's concept of law overwhelm us, candor and fairness require that we acknowledge its strengths. At its best, Angelo's legal theory represents an effort to find in law safety from arbitrary power, to find protection in law's objectivity and impersonality. Arbitrariness is the negation of the law. Rigid adherence to rules regardless of consequences is one way to prevent government from showing favoritism or abusing discretion. As Judge Posner has noted, "In our society the exercise of power by appointed officials . . . is tolerated only in the belief that the power is somehow constrained."[32] That is, after all, the core of the slogan of our own founders: "a government of laws, not of men."

This potential for good shows through to some extent in the choice of perpetrator in *Measure for Measure*. To Angelo's credit—and there is not much to say to Angelo's credit—he enforces the law not against a poor, defenseless, friendless, uneducated character from the Viennese underclass, but against Claudio, a "gentleman" who "had a most noble father" (2.1.6–7). It is not often in Shakespeare, in literature, or in life that an unpopular law is enforced against a defendant of means from the upper class. Insofar as Angelo's law enforcement did not swerve because of Claudio's social status, Angelo acted in the highest tradition of blind justice that draws no distinction among defendants.

But the virtues of Angelo's theory of legal interpretation, while real enough, can be pushed too far, as in *Measure for Measure*. Those virtues are outweighed by defects. But we see Angelo's theory as, in Posner's phrase, an abuse of a good thing, not the essence of a bad thing. Shakespeare portrays Angelo's view of law as something apart from man, as an inhuman obstruction that can become intolerable and self-contradictory and lead to repressive legalism. Despite the extenuating circumstances of the antifornication law not being enforced for several years and of Claudio's marriage contract with Julietta, Angelo refuses to act leniently toward Claudio. For Angelo, such leniency would amount to tampering with the law, because for him the law is a set of rigid rules inflexibly applied, quite apart from human feeling. Nor does the severity of the death penalty deter Angelo from his course.

In vivid contrast to Angelo's legal views are those of the duke of Vienna and Escalus, Angelo's deputy. Both the Duke and Escalus take a more moderate view of law, seeing it as administered by people and softened by realism, politics, equity, mercy, justice, discretion, and flexibility. This concept of law requires law and authority to be exercised with largeness of mind and understanding, lest a tyrannically strict construction result. The spirit of the law, not the letter, should inform the decision. According to the duke and Escalus, a judge can and should make the law in interpreting it. To dispel any doubt on which side Shakespeare comes out, the duke, at the end of the play, shows his appreciation: "Thanks, good friend Escalus, for thy much goodness" (5.1.527).

That Angelo has misconstrued the duke's intentions seems indisputable. Although Angelo hid behind the letter of the law in saying that the law, not he, had condemned Claudio, the duke had told Angelo:

> Your scope is as my own,
> So to enforce or qualify [that is, moderate] the laws
> As to your soul seems good.
>
> (1.1.64–66)

That vital qualification—"As to your soul seems good"—clearly shows that the duke was reposing discretion in Angelo, a discretion that Angelo either did not recognize or could not exercise, but a discretion that undercuts his wooden and mechanical application of the law.

The inference that Angelo had discretion that he did not exercise is borne out by several other passages. Underscoring that discretion, not law, is the determining factor, the duke tells Angelo, "Mortality and mercy in Vienna / Live in thy tongue and heart" (1.1.44–45). Likewise, Escalus, after failing to persuade Angelo to be merciful toward Claudio, says, "Be it as your wisdom will" (2.1.32). At one point, even Angelo seems to recognize that in reality he, not the law, condemns Claudio. To Isabella's pleas to spare Claudio's life, Angelo replies, "I will not do't" (2.2.52). She has a fine ear for distinctions and asks, "But can you if you would?" (2.2.52). Angelo, however, slams the door shut on the possibility of his exercising discretion with a peremptory "Look what I will not, that I cannot do" (2.2.53).

In his discussion of *Measure for Measure*, Posner follows most commentators in focusing primarily on the play's different theories of law. Almost all of his remarks are far-ranging, useful, and insightful, but his greatest contribution is his "Table of Opposed Conceptions of Law."[33] To illustrate the two basically different views of the law in *Measure for*

Measure (and *The Merchant of Venice*), Posner constructs two lists. On the left-hand side Posner puts those words and phrases associated with law as a disembodied set of rules favored by Angelo: government of laws, foundation, law, rule, logic, rigid, right answers, precedent, objectivity, letter of the law, impossibility, strict construction, judge finds law. On the right-hand side are those words and phrases associated with the concept of law as equity favored by the duke and Escalus: government of men, realism, mercy, justice, discretion, policy, flexible, natural law, subjectivity, needs, loose construction, spirit of the law, judge makes law. Posner's table helps considerably in grasping the legal continuum, the theoretical template underneath *Measure for Measure*. It also shows that both concepts represent good ideals, though too much of either could cause problems.

THE ART OF JUDGING

Right from the outset, Shakespeare undercuts Angelo's theory of legal interpretation and his fitness as a judge. The duke's first speech, significant as all opening comments are in Shakespeare, highlights the role of human judgment and discretion in administering the law. Talking to Escalus, his trusted aide who will turn out to embody the qualities of a true and good judge, the duke says that because Escalus well understands "the properties" of government, and "your worth is able," all that the duke has to do is allow the judgment of Escalus to take over. Escalus, unlike the rigid Angelo, is keenly aware of the blend of proper elements for interpreting and applying the law: "The nature of our people, / Our city's institutions and the terms / For common justice" (1.1.9–11). Put another way, the duke is saying that given Escalus's fine qualities, he need only give Escalus the requisite authority and leave him to exercise it in accordance with his considerable abilities. (Why the duke leaves the unfit Angelo rather than the more suitable Escalus in charge is unclear, except for dramatic effect.)

Measure for Measure is a play guaranteed to wake judges from complacency and set them worrying about the fallible nature of human judgment. Shakespeare quickly shifts from the question of the criminal's guilt to the far more interesting question of the guilt of the judge. Shakespeare asks the final, fundamental, subversive question: is any man or woman fit to sit in judgment on a fellow human being? Shakespeare thus challenges all the assumptions of society. He subjects human justice to a devastating cross-examination.

Even Shakespeare's prescription for a good judge resonates today. As we from time to time consider nominees for the Supreme Court and lower courts, we should remember the opening speech in *Measure for Measure*.

A judge should understand "the nature of our people," that is, what they are inherently capable of doing or not doing. A judge should also understand our "institutions," political and otherwise, with the appropriate respect for tradition and for potential. Finally, a judge must know "the terms for common justice," that is, have a good practical sense of what is right and wrong.

As events unfold, Shakespeare makes us understand that he thinks law should not be divorced from human feeling. Angelo's fall represents the futility of his narrow and rigid legalism, of enforcing law too strictly. But Shakespeare does not go to the other extreme either, and favor law that is not enforced or is totally arbitrary. Rather, he recognizes—as we should—that law also includes moderating doctrines, such as equity. Law is not fully law if it is inflexible application of rules; the moderating doctrines are as much a part of law as anything else.

The prudent theory advanced by Shakespeare, and congenial to ourselves, is that law should be enforced, but in moderation. Moderate enforcement or discretionary nonenforcement must give due recognition to the realities of human nature. It is no violation of the rule of law if aggravating and mitigating circumstances are taken into account in administering the law. A strict and rigorous legalism has always been rejected, as has an arbitrary, haphazard enforcement of the law as well.

This dialectic of legal theories is ever present. One could, for example, interpret *Bowers v. Hardwick* (and many other current cases) in light of this conflict. The Supreme Court majority in *Bowers* seems to echo Angelo in interpreting the Georgia anti-sodomy law as a valid statute. The majority declines to exercise any discretion in upholding the law, so as to avoid the "imposition of the Justices' own choice of values," and thereby refuses to find any constitutional protection.[34] Unlike the majority, the minority seems more willing to soften the rigor of the law and to make an effort to interpret the Constitution in a way more congenial to critics of the statute. The dissenters are willing to make law in the service of a more flexible search for the right answer.

The theory of legal interpretation favored in *Measure for Measure* is still with us. Formal laws may have unjust results unless tempered by equity; rigid interpretation of formal rules is fraught with risk.

TEACHING A NEW KING

Interesting as they are, the many legal themes in *Measure for Measure* were no mere idle dramatic references. Shakespeare, who wrote the play in 1604, used them to tutor King James I, the Scottish king who ascended the English throne upon the death of Queen Elizabeth I in 1603. Scot-

land's law differed from England's, especially in having no separate jurisdiction for equity. With his play, the first performance of which was given
privately to the new monarch on December 26, 1604, Shakespeare meant
to teach James, in the first year of his reign, how to govern in view of
English jurisprudence, precedent, and case law.[35]

Shakespeare's audacity was tempered by his art. He made the duke a
flattering imitation of King James. The playwright warned James against
using law to interfere arbitrarily with the fabric of society. The Bard
showed the new king from a different background how impractical it is to
try to alter custom by rigid application of law. He demonstrated in art the
disruption caused by personal and arbitrary manipulation of the judicial
system. Through the medium of literature, Shakespeare told James to be
humane and just, and to follow English precedent, interpretation, and
equity in his judicial capacity. It was a lesson the Stuarts should have
learned better.

MEASURE FOR MEASURE REDUX

Measure for Measure astounds us with the timeliness of its comments
about human nature and the nature of law. It was relevant in 1604 and it
is ever so relevant today. The play supplied the unacknowledged cultural
backdrop for a rash of recent real cases. In 1990 Wisconsin and Connecticut charged a number of people with the crime of adultery. Amid divorce
and custody battles, estranged spouses swore out the criminal complaints. No one in either state could recall the last time a prosecution
sought to enforce that law, but some lawyers thought it might have been
in the early part of this century.

The similarities to *Measure for Measure* did not end there. One of the
prosecutors, sounding a lot like Angelo, defended what he did by saying,
"The law is on the books. There was strong evidence presented to me of
a violation. For me to decide not to prosecute would be, in effect, to
declare the statute null and void." He might as well have quoted Angelo:
"The law hath not been dead, though it hath slept. . . . Now 'tis awake"
(2.2.92–95). Yet favoring repeal of such statutes can border on political
suicide; constituents flood legislators' offices condemning repeal as anti-
family and immoral. *Measure for Measure* was surely a relevant literary
precedent.[36]

Measure for Measure faces in a number of directions. It looks with
trepidation toward the political and legal changes that may be wrought
by a new monarch. It finds uncanny parallels in a recent precedent from
America's highest court relating to the enforcement of morals through
law. And it prefigures Shakespeare's other explicitly legal play, *The Mer-*

chant of Venice, whose similarities and differences on many of the same basic legal issues make them twin plays that should be considered together. *Measure for Measure,* with its important lesson about avoiding rigid interpretation of formal rules that can have unjust results unless tempered by equity, sets up the related lessons in *The Merchant of Venice.*

FIE UPON YOUR LAW!

THE MERCHANT OF VENICE

THE MERCHANT OF VENICE, Shakespeare's other obviously "legal" play, has important parallels to *Measure for Measure*. The most significant parallel from a legal point of view is that both plays are generally understood to stand for the same concept of law and legal interpretation: formal laws may have unjust results unless tempered by equity. In both plays, the spirit of the law is in tension with the letter of the law, equitable discretion and mercy conflict with strict justice, and in the end mercy supposedly vanquishes the legalistic approach. One lesson we come away with from both plays is that we should avoid rigid interpretation of formal rules.

Other significant parallels exist too. Shylock and Angelo, for example, have common traits. Both stand or fall on legalisms. Both misuse the law, one the law of contracts and the other his legal authority. And both lead austere lives while being subject to destructive passions and emotions. Similarly, Portia resembles Isabella, first, in being the agent who upsets the nasty plans of a villain and, second, in pleading for mercy. Given these parallels, one can readily understand why *Measure for Measure* and *The Merchant of Venice* are often considered Shakespeare's twin legal plays.

Yet these similarities between Shakespeare's two legal plays should not hide their crucial differences. Closer analysis from a legal vantage point exposes the differences, reveals more complexity, and opens up more understanding of these great plays. Portia's resemblance to Isabella, for instance, goes only so far. Although Portia delivers a great speech about mercy, she does not act mercifully. Isabella, in contrast, does match act to word; she is liberated from her passion for revenge to a feeling of sympathy. Likewise, Shylock's personality remains what it has always been (avaricious and vengeful), while Angelo had to be introduced to evil. Finally, and perhaps most vital of all, *The Merchant of Venice* differs from *Measure for Measure* in underscoring a basic legal counterprinciple: strict adherence to formal rules is often necessary to do justice, especially for an outsider.

The Merchant of Venice is surely the Shakespearean play most closely linked in the popular mind with law. The crucial trial scene sears the legal and popular conscience like nothing else in Shakespeare. Over the centuries, *The Merchant of Venice* has spawned more commentary by lawyers than any other Shakespeare play.

Commentary on the legal aspects of the trial in *The Merchant of Venice* is divided. One critic, not a lawyer, thinks the trial scene is so controversial that each reader must decide, like a Supreme Court justice, where to stand in the conflict.[1] The vast majority of commentary—an eight-to-one ratio—agrees with Portia's ruling.[2] For such observers, the ruling of the court was a victory of the liberating spirit over the deadly letter of the law, of mercy over legalism, of reasonable discretion over Shylock's demand for literal-minded justice, of love and mercy over cold justice. According to these majority commentators, Shylock was a monster—villainous, usurious, malevolent, savage, repellent, deformed by hatred and greed—who got just what he deserved, severe punishment for his miserly vengefulness. If viewers accept this concept of Shylock, they can easily see him as a comic villain and laugh at his miserable fate. The consensus view is that the play dramatizes the struggle in Shakespeare's England for supremacy between the common law courts and the equitable Court of Chancery.

The minority view disagrees with Portia's judgment.[3] Those dissenters see Shylock as a victim of injustice, as the hero of the play, shown no mercy by Portia, and trapped by secret legalities. Rather than a fiend, Shylock strikes the minority as a tragic victim of religious and ethnic prejudice, more sinned against then sinning. Portia's judgment seems, to these contrarians, to be a triumph of vengeance in the guise of justice. The more I think about *The Merchant of Venice*, the more I find myself in this camp.

The minority view of Portia has got it right, I think, for reasons apart from the obvious. A new look may show that the debate over Portia's judgment has failed to appreciate fully a crucial piece of nonobvious evidence. The suggestion made here is that the majority view favoring Portia has neglected the vital link between the trial scene and a prominent theme in the play: that things are not always what they seem. The minority commentators do not make the same error. Rather than accept the trial scene at face value, they—if only subconsciously—take to heart the play's theme about misleading appearances and, perhaps more faithfully to Shakespeare's purpose, come out criticizing Portia and supporting Shylock.

As the sharp split of opinion might indicate, *The Merchant of Venice* has a persistent and uncanny grip on human imagination. Shakespeare's play strikes at the subconscious with a force extremely rare in literature, even in classics. When Dustin Hoffman played Shylock in London and on Broadway in 1989 and 1990, it was an international cultural event. Part of what makes a classic is its capacity over time to yield new and different meanings. *The Merchant of Venice* has this ability to be meaningful to successive generations of viewers. Each playgoer brings not only the spirit of the age but also personal experience and sensibility, a unique response and attitude toward the play.

The sensibility and response of a lawyer may find new meaning in *The Merchant of Venice*. To someone trained in the law, the important and lasting message of *The Merchant of Venice* has an overwhelmingly legal cast. Although at its core *The Merchant of Venice* is about the complexity of the human spirit, the play is in many fundamental ways about law and about the need for law to reflect the folkways and mores of the community. The classic trial scene in act 4 is the climax of the play. But even apart from the trial scene, the entire play is from start to finish dominated by several legal themes. It is impossible to understand the play fully and in all its richness without grasping these legal themes.

The legal themes occur in the context of an attempt to enforce a contract. The main action in the play turns on a civil lawsuit, the material facts of which are simple, undisputed, and well known. Plaintiff Shylock is a Jewish moneylender; defendant Antonio is a Christian merchant in Venice who needs funds to help his friend Bassanio woo an heiress, Portia. The parties enter into a written agreement whereby Shylock departs from his usual practice of charging interest and lends money interest-free to Antonio. The loan agreement provides a grisly penalty—if Antonio fails to repay the loan on time, Shylock could cut out a pound of flesh nearest Antonio's heart.

On first hearing Shylock's loan terms, Antonio's companion says, "I like not fair terms and a villain's mind" (1.3.178). Every lawyer who ever drew a contract knows the importance of good faith: an honest person acting in good faith will abide by the sense of a contract however expressed; a villain will look for a way out of a contract no matter how tightly drawn. A lawyer can learn a lot about contracts, what to do and what not to do, and how to make them airtight and to protect against this or that contingency. But a handshake between honorable people can often be the best contract. And sometimes letting people off the hook and letting them out of a commitment can be far more effective than holding them to the commitment, as Shylock comes to learn.

Antonio's ships do not come in on time and the repayment date passes. Shylock, whose normally high level of resentment against Antonio's anti-Semitism is raised to irrational revenge on learning of his daughter's eloping with a non-Jew, now sues for deadly specific performance. Spurning repayment several times over, he wants his pound of flesh. At the trial, Judge Portia presides in the guise of Balthasar, a learned young doctor of laws recommended by Dr. Bellario, a noted jurist in Padua. Portia-Balthasar tells Shylock, "Of a strange nature is the suit you follow" (4.1.174), which is Shakespeare's way of saying it is what lawyers today would call a "case of first impression."

LIBERTY OF CONTRACT AND ITS LIMITS

One key to explaining the strange case of *Shylock v. Antonio* is the conflict between two legal doctrines: liberty of contract and limitations put on that liberty by public policy. The trick is to think of the contract in Shakespeare's play as void against public policy. Shylock wants the court to uphold freedom of contract, and asks to have his contract enforced according to the clear and unambiguous terms freely agreed to by the parties. From Shylock's point of view, the case is ripe for summary judgment.

Liberty of contract is of bedrock importance to Shylock. The ability to structure transactions as parties wish facilitates commerce and helped to overcome the economic inertia of feudalism. Equally important, that same ability shifted the focus away from one's inherited status by way of family or religion as a detriment to consensual agreements. This movement from status to contract, popularized by a famous passage in Henry Sumner Maine's nineteenth-century book *Ancient Law*, created social and economic mobility and allowed far more individual freedom. People have more rather than less freedom if they are allowed to make a legally binding contract, even though by making it some freedom is surrendered while the contract is in force.

Shylock seeks a literal reading of the contract. The contract says a pound of flesh of Shylock's choosing, and Shylock will settle for only that: "So says the bond, doth it not, noble judge? / 'Nearest his heart'—those are the very words" (4.1.250–51). When Portia suggests that Shylock have a doctor at the ready to stop Antonio from bleeding to death, Shylock falls back upon a strict construction:

> *Shylock*   Is it so nominated in the bond?
> *Portia*   It is not so expressed, but what of that?
>   'Twere good you do so much for charity.
> *Shylock*   I cannot find it. 'Tis not in the bond.
>
>   (4.1.256–59)

Shylock here symbolizes literalness and technicality in the law, divorced from common sense, prudence, and practical wisdom.

By resting his case so heavily on legal technicality, Shylock draws the lines of battle on a treacherous field. Experienced trial lawyers know that getting one's adversary and the court to accept one's definition of the issues is half the battle, but here that tactic backfires. Shylock defines the issues in terms of literalness and technicality, and Portia reluctantly accepts his definition. But Shylock's reliance on technicality invites Portia to do the same, and Portia responds by giving a technical interpretation, but only after leading him on. "For as thou urgest justice, be assured / Thou shalt have justice more than thou desir'st" (4.1.313–14).

For a while, Portia appears to agree with Shylock's interpretation. She seems to accept the legality of the penalty clause, as she tells Shylock that "the Venetian law / Cannot impugn you as you do proceed" (4.1.175–76). She adds that the law clearly allows the stipulated penalty:

> For the intent and purpose of the law
> Hath full relation to the penalty
> Which here appeareth due upon the bond.
>
> (4.1.244–46)

And she looks as if she is ready to enforce it:

> Why, this bond is forfeit,
> And lawfully by this the Jew may claim
> A pound of flesh, to be by him cut off
> Nearest the merchant's heart.
>
> (4.1.227–30)

No wonder Shylock is emboldened to sharpen his knife.

Portia's attitude up to this point has three consequences. First, it persuades Shylock to view her as someone who "know[s] the law" and whose legal judgment is "most sound" (4.1.234–35) and authoritative. He calls Portia, "a Daniel come to judgement! . . . O wise young judge" (4.1.220–21), "a worthy judge" (4.1.233), "most learnèd judge" (4.1.301), "most rightful judge" (4.1.298), "a well-deserving pillar" (4.1.236) of the law. The second consequence is to raise Shylock's expectation of legal victory so that he rebuffs munificent settlement offers of three times the principal of the loan. This inflexible and rigid settlement posture on Shylock's part means the matter will go to judgment; there will be no compromise. (A trial lawyer who had been around the block a few times would have advised Shylock that it is always risky and dangerous to reject a settlement recommended by the trial judge, no matter how airtight the case might seem.) Finally, Portia's early tilt toward Shylock beautifully sets the stage for the dramatic reversal that comes next. By lulling Shylock into a false sense of security on the very brink of his success, Portia—and Shakespeare—highlight the suddenness and the extremity of the change in circumstances that happens.

Portia abruptly pulls the judicial string on Shylock by resorting to an even more literal and hypertechnical interpretation than Shylock's. "Tarry a little," she says ominously to Shylock, "There is something else" (4.1.302). Portia then points out that the contract says a pound of flesh but nowhere mentions blood. Therefore, she rules, Shylock must cut precisely one pound of flesh—no more, no less—and without shedding any of Antonio's blood, an obvious impossibility. Faced with such a hypertechnical reading, Shylock utters the incredulous cry of all disappointed litigants: "Is that the law?" (4.1.311).

It might be and it might not be. It could be argued with some force—part of the extensive literature has in fact done so—that Portia's interpretation is not the law.[4] To hold, as Portia does, that Shylock may take a pound of flesh but no blood is transparently absurd. Although no one in the play makes this rebuttal argument, the bond must have implicitly authorized what was necessary for Shylock to get his pound of flesh, that is, the shedding of Antonio's blood. Portia's interpretation is like granting an easement on land without the right to leave footprints.

From this perspective, Portia's judgment seems to be a quibble, a ludicrously literalist reading of the contract; an empty, hypertechnical legalistic interpretation that is illogical, useless, impossible, and absurd.[5] Portia shows herself to be as legalistic as Shylock. Portia and Shylock here demonstrate that law, literally construed, can be nonsense. They epitomize the empty and useless consequences of literalist and legalistic interpretation.

Portia's legalistic and hypertechnical "flesh-but-no-blood" construction is probably unnecessary. There are alternative rationales for denying Shylock's suit. Instead of resting her decision on interpreting the text of the bond, Portia could explicitly rely on public policy. Rather than ingeniously quibbling about the wording of the contract, Portia could have forthrightly addressed whether the bond was legal in the first place. It may be more accurate to understand Portia's ruling as in fact based on public policy, though explained by her in terms of construing contract provisions. We should perhaps focus on the result, not the rationale; and should watch what Portia does, not what she says.

Probably Portia's cram course with her cousin Dr. Bellario, the renowned legal expert in Padua who supposedly sent her to Venice in his place, taught her that liberty of contract has limits. She should have learned to ask the hardest question of all about freedom of contract: should every contract between consenting and adequately informed adults be enforced to the limit? Certain bargains, she had to have learned, are illegal, void, and unenforceable as against public policy. (Indulge me and assume for a moment the uncertain but useful proposition that the "void as against public policy" doctrine existed then and there roughly as it does here and now. This assumption is not that farfetched, for the doctrine is based more on common sense, fairness, and natural law than on technical legal concepts.) To find that public policy, Portia can look to legislation, legal precedents, and the prevailing practices of the community of people and their notions as to what makes for the general welfare.

Rather than a strained, legalistic interpretation, Portia could have invoked the public policy against absurd contracts such as Shylock's. No court in any civilized society would even entertain the thought of enforcing a contract penalty calling for the death of one party. It would be obviously unconscionable, like a contract of self-enslavement. Portia could have immediately relied on, as she ultimately does, the Venetian statute against attempted murder, not to punish Shylock but as a source of public policy. Portia would be on more solid legal ground here, especially when Shylock refuses to take three times the principal instead. Such a conclusion depends on no fine-spun parsing of contract terms but goes to the heart of the transaction—Antonio's heart.

Portia rules the contract unenforceable, both as to principal and penalty, but hardly stops there. She wheels on Shylock with legalistic fury, as she begins to deal with the second major phase of the case. According to the cited statute, Portia says Shylock must pay half his wealth to his intended victim, Antonio, and "the other half / comes to the privy coffer of the state" (4.1.350–51). It gets worse. Asked by Portia at the end of the trial scene "what mercy" he can show Shylock, Antonio reveals his determination to ruin his rival. Antonio slaps a trust on half of Shylock's current wealth, with the hated gentile son-in-law and runaway daughter as the ultimate beneficiaries. The cruel Antonio then compounds his lack of generosity by forcing Shylock to pledge by will to this same detested pair any assets he might acquire in the future. This vicious monetary punishment—which far surpasses the mere "fine" suggested by the presiding duke—is then even further aggravated, gratuitously and venomously. In the end, as the coup de grace, Antonio demands that Shylock convert to Christianity.

The legal underpinnings of Portia's ruling, even if she does not fully articulate them, should be familiar to us. The doctrine that contracts against public policy are void is still very much alive. Under the law of New York and a number of other states, for example, a usurious contract is void and unenforceable, and the usurious lender must forfeit principal as well as interest. The case reports are full of lenders who, caught in the web of such usury laws, plead as plaintively and as ineffectively as Shylock did, "Give me my principal and let me go" (4.1.333). The newly emerging "lender liability doctrine," which makes lenders in certain situations liable for damage they cause to borrowers, may trace its roots to the seminal case of *Shylock v. Antonio*.

Quite apart from public policy, other independent legal grounds exist for plausible rulings.[6] Portia could have refused the equitable remedy of specific performance on the ground that Shylock had an adequate remedy at law for damages, especially because he had been offered more than principal and interest. Indeed, mere tender of the principal plus interest could by itself suffice to rule against Shylock. Repayment was, after all, the only legitimate purpose of the contract.

Not everyone agrees with such legal objections to Shylock's suit. Several lawyers who have written on the play have concluded that Antonio's obligation is unconditional and automatic.[7] They argue that English common law and Roman civil law would prevent even the cash tender in open court from rescuing Antonio if Shylock were to insist on the penalty. Others contend that Roman law might have enforced Shylock's penalty against Antonio.[8] These arguments have the smell of the lamp about them, out of touch with practical realities. Despite such legalistic arguments, the contract simply would not be enforced—under medieval Venetian law, under Roman civil law, under the English law of Shakespeare's time, under current American law—or under any other civilized system of law.

Portia might also have denied enforcement because of fraud. It could be argued that Shylock proposed the penalty clause to Antonio as a jest; Shylock himself told Antonio that the bond was "in a merry sport" (1.3.144) and not meant seriously (which may well have been the case until Shylock's daughter Jessica elopes with her Christian lover and takes Shylock's jewels with her). But the severity of the penalty, the seriousness with which Antonio understood it, and the solemnity of sealing the contract in writing all make fraud less likely.

Two other possibilities come to mind. It might also be argued that the bond is an unenforceable gambling contract. Shylock's refusal to accept generous repayment is evidence that the bond is not an ordinary commercial guarantee at all, but truly a gamble on Antonio's life. A final legal ground might have been mutual mistake, for the play's last act reveals that three of Antonio's ships were not lost (as all had thought) but returned to harbor safely and with great profit for Antonio, who could himself now pay the debt. At the least, the court might have let Shylock have his principal, without the burden of the additional punishments. Why should Shylock, who kept up his end of the bargain, be the only loser, and such a big one at that?

But despite their availability, Portia takes none of these legal escape routes. Of course we must always remember that Portia is not a real judge, but merely a fictional character drawn temporarily into judicial service. Shakespeare wrote a play, not a judicial opinion. In such a context, the needs of drama trump the probabilities of the courtroom. And legalistic arguments based on technicalities provide good, efficient drama, much more so perhaps than longwinded and hard-to-expound legal principles and public policy. Besides, only a legalistic argument would have taught the lesson that technicalities and literalness beget technicalities and literalness. Portia's persnickety reading of the bond catches everyone, those in the play and in the audience, off guard, and allows the play to take a sharp, unexpected turn. Whether or not Portia's ruling was good law, it definitely is good theater as it turns the tables on Shylock's lethal vengeance.

LAW AND DISCRETION

Portia's ruling vividly illustrates a larger and ever present tension between rigid law and judicial discretion. Those who like Portia's decision (at least that part of it that saves Antonio's life) say it shows how strict law can and should be mitigated by equity. One theory holds that Shakespeare may have been demonstrating the cruelty of English law and its necessary mitigation by the new courts of equity.[9] From this perspective, Portia's ruling is a metaphor of the struggle between rigidity and flexibility.

Shylock, a descendant of the People of the Law, aligns himself with the rule of law. "I stand here for law," he cries (4.1.141). "I crave the law" (4.1.203). "If you deny me, fie upon your law!" (4.1.100). He seeks "law" and "justice" through a mechanical enforcement of the words of his contract. He relies on certainty and stability in the law. To the extent Shylock wants the judge to enforce contracts as written, he is an advocate of judicial restraint.

The need for certainty and stability in contracts generally is even more pronounced in the play's commercial setting. Then, as now, the ability to rely on contracts is of prime importance in commercial law. Even Antonio understands this requirement. "The Duke cannot deny the course of law," moans the bankrupt merchant,

> For the commodity that strangers have
> With us in Venice, if it be denied,
> Will much impeach the justice of the state,
> Since that the trade and profit of the city
> Consisteth of all nations.

> (3.3.26–31)

As Portia further explains:

> There is no power in Venice
> Can alter a decree establishèd.
> 'Twill be recorded for a precedent,
> And many an error by the same example
> Will rush into the state. It cannot be.

> (4.1.215–19)

In essence Shylock is saying—and up to this point Antonio and Portia agree with him—that a ruling in Antonio's favor will upset the entire reliability of commercial contracts under Venetian law, and discourage merchants and moneylenders from doing business in Venice. As a policy consideration, Shylock's position has some merit.

Shylock's legal stance is far from the harsh caricature often portrayed. Shylock is an outsider in Venice, an unpopular minority member who is discriminated against, a hated alien who lacks the same rights as his adversaries. For such a victim of discrimination, it is entirely logical and reasonable—as Posner insightfully points out in the most original, most important, and most liberating contribution of his book—to trust in the apparent severity of a rigid but certain interpretation of law than in the discretion of a system that has already shown its bias.[10] Discretion, as emerged in considering *Measure for Measure*, can become arbitrariness, and worse than injustice is arbitrariness, the negation of law. Power needs to be cabined. The majority does not require courts or law to protect its rights; a minority relies on law for protection precisely because it lacks the numbers to prevail in the political realm.

In this sense, Shylock stands for every minority member who ever sought protection in the safety of clear, precise, written law instead of the personal value judgments of a prejudiced local official. Shylock's concept of law—ridiculed for centuries, shunned by many readers of Shakespeare—turns out to have noble and attractive aspects that could be said to have animated our own civil rights movement.

For outsiders, the law of contracts is important. Law and order and the sanctity of contract are essential for them to compete in society. Their success depends on being scrupulous in obeying the law and abiding by contracts. Justifiable insecurity makes them that way.[11]

But Shylock begs the crucial question. When he claims to "stand here for law" and to "crave the law," he omits the key inquiry: what is law? He assumes that his rigid approach is the only one possible. He is wrong.

Bassanio has a glimpse of the flaw in Shylock's definition of law. Asking Portia to make an exception, Bassanio begs:

> And I beseech you,
> Wrest once the law to your authority.
> To do a great right, do a little wrong,
> And curb this cruel devil of his will.
>
> (4.1.211–14)

Bassanio here seems to concede that it would be "wrong" not to enforce the contract, though only a "little wrong." What Antonio's friend is really articulating is a theory of legal interpretation that involves balancing. It is the argument for discretion, for weighing policy considerations, for ensuring the "right" result.

Right after Bassanio makes his pitch for a discretionary legal approach, Portia, for a fleeting moment, assumes the role of protector of strict, unbending law. "It must not be," snaps Portia. It will be a bad precedent, which will lead to others. "It cannot be" (4.1.215–19). This has been and thus will ever be the argument made when legal interpretation is thought too creative. At this moment Portia and Shylock stand for the same concept of law. But not for long.

Portia soon breaks ranks and defines law differently than Shylock. She understands that to be sensible, law requires judicial discretion. The rigor of the law, she thinks, must be softened with equity and mercy and tempered by individual circumstances. When Portia speaks her moving "quality of mercy" speech (4.1.189–207), she puts into words an equitable concept of law that should inform all legal proceedings. To this extent, Portia is a judicial activist.

In finding a creative solution to a hard judicial problem, Portia, like King Solomon, shows what some might consider signs of greatness. Greatness on the bench—as elsewhere—lies in creativity. But such creativity underscores a basic problem in the judicial process. We expect judges to enforce the law, while knowing they must exercise discretion in applying it to the intractable facts of life. How much law and how much discretion (or justice) are appropriate in the decision of a concrete case? That is the question.

The Merchant of Venice thus sets up the ancient dilemma of rule versus discretion, of constraint versus leeway. Shylock symbolizes law as rigid rules; Portia personifies the spirit of equity. Perhaps because of Shakespeare's successful dramatic technique, our intellectual tradition tends to view Shylock's concept as bad and Portia's as good, but that is too simplistic. Both concepts are good, both are susceptible to abuse, and both are in frequent tension. This basic dilemma may be unavoidable; it may be embedded in the nature of a living legal system.

The implications of this dilemma are far-reaching. Although often discussed in terms of Measure for Measure and The Merchant of Venice, the tension between law and discretion can clearly be seen in the development of whole legal systems. The central legal dilemma so well illustrated in those two plays thus becomes a new way to measure and evaluate what a legal system is actually doing. Such a Shakespearean approach throws light in unexpected ways on, for example, American legal history.

Like The Merchant of Venice, the history of American law shows two different approaches to discretion in government, both of which are designed in theory to enhance and protect liberty. One approach, Shylock's, is to limit such discretion; the other, Portia's, is to encourage it. They are part of the conflict within consensus in our attitudes toward interpreting our basic law, the Constitution. These differing approaches to the same professed goal of greater freedom have been from the beginning of American history continually in tension, as the yin and yang of American constitutional law.

It is vital for us to learn that these differing currents join to define the American judicial tradition. The two jostling strains in American legal thought—Shylock's and Portia's—agree more than they disagree. Both are committed to individual liberty, the constitutional state, and the rule of law. Both have their reciprocal function in preserving society's values. Both have their indispensable roles in the dialectic of public policy. Both are indissoluble partners in the great adventure of the law.

MERCY STRAINED

Much has been written about the quality of mercy shown by Portia toward Shylock. We know she talks a good game: her moving "quality of mercy" speech during the trial has been read with pleasure, memorized by generations, and quoted to courts over and over again (4.1.181–202). One would think that the person who speaks those lines would feel and act on the sentiments behind them. One would hope that when such a person is in a position of power, she would season justice with mercy. One would expect merciful actions to match noble words.

One would be sorely disappointed. Portia's inconsistency between word and deed is vast. For the gulf between her preaching about mercy dropping "as the gentle rain from heaven" and her vengeful punishment of Shylock is unbridgeably wide. On one hand, she practically begs Shylock to be merciful, and on the other, she acts with extraordinary cruelty toward him only moments later. She could and should have stopped at merely denying Shylock's request for his pound of flesh. Is it absolutely necessary to appropriate all of Shylock's property? To put him under a death sentence? To make him convert to another religion? After all, Antonio did default on the loan. Is Portia's judgment fair? It certainly is not merciful. Portia's huge inconsistency and terrible meanness leave haunting doubts about her character.

Those doubts only grow larger. In addition to her hypocrisy and vindictiveness, we see her as a bigot, and not just a minor-league bigot, but a world-class, equal opportunity hate monger. We know she is prejudiced against Jews by her enthusiastically reaching out to rely on the harsh, anti-Semitic Alien Statute. And we also know she is a racist because of her comments about her African suitor's skin color. When the black prince of Morocco makes the wrong choice in the lottery for Portia, she exclaims with relief, "Let all of his complexion choose me so" (2.7.79). But the true scope of her prejudice is revealed before Morocco appears, as she and her maid Nerissa nastily belittle the various suitors' foreign ways (1.2.35–96).

To these character flaws, we add her jealousy of Antonio's suspect love for Bassanio. And on top of all these defects is her corruption as a judge in a case in which she is closely interested.[12] Portia, for all her cleverness and verbal agility, is—to me, at least—unattractive and infuriating, especially as a heroine.

For these reasons, I agree with William Hazlitt, who in the early nineteenth century wrote, "Portia is not a very great favorite with us."[13] To be sure, Portia has for the most part enjoyed good press over the centuries but it mystifies me that so sensitive an observer as Richard Weisberg can refer to Portia as an "exquisite heroine."[14] She strikes me more as the "eloquent mouthpiece"[15] than the lawyer's professional paradigm. She may be quick and legalistically agile, but more judges like Portia would in reality cause a revolution by litigants and lawyers. By going beyond simply denying Shylock's suit and cruelly punishing him, Portia makes herself no more of a hero than the infamous Judge Jeffries, who was notorious for his ruthless rulings during England's Glorious Revolution.

THE CASKET GAME: APPEARANCES DECEIVE

The notion that Portia may not be the heroine she appears to be becomes a crucial aid to interpreting the play as a whole and its legal meaning in particular. The most often repeated theme in the play is that appearances deceive. It shows up in several speeches, as well as in the casket game. Shakespeare's characters refer, for example, to "a villain with a smiling cheek" (1.3.99), and a "goodly apple rotten at the heart" (1.3.100). One says, "O, what a goodly outside falsehood hath!" (1.3.101). If a central message of the play is that we should distinguish between appearance and substance, what are we to make of Portia's and Antonio's apparent triumph in the trial scene? Who, in reality, is the hero, and who the villain?

Even the casket game for picking Portia's husband can be read as a metaphor for law and justice. Portia's dead father's will insisted that her prospective suitors choose among three caskets—gold, silver, and lead— only one of which contains her picture. The suitor who picks the right casket can marry Portia. On the surface, this trial of the caskets seems unrelated to law, but as the play and the casket trial teach, things are not always what they appear.

Consider the evidence. During the casket trial, the characters refer several times to Fortune and "blind Fortune" (2.1.36), and Jessica says once, "Love is blind" (2.6.36). Justice, like Fortune and Love, is also supposed to be blind. Next, Portia says to one of her unsuccessful suitors, "To offend and judge are distinct offices" (2.9.60), which means, "You willingly chose the trial of the caskets; you should not presume to judge the verdict." A further linking of the caskets to law occurs when Portia's maid says, "Hanging [i.e., the results of law] and wiving [i.e., the results of the casket trial] goes by destiny" (2.9.82). This in turn brings out the uncertainty of litigation generally, which is surely reinforced by both the play's express language and stunning outcome.

The casket game can be read as a way to think about law and legal interpretation. Think of Portia's father's will as law. Just as "the will of a living / daughter [is] curbed by the will of a dead father" (1.2.23–24), so too is our desire to govern ourselves constrained by the dead hand of the past. Like Portia's father's will, our law—constitution, statutes, common law—represents the past. In interpreting the Constitution, for example, in choosing how to apply it, we must—it is often said—defer to the intent of the framers, who have long since departed the scene, rather than adapt to new circumstances. In this sense, we are in the same predicament as Portia, who complains, "The lott'ry of my destiny / Bars me the right of voluntary choosing" (2.1.15–16). And yet Portia's song to Bassanio allows her, by interpretation, to bring about the outcome she wants.

Legal interpretation is at the core. How to interpret Portia's father will is one such issue. How to interpret Shylock's contract with Antonio is another. For us, it would be how to interpret the Constitution.

The three caskets are themselves compelling evidence of a legal theme. The winning lead casket bears an inscription that continues the subtheme of chance: "Whose chooseth me must give and hazard all he hath" (2.7.9). So it is with litigation. The silver casket, a loser, says, "Who chooseth me shall get as much as he deserves" (2.7.7), which is one definition of justice. Later, Portia adds to that definition: "In the course of justice none of us / should see salvation. We do pray for mercy" (4.1.195–97). But it is the gold casket that is the most convincing.

The gold casket's legend is: "Who chooseth me shall gain what many men desire" (2.7.5). It symbolizes the gulf between appearance and reality; inside it says, "All that glisters is not gold" (2.7.65). When Bassanio considers which casket to pick, he repeats the underlying theme: "So may the outward shows be least themselves. / The world is still deceived with ornament" (3.2.73–74). And the very first example to his mind of an "outward show," of a misleading appearance, is legal:

> In law, what plea so tainted and corrupt
> But, being seasoned with a gracious voice,
> Obscures the show of evil?
>
> (3.2.75–77)

After twenty years of practicing law, I can only say, 'Tis true, 'tis true.[16]

We should take Shakespeare's hint and link the casket game theme—that things are not always what they seem—to the trial of *Shylock v. Antonio*, the legal show in the play. Shylock's contract with Antonio appeared clear and unambiguous, but Portia showed that it was not what it appeared. Even Portia herself is not what she seems. As the wife of Antonio's best friend, for whom the loan was made, she is anything but a disinterested judge. Her bias removes the blindfold from justice. Indeed, Portia is neither a man nor a lawyer. And in spite of her speech about mercy, she is unnecessarily cruel to Shylock. Does all this mean Portia is a fraud? That justice is a fraud? Or merely uncertain?

More comprehensively, does the misleading appearances theme bear on the majority and minority views of Portia and Shylock in the play? I think it does. The majority view—that Shylock is a villain routed by a good and wise Portia—is what the play *appears* to support. Like Portia's failed suitors, the majority commentators are taken in by surface features of the trial scene: "The seeming truth which cunning times put on / To entrap the wisest" (3.2.100–101). This overwhelming majority ignores Shakespeare's warning, from the mouth of another failed suitor (Aragon), about "the fool multitude, that choose by show, / Not learning more than the fond eye doth teach, / Which pries not to th' interior" (2.9.25–27). But the minority view—that Shylock is a victim of injustice—follows more closely the theme of the play, wholly accords with Shakespeare's text, and like Bassanio's correct choice of the lead casket, goes behind appearances to essence.

EQUAL PROTECTION

From a slightly different legal viewpoint, the play shows what happens when society denies a person equal protection of the laws. Shylock's hate and revenge—what he calls the "ancient grudge" between Jews and Christians (1.3.45)—arise from the suffering, humiliation, injustice, and prejudice he and his co-religionists have borne. Shylock is not a cardboard figure of evil, but a complex and somewhat sympathetic man who has suffered much. We feel this with the intensity of his eloquent "Hath not a Jew eyes?" speech (3.1.54–68). As a non-Christian, Shylock could not even become a citizen of Venice. And it is this discrimination that makes the crucial Venetian law—the vile Alien Statute—apply to him:

> It is enacted in the laws of Venice,
> If it be proved against an alien
> That by direct or indirect attempts
> He seek the life of any citizen . . .

> (4.1.345–48)

This Alien Statute deserves strict scrutiny, for it is an outrage, at least to twentieth-century readers. Curiously, this odd and sinister law, so central to the play's outcome, has largely escaped careful legal analysis. In a new, pathbreaking paper, Peter Alscher, a businessman with a Ph.D. in English literature, has brilliantly refocused our attention on the vices of this law. As Alscher points out, the law gives the state incredible power. If the statute is violated, the state has the legal authority to take all the property of a Jew or any other alien. Half goes to the Venetian citizen whose life has been threatened and half to the government. The law also allows the state to execute the offender. These are heavy punishments indeed.

The harshness of the penalties under the Alien Statute is by no means matched by the severity of the crime for which they can be imposed. The law prohibits not only direct but also "indirect attempts" on the life of any citizen and includes merely "contriving against" such a life. The statute appears to apply even when the offender acts in self-defense or when no bodily harm is actually done. Ignoring the salutary distinction made by Isabella in *Measure for Measure*, the Alien Statute can be invoked not only for actions but also for intentions to act. The statute might be interpreted by Venetian citizens to prosecute "contriving against" a citizen's livelihood as well as his life, since property is the foundation of life. Conceivably, if an alien seeks repayment of a loan made to a citizen, such action itself could amount to "contriving against" the citizen's life.

These objections are nothing as compared to the fundamental flaw of the Alien Statute, which is its denial of equal protection of the laws. It discriminates against aliens (including Jews). There is no comparable Citizen Statute. A citizen who indirectly "contrived against" the life of an alien would not be subject to the same penalties. By virtue of this law, a Jew does not have the same rights as a citizen of Venice. This is the real vice of the Alien Statute: it constitutes unequal treatment by the state, takes away the civil rights of Jews, and deprives Jews of the right to private property. It would be clearly unconstitutional under U.S. law.

A basic and obnoxious defect indelibly taints the Alien Statute. It embodies anti-Semitism and encourages persecution against Jews. By making Jews' hold on life and property precarious, it foreshadows the infamous Nuremburg Laws of our own century and reminds us of Jim Crow laws in this country and apartheid in South Africa. What strikes a modern reader is that no one in the play—not even Shylock—challenges or contests this law. Everyone seems to accept the awful premise of the Alien Statute. Have fundamental sensibilities changed that much? Faced with the Alien Statute, we should cry out, as Shylock cries out earlier, "Fie upon your law!"

Despite these deeply offensive qualities, the Alien Statute's application to Shylock has not drawn unanimous disapproval. On the contrary, the overwhelming majority of commentators object not at all. But in the eyes of the minority, invoking the Alien Statute against Shylock is a horrible miscarriage of justice. After all, Shylock had no prior warning of this infuriating law. Rather, Portia previously told him that no other legal obstacle blocked his suit. For example, Portia asks Shylock to show mercy or else "this strict court of Venice / Must needs give sentence 'gainst the merchant there" (4.1.201–2). And Portia brings up the Alien Statute for the first time only after Shylock has withdrawn his demand for a pound of flesh.

Taking all of the factors into consideration, Alscher proposes a balanced resolution of the trial scene. In a dazzling set of new stage directions, Alscher makes the Alien Statute the true villain of the play. To challenge and eliminate this evil law, he introduces the statute itself as a paper scroll prop in the play. As Portia reads the scroll statute in Alscher's version, she has picked up Shylock's knife and uses it to point to the words. When finished, after saying that Shylock's life is at the mercy of the duke, Portia gives Shylock's knife to Antonio, who starts and then stops in an effort to kill Shylock. The high point in Alscher's directions comes when Antonio raises high the knife and, for one potentially transforming moment, considers plunging the knife through the scroll.[17]

But Shylock is not only a Jew; he is a symbol for any group that feels itself oppressed. Substitute African-Americans, women, or any other such group, and we understand the strength of their impatient feelings for full equality. We are all outsiders now, and Shylock looks better to us. Shakespeare's play thus becomes a dramatic representation of the common-sense wisdom of the equal protection requirement of the Fourteenth Amendment. Rather than anti-Semitic, the play can plausibly be read as pro-minority rights. It shows how inequality before the law breeds dangerous and divisive discontent, never a good thing in any society.

For at least one group—women—the play stands out as an example of triumph over inequality. Portia defies the codes of her milieu by assuming a commanding position of authority and respect as lawyer and judge in a man's world. She is skillful, witty, and learned. Despite occasional criticism from contrarian commentators like myself, Portia's name has become synonymous with eloquence and wisdom in a female attorney or judge. John Mortimer, the English lawyer and writer, has his fictional London barrister, Horace Rumpole of the Bailey, often refer admiringly to his female colleague Phillida Trant as "the Portia of our chambers." And at least one colleague on the Supreme Court has complimented Justice Sandra Day O'Connor—She Who Really Must Be Obeyed—as "the Portia that now graces our Court."[18]

Portia, moreover, rebels at the lack of choice in marriage. Intelligent and ambitious, Portia feels that society and her father's will fetter her choices. She is not resigned to her lot; she takes control.

But here too Portia's feminist triumph may not be all that it appears. Once the trial is over, Portia resumes her demure domestic role in which she had previously called Bassanio "her lord, her governor, her king" (3.2.165). Some feminist! Portia almost seems like two different persons: one the clever, forceful judge, the other a passive princess. And her rebellion over lack of marriage choice is more verbal than real: she complains but still submits to the marriage lottery. In sharp contrast, Shylock's daughter Jessica talks less but rebels more by running away from her father and marrying out of her faith. In this sense, Jessica may claim equal or better title as feminist heroine of the play.

ACT 5's OVERLOOKED LEGAL SIGNIFICANCE

The play's fifth act has often been neglected, but this would be a serious mistake, particularly from a legal point of view. Act 5 has the three sets of young lovers—Jessica and Lorenzo, Nerissa and Gratiano, and Portia and Bassanio—playfully bantering on the island of Belmont, where Portia lives. Coming as it does right after the tremendous tension of the trial scene in act 4, the final act strikes many as anticlimactic and even superfluous. In fact, throughout much of the nineteenth century, English productions of The Merchant of Venice simply stopped the play after Shylock's humiliation at the end of the fourth act, dropping the last act entirely. Now, thanks to Richard Weisberg, we know just how much of an error it would be to overlook act 5.

Weisberg, in his 1992 book Poethics, sets forth an original and persuasive case for the crucial importance of act 5 to the underlying legal themes of Shakespeare's play.[19] Unlike almost all other legal commentators on The Merchant of Venice, Weisberg goes beyond concentrating on the trial scene. According to Weisberg's trailblazing analysis, act 5 is filled with legal imagery and talk of promises that represent a turnaround of the play's legal momentum. By the end of the play, Shylock may be vanquished, but his legalistic mindset has triumphed; everyone becomes as legalistic as Shylock.

The great change in Portia's attitude in act 5 is hard to miss when we compare it to what happened in act 4. At the trial, Shylock stood for sanctity of contract, the keeping of promises, and verbal expressions of commitment. The courtroom attack on Shylock was an attack on verbal obligation. Antonio, Bassanio, and their Venetian friends were casual oath breakers and outright racists. Portia's ruling, however disguised in its own legalisms, encouraged lighthearted breaches of contract and the failure to take seriously the making of a sacred oath. Equity won over law.

But all that changes in the often neglected act 5. There Portia and Nerissa chide their lovers for giving away their wedding rings. Portia lectures Gratiano with words equally applicable to Bassanio:

> You were to blame, I must be plain with you
> To part so slightly with your wife's first gift,
> A thing stuck on with oaths upon your finger,
> And so riveted with faith upon your flesh.

> (5.1.166–69)

Now we have Portia, the symbol of equity, stressing the importance of oaths and their physical representation—rings. She asks Bassanio for "an oath of credit" that he will be faithful and never again give away her ring (5.1.245). Portia, having in act 4 allowed it as a judge, forbids oath breaking in act 5. By play's end, law prevails over equity, oaths over breaches, and Shylock's ethical system over the Venetians' casual attitude toward obligations. Portia in effect adopts Shylock's values.

AN IMAGINARY APPEAL

Given what we now know, we can go beyond Shakespeare and imagine a new sixth act in the play describing Shylock's appeal of Portia's ruling. We can disobey the warnings of some critics and, for heuristic purposes, read into the play our own contemporary legal rules and social attitudes.[20] We can knowingly make the error of historicism and judge the trial not by medieval English or Venetian law, but by our modern American law. Such a technique may not make good literary criticism, nor may it be entirely fair to Shakespeare, but it does illustrate progress in the law.

Undoubtedly, Shylock would on appeal take advantage of the guiding hand of counsel. He would not make the mistake of representing himself a second time. After reviewing the record and doing some preliminary research, appellate counsel would advise Shylock of several arrows in his appellate quiver.

If I were Shylock's counsel on appeal, I would advise him to divide the appeal into two separate aspects, one dealing with the penalties imposed on him and the other with enforcing the underlying contract. I would attack most vigorously that part of the trial court's ruling that confiscated Shylock's wealth and made him convert to another religion. I would recommend such an appellate strategy because it stands the greatest likelihood of success and, if successful, would reverse the worst elements of Portia's decision. At least it would make Shylock whole, putting him back to where he was before the trial.

The appellate attack on Shylock's punishments would have a number

of prongs. I would start with the most attractive one, the argument based
on Shylock being denied equal protection of the laws. For the first aspect
of the equal protection argument, I would stress the pervasive prejudice
that marked the whole trial. Then I would argue that the Alien Statute, on
its face and as applied, discriminated against Shylock by deeming him an
alien by virtue of his religion and treating him differently for that impermissible reason.

Next I would group a cluster of arguments. I would try to show that
the trial denied Shylock procedural due process because the trial judge
was biased and not a lawyer. Then I would argue that Shylock's punishment was unconstitutional in that it was cruel and unusual. That Shylock
was punished at all constitutes a separate but related argument. Shylock
brought a civil suit for breach of contract that somehow got transformed
into a criminal case against him. That is something an appellate court
might frown upon. As for that part of the penalty requiring Shylock to
convert from Judaism to Christianity, I would argue that it violated Shylock's fundamental right to free exercise of his religion, as well as the
basic ban against establishing a state religion.

With respect to the second major issue on appeal—enforceability of the
underlying bond—I would tread gingerly. I would not advise Shylock to
press for specific performance, but rather to abandon that claim in favor
of possibly receiving principal plus interest. I would give that advice on
the basis of pragmatic judgment and in an effort to salvage for Shylock
the most out of the difficult situation. Having been so humiliated in court
the first time, I would hope Shylock would be receptive to practical legal
advice in his own best interest.

I would still discuss the enforceability of the contract, except for the
penalty. I would concede at the outset that Shylock no longer seeks his
pound of flesh. But I would maintain that Shylock's substantive due process was denied because his liberty of contract was infringed. Although
the contract penalty may be against public policy, the parties were of
relatively equal bargaining power, and therefore it is wrong to speak of
the penalty as unconscionable in the usual sense of one party using economic leverage to overreach a weaker, uninformed party. I would stress
that, at least as to principal and interest, Portia erred by failing to enforce
the contract and thereby jeopardized stability and certainty in Venetian
commercial law. The next argument would be that to deny Shylock principal and interest would give Antonio a tremendous windfall, especially
since three of his ships did return safely.

If I were Antonio's counsel on appeal, I would have plenty to say too.
As to Shylock's arguments about the desirability of enforcing commercial
contracts as written, I would obviously rely heavily on the public policy
against such penalty clauses and provide alternative grounds for the trial

court's nonenforcement. I would stress that forfeiture of principal and interest is common enough for lenders who violate public policy. And if such forfeitures are permissible for something as innocuous as usury, I would argue that far more severe legal penalties are justifiable for a lender seeking the death of a borrower. To defuse the equal protection argument, I would say that the statute should be interpreted to apply to all persons regardless of whether they are aliens or Jews. As for the other alleged errors, I would argue that they were at most harmless.

Although speculation about how appellate courts will rule is risky in real cases, an imaginary appeal gives us more license. My prediction is that on appeal the decision would be affirmed in part and reversed in part. The unenforceability of the loan agreement would be affirmed on the grounds of public policy, but the penalties beyond forfeiture of principal would be reversed on the three grounds: equal protection, procedural due process, and freedom of religion. The (no doubt) all-male appellate panel would make a criminal reference to the district attorney about Portia practicing law without a license.

Freedom of Speech

Shakespeare's portrayal of Shylock has generated controversy for centuries. There have been those who have believed that *Merchant* is anti-Semitic in its unflattering picture of Shylock. Such perceived anti-Semitism has led some to question whether the play should be produced at all during periods of actual or incipient anti-Semitism. According to Harold Bloom, "The play, honestly interpreted and responsibly performed . . . would no longer be acceptable on a stage in New York City, for it is an anti-Semitic masterpiece, unmatched in its kind."[21] Others have gone further and doubted whether the play, given its clear anti-Semitic slant, should even be taught, especially after the Holocaust.

The gist of the controversy is the concern that, in light of Shakespeare's influence and position, we may unleash dark forces by opening the public to Shakespeare's negative picture of a Jew. No right-thinking person, the argument goes, would wish to publicize Shakespeare's voice as part of the anti-Jewish chorus in our midst. As a matter of historical fact, the play has at times been used for anti-Semitic purposes. It has induced prejudice and led to a bad image for Jews.

The threshold response could be to deny that *Merchant* is anti-Semitic. It is, above all, a play, and one might first ask if it is expressing anti-Semitism or describing anti-Semitism. Then we might recall the play's theme of deceitful appearances and wonder again if what appears to be anti-Semitism really is so. The play is equally critical of other groups, especially Christians, who come in for some very harsh scrutiny. Careful observers will note several almost majestic qualities in Shakespeare's "Jew of Venice." Shylock stands for: (1) loyalty to his community and his family (note especially his poignant speech about his late wife's gift of a ring, and compare it with the other characters' treatment of rings); (2) unflagging honesty in his view of situations and individuals (listen to Shylock speak, simply and without the grandiloquent falsity, of the Venetians); (3) literalism and a sense of justice (compare Shylock's approach to the commercial contract with Bassanio's, that same Bassanio who uses his friend Antonio's credit to finance a project designed to win for himself Portia and her wealth).

These admirable qualities in Shylock meet their polar opposites among the rest of the characters. Portia's performance at the trial is flawed by fundamental hypocrisy. And Antonio and Bassanio more than match Shylock's revenge quotient. All in all, we might reasonably conclude that the play is generally evenhanded.

But even if we assume, for the sake of argument, that *Merchant* is anti-Semitic, it does not necessarily follow that it should be banned from the stage or from the classroom. Of course, theatergoers need not attend performances of *Merchant* if they do not wish to. To press for censorship or a boycott or a blacklist, however, is to raise serious questions of freedom of expression, involving rights of artists to produce and audiences to see. It is reminiscent of misguided attempts to take *Huckleberry Finn* off the library shelves because it is allegedly racist or benighted efforts to fire actors for political reasons.[22]

Objections to *Merchant* on grounds of anti-Semitism call to mind the overall subject of government funding for the arts. In 1990 Senator Jesse Helms of North Carolina objected to several grants made by the National Endowment for the Arts, primarily because he regarded the funded work as obscene. Regulations prohibiting federal support for art that might be considered obscene have been challenged in court, and Congress has considered restricting grants to works that do not denigrate racial or religious groups or the handicapped, or otherwise meet general standards of decency. Under such a restriction, many Shakespeare plays in addition to *Merchant* might be suspect. Several of the plays have sexual themes and bedroom tricks that might strike some latter-day sexually repressed Bowdler as obscene.[23] And might not *Othello* and *Richard III* be considered derogatory of racial groups or the handicapped? These are large First Amendment questions.

REVENGE THROUGH LAW

Another theme, important in Shakespeare generally and particularly for his legal themes, permanently marks *The Merchant of Venice*—the theme of vengeance through law. *The Merchant of Venice* is a "revenge play," common enough in Elizabethan times, in which crucial dramatic action turns on a major character's thirst for revenge. With *Merchant*, Shakespeare puts a special twist on the standard revenge play by having Shylock seek to get even by using the law. Shylock does not take the law into his own hands and carry out private vengeance on Antonio through private violence. Rather, Shylock takes him to court, where the moneylender attempts to enforce his legal rights to the limit, without pity, and even though Antonio's death might result. The legal system, in Shylock's hands, itself becomes the means for revenge.

The play is explicit about the theme of vengeance through law. After Jessica runs away with Shylock's jewels and money, and after Antonio is in trouble, Shylock is whipped up into a vengeful frenzy. "Let him look to his bond" (3.1.41–44), Shylock says over and over again, believing he still has one way of getting back at Antonio. When Shylock's colleague Saler asks what good will enforcing the bond do, Shylock answers that "it / will feed my revenge" (3.1.49–50).

Then immediately follows Shylock's "Hath not a Jew eyes?" speech, during which he makes even clearer his use of legal process to work revenge:

> And if you wrong us
> shall we not revenge? If we are like you in the rest,
> we will resemble you in that. If a Jew wrong a Christian,
> what is his humility? Revenge. If a Christian wrong a
> Jew, what should his sufferance be by Christian
> example? Why, revenge. The villainy you teach me I
> will execute, and it shall go hard but I will better the
> instruction.
>
> (3.1.61–68)

Just in case we somehow miss the point, Shakespeare has Shylock repeat it before the start of the trial scene. "I'll have my bond. Speak not against my bond / I have sworn an oath that I will have my bond" (3.3.4–5).

Shylock's use of litigation for revenge has a modern ring to it. It is a late development in the long evolution of law from violent private revenge to public enforcement by disinterested persons in a trial at law. In contrast with early use of revenge as a substitute for law, *Merchant* depicts the more recent phenomenon of vengeance through law. Venice is cosmopolitan and civilized; it has laws and a legal system for resolving disputes. Venetians go to law instead of doing bodily harm to those of their neighbors against whom they have claims.

Still, the thin veneer of civilization hardly wipes out so strong and deep-seated an emotion as revenge. Wise politicians and lawmakers know this psychological fact and, acting on it, create institutions and encourage habits to provide socially acceptable and orderly ways for venting vengeful feelings. "Law channels rather than eliminates revenge," as Judge Posner puts it, "replaces it as system but not as feeling."[24] Under the circumstances, nothing would mollify Shylock but revenge. Better it should be revenge through law than revenge as a substitute for law.

Despite its modern and salutary aspects, Shylock's use of law for revenge distresses us. It is as if Shylock is abusing modern law, as if he is abusing his legal rights. He uses the means of the law for a bad end or purpose. In doing so, Shylock also does something nasty to himself, so misusing the law that he loses part of his mental and emotional balance and even some essential element of his humanity. Shylock is the embodiment of a character familiar to law offices today: the person obsessed with litigation. A victim of litigation psychosis, Shylock lives to inflict pain on his enemies through lawsuits. Any lawyer who has handled an emotion-laden litigation—a bitter divorce case or a child custody battle—or defended a pro se case knows the symptoms.

Shakespeare seems to take a dim view of Shylock's use of revenge through law. To be sure, one must always be careful when attempting to impute values or views to an author from his dramatic literature. But even approaching the subject with diffidence, we can fairly conclude that Shakespeare in *The Merchant of Venice* rejects revenge. His portrayal of Shylock's ignoble quest through law, his handling of the trial scene, the very language and action—all reflect a view of law in which the primitive impulse of revenge is disapproved. This theme, and the role of revenge in the evolution of law, figures prominently in other Shakespearean plays, especially *Hamlet* and *Julius Caesar*.

CLASSIFICATIONS

Classifying *The Merchant of Venice* has always been hard. Tradition lists it as a comedy, but that is troublesome, unless the play was originally meant to be humorous, as it probably was, with Shylock the butt of the laughter. Of course, the comedy label does not necessarily imply humor, but according to conventional structure, only that a sudden reversal of fate occurs and that a reconciliation of sorts takes place at the end of the play. By that definition, the play would be a comedy, though certainly a dark one. Except for a few hilarious scenes with Lancelot Gobbo, there is nothing funny about this play today; it is, for the most part, anything but humorous. It is, truly speaking, neither a comedy nor a tragedy nor a history. It is a dramatic crystal of many legal issues, a rich text for a law school seminar. If a category is needed, let us invent one called legal parable.

As a legal parable, *The Merchant of Venice* may have influenced contemporary judges and changed the course of English legal history. King James I asked to see two performances of the play on two consecutive days. The leading modern champion of Shakespeare's impact on English jurisprudence, W. Nicholas Knight, insists that the 1616 case of *Glanville v. Courtney* demonstrates the play's effect. In that case, which was a suit on a bond, Lord Coke, acting as chief justice of the common law courts, entered judgment for plaintiff. But the lord chancellor, Lord Ellesmore, issued an injunction to prevent enforcement of the bond. The result is considered to be a victory of equity over the common law, with the Crown siding with equity, just as the duke did in *Shylock v. Antonio*.

Based on these facts, Knight speculates that the result in *Glanville v. Courtney* was due to *The Merchant of Venice*. If I understand Knight correctly, he is arguing that since *Glanville* was decided by judges who must have seen *Merchant*, then *Merchant* must have contributed to the legal result.[25] Such an argument is difficult to respond to. Knight's theory is possible, but no proof exists for it. The highly speculative nature of Knight's conclusions, provocative and fascinating though they may be, does not warrant the exaggerated style of certainty in which they are expressed.

And yet others have sided with Knight on this point. A nineteenth-century lawyer, on whose work Knight draws, also thought that the result in *Glanville* was due to Shakespeare's ideas. More recently, Harlan F. Stone, a justice of the Supreme Court for two decades in this century, once said that, "Often, in listening to *The Merchant of Venice*, it has occurred to me that Shakespeare knew the essentials of the contemporary conflict between law and equity."[26]

Whatever the impact on seventeenth-century lawyers of *The Merchant of Venice*, we can surely appreciate its influence over us. We can feel the power of the theatrical experience in our professional as well as personal lives. The play is about human character, but it is also about law, liberty of contract and its limits, law and discretion, the meaning of mercy, the legal symbolism of the casket game, equal protection, and other legal themes.

The more often I see the play, the larger it looms in my experience. Familiarity has only deepened its hold on my attention and brought me closer to the spirit that animated it. More than ever before, it now stands separate and lonely in its tragic splendor. As I enter a courthouse, I think of Shakespeare's warning, "You must take your chance" (2.1.38). And as I leave a spiritually liberating performance of *The Merchant of Venice*, I hear over and over again in my mind what Portia says to Shylock, and what Shakespeare means the whole play to say to all of us: "The law hath yet another hold on you" (4.1.344).

Chapter Five

SKULL OF A LAWYER

HAMLET

SHAKESPEARE tightens his legal hold on us with *Hamlet*. If *The Merchant of Venice* shows the misuse of law as an instrument of revenge, *Hamlet* illustrates a related theme: how law can benefit society by properly and usefully taming, channeling, and sublimating the hard-to-control passion for revenge. Of course, there is much, much more in *Hamlet*.

"*Hamlet* is pound for pound . . . the greatest play ever written. It towers above everything else in dramatic literature. . . . Every time you read a line it can be a new discovery." So wrote Laurence Olivier, one of the most memorable Hamlets, in his 1986 book *On Acting*. Many would agree.

One of the reasons for *Hamlet*'s greatness, according to Olivier, is that "it lends itself to so many changes and interpretations." We are continually "finding new meanings in the text" and are dazzled at its "forever being fresh." You can read it and view it as many times as opportunity permits "and still not get to the bottom of its box of wonders." No matter how familiar the play becomes, "the questions keep coming up, and always will. Was Hamlet this? Was he that? Did he do this, did he do that?"[1]

With everything that has been written about *Hamlet* no one book or article tells it all. More remains to discover—new reflecting facets for new generations. For instance, one generation, influenced by Freud, explained the play in terms of the Oedipal complex.[2] But even if we subscribe to that psychological theory, we need not go so far as to let the play—an extraordinary exploration of the human mind—be only about that.

Among the many meanings in *Hamlet* are distinctly legal themes. This is, but ought not to be, a controversial statement. Posner, for instance, would argue about it. He recognizes that *Hamlet* is an example of revenge literature and that "perhaps legal training can enable one to say something fresh" about such literature. But later, Posner surprisingly seems to say the opposite. In a line that begs for a response, Posner proclaims it "unlikely that a *Hamlet* scholar will have anything useful to say about the Constitution or a constitutional scholar anything useful to say about *Hamlet*."[3] Such rigid, compartmentalized thinking limits the exploratory scope and tentative conclusions of law and literature as a new approach.

On one level *Hamlet* can be used to illustrate the pitfalls of wooden legal interpretation. Justice Thurgood Marshall, who as a civil rights lawyer had argued against mechanical deference to old legal rules, pointed out these pitfalls while dissenting in a 1976 Supreme Court case. To apply an old rule of law "blindly today, however," Marshall wrote, "makes as much sense as attempting to interpret Hamlet's admonition to Ophelia, 'Get thee to a nunnery, go,' without understanding the meaning of Hamlet's words in the context of their age."[4] Marshall added in a footnote, "Nunnery was Elizabethan slang for house of prostitution." But this is only the first level of legal meaning in *Hamlet*. Others, far more important, abound.

REVENGE VERSUS RULE OF LAW

The most basic legal theme in *Hamlet*, not discussed in standard Shakespeare criticism, explores nothing less than the struggle for the rule of law. To develop this large legal theme, Shakespeare uses Hamlet to depict the uncertain battle within human nature between the primitive passion for revenge and the more civilized law against individual retaliation. *Hamlet* shows the evolution of law and order out of vengeful barbarism.

Hamlet is a play filled with revenge. Three separate revenge tragedies go on at the same time. The main action is about Hamlet's revenge against Claudius for murdering Hamlet's father. In addition, Laertes seeks revenge against Hamlet for killing Polonius, Laertes' father. And in the background is Fortinbras's revenge because Hamlet's father killed Fortinbras's father. Shakespeare piles revenge upon revenge.

Revenge in tragedy serves an important function. It is an act in response to an earlier transgression that has upset the moral equilibrium. The first crime puts the moral world out of kilter and creates a tension. Revenge can be seen as a positive act of retribution that brings the moral norms of society into balance again. In *Hamlet*, the total effect of so many simultaneous revenge tragedies is to neutralize the sense of restoring moral balance. By the end of the play, after all the main characters have died, Fortinbras restores order and moral law.

Everyone assumes Hamlet has a duty to seek revenge. All literary criticism proceeds on that assumption, and holds that he should have killed Claudius much sooner than he did. According to tradition, it is precisely Hamlet's delay in avenging his father's death that is his basic weakness and that leads to disaster. The oceans of ink analyzing and interpreting *Hamlet* all start from the headwater of blood revenge.

The assumption that Hamlet ought to have sought revenge needs to be challenged. We should consider the possibility that Hamlet ought *not* to have killed Claudius. We need to explore the thesis that Hamlet's delay does him credit, that Hamlet's indecision was an effort not to yield to the passion for revenge. We need to weigh the proposition that Shakespeare wanted us first to believe that Hamlet should kill Claudius so that we might undergo his agony with him, but that Shakespeare did not want us to persist in that belief.

From this fresh, non-Euclidean perspective, whole new legal vistas appear. Hamlet's dramatic struggle then becomes an effort to transcend a lower morality and move beyond a rule of force and private vengeance. Hamlet represents humanity's effort, faced with forces that would drag it backward, to ascend to a higher level. Hamlet symbolizes the battle between the primitive morality of personal vengeance and the modern rule of law, a turning point in the growth of the law from barbarism to civilization.

This battle shows through in Hamlet's "To be, or not to be" soliloquy. What if this most famous of Shakespearean speeches is not about suicide, as is commonly thought, but instead about revenge? If so, then Hamlet's comment "conscience doth make cowards of us all" takes on more meaning, as well it should. Among life's hardships listed in this soliloquy, hardships that Hamlet thinks could be cut through in an instant, are the inactivity, ineffectiveness, and slowness of legal process:

> For who would bear the whips and scorns of time,
> Th'oppressor's wrong, the proud man's contumely,
> The pangs of disprized love, *the law's delay*,
> The insolence of office, and the spurns
> That patient merit of th'unworthy takes,
> When he himself might his quietus [i.e., settlement] make
> With a bare bodkin [i.e., dagger]?
>
> (3.1.72–78 [emphasis added])

Should Hamlet—or any of us—put up with "the law's delay" or instead seek speedier private revenge? That question is the most crucial and basic legal question posed by *Hamlet*.

In this sense, Hamlet shows in the struggle of one man a critical moment in the evolution of law. In biology, we hear how "ontogeny recapitulates phylogeny," which means that individual development (ontogeny) duplicates the evolution of the species (phylogeny). In *Hamlet*, Shakespeare may have used his protagonist to show the agony and uncertainty of the species' upward climb to the rule of law. Such a theory is fruitful.

This theory, fruitful or not, is also controversial. A. C. Bradley, for example, rejected it almost a century ago. According to Bradley, the play's text belies any reading that Hamlet had moral scruples about avenging his father's death. Bradley even goes beyond this "ordinary conscience" theory to set up and then knock down what he calls a "deeper conscience" approach. In describing this "deeper conscience" theory, Bradley anticipates my own theory. He says that Hamlet, on the conscious level, was sure that he ought to obey the ghost. But, argues Bradley, in the "depths" of Hamlet's "nature, and unknown to himself, there was a moral repulsion to the deed." The "conventional moral ideas of his time," Bradley continues, told Hamlet "plainly that he ought to avenge his father; but a deeper conscience in him, which was in advance of his time, contended with these explicit conventional ideas." Hamlet fails to recognize this "deeper conscience," Bradley surmises, precisely because it "remains below the surface."[5] But after this illuminating insight, Bradley winds up disappointingly by cavalierly saying that "we must reject" this interpretation because Shakespeare meant us to assume that Hamlet should have obeyed the ghost.

Regardless of what Shakespeare actually intended, Bradley's criticisms do not undercut the theory put forth here. I am not offering my version of the "deeper conscience" theory as a complete explanation for all of Hamlet's conduct in the play. I know the error of isolating one element of his character and treating it as the whole. My purpose is far more limited and does not turn on Shakespeare's actual specific intent. Quite apart from Shakespeare's intent, Hamlet's behavior fairly gives rise to the "deeper conscience" theory, and that theory then becomes a legitimate subject for meditation on a legal theme. The meditation stands (or falls) on its own, even if I am possibly misreading Shakespeare.

Revenge, of course, is a primitive, if natural and understandable, human impulse. It dominates the early stages of all legal systems. "The early forms of legal procedure," wrote Oliver Wendell Holmes in *The Common Law*, "were grounded in vengeance."[6] The biblical concept of "an eye for an eye"—*lex talionis*—is, if taken literally, the hallmark of such early systems of law. It gave the title to Shakespeare's other play *Measure for Measure* and finds voice in the duke's speech in that play.[7] On its face, it reflects the morality of primitive, more violent times when the impulse of revenge was gratified by retaliatory measures on the part of the individual who suffered the crime committed, or of his relatives in the case of murder.

In time the bloody, vengeful "eye for an eye" rule came to be interpreted so as to be a step away from vengeance. Up until then, the norm was to wipe out the family, clan, village, or countryside to retaliate for a perceived transgression against you or yours. But an "eye for an eye" became a limitation on revenge, the beginning perhaps of our concept that punishment should bear some relationship to the offense.

Scholars of Jewish law insist that the concept of "an eye for an eye" has been misunderstood and that it was never meant to be taken literally. Jewish jurisprudence has interpreted "eye for eye" as meaning appropriate monetary compensatory damages. Thus the true meaning of "an eye for an eye" is that the person who caused the harm should be assessed monetary damages commensurate with the loss inflicted (the *value* of an eye or a tooth). Far from epitomizing vengeance, the "eye for eye" rule, so interpreted, means a measure of compensatory damages, one of the foundations of our "modern" system of justice, particularly the law of torts. It is unclear whether such an interpretation existed from the beginning of the rule or whether it became a revisionist interpretation to adapt a primitive rule to more modern notions.

Regardless of the real meaning of "eye for eye," in *Hamlet* primitive morals are embodied in three characters. Laertes and Fortinbras take their respective revenges without hesitancy or self-doubt, in contrast to the reluctant and more thoughtful Hamlet. But more than those two, the most powerful symbol of the primitive morals is the ghost of Hamlet's dead father. The ghost, a violent warrior king in battle dress, orders Hamlet to seek revenge by killing Claudius. The older, more warlike and violent generation tells the younger generation to carry on the endless violence.

But revenge begets more revenge, violence leads to more violence. Certainly that is the message of several of Shakespeare's other plays, as well as history and experience. Shedding blood tears the fabric of human society. Private blood revenge is barbaric, a vestige of the Hobbesian state of nature, where each man is a law unto himself. As George Bernard Shaw wrote in *Caesar and Cleopatra*, "To the end of history murder breeds murder, always in the name of right and honour and peace, until the gods are tired of blood and create a race that can understand."

To tame such barbarism is one of the chief functions of law. In his essay "Of Revenge," Francis Bacon writes, "Revenge is a kind of wild justice, which the more man's nature runs to, the more ought law to weed it out. For as for the first wrong, it doth but offend the law; but the revenge of that wrong putteth the law out of office."[8] Law, by forbidding private revenge, tries to take the wildness out of justice. As time passed, people realized that violent self-help was no answer.

A major purpose of law is to discourage private vengeance by allowing the legal system alone to mete out punishment. Criminal law really began when the state assumed the function of revenge and took away the right of retaliation from individuals. Hamlet's hesitancy comes from his being on the cusp of discovering criminal law.

Hamlet reflects this civilizing function of law by struggling to resist the primitive call for revenge. He does not simply obey his father. He does not immediately kill the king. He doubts blood revenge. Hamlet, the more educated and civilized younger generation, fights within himself to repudiate the lower morals of violence.

This aspect of Hamlet's struggle against violence is overlooked by psychological theories that stress Hamlet's Oedipal complex. In *Civilization and Its Discontents*, Freud argues that civilization requires the curbing (or sublimating) of violent impulses. If Hamlet did avenge his father's death, he would have violated Freud's basic rule of civilized conduct. Hamlet is thus caught in a Freudian dilemma: if he seeks revenge, he is uncivilized; if he does not seek revenge, he is a victim of the Oedipal complex. No wonder Hamlet is confused.

Hamlet's repudiation of revenge is in keeping with his high view of humanity. "What a piece of work is a man!" he says. "In action how like an angel! In apprehension how like a god!" (2.2.305–8). Hamlet's mind was focused on lofty aspirations: reading, philosophy, civilization. And civilization means law. Hamlet drew back from killing his uncle because he did not want to degrade himself, descending to Claudius's level and becoming a murderer.

The outcome of Hamlet's war with the primitive moral code is less important than the war itself. After the play within the play, Hamlet seems to yield to irresistible forces from underneath. Having given up the struggle, he speeds onward to violent destruction. But the point is not that Hamlet, in a rush of emotion, finally kills Claudius. The crucial point is that Hamlet was won to the side of violence only after a long inner struggle. At least Hamlet struggled mightily, and in that mighty struggle we see an important part of legal history.

But Hamlet is only a transitional figure in legal development. To be sure, he does not oppose private revenge with a clear-cut moral theory of his own. Yet new moralities do not spring into existence in the face of entrenched custom in full-fledged conscious and conceptual form. Hamlet is humanity yearning to emerge from the violent state of nature. Hamlet's mind is the law's battleground.

Hamlet's great struggle is in part our own, though we have learned to channel the passion for revenge. Revenge still plays a role in our law, both civil and criminal. Holmes, for example, concluded that "the various forms of [civil] liability known to modern law spring from the common ground of revenge."[9] Criminal law's link to revenge is even more obvious. In the famous words of Sir James Stephen, "The criminal law stands to the passion for revenge in much the same relation as marriage to the sexual appetite."[10] America's recent return to use of the death penalty surely reflects, at least in part, the continuing potency of revenge in our law.

Posner's book *Law and Literature* points in the right direction but stops far short of fully exploring the crucial link between the revenge theme in *Hamlet* and the development of law. Posner unfairly criticizes "literary lawyers" for their alleged neglect of revenge as a literary theme, specifically as a theme in *Hamlet*. Posner is right to stress the importance of the revenge theme for the law and literature movement, though he too fails to do that theme justice.

Like Hamlet, Posner comes to the brink of discovery, but then shies away. To his credit, Posner does recognize that "*Hamlet* is a powerful argument for the rule of law," and that revenge is "a primitive form of law, an antecedent and template of modern law, and an argument for modern law."[11] But he does not go far enough; he does not connect Hamlet's paralysis of will to the evolution of law. Posner's theory is that Hamlet's inaction is due to his being temperamentally unsuited to play the revenger's role. That may be so, but it totally misses the point that probing Hamlet's temperament reveals his very indecision to be a crucial node in the history of law and morals.

The lesson of *Hamlet* radiates even more broadly. It shows humanity grappling with a basic choice: civilization and law or violence and chaos. One can only wonder how Hamlet would have solved his problem if he had had an opportunity to talk over the centuries with Justice Holmes. Holmes admitted the importance of vengeance and even went so far as to say that "the law does, [and] ought to, make the gratification of revenge an object." But Holmes saw that such passion needs to be channeled. "If people would gratify the passion of revenge outside of the law," Holmes wrote, "if the law did not help them, the law has no choice but to satisfy the craving itself, and thus avoid the greater evil of private retaliation. At the same time, this passion is not one which we encourage, either as private individuals or as law-makers."[12] Holmes, a Civil War hero who charged through life, was no Hamlet; but, a thoughtful man, he understood Hamlet's predicament.

ILLEGAL AUTHORITY

A different legal theme in *Hamlet* perhaps as pervasive as revenge is of constitutional magnitude. "Something is rotten in the State of Denmark" (1.4.90). We are met at the outset with corruption and decay in the state: an illegal seizure of power. Claudius has murdered his brother the king, Hamlet's father, and usurped his place on the throne. Law in the sense of properly constituted authority, so essential to society, is missing. We are, as a result, plunged into a lower level of law and social organization.

This particular theme of constitutional law—the consequences of improperly constituted authority—shows up again and again in Shakespeare. *King Lear* and *Macbeth* have it, as do *Measure for Measure* and several of the histories (for example, *Richard III* and *Henry IV*). Indeed, *Macbeth* became the basis for *Macbird*, a controversial 1960s American satire that compared Lyndon Johnson to Macbeth as a usurper.

A MELANCHOLY LAW STUDENT?

Against the constitutional law backdrop unfolds the central mystery of
the play: Hamlet's hesitancy in seeking to obtain revenge for his father's
murder. Of the many explanations for Hamlet's indecision, one of the
most common stresses Hamlet's contemplative nature and his inability to
take action. Hamlet has supposedly overdeveloped his intellect at the expense of action or will. He loses himself in abstract trains of thought at
the risk of diminished contact with external reality.

Hamlet is a student afflicted with the student's disease of melancholy.
He seems to be the victim of too much study. "To spend too much time
in studies," wrote Shakespeare's contemporary Francis Bacon (a lawyer)
in one of his famous essays, "is sloth."[13] And the Bible tells us that "much
study is a weariness of the flesh."[14] But what was Hamlet studying? Law,
perhaps. Maybe the book every Hamlet, almost always dressed in barrister's black, has in his hand is a law book. Of course this is rank speculation, not fact, but it is suggestive.

Considering Shakespeare's London environment, and the audiences
for whom he wrote, Hamlet may be a reflection of a gloomy young student from the Inns of Court, which certainly influenced Shakespeare.
Hamlet in some ways symbolizes the fin de siècle atmosphere in the late
1590s in the Inns of Court. Widespread skepticism and pessimism, despair and profound discouragement, were voiced by many thoughtful
men of the age. Hamlet's passing remarks on the hollowness of life and
the futility of heroic action are typical of many intellectuals of the last
decades of the sixteenth century.

HAMLET'S LAWYERLY TRAITS

Whether or not Hamlet is a melancholy law student, he exhibits some
lawyerly traits. One could say that Hamlet hesitates to kill Claudius because the prince, in lawyerly fashion, wants hard evidence of his uncle's
guilt before he acts. The word of a ghost is scarcely the most compelling
proof. Like a lawyer, Hamlet is fond of quibbles and wordplay, which he
uses to mystify, thwart, and annoy. This shows a nimbleness and flexibility of mind characteristic of Hamlet and many lawyers. They are manipu-
lators of words.

"Words. Words. Words," cries out an exasperated Hamlet (2.2.195)
when Polonius asks what he is reading. But Hamlet's apparent dismay at
so many words can be turned back on him, as it can on lawyers generally.
For it is Hamlet who, confronted with situations calling for action, retreats into "Words. Words. Words."

Hamlet's much criticized hesitancy looks like equivocal legalizing, his postponements resemble legalistic delays. As Richard Weisberg astutely notes in *The Failure of the Word*, "Hamlet's procedures are those of a lawyer, not an aristocrat or hero. Everything must be proven to him, even the self-evident. . . . endless cross-examination and prolix argumentation become his mode."[15]

The key to Hamlet's "legalistic proclivity," as Weisberg calls it, is his verbosity. Hamlet, like many lawyers, talks too much. An inactive, wordy character, he prefers the safety of words to the risks of action. He is "sicklied o'er with the pale cast of thought" (3.1.87). Speech, for Hamlet, replaces action. He uses words to hide from reality, to recast reality—and his futile wordiness prevents him from doing anything to right the wrong he so keenly feels. Rather than act, Hamlet, like many a motormouth lawyer, talks.

Bradley puts a different spin on this point. Unlike Weisberg, who did practice as a lawyer, Bradley, an academic who never studied law, perceives the lawyer as a person of affairs, of action—not mere thought. Thus, from his perspective as an academic who is respectful of worldly and businesslike attorneys, Bradley, in commenting on *Hamlet*, observes that "a mere student is likely to be more at a loss in a sudden and great practical emergency than a soldier or a lawyer."[16] It is fascinating to speculate whether Bradley would have held the same opinion, would have regarded lawyers the same way, if he, like Weisberg, had been trained as a lawyer and practiced at the bar.

In any event, were Hamlet a judge, he would likely be an exemplar of judicial self-restraint. He might agree with Justice Louis Brandeis's comment, "The most important thing we do is not doing." As lawyer or judge, Hamlet would probably justify his psychological reluctance to act by relying on the self-denying ordinances of judicial restraint: lack of justiciability, mootness, ripeness, and political questions. Hamlet is a model for lawyers who are verbose, passive, hypertechnical, long-winded, persnickety, and more concerned with process than with substance.

A modern Hamlet in judicial robes was Felix Frankfurter. An apostle of judicial restraint, Frankfurter—who served on the Supreme Court from 1939 to 1962—wrote many long judicial opinions rationalizing his inaction with what now seem like unconscious excuses. Frankfurter's Hamlet-like torrent of words relied on the "passive virtues" of constitutional jurisprudence and was filled with self-doubts about the Supreme Court's competence and endless second guessing. Just as Hamlet's vengeance took the form of words and most of the reasons he assigned for his procrastination are evidently not the true reasons, so too Justice Frankfurter's reaction to social wrongs, injustice, and other substantive issues often took the form of retreating into language, of saturating many pages of the United States Reports with excuses for not acting.

In view of these similar personality traits, we are not surprised to find the cultured Supreme Court justice, a former Harvard law professor, invoking the melancholy prince in a judicial opinion. The case, a relatively obscure one decided in 1949, turned on a question of whether a federal law regulating interstate commerce covered handling of irrigation water in agriculture despite an exemption for individuals "employed in agriculture." The Supreme Court held that, regardless of the exemption, the federal statute did indeed cover the irrigation activity. Justice Frankfurter went along with the Court's majority, but wrote, as he often did, a separate concurring opinion to express his doubts about the Court's reasoning.

His doubts led his civilized mind back to *Hamlet*. Frankfurter did not see how the Court could simultaneously hold that the employees were engaged in production of agricultural crops for commerce and that they were not engaged in agriculture. Faced with what he saw as a mutually exclusive choice, a clear either-or situation, this is what Frankfurter stated: "If the Court could say 'To be or not to be: that is the question,' it might reasonably answer in support of either side. But here the Court tells us that the real solution of this dilemma is 'to be' and 'not to be' at the same time." Frankfurter called this illogical sleight of hand "a unique contribution to the literature of statutory construction," but could "only regret the great loss to the literature of the drama that this possibility was overlooked by the Bard of Avon." Frankfurter could not resist winding up his literary-philosophical detour by noting, "It will probably now be as great a surprise to the proponents of the agricultural exemption as it would have been to Shakespeare, had it been suggested to him."[17] One might sometimes criticize Frankfurter's judicial restraint as maddening, but even so he occasionally wrote superb prose, informed by wide and deep reading.

Practicing lawyers are also subject to the Hamlet syndrome. Hamlet is like equivocating lawyers ("on the one hand . . . , on the other hand") who are so paralyzed by seeing all sides of every legal issue, by everlasting brooding on the legal pros and cons, that they cannot advise one course of conduct or another. Of course, it is important for lawyers to be aware of risks and to see counterarguments, but not to the point where they are insensitive to excessive thought. A mind so fully absorbed by speculation and reflection may leave no impulse toward action left in the lawyer's consciousness. Such Hamlet-like qualities of attorneys—the inability to act and take risks—bewilder clients who are men or women of action.

Skull of a Lawyer

Hamlet himself attacks the clever, equivocating, dissembling language of lawyers in the gravedigger scene. He points to a skull in the graveyard and meditates aloud:

> There's another: why might not that be the skull
> of a lawyer? Where be his quiddits [i.e., subtleties] now, his quillets
> [i.e., evasions],
> his cases, his tenures, and his tricks? Why does he
> suffer this rude knave now to knock him about the
> sconce [i.e., head] with a dirty shovel, and will not tell him
> of his action of battery? H'm!
>
> (5.1.95–100)

Note Hamlet's pointed reference to the putative lawyer's quiddities, quillets, and tricks, as if anyone could miss it. Critics often say Hamlet's speeches more than those of any other character reflect Shakespeare's own thoughts. One wonders, then, and especially in light of the ambiguity of the famous antilawyer line in *Henry VI, Part 2*, if Hamlet's faintly antilawyer speech in the graveyard, with its snide reference to lawyers' "tricks," is the real Shakespeare.

For Hamlet, the lawyer's skull becomes almost as evocative as the madeleine became for Proust. Hamlet continues his meditative and mild mocking of the skull of the imaginary lawyer:

> This fellow might be in 's time
> a great buyer of land, with his statutes, his
> recognizances, his fines, his double vouchers, his
> recoveries: is this the fine of his fines and the recovery
> of his recoveries, to have his fine pate full of fine dirt?
> Will his vouchers vouch him no more of his purchases,
> and double ones too, than the length and breadth of a
> pair of indentures? The very conveyances of his lands
> will hardly lie in this box; and must th'inheritor himself
> have no more, ha?
>
> (5.1.100–109)

From this long speech, much longer than any other in the gravedigger scene, we can at least infer that Shakespeare had a special feeling toward lawyers, even if at this point it is tinged with the fatalism of Ecclesiastes and Thomas Gray's "Elegy Written in a Country Churchyard."

But wait a minute. Let us stop a while and consider Hamlet's interesting meditation on "the skull of a lawyer." We ourselves might profit from meditating on Hamlet's meditation, and the result of that metameditation may be surprising.

What prompts Hamlet to ask, "Why might not that be the skull of a lawyer?" Is there something that distinguishes a lawyer's skull from other people's skulls? Does the shape of a lawyer's skull bear some telltale mark? Perhaps Hamlet noticed a brow that suggested caginess, or a high-domed forehead indicating great intellect. Or maybe the skull was Neanderthal in shape and reminded Hamlet of some overly aggressive lawyers he knew. Or there might have been a dent in the skull, reflecting a blow from an angry adversary or a disappointed client.

However fertile ground for speculation is the outside of a lawyer's skull, the inside of a lawyer's skull—a lawyer's methods and channels of thought—is even more tantalizing to consider. Many nonlawyers are fascinated and puzzled by the legal mentality. How does it differ from the thinking of musicians, writers, or scientists? How do lawyers make legal arguments? What do lawyers mean when they say the holding of one case should embrace the different facts of another?

But the legal mentality is only a part of the lawyer. It does not include the lawyer's personality, the life the lawyer leads, the lawyer's world. For centuries people have observed the changes that occur—and not all for the better—when one studies law. Recall Edmund Burke's memorable comment that the study of law sharpens the mind by narrowing it. Yet during the last several decades, law professors have boasted and prided themselves on their ability to take new college graduates with mush-filled minds and, in the first year of law school, make them think like lawyers. What does it mean to grow a lawyer's skull, to "think like a lawyer"?

Thinking like a lawyer involves several qualities, two of which—analysis and narrative—come quickly to mind. Analytical power, the ability to give reasons, to explain oneself in a logical way, is a primary tool of lawyers. Early on a new law student learns not to say simply that the result of a particular case is right or wrong, but to justify praise or criticism of the result, to explain systematically and theoretically why one likes or dislikes a decision. Unless it can be put into the form of logic, emotion tends to be subordinated by law school. But mentally agile and verbally facile law students and lawyers have little trouble in importing emotion by way of basic value choices to be used as axioms or postulates of legal logic or policy considerations.

Of equal importance in thinking like a lawyer is the type of logic used. From about the end of the Civil War until World War I, legal thinking in America was primarily cast in the form of deductive logic. A legal principle would constitute a major premise; a set of facts would come either within or without the major premise; and a legal conclusion or judicial finding would necessarily follow. Such formalist legal thinking, as it was called, eventually gave way to a more inductive method. Lawyers are taught to reason by analogy: does the new set of facts fit better under legal rule A or legal rule B? But under either approach, the logical form of legal reasoning and argument still controlled.

Thinking like a lawyer also involves suspending judgment, much as the reader of poetry or fiction must willingly suspend disbelief. A lawyer may have to argue either side of any case or question, so one should not come to an opinion too quickly. This turn of mind tends to render the lawyer less judgmental generally and more tolerant of human foibles. The practice of law gives one a front row seat at the human comedy. One sees all kinds of human error, stupidity, passion, negligence, overreaching, loss of control, vice, greed, violence—in short, the whole gamut of human behavior. Such exposure teaches restraint in moral judgment and makes one wonder if any of us are completely immune to such lapses, at least temporarily.

With time and experience and courtroom scars, today's attorney learns the only true way to think like a lawyer. The logical form, we eventually discover, is something of a delusion, often masking the real ground for deciding a law problem one way or another. The longer one practices law, the more one finds that for every legal principle there is a counter-principle, and that legal authorities can be found to support almost any reasonable proposition of law. Given such lack of direction, the lawyer often finds that the ultimate ground for decision is something beyond logic and precedent, is some emotional attachment, some basic, constitutional value, some policy people feel much attached to—which frequently tips the scales against mere logic. To think like a lawyer means to identify the key policy consideration that will determine the outcome.

A lawyer's mode of thought also has distinctive similarities to those of a playwright. A lawyer, like a playwright, depends on narrative, the ability to tell a story. Both use the power of illusion and persuasion. The playwright takes reality and, by imagination, makes it into fantasy, while the lawyer takes real-life disputes and, also by no less a form of imagination, transmits them into illusory concepts of law and legal castles out of thin air.[18] Even conducting a trial is largely the telling of a story that is a function of opening and closing statements, the substance and sequence of witnesses' testimony, the nature and order of questions on direct and cross-examination, the use of documentary and demonstrative evidence.

"Might it not be suggested," James Boyd White has written, "that the central act of the legal mind, of judge and lawyer alike, is the conversion of the raw material of life—of the actual experiences of people and the thousands of ways they can be talked about—into a story that will claim to tell the truth in legal terms?"[19]

The nature of the relationship between legal thinking and art in its broadest sense has yet to be understood. We know that a large number of creative writers started out studying or practicing law. We also know that some great composers (e.g., Stravinsky, Handel, Schumann) and painters (e.g., Matisse, Kandinsky) began the same way. These facts by themselves justify exploring the link between law and art to see if there is something in the study of law especially conducive and congenial to the creation of art. Of course it may be nothing more than a reaction to the law and the confining rigidity of legal reasoning—the desire to escape from what the incipient artist sees as the dull, dry, prosaic prison of the law to the exciting, imaginative, and stimulating realm of art. Or we may discover that the tension between law and everything else could be a creative one. A full study of the effect of legal training on artistic creativity remains to be made, and when it is done it will connect with Shakespeare and other great creative artists who are linked with law, and unlock more of them than we now have.

Thus Shakespeare might have much to ponder, through the character of Hamlet, over the skull of a lawyer. Shakespeare-Hamlet could wonder how a lawyer's mind takes these two apparently discordant and inconsistent thought processes—analysis and narrative—and reconciles them in a single work of the imagination. Yet for all his wit, Hamlet's gentle attack on the dead lawyer really seems to be an attack on himself. Does he not act with a lawyer's head as he sees only too well both sides of the revenge issue? Are not Hamlet's own speeches filled with quiddits and quillets?

SELF-DEFENSE

Among the legal quiddits in *Hamlet*, indeed in the same gravedigger scene, is Shakespeare's satire of an early form of self-defense in English law. The legal doctrine known as *se defendendo* was in use for four hundred years leading up to Shakespeare's time whenever a fight occurred and one party retreated as far as he could go before resorting to force. If, with his back literally against the wall, he then killed the aggressor, *se defendendo* spared the defendant from the death penalty. Killing *se defendendo* was called excusable homicide. But the defendant, though saved from execution, still had to forfeit his property as expiation for his having taken human life.

To avoid the harsh result of forfeiting all his property on a successful plea of *se defendendo*, the defendant had to argue that the death of the victim was not the defendant's act at all. If the killing were not the act of the defendant, there was nothing for the defendant to expiate and the jury could find him not guilty without the defendant having to forfeit his goods. The trick is a metaphysical delight. A famous example is the distinction between a defender's stabbing a victim and a victim's impaling himself on the defender's motionless sword.

In *Hamlet* Shakespeare ridicules the logic chopping surrounding *se defendendo*. If Ophelia killed herself by her own hand, as she appears to have done, she was not entitled to a Christian burial. When one gravedigger tells the other that Ophelia is entitled to a Christian burial, the other, dumbfounded, asks, "How can that be unless she drowned herself / in her own defence?" (5.1.6–7). His friend responds, "Why, 'tis found so." To which the first gravedigger says:

> It must be 'se offendendo', it cannot be else;
> for here lies the point: if I drown myself wittingly, it
> argues an act; and an act hath three branches: it is
> to act, to do, to perform. Argal [i.e., therefore] she drowned herself
> wittingly. (5.1.8–12)

He further explains the legal doctrine:

> Here lies the water—good.
> Here stands the man—good. If the man go to this water
> and drown himself, it is, will he, nill he, he goes. Mark
> you that. But if the water come to him and drown him,
> he drowns not himself, argal he that is not guilty of
> his own death shortens not his own life. (5.1.14–19)

After hearing such a tortuous explanation, the other gravedigger can only shake his confused and doubting head and ask, "But is this law?" (5.1.20). Shakespeare's witty mention of *se offendendo*, with the final question translated as, "But could anything so ridiculous be law?" underscores the jurisprudential hairsplitting.

In time, the hairsplitting on this particular point became unnecessary. By 1532 Parliament passed a statute correcting the flaws in *se defendendo*. This new law, in effect during Shakespeare's life, made justifiable homicide subject to total acquittal without any forfeiture of the defendant's goods. Hamlet's remarks about lawyers' quiddities and quillets are more understandable in light of the earlier exchange about the lawfulness of Ophelia's burial.

The Guilty Conscience

One particular scene in *Hamlet* emphasizes Shakespeare's deep understanding of psychology as it relates to the guilty conscience. It reminds us of Dostoyevsky's portrayal of Roskolnikov's eventual unburdening of his guilt-ridden conscience in *Crime and Punishment*. Hamlet comes up with the idea of having a play "something like the murder of my father" (2.2.597) performed for Claudius to see if the king will betray himself. "I have heard," Hamlet says,

> That guilty creatures sitting at a play
> Have by the very cunning of the scene
> Been struck so to the soul that presently
> They have proclaimed their malefactions;
> For murder, though it have no tongue, will speak
> With most miraculous organ.
>
> (2.2.591–96)

So confident is Hamlet that he exclaims, "The play's the thing / Wherein I'll catch the conscience of the King" (2.2.606–7).

The device of the play within a play bears not only on the psychology of the guilty party, but also on trial tactics. In real life we rarely if ever see a Perry Mason scenario where a guilty person simply breaks down and confesses in court to some heinous crime. Jack Nicholson's courtroom admission in the film *A Few Good Men* is unusual in the extreme. Life is more complex than that, and human defense mechanisms a bit stronger. Nonetheless, demeanor and demonstrative evidence are important parts of the trial process. At a trial it is often possible to try to recreate, at least mentally and subconsciously, the conditions surrounding the event in question. Trial props and carefully crafted questioning can help develop a mood of emotional participation by the witness in the trial process itself. Although psychopaths may be immune to such techniques, the rest of us—like Claudius—will react in varying degrees.

In the hands of a master, the technique can be a powerful tool. Such a master was Earl Rogers, a famous and colorful criminal lawyer in California in the early 1900s. Following Hamlet's suggestion, Rogers tried, by his questions on cross-examination, to hypnotize lying witnesses back to the events, to relive the truth of what happened so powerfully that sooner or later it would clash with the lie. The idea was to make the witness forget what was truth and make a mistake. "It takes only one mistake," Rogers used to say.

Using such subtle cross-examination to catch the conscience of the witness, Rogers once had the rare pleasure of hearing the prosecution's chief witness unwittingly implicate himself as the murderer. As told by his daughter Adela Rogers St. Johns in her biography of him called *Final Verdict*, Earl Rogers assembled various props in the courtroom—a poker table with four chairs—to resemble the scene of the crime. After questioning the witness in great detail about the murder itself, Rogers moved on to what happened later. With the story of the murder behind him, the witness relaxed his guard and made a fatal mistake.

Q. You told him [the policeman] Boyd had killed Yeager?
A. Yes, I said he shot him.

Q. What did you do then?
A. I went to the washroom.

Q. To the washroom?
A. Yes, yes. . . .

Q. Did you wash the powder burns off your hands?
A. Did I? Did I?

Q. Yes, Mr. Johnson. Yes. You did.[20]

To those in the courtroom, the questions and answers damned the witness in a way the cold record cannot recreate exactly. The witness thought his trip to the washroom did not matter, so he freely talked about it before realizing his error. But he would not have had powder burns unless he, and not the defendant, had pulled the trigger. In effect, he practically confessed to murder on the witness stand. It was a triumph of applied psychology, of Rogers overpowering the witness's guilty mind, of Hamlet's technique succeeding.

THE INSANITY DEFENSE

Even the insanity defense is part of Shakespeare's play. Hamlet pleads it when Laertes, unhampered by the hesitancy that so plagues Hamlet, seeks revenge for the death of Polonius, his father. Face to face with Laertes' wrath, Hamlet claims to be beset "with sore distraction" (5.2.176).

"What I have done," Hamlet says, referring to his killing of Polonius, "I here proclaim was madness. / Was't Hamlet wronged Laertes? Never Hamlet / . . . His madness is poor Hamlet's enemy" (5.2.176–85). But inasmuch as Hamlet at one point says he intends to put "an antic disposition on" (1.5.173), scholars have long debated whether his madness was feigned. Time and psychological advance may have improved the legal definition, but Shakespeare's portrayal of Hamlet's insanity defense has worn well.

To discover a few legal themes in *Hamlet* is itself a bit like the gravedigger scene. We rummage through pieces of the old play and, fastening on a few suggestive parts of the play's skeleton, meditate on their larger meanings. But *Hamlet* has many interpretations, it is so indeterminate that no definitive or single correct interpretation emerges.[21] We never get to the bottom of *Hamlet*. If we are criticized for finding too much law, perhaps we can seek refuge in Olivier's comment about how he as an actor tries to affect his audiences. Like Olivier, the literary lawyer is "trying to persuade them to believe it, to see it my way."[22]

Chapter Six

LIBERTY! FREEDOM! TYRANNY IS DEAD!

Julius Caesar

THE LEGAL LINK between *Hamlet* and *Julius Caesar* is close. The obvious tie between the two is that both are plays of revenge. But there is another, deeper connection. Hamlet, a man with a double personality on the subject of revenge, appears as two characters in *Julius Caesar*. Hamlet, the divided man, splits by a process of dramatic mitosis into Brutus and Antony. The strife between his two selves is replaced by the strife and contrast between Brutus and Antony. Hamlet, with one foot in the vengeful past and one foot in the more civilized future, divides into his components, looking forward with Brutus, looking back with Antony.

In both plays, murder is the occasion for revenge. In *Hamlet* it is the murder of Hamlet's father; in *Julius Caesar*, it is the assassination of Caesar. Both murders unleash a consuming passion for revenge. Both involve fathers and sons: Antony was Caesar's surrogate son, and Brutus was treated by Caesar like a son. As the Ghost haunts Hamlet, so too does Caesar's ghost haunt Brutus. Given such similarities in emotional context, it is fascinating to see how Shakespeare depicts the different attitudes of the main characters in *Julius Caesar* toward the duty of revenge.

Brutus symbolizes a modern view of political justice that does not stress the emotional component of revenge. He is abstract and impersonal, without depending on such primitive emotions as revenge. For Brutus, Caesar's murder is necessary as a matter of ideals. Caesar's ambition threatened civic virtue, individual freedom, and self-government. Brutus believes he acts for the most rational and high-minded of reasons. As the play unfolds, we see that Brutus's ideas about revenge were premature and too advanced for the world of *Julius Caesar*, and perhaps too idealistic for any era in their unrealistic demands on human nature.

Just as Hamlet ultimately gave in to the instinct for revenge, so too does Brutus's unemotional attitude suffer defeat at the hands of Antony's vengefulness. Antony is mad for revenge out of personal loyalty to Caesar. He understands the important role of emotion, of blood connections and personal attachments. He acts and trades on the powerful emotional loyalties that mark a society in which vengeance is an organizing principle. Antony grasps the emotional side of human nature.

Despite all this emotional turmoil, when the late Joseph Papp produced

Julius Caesar at the Public Theater in 1988, *New York Times* drama critic Frank Rich thought it was wrongly staged as a "pedantic civics lesson." Rich opened his review in a startling way. "The worst thing that ever happened to *Julius Caesar*," wrote Rich, "was its adoption by teachers nationwide as the ninth-grade student's ideal introduction to Shakespeare. In countless classrooms, *Julius Caesar* became the play that was Good for You—a sodden launching pad for earnest discussions about the perils of democracy, despotism, mob rule and . . . Are you dozing yet?"[1] Dozing? How can anyone nod off discussing as exciting a play as *Julius Caesar*? Whose mind is so inert that it can see the "civics lesson" of the play as "pedantic"?

The "civics lesson" of *Julius Caesar* is anything but. It is a vital, large, grand Shakespearean concept of law that goes far beyond the role of revenge in the law. With *Julius Caesar*, Shakespeare deals not with petty lawsuits, but with the overall legal framework of society; not with forms of action, but with constitutionalism. When we come to *Julius Caesar*, we see classical republicanism at work in a society riven by faction. We see a study of ends and means in the law. And, not least, we see in *Julius Caesar* an unforgettable example of oral advocacy.

Oral Advocacy

Oral advocacy, that special skill of good courtroom lawyers, provides the turning point in *Julius Caesar*. The play's crucial oral advocacy takes the form of funeral orations by Brutus and Antony over Caesar's corpse. Before those funeral orations, the play moves in one direction—toward the assassination of Caesar. After Brutus and Antony speak, the tragedy goes in an entirely different direction—to the final destruction of the conspirators and their repudiation by the Roman people. The funeral oration scene is the play's apex.

By dwelling a bit on the funeral orations, by viewing them as closing arguments to a jury, we can learn something about oral advocacy. We can compare and contrast the rhetorical styles of the two speakers. We can try to discover, for example, why Antony's speech succeeds so much more than Brutus's.

Shakespeare is right to make the play turn on oratory, for oratory was important in Caesar's Rome. The politics of republican Rome and the development of the legal profession created a wide demand for public speaking. In the Forum and in the courts, Roman orators commanded attention and distinguished themselves. Schools of rhetoric grew up and books were written about rhetoric, rules of composition, prose rhythm, and delivery.

Two of the greatest Roman orators are characters in the play, although they do not deliver the funeral orations. Cicero, whom Shakespeare gives a minor role, was easily the most famous and eloquent of Roman orators, having won his reputation from political speeches and courtroom arguments, some of which have been preserved and are still read. So renowned was Cicero that even Caesar wrote to him, "You have discovered the treasures of oratory, . . . You have gained a triumph to be preferred to that of the greatest generals."

Such a compliment from Caesar was meaningful not merely because of Caesar's achievements as a great general. Caesar himself was also an accomplished orator. As a successful leader of men in war and in politics, Caesar had developed an effective writing and speaking style. Although not as emotional or as passionate as Cicero, Caesar's simple and direct style ranked him second only to Cicero in eloquence.

Under this arch of Roman eloquence, the funeral orations in *Julius Caesar* become that much more fascinating. Caesar having just been killed, the conspirators want Brutus to reassure the people that all is well, that there is no cause for alarm, and that Caesar's death was necessary to prevent tyranny. Antony, Caesar's close friend, feigns solidarity with the conspirators and persuades them that he too should say a few words over Caesar's body. Posner gives us an excellent discussion of the two speeches.[2]

Brutus speaks first, briefly and in prose, appealing to his listeners' sense of abstract values. He wraps his conduct in his well-known personal virtue. He asks his listeners to "believe me for / mine honor" (3.2.14–15) and reminds them how much he loved Caesar, who was rumored to be Brutus's father and who had always treated Brutus with kindness. But outweighing these abstract ties was yet another abstraction: Brutus's duty to his city. If someone asks "why Brutus / rose against Caesar, this is my answer: not that I loved / Caesar less, but that I loved Rome more" (3.2.21–22).

Brutus tries to explain what he means in terms of political abstractions. "Had you / rather Caesar were living, and die all slaves, than that / Caesar were dead, to live all free men?" (3.2.22–24). Essentially, Brutus attempts, with some rhetorical flourish, to justify Caesar's murder as necessary to block Caesar's ambition and to preserve freedom and "a place in the commonwealth" for each citizen (3.2.43). Brutus slew Caesar, he tells the crowd, "for the good of Rome" (3.2.45).

Brutus's short speech appears to succeed. Carefully constructed, it builds on rhetorical devices such as repetition and antithesis ("loved Caesar less," "loved Rome more"). The people seem to react favorably. They say, "This Caesar was a tyrant. . . . We are blest Rome is rid of him" (3.2.70–71). They cheer Brutus and even exclaim, "Let him be Caesar" (3.2.51).

But that very exclamation—"Let him be Caesar"—shows that something has gone wrong with Brutus's speech, even before Antony opens his mouth. Instead of shrinking from all dictators, as Brutus intends, the crowd wants Brutus to take Caesar's place. Brutus's basic message went right by his audience. They did not "get" it.

Refined and graceful, Brutus's speech is nonetheless fundamentally inept. Its elaborate rhetorical structure is so obvious and affected that listeners know they are hearing a formal utterance, which distances audience from speaker. Brutus's formal style and structure lack emotion: his dwelling on abstraction is dry and bloodless, devoid of passion. The Roman people had too often heard such abstractions as the "good of Rome" serve as masks for greed and power. Nor does Brutus elaborate his charge of Caesar's ambition.

The crowd's missing his point prefigures the short life of Brutus's apparent oratorical success. As often happens with a jury's reaction to a lawyer who speaks, Brutus's seeming victory lasts only until his adversary, Antony, begins *his* speech. Of course, that is the point of the adversary process: to allow each side an opportunity to persuade before the listeners decide. The vivid contrast with Antony's speech exposes the deep and many flaws in Brutus's speech.

Where Brutus speaks briefly, Antony speaks at length, and in verse. Where Brutus is cool and abstract, Antony is hot and concrete. Unlike Brutus, Antony uses vivid and vital expressions interwoven with wit and innuendo. As successful and effective as Brutus's speech appears to be, Antony's is in reality that much more successful and effective. And Antony accomplishes this by overcoming the problem of the crowd still being on Brutus's side as Antony begins speaking.

From the start, Antony speaks by subtle and clever indirection. He says, "I come to bury Caesar, not to praise him" (3.2.75), but he means just the opposite. He says to the crowd, "Let me not stir you up" (3.2.205), when that is exactly what he intends. Antony refers to "the noble Brutus" (3.2.78) and, in an oft-repeated, increasingly sardonic refrain (so effective it has long since become a cliché), to the conspirators as "honourable men" (3.2.83, 84, 88, 95, 100, 125, 128, 152), when in fact he thinks precisely the contrary.

Antony's use of ironic repetition of "Brutus is an honorable man" has been used as a point of reference in a modern case concerning a criminal defendant's constitutional rights. In *Lakeside v. Oregon*, the Supreme Court in 1978 upheld a conviction where the trial judge, over the defendant's objection, instructed the jury not to draw an adverse inference from the defendant's exercise of his constitutional right not to testify. On appeal, the defendant unsuccessfully contended that the judge's instruction, ostensibly for the defendant's benefit, actually drew attention to his failure to take the witness stand. In dissent, Justice John Paul Stevens—the same justice who in another case commented on what Shakespeare meant when he wrote "kill all the lawyers"—cited Antony's funeral speech and wondered "if the Court would find petitioner's argument as strange if the prosecutor, or even the judge, had given the instruction three or four times, in slightly different form, just to make sure the jury knew that silence, like killing Caesar, is consistent with honor."[3]

Antony deprecates his own efforts—"I am no orator as Brutus is" (3.2.212)—even as he displays oratorical skill far superior to that of Brutus. Self-deprecation is an old courtroom lawyer's trick, apparently at least as old as ancient Rome. Whenever you hear an adversary say something like, "I'm just a country lawyer," watch out for the dagger. Some lawyers imitate Antony and deliberately assume the role of an underdog fighting an earnest contest against a superior adversary. You may occasionally see the interesting spectacle of two cunning trial lawyers each praising the other as the greatest advocate of all times and personally assuming the role of just an ordinary, honest plodder whose client's only hope is that the jury will protect his or her interests in spite of the unequal representation.

Unlike Brutus, Antony takes his time to build to a suspenseful climax. He begins slowly, swaying the crowd bit by bit, charming them gradually. At first he refuses to read Caesar's will. His initial cautious restraint becomes fervid eloquence when his pent-up feelings finally overflow. Anyone who has ever summed up to a jury knows the challenge—and the technique.

Antony even knows how to use demonstrative evidence to great effect, relying on it at exactly the moment of maximum emotional impact. In Antony's case, the demonstrative evidence includes Caesar's will, the torn and bloody robe that Caesar wore when he was stabbed, and even Caesar's corpse. Like an aggressive prosecutor, he raises Caesar's mantle before the crowd, points to the holes made by the conspirators' dagger thrusts, and marks the stains from Caesar's blood. No trial lawyer ever used demonstrative evidence to greater effect.

One is reminded of a famous forensic moment in the 1979 triple murder trial of Jeffrey MacDonald, memorialized forever in the true crime best seller *Fatal Vision* by Joe McGinniss. Although MacDonald had denied killing his pregnant twenty-six-year-old wife and his two young daughters, the government was able to persuade the jury of MacDonald's guilt by using Marc Antony's tactic. A forensic expert witness testified for the government that the bloody holes in MacDonald's pajama top, when folded as it was on the night of the murder, matched the unusual pattern of ice-pick wounds on MacDonald's dead wife's chest and her pajama top. It was a climactic point of the trial, and when coupled with testimony that MacDonald's folded pajama top was found lying on his wife's body, it sealed MacDonald's fate just as effectively as Antony's use of the same technique worked magic on his listeners.[4]

"If you have tears, prepare to shed them now" (3.2.168), Antony cries as he whips up the crowd's emotions beyond control. Throughout, Antony uses emotion rather than reason to make his case. He destroys reason with emotion. Yet as he does so, even as he plays on the emotions of his audience, Antony denies his inflammatory intent. It works. And Brutus having already left, there is not even any rebuttal.

The frenzied listeners are now ready to return the verdict sought by Antony: they proceed to chase the conspirators and to burn their houses. And sly Antony, who had previously said,

> I have neither wit, nor words, nor worth,
> Action, nor utterance, nor the power of speech,
> To stir men's blood,
>
> (3.2.216–18)

later says:

> Now let it work. Mischief, thou art afoot.
> Take thou what course thou wilt.
>
> (3.2.253–54)

Whatever we may think of the Roman mob for being incited by such an emotional speech, we must envy Antony's persuasive skill as an orator.

The funeral orations in *Julius Caesar* are an extraordinary example of how Shakespeare can bear on the law. One can learn much about effective oral advocacy from the speeches of Brutus and Antony. They repay study. A lawyer should ponder them before making an oral argument or summing up to a jury.

Brutus's speech is, as Posner explains convincingly, weak for several reasons. It is conspicuously rhetorical, which puts the audience on guard. It fails to engage the audience by dialogue. It is abstract and lacks detail or anecdote. It fails to appeal to the concrete self-interest of the audience. It fails to present evidence to support the crucial charge (Caesar's ambition). Finally, Brutus waives rebuttal by leaving before Antony speaks.

Antony avoids these weaknesses and adds a number of powerful strengths of his own. He offhandedly and without pomp tries to defuse a hostile audience. He promptly deals with Brutus's charge of ambition, attempts to answer, and knows that Brutus will not be around to rebut what Antony says. Unlike Brutus, Antony displays emotion. He uses props, physical evidence, and visual aids. He tells an anecdote. He proceeds in dramatic fashion. He disclaims oratorical ability in a successful attempt to disarm the audience. He uses the terms of the will to appeal to the audience's concrete interests and sense of gratitude. He invites frequent interruption to create the impression of conversation rather than monologue. He moves about the stage.

Antony thus uses a variety of devices, and a good courtroom lawyer would do well to consider Antony's example. He or she should try, like Antony, to be "concrete, vivid, personal, conversational, versatile, dramatic, [and] empathetic with his [or her] audience."[5] Antony gives a supreme example of effective persuasion, of a speaker whose will dominates his listeners and motivates them to act.

The key to Antony's success and Brutus's failure in oral advocacy goes beyond technical and stylistic differences. Why one failed and the other succeeded in moving his listeners was a direct result of one's failure and the other's success in understanding his audience. Antony knew what to touch in his audience, how to connect his subject with the most vital concerns of the audience, how to appeal to each listener. Antony did not bury his points in abstractions, but clad them in the garb of truly permanent human problems. And Antony did all this without the audience becoming aware of him or his artistic technique.

In comparing Brutus and Antony as orators, we are reminded of the comparison drawn between two other classical orators: Cicero and Demosthenes. When Cicero finished an oration, the people would say, "How well he spoke." But when Demosthenes finished speaking, the people would say, "Let us march." Brutus was like Cicero, and Antony like Demosthenes. Brutus won respect, but Antony started a riot.

He Loved Rome More

Funeral orations in ancient times supply us with more than examples of oral advocacy. Probably the most famous came not from Rome, but from ancient Greece. In 431 B.C. Pericles delivered his celebrated funeral oration to the people of Athens. An eloquent exposition of the democratic ideal, that funeral speech articulated a legal theme important in *Julius Caesar* and in today's American constitutional thinking.

"Here each individual is interested not only in his own affairs but in the affairs of the state as well," declared Pericles. "Even those who are mostly occupied with their own business are extremely well-informed on general politics—this is a peculiarity of ours: we do not say that a man who takes no interest in politics is a man who minds his own business; we say that he has no business here at all." None of the fallen Athenian soldiers whom Pericles celebrated "weakened because he wanted to go on enjoying his wealth."

There it is: a forthright statement of classical republicanism, of the search for the republic of virtue, contained in an idealized but substantially true picture of Athenian life. Classical republicanism is a type of civic virtue that both allows and requires the citizen—as a central facet of citizenship—to take an active part in public affairs, even if such participation interferes with the citizen's individual private or economic life. Individual self-interest is subordinated to civic good. It is at once an obligation and an opportunity to perform public service, a concept at the core of a political philosophy based on citizen participation.

Classical republicanism did not end in Athens. The aspiration for a republic of virtue was a central element in classical philosophy. That aspiration also animated the Roman republic until the death of Julius Caesar. Although the common people could not hold political office in republican Rome, they did have the right to vote for magistrates from among the patricians, who, as members of the class supposedly representing virtue, had a civic duty to take part in political life.

Through every scene of *Julius Caesar* classical republicanism shines. It supplies the clincher to Cassius's appeal to Brutus to join the conspiracy. After reviewing Caesar's attempts to assume power and destroy the republic, Cassius persuades Brutus by invoking the republicanism of their ancestors, their founders:

> O, you and I have heard our fathers say,
> There was a Brutus once that would have brook'd
> Th'eternal devil to keep his state in Rome
> As easily as a king.
>
> (1.2.160–61)

Cassius's pointed reference to the elder Brutus brims with classical republican symbolism. In 508 B.C. the elder Brutus, from whom the younger Brutus was supposedly descended, led a successful revolt against the cruel Tarquins, a line of Etruscan kings not chosen by the Roman people. Expulsion of the Tarquins led to the birth of the republic. The elder Brutus elevated public good over private feeling when, as first consul, he refused to pardon his two sons arrested for conspiring to restore the hated Tarquins. In a poignant example of civic virtue, rendered unforgettably by Jacques-Louis David's painting in the Louvre (*Brutus Seeing the Bodies of His Sons*), he allowed the law to run its course and execute his children.

The appeal of Cassius succeeds. A man renowned for virtue, Brutus joins the conspiracy because he thinks it noble. Although Caesar has been kind to him, and he loves Caesar, Brutus, like his public-spirited ancestor of great fame, puts public good above personal feeling. He truly believes the conspirators are trying to protect the Roman republic from tyranny. Brutus understood virtue to be part of the life of the good citizen, and that he must recognize the common good and act on it.

This same strain of classical republicanism emerges, at least in the minds of the conspirators, when the assassination occurs. As Caesar falls, Cinna shouts, "Liberty! Freedom! Tyranny is dead!" (3.1.77). Casca echoes the sentiment: "Liberty, freedom, and enfranchisement!" (3.1.80). And Brutus joins in with: "Peace, freedom, and liberty!" (3.1.111). Cassius, giddy with self-importance, sees the assassination as a "lofty scene" to "be acted over, / In states unborn and accents yet unknown" and the conspirators will "be called / The men that gave their country liberty" (1.3.113–119). They see themselves as eternal symbols of freedom and public-spiritedness against tyranny and private ambition.

That classical republicanism was behind Brutus's actions (even if not the other conspirators') is confirmed by Brutus's funeral oration, in which he appeals to civic virtue. "Not that I loved / Caesar less, but that I loved Rome more" (3.2.21–22) is how Brutus puts it. Caesar tried to steal the political rights of Roman citizens, Brutus explains. "Who / is here so rude that would not be a Roman? . . . Who is here so vile that / will not love his country?" (3.2.30–33). Brutus did what he did—assassinate Caesar—not for any private gain, not out of base self-interest, but "for the good of Rome."

At the end of the play, even Antony, without the irony that marks his funeral speech, calls Brutus "the noblest Roman of them all" (5.5.67). He describes how only Brutus of all the conspirators acted solely out of patriotism. Antony talks of Brutus acting with a universally honorable purpose (unmixed with selfish considerations) and for the sake of the good of all the Romans in common. "This was a man!" exclaims Antony (5.5.74).

The classical republicanism exemplified by Shakespeare's Brutus slumbered at the end of the republic, but its sleep did not last forever. After the decline and fall of the Roman empire, and the long night of the dark ages, the Renaissance reawakened classical republicanism. The ideal of civic virtue captured the human imagination again in the revival of civic humanism in the Renaissance. As part of the renewal of interest in ancient Greece and Rome, Renaissance minds found classical republicanism congenial to their outlook.

Machiavelli, for example, wrote a number of important works in political theory championing the principles of classical republicanism. Even five hundred years later, his *Discourses* and *Histories* remain monuments of classical republicanism. Shakespeare was part of the Renaissance flowering, and his portrayal of political principles in *Julius Caesar* was the product and fulfillment of that Renaissance moment of rediscovery of classical republicanism.

We are now in the midst of a second rediscovery of classical republicanism. Our rediscovery began in 1975 with the publication of a crucial book, *The Machiavellian Moment: Florentine Political Thought and the*

Atlantic Republican Tradition, by J.G.A. Pocock, a history professor at Johns Hopkins. According to Pocock, the American form of government was largely based on classical republicanism; the "last great pre-modern efflorescence" of that tradition "took place in the American colonies," and "the American Revolution and the Constitution in some sense form the last act of the civic Renaissance."[6]

Pocock assembles and lays bare an impressive wealth of evidence to show, despite Charles Beard's *Economic Interpretation of the Constitution*, that our founders acted on classical republican principles, that in their personal and public lives they were motivated by civic duty and virtue more than financial gain, and that their essential notions of political philosophy had much in common with the republican tradition.

It took a while for Pocock's provocative views to generate great interest. At first, widespread reaction was slow. *The Machiavellian Moment*, a long and dense book, was not an easy read or on anyone's bestseller list, and it remained for a few years the private preserve of professional historians. But then, in what can only be described as an extraordinary intellectual phenomenon, word of it began to spread beyond the professors of history. People started to glimpse the implications of Pocock's ideas.

Pocock's book did nothing less than send debate about American constitutionalism off in an entirely new direction; it reordered the lines of inquiry for those who have come after. Since about the early to mid-1980s and continuing to the present, classical republicanism has become one of the most talked about, written about, and controversial topics among those who think seriously about American constitutional law. In the law schools, it is at least as important as the debates over "originalist" interpretations of the Constitution, the critical legal studies movement, law and economics, or feminist legal doctrine. Pocock's rediscovery of classical republicanism is probably the most exciting thing to happen to American constitutionalism in decades.

"There is a tide in the affairs of men," Brutus says in *Julius Caesar*, and Pocock took it "at the flood" (4.2.270–71). He had good timing. With the bicentennial of the Constitution in 1987, Pocock's seminal book caught the legal imagination at just the right moment. Though published twelve years before the bicentennial celebration, the book needed that time to gestate and percolate in readers' minds so that it could explode on the scene when everyone was looking for some new angle of vision on the origins of constitutionalism in this country.

It is impossible to tell when the current fashion for classical republicanism will fade, if ever. The July 1988 issue of the *Yale Law Journal*, for instance, featured a symposium titled "The Republican Civic Tradition." New books and articles on classical republicanism continue to be published.

Even today we go on debating whether the United States has been or can be a republic of virtue. The framers of our republic saw the maintenance of a republic of virtue as the overriding goal of statecraft. But they also saw that self-interest often blocked the general good. Some historians of social thought argue that the framers of the Constitution abandoned the idea of a republic of virtue as a working principle of public life. Others argue the opposite.

At least part of that tradition quickens *Julius Caesar*. In his stirring 1765 speech in the Virginia House of Burgesses opposing the Stamp Act, twenty-nine-year-old Patrick Henry, a lawyer, referred to what happened on the Ides of March in 44 B.C. "Caesar had his Brutus," firebrand Henry thundered, "Charles the First, his Cromwell; and George the Third [a pause here punctuated by shouts of "Treason! Treason!" from some burgesses] *may profit by their example.*"

The public-spiritedness exemplified in *Julius Caesar* also bears directly on what it means to be a lawyer. As Anthony Kronman argues in his 1993 book *The Lost Lawyer*, American history long held aloft the ideal of the "lawyer-statesman," who, like Patrick Henry and other American revolutionary leaders, combined practical wisdom with care for the public good, who were leaders in public life. The value of public service and the virtue of civic-mindedness associated with it are qualities that should be of special importance to lawyers, traits promoted by the experience and professional duties of lawyers. Now, according to Kronman, that professional ideal unfortunately seems outmoded and has come under attack.

Cassius may well have been right. Our debate over "lofty" classical republicanism is taking place, as Cassius foretold, "in states unborn and accents yet unknown" to the conspirators. And we do focus that debate on "the men that gave [our] country liberty."

ROLE MODEL FOR IMPERIAL PRESIDENTS

Julius Caesar illuminates constitutionalism in general and separation of powers in particular. To be more precise, Shakespeare explores the contest for power in ancient Rome between the executive and the legislature. This constitutional contest holds special interest for us, since we have witnessed a similar contest throughout most of our own national history.

The American power contest forms the core of Arthur Schlesinger's 1973 book *The Imperial Presidency*. "This book," writes Schlesinger in his foreword, "deals essentially with the shift in the *constitutional* balance—with, that is, the appropriation by the Presidency, and particularly by the contemporary Presidency, of powers reserved by the Constitution and by long historical practice to Congress."

Schlesinger invokes *Julius Caesar*: "Through history the media of mass opinion—newspapers and, in more recent years, radio and television—had provided an unwritten check on Caesarism." Schlesinger then quotes Shakespeare's Caesar: "Who is it in the press that calls on me? / I hear a tongue shriller than all the music" (1.2.17–18).

Julius Caesar and *The Imperial Presidency* have a fundamental affinity. Their basic concerns are similar. According to Schlesinger, President Kennedy's former assistant, a serious problem arises from "a larger concentration of authority in the Presidency." Adds Schlesinger, "The expansion and abuse of presidential power constituted the underlying issue." At stake, in Rome and America, were "the unwritten restraints of the republican ethos."[7]

Americans of the Revolutionary War era picked up many of their ideas of republicanism from theatrical productions of, among other things, *Julius Caesar*. As a result, it is difficult to tell if people were more influenced by the historical Caesar or the Shakespearean Caesar, or if they could even tell them apart. Joseph Addison's play *Cato*, based on a noble Roman's republican resistance to Caesar's tyranny, was George Washington's favorite serious drama. Washington saw it several times and had it staged to inspire his troops. To these American rebels, Caesar symbolized tyranny, the despotic, unrepresentative English government they sought to throw off, and the republican conspirators were brave freedom fighters like themselves.

One Anti-Federalist tract published in January 1788 and signed, appropriately enough, with the pseudonym Brutus, argued:

> The liberties of the [Roman] commonwealth were destroyed, and the constitution overturned, by an army, led by Julius Caesar, who was appointed to the command, by the constitutional authority of that commonwealth. He changed it from a free republic, whose fame had sounded, and is still celebrated by all the world, into that of the most absolute despotism.[8]

This same Anti-Federalist paper reminded its readers of just how close America had come to the Roman republic's fate. After the victory at Yorktown but before a peace treaty, leading officers in the Continental Army, angry over not being paid, talked seriously of refusing to demobilize, of threatening the state governments with violence, and of illegally setting up a military government under Washington or, if Washington refused, under a more amenable military leader. In March 1783 the commander in chief, with some difficulty, scotched the conspiracy. "But had the General who commanded them been possessed of the spirit of a Julius Caesar," wrote our American Brutus, "the liberties of this country had in all probability terminated with the war."

"It remains a secret, yet to be revealed," continued the Anti-Federalist

Brutus, "whether this [conspiratorial] measure was not suggested, or at least countenanced, by some, who have had great influence in producing the present system [i.e., the proposed Constitution]." It is a secret no more; we now know that Alexander Hamilton and Robert and Gouverneur Morris, founders all, played a role in and endorsed the military intrigue.

Is it any wonder, then, given these opposing strains in American thinking from the beginning, that the political problems and tensions in *Julius Caesar* have been continuing problems and tensions in American constitutional law? The delegates at the Philadelphia Convention had to work out a division of authority between the legislative and executive branches. Yet Schlesinger, even with his two Pulitzer Prizes, neglects, in a work about an overpowerful executive, to mention the military coup that failed at the start of our history as a nation. Surely that experience has tempered our national perspective. We can hardly be surprised if other Americans have felt about other presidents what Justice Joseph Story said of Andrew Jackson in 1834: "Though we live under the form of a republic we are in fact under the absolute rule of a single man."[9]

Both Caesarism and the imperial presidency thrive on weakness in other branches of government. Lack of a strong central authority creates a power void that needs to be filled (as Shakespeare demonstrated in *Richard II* and elsewhere). The weakness of the Roman republic in Caesar's day encouraged aristocrats to seize power. A corrupt and feeble Roman Senate in a time of general disorder made the government a tempting prize.

In American history we have seen how presidential power expands when Congress fails to assert itself. As Justice Robert Jackson warned in the 1952 *Steel Seizure* case, "only Congress itself can prevent power from slipping through its fingers."[10] Schlesinger makes the same point when he says about the Vietnam era that the House and the Senate "had to reclaim their own dignity and meet their own responsibilities."[11]

Into the Roman power vacuum charged an energetic Caesar, accumulating power with accelerating speed. In 50 B.C. Caesar was on the verge of starting a civil war by illegally leading his legions on Rome. In 46 B.C., when Caesar returned to Rome, the Senate, frightened at his power, made him dictator for ten years. In 44 B.C., just before the events in Shakespeare's play, Caesar took the Duvalieresque title of "dictator for life."

The monarchist in democratic clothing is not unheard of in American political history. From time to time a leader will misuse democracy for nondemocratic ends. This is precisely what Schlesinger seems to be saying: "The belief of the Nixon administration *in its own mandate* and in its own virtue, compounded by its conviction that the republic was in mortal danger from internal enemies, had produced an unprecedented attempt to transform the Presidency of the Constitution into a *plebiscitary Presidency.*"

Caesar the monarchist hides his motives and acts like a populist and a demagogue. He leapfrogs the old order (represented by the Senate and Brutus and Cassius) by going over their heads to the people themselves. He bribes the people by redistributing land, by offering Roman citizenship to conquered peoples, and by building public works. In the play, Shakespeare has Antony stress in the funeral speech how Caesar's will left money for each Roman citizen and his large private gardens as a public park. The people have become depraved and corrupted, and Caesar took full advantage of it.

Here Shakespeare has put his finger on a perennial objection to democracy, an objection heard from some of our founders as well as from our political pundits in every election year. In *Julius Caesar*, Shakespeare shows that unscrupulous politicians can sometimes flatter, buy, and mislead a fickle people and turn them into a mob, that the people are more interested in base than noble things, and that the people do not always know what is right.

Sound familiar? It should. Such sentiments are scattered throughout the debates of our own Constitutional Convention. Roger Sherman of Connecticut argued that the people "should have as little to do as may be about the government. They want information and are constantly liable to be misled." The people, Elbridge Gerry of Massachusetts told the delegates, "are the dupes of pretended patriots" and "are daily misled into the most baneful measures and opinions by the false reports circulated by designing men."

As these comments recognize, the spirit of the people plays a vital role in the success of any democratic government. Corruption of the people was the key to the mastery of Rome. By 44 B.C. the Roman people had lost the republican spirit, the spirit of free government. Likewise for America, as Schlesinger states: "In the end, the Constitution would live only if it embodied the spirit of the people."[12]

Precisely to quell such antidemocratic fears was a major aim of the Constitution's separation of powers, with its system of checks and balances. Sometimes a president will invoke the buzzword *democracy* to try to trump the separation of powers; he may, like Caesar, go over he heads of Congress or the Supreme Court directly to the people. Having won election or reelection, a chief executive may feel he, rather than a coordinate branch of government, better reflects the will of the people. Certainly such feelings were behind Franklin Roosevelt's ill-starred court-packing plan in the late 1930s and in Richard Nixon's behavior as president.

To such growth of power there is often a strong republican reaction.

The Roman conspirators saw their political heritage and human liberty threatened by Caesar. The republican constitution, unwritten though it may have been, was for them still the only possible constitution; it *was* Rome. To save Rome, they kill Caesar.

How different is this from what happened following Watergate? In words reminiscent of what fueled the Roman conspirators, Schlesinger writes: "By the 1970's the Constitution was out of balance, and the balance had to be restored or the republic would lose its original point."[13] In one case, the leader was assassinated; in the other, he resigned, under threat of impeachment, his political career "killed." In both cases, the head of a republican state could not stay in office without endangering the republican values on which the state was based.

Julius Caesar's constitutional lesson for us is of the first magnitude. Roman politics always involved competition between nobles, but traditionally kept that competition within certain limits. Before the end of the Republic, all the senators accepted the system and each senator subordinated himself to the Senate as a whole. Up to that point, a widespread sense of obligation kept the republican system working. Acceptance of governmental *process* over particular *result* made the crucial difference.

ENDS AND MEANS

A standard reading of *Julius Caesar* interprets the play as a comment on process and result, on ends and means. Critics who adopt this view focus on Brutus, who, they say, had a noble aim—to save Rome from tyranny—but used an ignoble method, murdering his friend Caesar. Inasmuch as the end did not justify the means, according to this view, Brutus failed.

This, the tragedy of Brutus, poses the question: what happens when one does evil for the sake of a greater good? Can a private crime accomplish a public good? Can a moral, lofty end be attained by immoral means of low character? Does the end justify the means?

The play's problem of ends and means, however, transcends poor Brutus. By shifting the focus to Caesar himself, we see how he was, ironically, guilty of the same tragic flaw. And in Caesar's flawed behavior we perceive larger constitutional and legal themes of process and result. Ultimately we glimpse how the law copes in various ways with the problem of ends and means.

Perhaps it is ironic that Caesar, no less than Brutus, confuses ends and means. For Caesar, an able and effective administrator and statesman, himself used improper means to achieve good ends of government. In the interest of quick, efficient, and intelligent rule, Caesar pushed through his laws, some of which were urgently needed, over constitutional objections. He demeaned and ignored the Roman Senate. A military man used to command, Caesar failed to grasp that his own illegal means, his violation of process, would so alienate the republicans.

No doubt Caesar rationalized his actions to himself on the ground of necessity. It was "necessary" to circumvent or override the Senate; the problems of government needed immediate solution. "Necessity" made him dictator; "necessity" justified all his actions.

The conspirators use the same rationalization. Brutus tells his colleagues to spare Antony but to kill Caesar "boldly, but not wrathfully" (2.1.172).

> This shall make
> Our purpose *necessary*, and not envious;
> Which so appearing to the common eyes,
> We shall be called purgers, not murderers.
>   (2.1.177–80 [emphasis added])

Both Caesar and the republicans anticipated Milton's famous passage in *Paradise Lost* when, after Satan makes some remarks, the poet observed: "So spake the Fiend, and with necessity, / The tyrant's plea, executed his devilish deeds." Caesar and the conspirators invoke "necessity, the tyrant's plea."

Throughout history "necessity" has often been the rationalization for infringing liberty. To those who destroy freedom as a means to an end, the end always justifies the means. Even in American constitutional history, "necessity" has bred some extraordinary doctrine from some of our most democratic national leaders.

"A strict observance of the written laws," Jefferson wrote in 1810 after he left the White House,

> is doubtless one of the high duties of a good citizen, but it is not the highest. The laws of necessity, of self-preservation, of saving our country when in danger, are of a higher obligation. . . . To lose our country by a scrupulous adherence to written law, would be to lose the law itself, with life, liberty, property and all those who are enjoying them with us; thus absurdly sacrificing the end to the means.[14]

Was Jefferson advocating the idea that necessity might be a higher law than the Constitution?

Lincoln, faced with the crisis of civil war, tried to constitutionalize the law of necessity. The controversy stirred by Lincoln in suspending habeas corpus was enormous. Secession and rebellion, Lincoln told Congress in 1861, "forces us to ask: 'Is there, in all republics, this inherent and fatal weakness?' 'Must a Government, of necessity, be too *strong* for the liberties of its own people, or too *weak* to maintain its own existence?'"

Later, Lincoln rephrased the question: "Was it possible to lose the nation and yet preserve the Constitution?"[15] Relying on the war power, Lincoln seemed to be arguing that the Constitution was different in war than in peace, that "Measures otherwise unconstitutional might become lawful by becoming indispensable to the preservation of the Constitution through the preservation of the nation." In other words, the end justifies the means.

In December 1939 Winston Churchill, then First Lord of the Admiralty and confronted with his own crises, adopted the Jefferson-Lincoln approach. Authorizing the British seizure of neutral ports to deprive Nazi Germany of iron ore from Norway, Churchill brushed aside neutrality objections based on the covenant of the League of Nations. "The letter of the law," said Churchill, "must not in supreme emergency obstruct those who are charged with its protection and enforcement.... Humanity, rather than legality, must be our guide."[16]

Jefferson, Lincoln, and Churchill were anything but tyrants. Of all leaders in world history, they were among the most sensitive to liberty, individual rights, and the democratic process. At the same time, though, they showed that the temporary exercise of nondemocratic and extralegal powers may be called for. This is a paradox that perhaps can only be justified during actual war.

In 1866, after the battlefield fighting in our Civil War was over, the Supreme Court in *Ex Parte Milligan* rejected Lincoln's view and declared that the Constitution worked "equally in war and in peace." Rebuking Lincoln for suspending habeas corpus, the Court announced: "No doctrine involving more pernicious consequences was ever invented by the wit of man than that any of [the Constitution's] provisions can be suspended during any of the great exigencies of government. Such a doctrine leads directly to anarchy or despotism, but the theory on which it is based is false; for the government, within the Constitution, has all the powers granted to it which are necessary to preserve its existence." In a pithy sentence, the Court summed up its position: "A country preserved at the sacrifice of all the cardinal principles of liberty, is not worth the costs of preserving."[17]

Similar issues arose when President Truman seized the nation's steel mills during a labor strike in the middle of the Korean War. Concurring in the Supreme Court's decision to uphold the mill owners' legal challenge to Truman's action, Justice Robert Jackson explicitly opposed "the unarticulated assumption ... that necessity knows no law."[18] Jackson knew, as history had taught, that necessity might become the pretext for usurpation.

Yet the government argument based on "necessity" is still with us and will be forever with us. Sometimes the "necessity" takes the form of national security, as we saw in the 1971 *Pentagon Papers* case, or when the government refuses to turn over names of informants or sensitive classified documents in criminal cases. The recent erosion of the exclusionary rule involving illegal searches is based on the assumption that the "necessity" for evidence has to be balanced against the shield of the Fourth Amendment.

Probably the most startling recent example was the Iran-Contra affair. As the congressional hearings in 1987 showed the world, Oliver North and his cohorts thought their noble ends (noble to them, that is) justified their questionable means (even they knew the means were at least questionable). North's tragic flaw was that in his sincere zeal to promote democracy, he helped subvert it. In his desire to defend and protect the Constitution he swore to uphold, he trampled some of its most fundamental precepts.

"Ends and means" is a vital concept in our law generally, as pointed out by Thomas Sowell in his 1988 book *A Conflict of Visions.* Sowell divides political, social, and legal thinkers into two main groups. One group, what most of us might think of as conservative, has a "constrained vision" that sees human beings as inevitably limited in both sympathy and knowledge and that places great value on economic, social, and legal *processes* as the way to progress. The other, more liberal group adheres, according to Sowell, to an "unconstrained vision" that is based on faith in the moral perfectibility of humankind and in the power of human reason. It focuses on *results.*

This conflict between "processes" and "results" plays itself out in the law in interesting ways. Sowell argues that advocates of the constrained vision believe that enforcement of just rules is the key regardless of a variety of outcomes, that individual rights are instrumentalities of social processes. For the opposing unconstrained vision, "justice is . . . a question of outcomes" and individual rights are vital in and of themselves.[19]

Sowell uses affirmative action cases and sex-difference cases as examples of legal rationales pitting process against result. For example, Sowell argues that affirmative action programs reflect the unconstrained vision of achieving results (greater minority employment) at the expense of process (color-blind evaluation).

This may seem a long way from *Julius Caesar,* but not really. The question of ends and means never goes away, particularly in the law. As Shakespeare says in the play, in a passage bearing heavily on legal interpretation: "But men may construe things after their fashion / Clear from the purpose of the things themselves" (1.3.34–35). In terms of democratic government, political leaders must understand what Caesar did not: that the democratic process, the means, is more important than any particular result, the end—that in fact the democratic means *is* the most important end.

Chapter Seven

THE LUNATIC, THE LOVER,
THE POET—AND THE LAWYER?

A Midsummer Night's Dream

PLAYS OF Shakespeare that appear to have little or nothing in common sometimes reveal genuine affinities upon a closer look and with a free play of the mind unhampered by centuries of prior criticism. Normally one would not speak of two such seemingly disparate plays as *Julius Caesar* and *A Midsummer Night's Dream* in the same breath. Yet despite their vastly different settings, certain basic legal themes in *Julius Caesar* do show up again in *A Midsummer Night's Dream*. Just as *Julius Caesar* turns on a violation of law for the good of the state, for example, so too *Dream* illustrates and sparks thought on civil disobedience. Likewise, the theme of democracy and popular sovereignty in *Julius Caesar* becomes the high point, the "most rare vision" of *Dream*. So, despite the lack of any apparent nexus, the two plays share some similar legal themes.

We do not usually think of *A Midsummer Night's Dream* as a play about reality at all, much less a serious play about law. We regard the play as a comedy. *Dream* is one of Shakespeare's most durable comedies, about mixed up lovers, fantastic dreams, magical love potions, and invisible sprites that make things turn out all right in the end. The fairy queen even falls in love with an Athenian craftsman while he has the head of an ass.

Such apparent silliness misled famed English diarist Samuel Pepys, after viewing a London performance in 1662, to describe *Dream* as "the most insipid ridiculous play that ever I saw in my life."[1] But whatever his merit as a diarist, Pepys failed as a drama critic, at least this time. He totally—if understandably—misjudged *Dream*. It is a mistake to think of *Dream* as no more than an insignificant bit of Shakespearean fluff, without any legal meaning.

DEFINITELY NOT THE SILLIEST STUFF

Pepys and many others make the mistake of overlooking the key passage in the final act about the audience's response to the play within the play. As Quince's inept actors put on *Pyramus and Thisbe* for Theseus, Hippolyta, and their guests, Hippolyta sounds much like Pepys (even in syntax) when she complains: "This is the silliest stuff that ever I heard" (5.1.209). But Theseus explains to Hippolyta and the rest of us, "The best in this kind are but shadows, and the / worst are no worse, if imagination amend them" (5.1.210–211). To this, Hippolyta retorts, "It must be your imagination, then, and not / theirs" (5.1.212–13).

This brief exchange between Theseus and Hippolyta provides a crucial clue to understanding the essence of *Dream*. With those comments, Shakespeare refers not only to *Pyramus and Thisbe*, but also to *Dream* itself. He tells the audience not to be put off by all the apparent absurdity, but as in *The Merchant of Venice*, to look beyond appearances. This exchange means that the audience must use *its* imagination to interpret the play correctly, to derive all its proper, if hidden, meaning.

Having found this clue, we can perhaps do better than Pepys and see past the surface nonsense in *Dream*. The superficially frivolous events of *Dream* take on greater meaning; they are by no means silly, "if imagination amend them."

It requires but little imagination to see some of the serious aspects of *Dream*. Though a comedy, *Dream* has lines, so often quoted they have become clichés, of great sober insight. "The course of true love never did run smooth" (1.1.134) and "Love looks not with the eyes, but with the mind" (1.1.234) are two of the most memorable. From its dream perspective, the play foreshadows Freud, particularly regarding irrational fantasies of unconscious libido.

Nor is this all. Among the serious aspects of *Dream* are several concerning law. From the opening scene, the play, like other Shakespeare works, says something about the rule of law, irrational and inflexible laws, how to respond to an unjust law, and the fragility of law. The play also encourages a large role for a lawyer's imagination and creativity in interpreting the law. Finally, the play's zenith, when Bottom the Weaver wakes from his dream, symbolizes the growth of democratic law. These are hardly "insipid" or "ridiculous" points, in spite of Pepys.

The entire dramatic action in *Dream* starts with a legal conflict. In the first scene, we meet Egeus, an Athenian whose daughter Hermia wants to marry Lysander. But Hermia's father, like other fathers before and since, objects and wants her to marry someone else. When Hermia disobeys, Egeus invokes an Athenian law that punishes a daughter, if she marries without her father's consent, either with death or life imprisonment in a convent.

This legal conflict resonates loudly even in our late twentieth-century ears, which in itself is extraordinary. Shakespeare wrote *Dream* in 1594–96 about events in ancient Greece, but it has a modern ring to us. We observe the tension between Egeus and his daughter Hermia and we inevitably think of our contemporary family relationships. We wonder about patriarchy and the rights of women. We almost expect an appearance by an earnest public interest lawyer from the Athenian Organization for Women.

But, alas, no such legal defender of the rights of women comes to Hermia's rescue. Instead, Egeus hales his headstrong daughter before Theseus, duke of Athens, and asks the duke to enforce the irrational and harsh (not to mention sexist) Athenian law:

> I beg the ancient privilege of Athens:
> As she is mine, I may dispose of her,
> Which shall be either to this gentleman
> Or to her death, according to our law.
>
> (1.1.41–44)

Shakespeare frequently uses this kind of irrational law as the mainspring for action. *The Comedy of Errors*, for example, opens with a law punishing foreigners simply for being foreigners. In *Measure for Measure*, everything turns on resurrecting a neglected law prescribing the death penalty for nonmarital sex. And at the heart of *The Merchant of Venice* is the conflict over enforceability of a contract for a pound of flesh as surety for a debt. *Dream* therefore has more in common with these plays than their designation as comedies.

One common theme in these plays is the tension created by the seeming inflexibility of law. In each, the person in authority declares that he has no power to abrogate or soften the law, which must be enforced in all its rigor. In *Dream*, Theseus warns Hermia:

> For you, fair Hermia, look you arm yourself
> To fit your fancies to your father's will,
> Or else the law of Athens yields you up—
> Which by no means we may extenuate—
> To death or to a vow of single life.
>
> (1.1.117–21)

Egeus gives voice to this rigidity later in the play, after the young lovers are caught in the enchanted forest. "I beg the law, the law upon his head" (4.1.154), cries Egeus, referring to Hermia's lover. Egeus here echoes no one so much as Shylock, who in his own climactic trial scene shrieks, "If you deny me, fie upon your law! . . . I stand here for law. . . . I crave the law. . . . I charge you, by the law" (*The Merchant of Venice* 4.1.100, 141, 235)

But both Egeus and Shylock learn that law is complex and subtle, requiring more than wooden application. In Egeus's case, his complaint against his daughter evaporates when the father's chosen suitor falls in love (aided by those mischievous sprites) with Hermia's friend Helena. For Shylock and the characters in the other plays, they find the authority figure, after disavowing the power to abrogate the law, doing just that. And so the alternating rhythm of law and equity continues.

But if equity or events fail to solve the problem, *Dream* offers another possible response to a harsh, inflexible, irrational, unjust law. Rather than submit to such a law, Lysander and Hermia flee the jurisdiction. The couple leave Athens and go to Lysander's rich aunt's house, where "the sharp Athenian law / Cannot pursue us" (1.1.162–63). When Theseus, Egeus, and the others catch up with the lovers, Lysander explains, "Our intent / Was to be gone from Athens," and thereby beyond "the peril of Athenian law" (4.1.150–52).

The lovers' response differs entirely from that of the most famous victim of "sharp Athenian law"—the philosopher Socrates. Faced with "the peril of Athenian law," Socrates turned down a chance to escape and instead submitted to what he saw as the rule of law. Perhaps Lysander and Hermia did what Socrates should have done. Perhaps they, at the start of their lives together, felt more of a need or desire to live than the aged philosopher. Perhaps Shakespeare, like Sophocles in *Antigone*, is telling us something important about civil disobedience and the rule of law. Should one's parents be disobeyed for love? Should one's country's laws be disobeyed for personal conscience or individual morality? Maybe it is more than coincidence that the setting is Athens.

Were Lysander and Hermes right to flee the clutches of what they regarded as an unjust law? Or was Socrates correct in choosing not to escape from prison, as he could have, after the jury had sentenced him to death? Shakespeare implicitly asks those very questions.

In sharp contrast to Socrates, Lysander and Hermes are young, student-age lovers, alienated from a harsh legal system they neither created nor understand. They do not want to die, nor do they want to live under intolerable conditions. Exile holds no fears for them.

Dream suggests, in more ways than one, that the rule of law is fragile. Athenian law and civilization are cruel and irrational in allowing a father to ask for his daughter's death just for marrying against her father's will. So the lovers run away to the forest, which symbolizes nature, neither so cruel, so irrational, so civilized, or so riddled with law. "The better the society," wrote Grant Gilmore in *The Ages of American Law*, "the less law there will be."[2] Beyond this anticipation of Rousseau and romanticism, the play shows that our instincts are also nature, and they are as irrational as the civilized world, and difficult to govern by law.

Shakespeare drives home the point at the end of the play. Theseus, ruler of Athens and symbol of the law, goes to sleep, as do his guests. The sprites then appear with their magical powers of good or mischief. Their appearance and their special powers suggest that Theseus (that is, the law) is not as supremely the ruler of his world as seemed at first. Maybe our "vaulting ambition" to have law control nature was running through Puck's mind when he exclaims, "Lord, what fools these mortals be!" (3.2.115).

A THEORY OF LEGAL INTERPRETATION

An important but hidden aspect of A Midsummer Night's Dream is its expansive theory of legal interpretation. For Dream can plausibly be read as advocating an imaginative, creative, activist approach to interpreting law. One can go even further and find in Dream support for a theory of constitutional interpretation more in accord with the "living document" view than with former Attorney General Edwin Meese's controversial "jurisprudence of original intent." All of this legal potential adds new texture to the play's meaning.

Dream is a play about the benevolent and positive creative powers of imagination. Through the first four acts, we see how imagination affects the characters and especially their romantic lives. Then in the fifth and final act, Shakespeare ties things together and explicitly sums up his view of imagination. At the start of the last act, Shakespeare makes clear that he believes imagination is a "shaping" force that can "apprehend / More than cool reason ever comprehends" (5.1.5–6). It is this salutary view of imagination that informs Shakespeare's theory of legal interpretation.

Shakespeare's theory of legal interpretation makes its appearance in that revealing and vital exchange in act 5 between Theseus and Hippolyta about their reactions to Pyramus and Thisbe, the play within the play. Hippolyta thinks the unpolished performance of Pyramus and Thisbe was dreadful, absolutely "the silliest stuff that ever I heard" (5.1.209). Theseus answers her by pointing out that such plays are not silly "if imagination amend them" (5.1.211). And then Hippolyta adds, "It must be your imagination, and not theirs" (5.1.212–13).

This conversation, however brief and simple it appears on its face, expresses a powerful theory of interpretation applicable to law as well as other fields.

Dream's theory of interpretation contains two interdependent components. The first requires the use of imagination to interpret the words—"if imagination amend them." The second makes it the audience, not the performers, whose imagination is called for—"It must be your imagination then, and not theirs." Thus, on its most obvious level, the exchange between Theseus and Hippolyta means that an audience must use its imagination, its creative power, to give and find substantive meaning in a stage performance. The audience, far from being passive, has a creative function as it constructs (and not merely registers) the play.

But the theory implicit in this Shakespearean dialogue is not limited to

plays. It has general application. More broadly yet still properly understood, Shakespeare in *Dream* is summoning any audience—whether of
playgoers, readers, or lawyers—to use its own imagination, based on its
own unique perceptions, experiences, and outlooks, to uncover the meaning of a play, a book, or a constitution. Without such audience participation, the play, book, or constitution remains flat and one dimensional and
never achieves its full power or true effect.

At this point, we are on familiar ground. For decades, literary criticism
has divided into two basic schools of interpretation: "author's intent"
and "reader response." The "author's intent" school thinks, as its name
implies, that the author's intent should control the interpretation of what
the author wrote.[3] For the "reader-response" school, the author's intent
is not determinative of the work's meaning, which really turns on a
reader's response to it. According to this theory, a work can mean different things to different people at different times. Based on *Dream*, Shakespeare comes down squarely on the "reader response" side of the debate
over interpretation.[4]

For reader-based theory, all interpretation is guided by the inter-
preter's own viewpoint and preliminary understanding. Reader-based
hermeneutics claims to deal with the present significance of a text. It concentrates on how the words become meaningful for different readers by,
in Shakespeare's words, allowing their imagination to "amend them."
One's perception of the writing is considered part of the work itself. The
reader-based school claims to assess, by a process of historical understanding, the correct interpretation grandly conceived. Its chief virtue is
said to be its power to keep texts alive and valuable.

If this is Shakespeare's position, it is a controversial one. Reader-based
interpretation, such as Shakespeare seems to be endorsing, has been
sharply criticized as subjective and relativistic. Absent determinate standards, cry the critics, interpretation will run riot and reflect nothing more
than personal values. Author-based adherents fear interpreters imposing
their own impressionistic readings and ending up in what some might
regard as the swamp of deconstruction. This is an ongoing debate.

The Shakespearean reader-based view of interpretation has profound
implications for law. It means that whoever interprets the law has a significant and shaping role to play. Imagination takes advantage of ambiguity, in the language of law as well as in the language of poetry. We can
paraphrase Theseus and then say that laws are neither silly nor irrational,
"if imagination amend them." And to achieve such reasonable legal interpretation, "It must be your [the lawyer's or judge's] imagination, and not
theirs [the drafters']." Seen this way, Shakespeare begins to look like a
judicial activist and a loose constructionist.

From *Dream*'s theory of imaginative dramatic interpretation, it is only
a small step to an activist theory of constitutional interpretation. If I am

reading *Dream* correctly, Shakespeare is encouraging a "living document" approach to interpreting the Constitution. Each audience, each generation, he might say, has to use its own imagination to interpret the Constitution for itself, lest constitutional law become the "silliest stuff." For Shakespeare the constitutional theorist, to be straitjacketed by the framers' intent—assuming such intent could even be determined—would minimize the life-giving role of imagination and might result in judicial interpretations qualifying as the "silliest stuff."

High on any short list of the silliest, least imaginative, and most pernicious judicial stuff would be the Supreme Court's notorious 1857 *Dred Scott* decision. In that case, the Court held that a slave who had sued his owner on the ground that his temporary residence on free soil had removed his slave status was not entitled to sue because neither he nor any other African-American was a citizen. The Court reasoned that the founders regarded African-Americans as no more than property and therefore without any rights of citizenship under the Constitution, including the right to sue.

Despite "change in public opinion or feeling," Chief Justice Roger Taney ruled that the Constitution "must be construed now as it was understood at the time of its adoption. . . . Any other rule of construction would abrogate the judicial character of this Court and make it the mere reflex of the popular opinion or passion of the day."[5] Of such stuff are civil wars made.

Shakespeare himself shows how his theory of legal interpretation would operate to avoid the "silliest stuff." In *Dream*, Athenian law will severely punish Hermia if she marries someone other than Demetrius, her father's choice. Shakespeare makes the legal problem go away by having Demetrius fall in love with someone else. Similarly, whatever else we may think of Portia's judgment in *The Merchant of Venice*, it certainly showed judicial creativity in evading the clear wording of a contract. Portia's imagination certainly did "amend" Shylock's contract with Antonio. And again and again in Shakespeare's plays, we see the conflict between strict and harsh law, on the one hand, and more reasonable and flexible equity, on the other.

No wonder the seminal book in the law and literature movement is titled *The Legal Imagination*. "The activities which make up the professional life of the lawyer and judge," wrote James B. White in that book, "constitute an enterprise of the imagination . . . the translation of the imagination into reality by the power of language." Although White refers to some of Shakespeare's works, he makes no mention of *Dream*. Yet surely the Theseus-Hippolyta colloquy in *Dream* buttresses White's claim that "the lawyer is at heart a writer, one who lives by the power of his imagination."[6]

There is another way to express Shakespeare's theory of legal interpretation. We need only amend one of Shakespeare's memorable lines from *Dream*. In the hymn to imagination at the start of act 5, Shakespeare writes, "The lunatic, the lover, and the poet / Are of imagination all compact [i.e., composed]" (5.1.7–8). In light of his theory of creative interpretation of law, perhaps Shakespeare's short list of imaginative types with "such seething brains" should now read: "the lunatic, the lover, the poet, *the lawyer*."

A MOST RARE VISION

The legal high point of *A Midsummer Night's Dream* comes, as Goddard explains, when Bottom the Weaver wakes from his dream.[7] This scene is Shakespeare at his best. In this extraordinary scene, Shakespeare turns a purely farcical incident into a vital parable. We see the awakening of imagination in earthbound man, which in turn allows for the Jeffersonian ideal, the great liberal hope of democracy—government by the people. Yet for all this dramatic significance, Bottom the Weaver is, according to nineteenth-century English critic William Hazlitt, "a character that has not had justice done him."[8] The wonderful insight of his waking up is usually reduced to an occasion for loud laughter. It is now time to do justice to Bottom.

This is what Bottom says when he wakes up:

> I have had a most rare vision. I have had a
> dream past the wit of man to say what dream it was.
> Man is but an ass if he go about t' expound this dream.
> Methought I was—there is no man can tell what.
> Methought I was, and methought I had—but man is
> but a patched fool if he will offer to say what methought
> I had. The eye of man hath not heard, the ear of man
> hath not seen, man's hand is not able to taste, his
> tongue to conceive, nor his heart to report what my
> dream was. I will get Peter Quince to write a ballad of
> this dream. It shall be called 'Bottom's Dream' because
> it hath no bottom.
>
> (4.1.202–13)

Bottom's short but sublime speech about his dream means much more precisely because of who the speaker is. Bottom and his friends represent the "bottom" of society, the common man. They are ordinary, rude workers, whose "tongue-tied simplicity" so pleases their ruler Theseus. But even among these rude fellows, Bottom stands out. He seems, like a child, to crave attention. One character in the play describes Bottom as having "the best wit of any handicraftman in Athens" (4.2.9–10).

And early on it is Bottom who, thinking about playing the role of a lion, says, "I will roar that I will do any man's heart good to hear me" (1.2.66–67). His speech on waking is that roar.

It is no accident that this representative common man takes on the head of an ass. Throughout history, the upper classes—the patricians of the world—have always thought of the masses as a lower order of beings, the swinish multitude, the herd, animals unfit for governing themselves. Thus arose the older, hierarchical notions of government and law, which viewed the mass of humankind as some beast of burden. In American constitutional history, the older view animated some of the founders, particularly Alexander Hamilton. To Hamilton, supporter of an aristocratic type of government, is attributed that most revealing and characteristic remark about the people being a "great beast."

In reaction to such divine right notions, Jefferson wrote, "The mass of mankind has not been born with saddles on their backs, nor a favored few booted and spurred, ready to ride them legitimately, by the grace of God."[9]

Bottom's speech, in the Jeffersonian mold, heralds a newer, more democratic view, where the masses are not beasts. Bottom and his friends are "hard-handed men, that work in Athens here, / Which never laboured in their minds till now" (5.1.72–73). This is the original miracle of the imagination. Bottom is aware of transcendent things when he wakes up. A creation has taken place within him. He struggles, in vain, to express it, and, in his very failure, succeeds. We see that as our imagination becomes more educated, certain kinds of lower behavior will not be possible to us anymore.

Bottom's metamorphosis, as reflected in his speech, signals the arrival of conditions that would permit the mass of men and women to lead lives of personal and political freedom. It is the poet's way of saying that even within the head of this foolish plebeian weaver a divine light can be kindled. The older hierarchical connections give way to a vision of a society of individuals living here on a plane of equality. "Democracy becomes possible. Nothing less than this is what this incident [in *Dream*] implies."[10]

Bottom is the Jeffersonian ideal, the great liberal hope. The school, the library, education, learning, culture—they are the great Jeffersonian instruments of making the people compassionate and humane, and awakening in their imagination the desire and the ability to govern themselves. Bottom and his friends now labor in their minds. This is, indeed, as Bottom says, "a most rare vision."

Bottom, Jefferson, and Lincoln are all-important figures in the history of popular government. Bottom's dream is democracy in the making and, after all, the scene of the play is ancient Athens, the cradle of democracy. Bottom's democratic roar on awakening "will do any man's heart good to hear."

Bottom is wrong when he says, "Man is but an ass if he go about t'expound this dream" (4.1.204). For expounding Bottom's dream, seen from its incipient democratic perspective, is an important and worthwhile task. Our eyes have been well and truly opened and some undreamed of possibilities have been raised by expounding Bottom's "most rare vision."

Chapter Eight

OLD FATHER ANTIC THE LAW

HENRY IV, PARTS 1 AND 2

WITH THE TWO parts of *Henry IV*, Shakespeare spins a new and important legal theme. Like *A Midsummer Night's Dream*, the plays about Henry IV offer a theory of legal interpretation and perceptive comments on the role of law in society. But then the Bard does something unique and central to understanding his attitude toward law and lawyers. In the two *Henry IV* plays, Shakespeare gives us the most unqualifiedly, unmistakably complimentary portrait of a sober, solid, fair-minded lawyer figure in all the canon. Shakespeare's highly favorable and especially respectful description of the lord chief justice in the two parts of *Henry IV* is a powerful and effective antidote to those who think Dick the Butcher's line about killing all the lawyers should be taken at face value only.

To etch his most positive portrait of a lawyer that much more deeply, Shakespeare sets up a contrast. Early in Shakespeare's *Henry IV, Part 1*, Falstaff, the great comic creation of Shakespeare, gives his own candid view of the rule of law. Chatting merrily with Prince Hal, Falstaff asks, "Shall there be gallows standing in England when thou / art king?" (1.2.58–59). Why, asks Falstaff, should a thief's courage be cheated of its reward "with the / rusty curb of old father Antic [i.e., that old screwball] the law" (1.2.59–60)? The very phrasing, the offhand but colorful reference to the law gone awry, catches our attention and makes us anticipate something special about the role played by "old father Antic the law" in *Henry IV*. The two parts of *Henry IV* continue the story begun in *Richard II*. At the end of *Richard II*, Bolingbroke, having successfully rebelled against Richard II, is crowned Henry IV. But both parts of *Henry IV* show that "uneasy lies the head that wears a crown" (*2 Henry IV*, 3.1.31).

King Henry is beset by troubles. He spends his time putting down new revolts by Hotspur and others who had originally helped the king achieve his power. Hal, the young prince of Wales, is a youth without any apparent sense of responsibility, who pains his father the king with the "bad element" he hangs around with. By the time *Part 2* closes, the new rebels are routed, Henry IV dies of natural causes, and ne'er-do-well Hal assumes the crown while foreswearing his past friends.

One of the underlying legal themes in *Henry IV* concerns the teaching *lawlessness as a general theme; a warning to leaders* [handwritten margin note]

function of government. Bolingbroke, the successful revolutionary, becomes, as Henry IV, a symbol of disorder. Under his reign, there is no lasting order. Lawlessness springs up all about him. One who acted as a street thug is king.

But *Henry IV* is not primarily about the educative role of government. According to a leading Shakespearean scholar, "the mainspring of the dramatic action" in *Henry IV* is legal.

In *The Fortunes of Falstaff*, published in 1944, John Dover Wilson, an English critic, argued that *Henry IV* hinges on "the choice . . . Hal is called upon to make between vanity and government."[1] Vanity is personified by Falstaff, and government by chivalry or prowess in the field (in *Part 1*) and justice (the theme of *Part 2*). In Wilson's analysis, Hotspur symbolizes chivalry and the lord chief justice stands for the rule of law or the new ideal of service to the state. *Henry IV* becomes a morality play, a struggle between vanity and government for possession of youth.

To choose vanity is, for Hal, to choose a disrespectful, even anarchic attitude toward law. He takes part in robberies. He even hits the chief justice, who sends Hal to jail. In this phase, Hal is always in trouble with the law.

Hal's antilegal attitude is the same as Falstaff's. He sees in Falstaff—and imitates—an entire absence of moral responsibility, a complete freedom. After Henry IV dies, and Falstaff thinks of his own influence over his friend Hal, Falstaff says, "Let us / take any man's horses—the laws of England are at my commandment . . . and woe to my Lord Chief Justice" (*Part 2*, 5.3.134–137). The law is "old father Antic the law."

Falstaff's interview with the chief justice nicely poses the basic choice facing Hal. When the chief justice asks for him, Falstaff tells a servant, "Tell him I am deaf" (*Part 2*, 1.2.67). In context, we can interpret this as "deaf to the law." And then a little later the chief justice upbraids Falstaff: "You hear not what I [i.e., the law] say to you" (*Part 2*, 1.2.121). In this interview, Falstaff comes off far wittier, which may help dramatize the choice for Hal.

In the same interview, Hal's friend speaks for Hal and youth in all times and in all places. Falstaff sums up generational conflict and youthful bridling at authority when he challenges the chief justice, in words that echo down to our own times: "You that are old / consider not the capacities of us that are young" (*Part 2*, 1.2.174–75). And soon after Hal inherits the throne, an adviser tells the chief justice, "Indeed I think the young King loves you [i.e., the law] not" (*Part 2*, 5.2.9).

But Hal's attitude changes. The lord chief justice of England, admirable symbol of the law, remains constant. Shakespeare portrays him throughout as sober, calm, incorruptible, fair, measured, and at all times fully in control of himself and the situation. The chief justice always speaks rationally and sensibly, without being overbearing or arch. He personifies justice in its eternal, ideal form.

The chief justice's symbolic role shows through, for example, in act 2 of *Part 2* when he restores order following Falstaff's arrest for nonpayment of a debt. Mistress Quickly sues Falstaff, and two officers come to a tavern to bring Falstaff into custody. A scuffle ensues until the lord chief justice and his men enter. "What is the matter?" asks the chief justice. "Keep the peace here, ho!" (*Part 2*, 2.1.63). The commotion subsides and the chief justice hears both sides, rendering judgment against Falstaff: "Pay her / the debt you owe her" (*Part 2*, 2.1.120–21).

But the real moment of truth—the theatrical moment of the play for the link between Shakespeare and the law—comes in the last act of *Part 2* when Hal has to make the choice of his life. Prince Hal has become King Henry V, and the chief justice recalls how he, the chief justice, has had, on occasion, to punish the wayward youth. The new king confronts the experienced, upright judge and sees the uncertainty in the judge's face.

The new king tells the judge, "You are, I think, assured I love you not" (*Part 2*, 5.2.64). The judge does not know if he will now be removed from office or, worse yet, punished by the new king for the judge's past strictness.

Bravely answers the chief justice, "I am assured, if I be measured rightly, / Your majesty hath no just cause to hate me" (*Part 2*, 5.2.65–66). "No?" responds the king with apparent sarcasm (though much depends on the actor's inflection).

> How might a prince of my great hopes forget
> So great indignities you laid upon me?
> What—rate, rebuke, and roughly send to prison
> Th'immediate heir of England? Was this easy?
> May this be washed in Lethe and forgotten?
>
> (*Part 2*, 5.2.67–71)

The chief justice's thoughtful comeback makes the play's legal symbolism explicit:

> I then did use the person of your father.
> The image of his power lay then in me;
> And in th'administration of his law,
> Whiles I was busy for the commonwealth,
> Your highness pleasèd to forget my place,
> The majesty and power of law and justice,
> The image of the King whom I presented,
> And struck me in my very seat of judgment.
>
> (*Part 2*, 5.2.72–79)

Then the chief justice goes on to tell the new king that he should think how he would feel,

> To have a son set your decrees at naught—
> To pluck down justice from your awe-full bench,
> To trip the course of law, and blunt the sword
> That guards the peace and safety of your person,
> See your most dreadful laws slighted . . .
>
> (*Part 2*, 5.2.84–87, 93)

The chief justice's cogent and dignified advocacy on his own behalf (and on behalf of law) moves the king. "You are right, Justice," answers Hal, and at last we know what his choice will be.

> And you weigh this well.
> Therefore still bear the balance and the sword;
> And I do wish your honours may increase.
>
> (*Part 2*, 5.2.101–3)

In an extraordinary passage, Shakespeare celebrates the notion that the law is supreme even over royalty. The playwright has Hal conjure up the possibility that one of his own sons would disobey the law, at which point Hal would say,

> Happy am I that have a man so bold
> That dares do justice on my proper son,
> And not less happy having such a son
> That would deliver up his greatness so
> Into the hands of justice.
>
> (*Part 2*, 5.2.107–11)

Hal returns the "unstained" sword of justice to the chief justice, reappoints him, and begs him to go on administering the laws of England in this "bold, just, and impartial spirit" (*Part 2*, 5.2.115).

Then and there the new king chooses law over vanity as the touchstone for his reign. He puts off vanity and adopts justice as his father and guide. To the chief justice, Hal says:

> You shall be as a father to my youth;
> My voice shall sound as you do prompt mine ear,
> And I will stoop and humble my intents
> To your well-practised wise directions.
>
> (*Part 2*, 5.2.117–20)

Shakespeare has created a portrait of a great judge and has paid an impressive tribute to the impartiality of courts.[2] So much for a superficial reading of Dick the Butcher's "Kill all the lawyers."

Here we have an allegory for all of us, lawyers or not. Each of us faces a choice similar to Hal's: youth standing between vanity and law or some other occupation. Somewhere around the time we finish college, consider what to do with our lives, decide whether to go on to graduate or professional school, and start to conduct our life's work, we first choose, as Hal chose, one over the other, profession over vanity. And then, as we live our lives in our work, we choose the way we will practice and conduct ourselves. Prince Hal is each one of us. This remembrance of choice quickens anyone's interest in the play.

There is proof of the large role of the law in Shakespeare's *Henry IV*. I find persuasive—and personally significant—the theory that the work is essentially a morality play about youth faced with a choice between law and vanity. But supplementing and even going beyond that theory is other evidence. Again and again Shakespeare makes us aware that the play is an allegory about law, sprinkled with casual but still stimulating legal references, some of which stay a while in the mind.

Consider the small but revealing matter of Mistress Quickly's lawsuit against Falstaff. In those days, lawsuits apparently began with more than a simple summons. Attachment of the person was the preferred method. In *Henry IV*, the two officers of the law who come to arrest Falstaff as a defendant in *Quickly v. Falstaff* are called Master Snare and Master Fang. Could Shakespeare have picked better allegorical names than Snare and Fang to reflect the dim, crabbed view debtors took of the law and its personnel?

Similarly, if the lord chief justice stands for the ideal element of the law, the mundane aspect of the law is represented by two local justices of the peace called Silence and Shallow. Justice Silence, true to his name, says almost nothing during the play. But Justice Shallow, hardly a deep fellow, is a fully developed character with many traits. The contrast between the lord chief justice and Justice Shallow could not be greater.

Shakespeare portrays Justice Shallow as a foolish old lawyer. Shallow makes several references to the time he spent as a young man at the Inns of Court (*Part 2*, 3.2.12–33, 275–83, 303–9). He reminisces about the wildness of his youth, his fighting, and his womanizing, for which he was then dubbed "lusty Shallow." At one point in the play a friend of Shallow even tries improperly to influence Shallow on behalf of a litigant. In the end, he comes off—especially in his dealings with Falstaff—as a stupid, gullible liar, ripe to be the victim of Falstaff's schemes.

Justice Shallow's allusions to the Inns of Court are significant. He refers to two by name—Clement's Inn and Gray's Inn; in only one other play, *Henry VI, Part 2*, does Shakespeare actually name another of the Inns (Middle Temple). We should recall that Clement's Inn is where Shakespeare's cousin John Greene had studied and Gray's Inn gave

Shakespeare one of his first big breaks by inviting him to put on *Comedy of Errors* there. All of this shows the influence of the Inns of Court on Shakespeare.

It may also show that Shakespeare had some firsthand knowledge of the carousing that sometimes went on at the Inns of Court, and that "lusty Shallow" was not the only one who earned such a sobriquet. Some surviving evidence indicates that Shakespeare followed Shallow's habits after a performance of *Twelfth Night* at Middle Temple in March 1602. According to the unexpurgated diary of John Manningham, a barrister of the Middle Temple:

> Upon a time when Burbage played Richard the Third there was a citizen grew so far in liking with him, that before she went from the play she appointed him to come that night unto her by the name of Richard the Third. Shakespeare, overhearing their conclusion, went before, was entertained and at his game ere Burbage came. Then message being brought that Richard the Third was at the door, Shakespeare caused return to be made that William the Conqueror was before Richard the Third. Shakespeare's name was William.[3]

The Bard might then have been called "lusty Shakespeare."

Both parts of *Henry IV* stress the virtues of settlement and compromise, virtues that should not readily be lost on lawyers. In *Part 1*, just before the crucial battle at Shrewsbury where Hotspur is killed, King Henry offers to pardon the rebels if they will lay down their arms. Worcester, emissary of the rebels, decides for his own reasons not to relay the "liberal and kind offer of the King" (5.2.2), which Hotspur would have accepted. After the battle, with the rebels defeated, the king confronts Worcester about the generous settlement offer and on getting no satisfactory response orders Worcester killed.

In *Part 2* another settlement conference takes place. The king's representative offers the king's promise of mercy and attention to the rebels' grievances. Everyone knows it will be the last chance to settle before the battle:

> we may meet,
> And either end in peace—which God so frame—
> Or to the place of diff'rence call the swords
> Which must decide it.
>
> (4.1.177–80)

If litigation is a type of war, then attempts to settle are akin to peace negotiations. Viewed this way, the double mention of settlement in *Henry IV* takes on meaning. Once again, the lawyer knows Shakespeare is

speaking about settling or calling down the swords. As almost every lawyer must have told a client at some time, the archbishop of York says:

> A peace is of the nature of a conquest,
> For then both parties nobly are subdued,
> And neither party loser.
>
> *(Part 2, 4.1.315–17)*

This is Shakespeare's version of the familiar lawyer's adage: "A fair settlement is better than a bad trial."

When the rebels have difficulty explaining their grievances, one of the
king's men says, "A rotten case abides no handling" *(Part 2, 4.1.159)*.
Now there's a thought that must have gone through lawyers' minds more
than once. How many rotten cases have attorneys handled? To what result? What is a rotten case?

Then there is a line full of special meaning about how a lawyer should
best plead a case. The chief justice says to Falstaff:

> Sir John, Sir John, I am well acquainted
> with your manner of wrenching the true cause the
> false way. It is not a confident brow, nor the throng
> of words that come with such more than impudent
> sauciness from you, can thrust me from a level consideration.
>
> *(Part 2, 2.1.111–16)*

This passage compresses in a verse a whole primer on advocacy. The
reader should linger on the lines a while, rolling them over delightedly in
his or her mind, and meditate about their meaning.

Ability to wield the written or spoken word is a lawyer's primary
weapon. Successful use of the basic technical skills of courtroom persuasion depend to a large extent on skillful use of language, on mobilizing
language to the advocate's ends. We try to persuade by using words.
Every great courtroom advocate grasps the vital importance of the written and oral word. "The power of clear statement," said Daniel Webster,
"is the great power at the bar."

"The throng of words" has double application here. Both sentimental
Richard II and pugnacious Hotspur—different personalities that they
were—were similar in their wordiness. Shakespeare gives them good
speeches, but in the end makes them both losers. They become victims of
words, and one wonders if that too is a lesson for lawyers.

"Impudent sauciness"—a lawyer *should* be bold, even irrepressible,
but there are limits. Overboldness runs the risk of sanctions; impudence
is an unpleasant trait. We all come across adversaries or colleagues
who have said and done things with "more than impudent sauciness."

On the other hand, if deference became the hallmark of the legal profession, the law's creativity, its independence and willingness to challenge authority, its very excitement, may to some extent be lost.

Which brings us back full circle to the lord chief justice. Might it not be suggested that the chief justice uses some of the very qualities he taxes Falstaff for using? After all, does not the chief justice in his occasionally difficult dealings with young Prince Hal and new King Henry V display a "confident brow" and rely on a "throng of words," and even on what some might characterize as an "impudent sauciness"? Yet when the chief justice employs these traits, they are good, praiseworthy, and for positive ends. The lesson may be that skills are only skills in the service of deeper aspects of personality and character; skills depend on the purpose to which they are put, means have to be related to ends. These purposes and ends come under scrutiny in *Richard III*.

Chapter Nine

FINAL VERDICT ON *RICHARD III*

THE TWO PARTS of *Henry IV* are plays in which Shakespeare's legal references are explicit. We have no doubt that Shakespeare alludes to law when he discusses the lord chief justice in *Henry IV*. Equally obvious is his intent to comment on lawyers and the law in *Henry VI, Part 2, The Merchant of Venice*, and *Measure for Measure*. But what we regard as legal issues in Shakespeare are not always expressly raised or necessarily intended by the Bard. Some aspects of Shakespeare's work, not law related on their face, have become so by the passage of time, developments in culture, and changes in legal doctrine. One of the most crucial of these legal issues for *our* society is vividly illustrated by *Richard III*.

What do Shakespeare's *Julius Caesar* and *Richard III* and Oliver Stone's film *JFK* have in common? They all raise a similar cultural and legal problem. In *Julius Caesar*, we have a dramatic tragedy about a historical fact—what we would now call a docudrama—that advocates one special view of a crucial event, the assassination of Caesar. With *Richard III*, Shakespeare also gives us a docudrama, but this time it is one that is often said to change important facts, to Richard's disadvantage. And the movie *JFK* is controversial precisely because it puts forth what many people think is a biased view of the assassination of President Kennedy based on distorted facts. The question posed by these three works of art and so many others is: how much leeway with historical truth, how much dramatic license, should an author have?

This question of a writer's fidelity to fact has become, among other things, a pressing and controversial legal problem. The media take increasing liberties with the truth, routinely blurring fact and fiction, and distorting real events to make dramatic or ideological points. When real people in our litigious age believe that false things have been said about them, they brood about how to regain their reputations. A popular way to vindicate oneself today is to sue for defamation, invasion of privacy, intentional infliction of emotional harm, fraud, or some other legal theory. Reconciling the value of one's reputation with the countervailing value of free expression defies easy solution, particularly in the realm of current historical events.

Whether or not Shakespeare had any thoughts about law in writing *Richard III*, the play is a paradigm highly useful for analyzing the important legal issue of authors' tendency to mix up fact and fiction, to mingle truth and speculation. The conventional wisdom is that the fusing of fact and fiction in a blender is a new problem. We tend to think that only a few decades ago we developed a new form, a kind of fiction that was reality, reality that was fiction: its artful practitioners, such as Truman Capote, Frank Conroy, and Tom Wolfe, caught our attention. We also tend to think that modern technology—film and television—has created the problem of docudrama.

Not so. The tension between "what is real" and "what is art" is an old phenomenon. Shakespeare's *Richard III* may well be the first significant docudrama. That Shakespeare wrote such a hybrid play gives us a good idea where he would probably come out in the legal debate. *Richard III* is Shakespeare's contribution to the current legal controversy between history and fiction, which ultimately boils down to a dispute over questionable testimony.

Lawyers are natural arbiters of questionable testimony. Who better than a lawyer to separate fabrication from hard fact and the bearers of false witness from the bearers of truth? Lawyers know that truth is a subtle blend of what is demonstrable and what cannot be disproved.

Analysis, especially by a lawyer, proceeds in the context of three simultaneous debates. First there is the historical debate over whether a writer (e.g., Shakespeare) has falsified the facts about a subject (e.g., *Richard III*). Then there is the legal debate as to proper standards for liability. Finally comes the cultural debate, which is really nothing less than a battle over history, the potential to alter dramatically the way truth is transmitted from generation to generation. If truth and fiction blur, will the result be an intellectual climate in which no fact, no event, and no aspect of history has any fixed meaning or content? If any fact can be recast, will there be any ultimate historical reality? *Richard III* helps us think about these issues.

HISTORICAL DEBATE

Richard III, Shakespeare's play about the battle of Bosworth Field in 1485 and the events leading up to it, is famous for its portrayal of Richard as an evil, tyrannical monster. According to Shakespeare, the malevolent Richard lost the battle to the good Henry Tudor, who then pronounced himself Henry VII and started the Tudor dynasty. Today we can look at *Richard III*, and Shakespeare's other so-called history plays, and reconsider their historical accuracy.

Loss of his crown was not the only thing that King Richard suffered at Henry's hands; he also lost his reputation. Richard III stands indicted at the bar of history, accused of numerous misdeeds, most notably the murder of his young nephews, Edward, prince of Wales, and Richard, duke of York. The verdict is the finding of guilty made by history (and helped along by Tudor historians and Shakespeare's influential play) against Richard. For half a millennium, history has blamed Richard III for the crime, which has come down through the ages as the murder of the princes in the Tower.

Now, however, a growing body of evidence seems to justify a motion on Richard's behalf for a new trial before the judgment seat of history. Passing judgment calls for careful weighing of the evidence regarding one of the most well-known events in the long and event-filled story of England. It is important to consider at least the possibility of a miscarriage of justice caused in large part by Shakespeare's unforgettable description of Richard as "this poisonous bunch-backed toad" (1.3.244).

The fate of the little princes in the Tower—the most famous mystery in the annals of English history[1]—has long been the subject of fierce controversy and dispute. In 1768 Horace Walpole published his *Historic Doubts on the Life and Reign of King Richard the Third*, which disagreed with the Shakespearean portrait. Since then, many books and articles have examined the murder from pro- and anti-Ricardian viewpoints, stirring doubts about history's (and Shakespeare's) verdict. In both America and England, societies have been formed to clear Richard's name.

The catalyst for many of these modern doubts is *The Daughter of Time*, a 1951 mystery novel by the late Josephine Tey. The book, still readily available in paperback, tells of a modern detective investigating the case against Richard and concluding that it was a frame-up by the Tudors, specifically by Henry VII. In 1984, as the dispute seemed to reach a crescendo, the British Broadcasting Company produced for television a modern trial by jury at the Old Bailey to determine if Richard was guilty or innocent of murdering the princes.

Recent books are forthright in disagreeing with Shakespeare. According to one of them, blaming Richard III for the murder of the princes is "totally without any factual evidence that would be accepted in any Court of Law."[2] A second asks, "Is it not time to concede that there are many good reasons for believing Richard innocent?"[3] "For every shred of evidence," claims yet another, "there were alternative explanations and other probable culprits."[4]

Yet our view of Richard III is more the result of literature than history or law. Our ideas are deeply colored by Shakespeare. According to a leading scholar, Paul Murray Kendall, "The dramatic exuberance of Shakespeare endowed the Tudor myth with a vitality that is one of the wonders of the world. What a tribute this is to art; what a misfortune this is to history."[5] More than any other source, Shakespeare's play *Richard III* has affected what we think even today of Richard's guilt or innocence.

The play has exerted a profound and crucial influence on history's negative verdict against Richard.

We quite properly are suspicious of history strained through the literary imagination. Shakespeare's word portrait of Richard is anything but innocent. In Shakespeare's play, Richard is physically deformed, a hunchback with a withered left arm. The physical deformity corresponds to an inner deformity: Richard is, in Shakespeare's drama, an awful ogre, fascinating as a snake.

Brother to King Edward IV, Richard, duke of Gloucester, wants the throne and power of England for himself—in Shakespeare's version. To clear the way, Richard kills their middle brother, Clarence; his own wife, Anne; the deposed King Henry VI and Henry's son Edward Lancaster, as well as King Edward's sons and heirs—the princes in the Tower. After exposure to Shakespeare's play, one feels certain that Richard deserved not only his death at Bosworth, but also his dismal reputation.

Certain material facts about Richard's life, which are undisputed, cast him in a better light. His loyalty to his brother Edward was a byword at court from the time Edward took the throne in 1461 until the king's death twenty-two years later. From 1471 to 1483 Richard served as his brother's "Lieutenant of the North." For more than a decade, he developed a highly personal and immensely popular style of government as the king's northernmost viceroy. Richard was responsible for useful legislation and wise administration. Nothing in Richard's conduct during this period of faithful service provides any preview of the later indictment against him.

The crucial events occurred in 1483. In April of that year, King Edward died of natural causes, leaving two young sons, aged twelve and ten. Edward IV's will proclaimed the elder boy king and Richard his protector until the boy's majority. Richard directed the prince of Wales to lodge at the Tower of London—at the time a major royal residence as well as a prison—until the coronation day, set for June 24, 1483.

That coronation never took place. One reason was the influence of Edward IV's widow, Elizabeth Woodville, and her large and ambitious family. While alive, Edward IV had showered the Woodvilles with land, money, and power. When the king died, the Woodvilles sought to control the throne through the new young king. Richard got wind of the Woodville plans and hastily flew south to London to take a stronger, more personal hand in matters. He then sent the younger brother, Richard, duke of York, to join the prince of Wales in the Tower. Neither prince was seen or heard from again.

Two days before the scheduled coronation, a new issue arose. A clergyman of St. Paul's Cathedral preached that the late king's sons could not take the throne because they were illegitimate. The illegitimacy claim grew out of a much earlier marriage agreement—a "precontract" like the familiar precontracts of marriage in *Measure for Measure*—between the late king and Lady Eleanor Butler, who had retired to a convent and died many years before. Such a precontract might well have caused the clergy to view the late king's marriage to Elizabeth Woodville as null and void, thereby disqualifying the princes from the line of succession under medieval law.

Soon after, on July 6, Richard III was crowned king of England. Rumors started that Richard had usurped the throne or done away with the princes in the Tower. After a first revolt, organized by the duke of Buckingham, failed in October 1483, a second effort, instigated by Henry Tudor and aided by the ousted Woodville faction, ended with success at Bosworth.

So much for the undisputed facts. All circumstantial, they yield inferences but by themselves prove nothing for certain about the death of the little princes. To probe further, we must consider more controversial evidence.

Several factors support history's verdict on Richard III. Richard's desire to be king gave him a potent motive to dispose of the princes. His prior murder of Hastings, a former associate who later opposed him, showed ruthlessness. It was impossible for anyone who was not a close associate of Richard's to have killed the princes because they were being kept in the Tower. Richard should therefore bear some of the responsibility for the deaths, since he placed the princes in the Tower.

To the popular mind, the legend was corroborated in 1674 when workmen in the Tower found the bones of two children. The bones in the Tower were declared to belong to the young princes and transferred to Westminster Abbey. Disinterred and examined by experts in 1933, the bones have been the subject of much dispute.

On the other hand, several factors favor Richard's defense. The princes might easily have been killed without Richard's knowledge or approval. There is no direct accusation, contemporary accounts being ambiguous or uncertain. Richard's general conduct as a fair governor is inconsistent with the alleged crimes. The precontract of marriage supports Richard. Victorious Henry Tudor failed to investigate the murders.

Finally, and perhaps most important of all, the general feeling persists that much of the evidence against Richard was distorted or biased. Henry VII himself had as much reason or more to want the princes dead.

A major part of Henry's claim to the English throne was that he was the only rightful living male heir of the Lancastrian-based line. After declaring the dead princes legitimate heirs, he married their elder sister, Edward's daughter Elizabeth, uniting the two warring factions. If the princes in the Tower were still alive, however, they held the true right of succession. It was vital to Henry that the children be legitimized only after they were dead and he was safely on the throne.

It becomes clearer, now, why the traditional accounts attributable to Tudor propaganda were necessary to justify the dynasty. The famous, traditional versions of Thomas More (who spent his childhood under the wing of John Morton, bishop of Ely, a sworn enemy of Richard III and later close henchman of Henry VII) and Shakespeare were written to flatter Tudor monarchs. Revisionist history to please those in power is hardly a new phenomenon. Part of the Tudor propaganda can actually be seen. Pictures of Richard III were actually altered to make him appear physically deformed.

"This is still an unsolved murder mystery," according to Aubrey Williamson's 1978 book *The Mystery of the Princes*. "It is the outstanding example," Williamson goes on, "of *assumption*, largely based on political propaganda, presented as *fact*."[6] According to A. P. Rossiter, "To think that we are seeing anything like sober history in this play is derisible naivety."[7] As Paul Kendall, a pro-Ricardian, concludes, "The available evidence admits of no decisive solution."

With characteristic fairness, sobriety, and style, Kendall elaborates: "What is inaccurate, misleading, and merely tiresome is for modern writers to declare flatly that Richard is guilty or to retain as fact the outworn tale of Thomas More. The problem goes more shades than are represented by the all-black or all-white which have hitherto usually been employed in attempts to solve this famous enigma."[8]

LEGAL DEBATE

What Shakespeare did to Richard III is not merely of academic historical interest. It is highly relevant to current legal and cultural developments. For more than fifteen years, television and films have used a controversial genre known as docudrama about historical events. As yet it is unclear how much First Amendment leeway a docudrama should receive, or how much fictionalization should be allowed in a work having the earmarks of factual truth and "presented as fact."

The King Richard effect is still at work, as Oliver Stone's film *JFK* shows. A docudrama of sorts, *JFK* provides one version of John F. Kennedy's assassination based on a controversial conspiracy theory of Jim Garrison, a prosecutor from Louisiana. When it was released, Stone's movie provoked much comment on the proper limits of dramatic license with the facts. Like *Richard III*, *JFK* is art and propaganda too. What if a generation of younger Americans, with no memory of 1963, were to form their ideas about John F. Kennedy's assassination solely from Oliver Stone's movie? Neither *Richard III* nor *JFK* stay close to the known facts; rather, they validate dark conjecture.

There are built-in constraints to this kind of debate. Thomas B. Costain, author of a balanced four-volume popular history of the Plantagenets, concludes in his final chapter that it is "unfortunate" that the only way to litigate the "indictment" of Richard III has been in the "Court of the Printed Word," with historians and writers acting as witnesses, as counsel, as pleaders, and finally as judges. Costain wonders what would the outcome be if Richard's case could be tried in court today under modern rules of evidence. "What a day it would be in court," Costain imagines, "if the central figures in this bizarre case could be summoned from the shades to take their turns on the stand and face a grueling examination and cross-examination."[9]

Costain's lament was answered in part by the BBC mock criminal trial of Richard III in 1984. That trial resulted in a verdict of not guilty. Perhaps the more interesting trial for us today would be an imaginary civil lawsuit by Richard III against Shakespeare and the Globe Theater for libel, slander, and invasion of privacy by portraying Richard in a false light.

At such a trial, the first question would, under our law, be whether Shakespeare's play was about a subject of general interest. To prevail on an invasion of privacy claim, a plaintiff must prove that a docudrama had no "public significance" or was not newsworthy. Privacy must inevitably give way unless the information does not command public interest. Since the events surrounding his reign are of public significance, Richard III could not get to first base on a strict privacy claim.

But Richard might have more of a chance under a false light and defamation claim. Even if invasion of privacy does not apply to a subject of general interest, a false light or defamation claim may arise if there is too much embellishment, fictionalization, or distortion so as to place the plaintiff in a false light. As far as defamation is concerned, where the subject involves a matter of legitimate public interest combined with an individual who exposes himself or herself to the risk of publicity, the plaintiff must prove that the statement was made with "actual malice," that is, that the statement is knowingly false or made with reckless disregard as to its truth or falsity.

Just imagine what it would be like to watch the privacy and defamation trial of *Richard III v. William Shakespeare et al.* All the evidence could then be put before the jury about the damage done to Richard's reputation. Each side could marshal its proofs, such as they exist. We can only contemplate with delight what testimony and documents might be introduced to show whether Shakespeare adequately verified his sources or whether he recklessly disregarded the truth or falsity of the facts he used about Richard. Ah, the mind so enjoys such dazzling thought experiments.

And yet when all the evidence is in, one still would soberly have to anticipate a verdict against Richard in this civil case, primarily because of the overarching importance of freedom of expression in our time. Contemporary attitudes toward the First Amendment have created a judicial atmosphere favorable to docudramas. As a result, publishers and broadcasters have generally prevailed in cases involving claims of harmful fictionalization in docudramas. Courts appear unconcerned with minor inaccuracies, guaranteeing "the leeway afforded an author who attempts to recount and popularize a historic event."[10]

Richard III's imaginary lawsuit against Shakespeare starkly sets forth the complex and daunting problems of defamation in fiction. Although the law in this field is far from settled, the relatively few decided cases agree that a plaintiff in a libel-in-fiction case must show that the defamatory publication identified the plaintiff. Of course, that is no barrier for our thought experiment: the plaintiff *is* the Richard III referred to in Shakespeare's play. In many other libel-in-fiction cases, identification is not so simple. The author may give a character a different name or otherwise try to disguise obvious identifying traits. But identification alone seems to be not enough.[11]

Identification alone is insufficient because a libel-in-fiction claim involves a confusing paradox. The plaintiff asserts an identification with the fictional character but denies that significant aspects of that character are true. The plaintiff must assert simultaneously that the story, novel, or play is "about" him or her to the extent that there are similarities between the plaintiff and the fictional character, but at the same time that "could not be about" the plaintiff because, in real life, he or she would never do the scandalous things ascribed to the character. The plaintiff's case thus becomes, "It's me, but it couldn't be me."[12] Put another way, Richard would have to claim that Shakespeare's play is about Richard, but that Richard was nothing like the awful character in Shakespeare's play.

This paradox was first articulated by a court in 1980 in *Geisler v. Petrocelli*. In the course of its opinion in *Geisler*, the court of appeals found a "disturbing irony" in such a case: "The more virtuous the victim of the libel, the less likely it will be that she will be able to establish this essential confusion in the mind of the third party."[13] The court's reference to "such a seeming contradiction" was the first time it appears in the legal authorities, and once mentioned, it has taken hold as the basic paradox of the libel-in-fiction field.

To overcome the ironies inherent in a libel-in-fiction claim, a New York court has proposed a hard test. The identity of the real and fictional personae, ruled the court, "must be so complete that the defamatory material becomes a plausible aspect of the real life plaintiff or suggestive of the plaintiff in significant ways."[14] The court went on to quote a law review article that stated, "Only when the immediate context of the allegedly defamatory statement convinces the reader of the statement's literal truth—when, that is, it ceases to be merely imaginary or plausible and begins to be believed—do damages to reputation, and thus liability, become possible."[15]

Like any plaintiff, Richard III would have a difficult time meeting such a standard. The test itself seems to be designed to minimize, if not exclude entirely, any possible libel-in-fiction plaintiffs. But freedom of speech is not the only precious freedom. Sometimes it is in tension with other fundamental rights. When such a clash occurs, we have to be intellectually honest with ourselves about what is involved. It is possible that our attachment to the principles of free expression can influence our judgment and temporarily hide the important values of reputation and privacy.

To be sure, defamation in fiction—such as would be raised by Richard III suing Shakespeare—is a thorny issue. In considering it, the courts have moved in different directions.[16] The trend seems to be against such cases, but the tentative results are far from conclusive. The final verdict on Richard III may depend on how that twentieth-century issue of libel law is ultimately resolved. Even if it is now impossible to reach any definite verdict, should it not be made clear that in all honesty the mystery of the princes has not been solved?

CULTURAL DEBATE

Surrounding the historical and legal debates over *Richard III* lurks a deeper and more fundamental cultural debate about the writing of history, biography, and other nonfiction generally. Should historical fiction be considered history in the conventional sense, and should it be judged as such? If history is, as historian Carl Becker once said, "a foreshortened and incomplete representation of reality,"[17] what distinguishes history from historical fiction? Might fictional history be "truer" than recorded history because of the novelist's special ability to capture essences of personality and motivation? Are facts more important than interpretations and resonances? Or if writers use real people and actual events, should they not be constrained by concern for truthfulness, by respect for the record and a judicious weighing of the possibilities? More broadly still, have we developed a growing habit of mind that refuses to acknowledge the old boundaries between reality and fiction?

These are questions of compelling interest. They have serious implications about the way we process reality and apprehend the world.[18] They make us think about Shakespeare's history plays and the possible differences between factual history and literary art. That is why an introduction to Bradley's *Shakespearean Tragedy* says, not by accident, "it is the paradox of the artist at work, showing truth by making lies."[19] It is easy to get caught in a confusing thicket of competing and seemingly inconsistent claims of factual accuracy and artistic vision.

I would propose a new, three-pronged way out of this literary-legal brier patch. My suggestion would be to identify and consider three different though related criteria: (1) genre, (2) nature of publication, and (3) expectations of readers or viewers. These interdependent factors point the way to a solution.

1. Genre

The controversy over factual accuracy stems in part from the ambiguity of art forms. Central to the criticism of certain art as inaccurate is the assumption that such art must be a recitation of accurate facts. But not all art carries—or should carry—the warning: "Caution. This artistic work contains some imaginary persons, events and conversations." Only certain forms of art depend on faithful history. It varies with the genre.

Fiction, poetry, and drama, for instance, all thrive without necessarily being anchored in historical facts, although such facts may supply a setting or background. Other genres, such as the nonfiction novel, blend fact and fiction. (Truman Capote's *In Cold Blood* and Norman Mailer's *Executioner's Song* are two well-known examples of the nonfiction novel.) Yet in all these genres, even those most dependent on imagination, the authors doubtless claim that they deal in truth and that their brand of truth is of a peculiarly profound and esoteric quality.[20] When Aristotle said that poetry is truer than history, he meant that literature supplied a more general truth than history. Literature renders in such a way as to make the understanding of its subject deeper, clearer, or more lasting. A true rendering of an inner reality is what a creative writer tries to convey in this type of work.

Other genres may call for careful and sensitive treatment. Autobiography, for example, is becoming more and more regarded as another form of prose fiction built on an overarching truth that is less "factual" than literary and psychological.[21] Film critics have acknowledged a distinction between artistic truth and factual accuracy. One film critic argued, in an article tellingly headlined "Facts Don't Always Give the True Story," that "films revolving around real individuals draw a distinction between what is authentic—technically faithful to the facts—and what is true." According to the critic, "the best of these films, even when they take liberties with facts, use real personalities to create a larger, more colorful reality than their source material may have had. On the other hand, when films are reverential about their models and slavish about their facts, they have a way of losing track of a larger truthfulness."[22]

Now we enter the difficult zone. Even historians debate whether a work of history must be scrupulously accurate or whether imaginative literary style, which may affect or distort factual accuracy, is permissible.[23] According to E. H. Carr, a leading English historian of the Russian Revolution, "The belief in a hard core of historical facts existing objectively and independently of the interpretation of the historian is a preposterous fallacy, but one which is very hard to eradicate."[24] Professional historians, whose task is to address facts and not fiction, thus disagree among themselves about the meaning and existence of faithful history. A creative and imaginative historian may use literary talent to subordinate facts to artistic or historical vision. Viewing history as having a literary as well as historical purpose, a writer may use artistic skills to mold facts with an eye toward the story's probability, coherence, and dramatic effect. But our tolerance is significantly different for journalism or other writing supposedly built on facts.

This difference is highlighted in the controversial libel suit in which the *New Yorker* magazine and one of its writers, Janet Malcolm, were sued for changing quotations and inventing conversations for articles.[25] The writer was quoted as saying that "she had acted only in an effort to get behind the facts to the truth."[26] Another account relates how "writers at *The New Yorker* have occasionally displayed a certain condescension toward the facts in their search for deeper truth," and that one writer, Alistair Reid, "admitted that he periodically fabricated facts in the magazine because 'there is a truth that is harder to get at and harder to get down towards than the truth yielded by fact.'"[27] After noting the widespread negative reaction to Reid's disclosure, one appellate judge wrote, "What Reid was criticized for doing pales by comparison to Malcolm's alleged transgression. . . . The criticisms leveled at Reid must fall far more harshly on a journalist who deliberately twists the words of real, named individuals she purports to be quoting."[28] After lower courts had thrown out the case on summary judgment before trial, the Supreme Court unanimously reversed and remanded the case for a jury trial in 1993, which ended in a unanimous verdict that the writer had fabricated five defamatory quotations.[29]

2. Nature of Publication

After genre comes the factor of where the art was published. An article in supermarket tabloids such as the *National Enquirer* or the *Star*, which regularly run stories about aliens giving birth, sightings of Elvis, and other scientific impossibilities, lacks a certain factual weight. It does not come with the imprimatur of accuracy that a nonfiction article in, say, the *New Yorker* has. The *New Yorker*, at least up until the Janet Malcolm litigation, had a "widely-acclaimed reputation for scrupulous accuracy

. . . that it nurtures assiduously."[30] In 1984 William Shawn, then the *New Yorker*'s editor, bragged, "We don't have a single fact presented as a fact that isn't one."[31]

But what about docudramas? "It's been noted time and time again," wrote a television critic, "that docudramas are generally, to put it delicately, flexible when it comes to facts."[32] People have learned to presume that docudramas are not necessarily completely accurate and that producers, scriptwriters, and directors have taken liberties for dramatic effect.

3. Expectations

Finally, we arrive at the real problem, the reader's or viewer's reasonable expectations. Advertising or marketing a book, a movie, a play, or a docudrama as a "true story" generates different expectations than advertising or marketing as "fiction." Readers and viewers are entitled to know what it is they are getting. They are left in a curiously uncertain position: are they reading history amplified by the empathy of the novelist or fiction dressed up in historical costume? By giving "categorical assurances to the reading public," Judge Alex Kozinski said in the Janet Malcolm case, "*The New Yorker* has induced a reasonable expectation of accuracy in the minds of sources and readers."[33]

If license is taken with the facts, an author has an obligation to use a disclaimer so as not to mislead his or her audience. This is exactly what author Joe McGinniss did with his controversial 1993 interpretive biography of Ted Kennedy, *The Last Brother*. Denied access to or cooperation by the subject or his family, McGinniss created some thoughts and dialogue and attributed them to figures in his book. A crucial point often overlooked is that McGinniss, unlike Janet Malcolm, told the reader precisely what he was doing, first in a prepublication excerpt and then in an explanatory author's note in the actual published book. McGinniss's readers thus knew exactly what they were getting. None of McGinniss's readers were tricked or deceived.[34]

Other authors, including Shakespeare, may not be so candid. Like a character in John Irving's novel *The World According to Garp*, readers might want to say to Shakespeare and other authors, "You have your own terms for what's fiction and what's fact, but do you think other people know your system?"

These three criteria—genre, nature of publication, and expectations of the public—can shed much needed light on the scope of an author's duty to the facts. The interplay of these criteria should resolve most, if not all, problems in this field. By measuring a particular work against these three factors we should be able to tell if ethics or the law have been violated. They are, for example, easily applied to *Richard III*.

In terms of genre, *Richard III* is a drama that, all other things being equal, need not be factually accurate. As for the nature of publication, the drama was, like other plays of the time, performed on the London stage, which surely did not carry with it any imprimatur of factual accuracy. Later publication in written form added nothing warranting the play's historical accuracy. The public's expectation, the last of our three factors, would probably have been to assume the truth of Richard's awful portrait. After all, a century of Tudor propaganda had conditioned the English to find Shakespeare's view of Richard III congenial. Thus we could conclude that Shakespeare did not, in this particular context, violate our criteria.

Shakespeare took one side—the fiction writer's side—on these legal issues. Today he would ally himself with Gore Vidal (author of *Lincoln* and other historical fiction), Don DeLillo (author of *Libra*), Simon Schama (author of *Dead Certainties*), and others, all of whom have subordinated facts to the telling of what they regard as deeper truth. Their intuitive refusal to spoil a good story by slavish adherence to fact enchants us. A modern Shakespeare would no doubt be assailed for his infidelity to facts by scholars and historians who believe facts are objective things, and that they differ from interpretations and opinions, which are inherently more subjective and impressionistic. But he would be in good company in a debate likely to continue for a long time without closure.[35]

Chapter Ten

MUCH ADO ABOUT SLANDER

OTHELLO AND MUCH ADO ABOUT NOTHING

IT IS HIGHLY ironic that Shakespeare should be accused of damaging Richard III's or anyone else's reputation. Concern for damaged reputation is an important, familiar, and repeated theme in Shakespeare's own work. It shows up in his plays, both tragedies and comedies, typically as slander of a woman's sexual reputation. Even his sonnets contain the same theme.

In the sonnets we probably learn Shakespeare's true feelings on the subject of damaged reputation, unfiltered and unmediated through a dramatic persona. In Sonnet 70, he writes:

> That thou are blamed shall not be thy defect,
> For slander's mark was ever yet the fair So thou be good,
>   slander doth but approve
> Thy worth the greater.

In light of what he is alleged to have done to Richard III's reputation, Shakespeare's stance in Sonnet 70 may seem inconsistent. But the attitude Shakespeare takes in Sonnet 70—that slander of a blameless woman only shows her virtue—is at least the same stance he takes in *Othello* and *Much Ado about Nothing*.

REPUTATION, REPUTATION, REPUTATION

On October 12, 1991, at about 5:00 P.M., Senator Alan Simpson, a member of the Senate Judiciary Committee, told Supreme Court nominee Clarence Thomas to take heart and read Shakespeare, particularly *Othello*. The occasion was the memorable second round of hearings into Thomas's fitness to sit as a justice of the Supreme Court. The second round of Senate hearings grew out of Anita Hill's lurid accusations of sexual harassment by her ex-boss Thomas while he was chairman of the Equal Employment Opportunity Commission. Watching the televised hearings in almost a hypnotic trance, the nation saw Senator Simpson, a lover of Shakespeare, tell Thomas he would find in *Othello* comfort for a troubled heart.

Then Senator Simpson proceeded to read aloud the following famous lines from *Othello*:

> Good name in man and woman, dear my lord,
> Is the immediate jewel of their souls,
> Who steals my purse steals trash; 'tis something, nothing;
> 'Twas mine, 'tis his, and has been slave to thousands.
> But he that filches from me my good name
> Robs me of that which not enriches him
> And makes me poor indeed.
>
> (3.3.160–66)

Senator Simpson obviously meant the passage from *Othello* to ease Judge Thomas's distress as his reputation came under awful assault and to show the media and the public the terrible damage that can be done to someone's good name. Surely that would be the most likely interpretation of what Simpson had intended, especially since the senator, a Wyoming Republican, was one of Judge Thomas's most vigorous supporters.

But anyone familiar with the whole of *Othello* and not just the single passage quoted by Simpson might put a different spin on the Thomas hearings. As Simpson knew, the words he cited were spoken by Iago to destroy Othello and Desdemona. With this knowledge in mind, one so inclined—a skeptic or a cynic, perhaps—might think of Senator Simpson as Iago placing each word carefully in the ear of Judge Thomas as Othello to inflame his anger against Thomas's accuser. Then, a Shakespearean free spirit might conclude, they both went after Anita Hill as Desdemona. Either reading of events is possible.

Senator Simpson may or may not have seen the New York Shakespeare Festival's production of *Othello* only a few months earlier. If he did, he would have found that *Othello* made the outdoor Delacorte Theater in Central Park echo with the sounds of wild jealousy, shake with the rage of uncontrolled anger, and yield to the deceit of misleading appearances. An American senator might well have felt at home.

Raul Julia was his characteristically magnificent self as the Moor tortured by jealousy, "the green-eyed monster" (3.3.192). But it was punk-like Christopher Walken whose leather-jacketed figure, strutting and swaggering though insecure, created a totally new, revelatory stage persona for the evil Iago. As we observed Walken's Iago work his famous villainy, we realized that *Othello*, as much as it is about anger, jealousy, and false appearances, is also a play about slander.

Slander in fact drives the play. Having been passed over for promotion, Iago seeks revenge on Othello by falsely accusing Othello's wife, Desdemona, of having an affair with Cassio, who got the job that Iago wanted.

This accusation, at first slyly and tentatively insinuated, but then boldly built on manufactured (if, to our eyes, thin) evidence, gnaws at the proud Othello until, overcome with jealous rage, he murders Desdemona. After this tragic deed, Othello learns of Iago's perfidy and of the false nature of the accusations and kills himself.

Take away the slander and there is no play, but to see the slander is just the start. With its insight into human nature, the play clarifies certain aspects of the law of slander. The play's action may even help explain why the First Amendment, no matter how much we believe in free expression, should not wipe out all libel and slander suits. Viewed in this light, Othello becomes a literary vehicle for thinking about the law of defamation.

This is not to say that other legal themes are unable to be mined from the rich ore of Othello. On the contrary, one could write about Iago's treachery toward Othello as a paradigm of breach of fiduciary duty. Or focusing on what led Othello to react the way he did, one could comment on the problems of fake proof. And considering Othello's rough treatment of Desdemona, one could even discuss the legal problem of battered women. But as interesting as each of these other legal themes may be, none of them deals with the fundamental legal theme of Othello: slander.

Slander depends on damaged reputation, and reputations are damaged throughout Othello. The play starts with Iago's resentment over the damage to his reputation when Cassio rather than he becomes Othello's lieutenant. Then Cassio loses his reputation—and position—by fighting and being drunk (at Iago's instigation) while on duty. Of course, it is on Desdemona's reputation that the play focuses. But Othello's reputation—as a judicious military leader and the husband of a faithful wife—hangs in the balance as well.

Othello's reputation has made him what he is. An outsider on several counts, he has achieved high status nonetheless because of his military reputation. Even his romance with Desdemona fed on tales of his military exploits. In the play itself, Othello performs no great military feat. The great victory over the enemy fleet is due to a sudden storm, not Othello's military genius. Still, he gains the credit.

Othello is a proud man who depends on his reputation. Reputation is his very essence. He sees himself in the opinions of the men about him. He is "other directed." His rewards are in the glory he receives from others, and he believes he deserves their admiration.[1]

But what happens if his reputation changes? A proud man has a tough time dealing with disgrace. Someone dependent on reputation becomes a slave of public opinion. When public opinion changes, he is lost. This part of the lesson Othello—and we—come to learn.

Cassio, Othello's former second-in-command, stresses the importance of reputation. Having been cashiered for misbehavior, Cassio bemoans his fate to, of all people, Iago, who engineered Cassio's downfall:

> Reputation, reputation, reputation, O, I ha' lost
> my reputation, I ha' lost the immortal part of myself,
> and what remains is bestial! My reputation, Iago, my reputation.
>
> (2.3.256–59)

Cassio's lament for his reputation is the sort of feeling behind some of our Supreme Court's attitude toward reputation. "Society has a pervasive and strong interest," the Court stated in 1966, "in preventing and redressing attacks upon reputation."[2] In the same case, Justice Potter Stewart, who charted an independent path on the Supreme Court, wrote a separate opinion in which he stressed that "the individual's right to the protection of his own good name reflects no more than our basic concept of the essential dignity and worth of every human being—a concept at the root of any decent system of ordered liberty."[3]

Iago, however, makes the case for each of us to be independent of public opinion. "As I am an honest man," responds Iago to Cassio's wailing, "I thought you had received / some bodily wound. There is more sense in that than / in reputation" (2.3.260–62). To Iago, at this moment anyway, lost reputation is no loss unless we make it so: "Reputation is an idle and most false / imposition, oft got without merit and lost without /deserving. You have lost no reputation at all unless / you equate yourself such a loser" (2.3.262–66).

Of course Iago is right—up to a point. Reputation does not necessarily reflect true virtue. And if someone is too dependent on reputation, too other directed, then that person is not really free at all, but a slave of public opinion—a fickle master at best. But taken at face value, Iago's comments here wipe out defamation as a cause of action.

Iago's belittling of reputation to Cassio contrasts sharply with what Iago says elsewhere. When Othello presses Iago to spell out the accusation against Desdemona, Iago, in his most famous speech, gives the classic defense of reputation, which Senator Simpson quoted to Clarence Thomas. In that speech, Iago calls people's reputation "the immediate jewel of their souls," while just one act earlier, he called reputation "an idle and false imposition." Which view does Iago really hold? Or does the answer depend on whatever view serves his purpose of the moment?

Iago intuitively understands how slander can damage a reputation. "Work on," he cries. "My medicine works. Thus credulous fools are caught, / And many worthy and chaste dames even thus, / All guiltless, meet reproach" (4.1.43–45).

Othello helps us understand why slander suits exist. All we have to do is look at Othello's reaction. He becomes, for all practical purposes, tem-

porarily insane with jealousy. Even if we think Othello acted on too little
evidence, we see here the epitome of the crime of passion, the ordinarily
sedate mind deranged by jealousy and sexual insecurity. In this sense,
Othello shows us a vivid picture of human nature, and human nature
being what it is, that anger and violence flow from certain accusations.
Iago's wife spits at her husband, "And your reports have set the murder
on" (5.2.194).

None of these mitigating factors necessarily means that Othello should
not be held responsible for his violent behavior. If Othello had sur-
vived and been tried for Desdemona's murder, it is unlikely that he would
have been acquitted. The best defenses he would have under our law
would be temporary insanity and heat of passion, but neither of them is
a sure winner. Much would depend on which particular test of insanity were used. And as to the heat of passion defense, it could be argued
that Othello's provocation (suspicion of adultery) does not appear serious enough to be legally sufficient, and there seems to have been enough
time between Othello's suspicion and his killing of Desdemona for a reasonable man to have cooled off.[4] But guilty or not, Othello wins our
empathy.

Jealousy, an easily recognizable emotion, makes *Othello* a constantly
popular play. Unlike some other themes in Shakespeare, jealousy has
never died. For this reason, according to Hazlitt, *Othello* "excites our
sympathy in an extraordinary degree. The moral it conveys has a closer
application to the concerns of human life than that of almost any other of
Shakespeare's plays."[5]

Part of the cause of Othello's jealousy may be the insecure male attitude toward female sexuality. In *Shakespeare Our Contemporary*, the
Polish writer Jan Kott insightfully observes that Desdemona may be a
victim of her own sensuality. Although Desdemona is faithful, she creates
an erotic climate that envelops not only Othello, but all men in her
orbit—Iago, Cassio, and Roderigo. Her sensuality and eroticism surprise,
amaze, and horrify Othello. By being erotic toward Othello, Desdemona
strikes him as having something of the slut in her. The more sensual Desdemona acts with Othello, the more readily Othello believes that she can,
or has, betrayed him.[6]

Precisely to prevent the tragedy of *Othello*, to avoid the violent consequences of avenging a damaged reputation, we have a legal cause of action for slander. The existence of such a cause of action operates as an
important safety valve. Redress in the courts, with all its attendant problems and defects, is still better than self-help. Vindication through the
legal system is a vital concept that, in the practical sense of keeping the
peace, justifies a cause of action for slander.

This reason alone, rooted in a realistic understanding of human nature, is enough to turn back the theoretical and abstract constitutional arguments occasionally advanced against the existence of suits for defamation. There are those, some of whom are intelligent, educated people of goodwill, who argue that the mere existence of a cause of action for libel or slander violates the First Amendment guarantees of free speech and free press. Justices Hugo Black and William Douglas took that extreme position with respect to the reputations of public figures. Others would go further and eliminate entirely the causes of action in private defamation cases, too. But *Othello* provides a clear and convincing case for approaching such a position with great skepticism, lest unavailability of legal redress lead to private violence.

Othello also makes us wonder about who has standing to sue. Desdemona, had she lived, could have sued Iago for slander. But what about Othello? Perhaps he could have argued that his reputation was hurt by being slandered as a cuckold. Or that his privacy was invaded by Iago portraying him in a false light. Maybe Othello would have had a claim for intentional infliction of emotional distress or prima facie tort (a catch-all legal category for misconduct that does not fall into any other category). After all, he threatens Iago, "If thou dost slander *her* and torture *me*" (3.3.373 [emphasis added]). And tortured Othello certainly was.

Othello asks the question whether someone is justified in telling one spouse that the other spouse has been unfaithful. For example, suppose you see your friend's husband at a restaurant holding hands with and kissing another woman. Should you tell your friend? In legal terms, the precise issue would be whether the speaker was "privileged" to pass on the information. Granted, Iago never believed in good faith the bad news he was giving Othello, but what if he had? And what if, despite Iago's good faith, the news about Desdemona had been false?

These issues became central to a 1930 English case, *Watt v. Longsdon.*[7] Decided by King's Bench, the various judges' opinions in *Watt* are a collection of short essays on morals as well as an appellate opinion about conditional privilege in libel cases.

The plaintiff, whose wife was in England, was managing director of a Scottish oil company operation in Morocco. The defendant was a director of the company in England. Another executive of the company in Morocco wrote a letter to the defendant in England in which he described marital infidelities of the plaintiff. The defendant showed the letter to the chairman of the company and to the plaintiff's wife, who sued the plaintiff for divorce. Although he did not take any steps to verify the accusations, the defendant believed them to be true. The plaintiff sued for libel.

In the lower court, the defendant won. The trial judge ruled that the publications were privileged and that there was no evidence of malice to go to the jury. On appeal, the three King's Bench judges considered the communication to the company chairman separately from the communication to the plaintiff's wife. All three judges held that the communication to the chairman was privileged, and all three held that the communication to the wife was not.

According to Judge Scrutton, "It is impossible to say" a stranger or a friend is "always under a moral or social duty" to communicate to a husband or wife information he receives as to the conduct of the other marriage partner; "it is equally impossible to say he is never under such a duty." His Lordship then ruled that "it cannot . . . be the duty even of a friend to communicate all the gossip the friend hears at men's clubs or women's bridge parties to one of the spouses affected." Winding up, Scrutton concluded that the decision must turn on the circumstances of each case, the judge being much influenced by the "general rule" that it is "not desirable for any one, even a mother-in-law, to interfere in the affairs of man and wife."

Judge Greer agreed. In his judgment, "no right minded man in the position of the defendant, a friend of the plaintiff and of his wife, would have thought it right to communicate the horrible accusations" contained in the letter to the plaintiff's wife. The information came "from a very doubtful source," Judge Greer continued, and "no reasonably right-minded person could think it his duty, without obtaining some corroboration of the story, and without first communicating with the plaintiff, to pass on these outrageous charges of marital infidelity of a gross kind" to the plaintiff's wife.

The whole theme of *Othello* can be summed up in terms of reputation. If there is one line that captures the essence of *Othello*, it is what Desdemona says, then in jest, to Iago when she arrives in Cyprus, a jest that takes on tragic dimensions in light of later events. Desdemona jokes, "O fie upon thee, slanderer!" That line is the play's essence.

On Filching Iago's Good Name

Iago's baneful influence grows and grows, even reaching to the *New York Times*. Hidden inconspicuously on the bottom of an inside page in December 1985 was a "Legal Notes" column by *Times* legal reporter David Margolick. Under the subhead "A Question of Value," he described a criminal case that turned on the meaning of robbery. A trial judge in New York City had ruled that snatching scrap paper with names and telephone numbers of clients could constitute robbery under New York law. The defendant's lawyer had argued unsuccessfully that the negligible value of the items taken undercut the notion of theft. The jury acquitted.

But like Homer on occasion, this time even Margolick, the astute reporter, nodded. His uncharacteristic slip came at the start of the story.

For his lead, Margolick wrote, "It was Polonius in Shakespeare's *Hamlet* who said, 'Who steals my purse steals trash.' " It was a clever and apt way to begin an article about a judge's legal definition of robbery. The only thing wrong was the literary reference.

The line occurs in *Othello*, as part of Iago's "good name" speech, the one cited by Senator Simpson. Iago's speech eloquently states the value of a person's reputation, explaining in unforgettable language and imagery the difference between loss of property and loss of name. It is one of those passages from Shakespeare quoted again and again.

Not surprisingly, it is a favorite quotation of lawyers and judges. The legal context is usually not confirmation hearings for Supreme Court justices or the criminal law. Rather, Iago's speech shows up most often in defamation cases, where reputation is at stake. Iago's lines are the classic statement on that subject.

The Supreme Court knows Iago's famous lines. In 1990, the Court's opinion in the leading case of *Milkovich v. Lorain Journal Co.* quoted it in full as part of preliminary remarks on the history of the law of defamation.[8] *Milkovich* involved the issue of whether, and if so how, fact and opinion should be treated differently for the purposes of libel under the free speech guarantees of the First Amendment. Writing for the majority, Chief Justice William Rehnquist set forth the complete text of Iago's "good name" speech to illustrate the traditionally high value put on reputation in our culture.

Iago's speech also cropped up in a 1984 New York case involving Jacqueline Kennedy Onassis. President Kennedy's widow sued in state court to enjoin an advertising campaign for Christian Dior designer products. In the advertising campaign, the defendants intentionally used a photograph of a woman who looked remarkably like Mrs. Onassis, so as to convey the false impression that Mrs. Onassis endorsed Dior products. In ruling for Mrs. Onassis, Judge Edward Greenfield wrote: "Shakespeare may not have been aware of advertising techniques, media hard-sell, or personal endorsements for product promotion, but the words he put in Iago's mouth were right on target."[9] The judge then quoted them.

Indeed, frequency of repetition has made Iago's comments almost a legal cliché. In a 1978 case, for instance, the highest court in New York State said, "In institutions, as with men and women, a good name is the 'immediate jewel of their souls.' "[10] Similarly, a California court in 1977 quoted Iago in full in a case involving "deprogramming" a cult follower, saying, "The same comparison may be drawn with a theft of one's beliefs."[11]

One court's reliance on Iago's "good name" speech deserves special note. In a 1978 federal case from Pennsylvania, a landlord sued a former tenant to recover the cost of cleaning the property at the end of the lease.

Judge Fogel began his opinion by quoting Iago's speech in full and itali-
cizing the line "Who steals my purse steals trash; 'tis something, nothing." The judge continued:

> The subject of this lawsuit concerns no one's good name; it does concern
> trash. While the actors in this saga do not quite reach the dramatic heights
> of an Othello or an Iago, the bitterness generated by this dispute between
> landlord and tenant with respect to the responsibility for cleaning up indus-
> trial land has produced quite a scenario (and has also provided us with more
> than one sideshow). It is the consequence of a long-standing business rela-
> tionship gone sour.[12]

Nor are Iago's comments about reputation his only claim to legal fame.
At least two courts have quoted Iago when faced with the task of evaluating a witness's credibility by reference to his demeanor.[13] In both cases,
the courts compared themselves to Othello as described by Iago:

> The Moor is of a free and open nature,
> That thinks men honest that but seem to be so,
> And will as tenderly be led by th' nose
> As asses are.
>
> (1.3.391–94)

Another court dealing with the credibility of a witness quoted Iago's line
that "men are men. The best sometimes forget" (2.3.234).[14]

Given the fame of Iago's speech, it is hard to confuse Iago with Polonius. One character is an arch villain who plots to plant in Othello's mind
a corroding belief in his wife's fidelity. The other is a pompous old fool
fond of spouting shopworn advice and of devising shabby schemes. No
two Shakespearean characters could be more different.

Even so, Shakespeare gives a passage to Polonius that would have been
fit for Margolick to cite. The case Margolick wrote about for his newspaper grew out of a street scuffle while the victim was going to make a
telephone call. The victim collided with the defendant, who then knocked
the victim down and took the papers he was carrying. With such facts,
Margolick could have appropriately quoted Polonius from the scene in
which he gives his son Laertes a "few precepts" to keep in mind while
away from home. Among those precepts is this one:

> Beware
> Of entrance to a quarrel, but being in,
> Bear't that th'opposèd may beware of thee.
>
> (Hamlet, 1.3.65–67)

Advice to avoid quarrels is good advice and quite relevant to a case having its roots in a street fight.

Poor Iago! Shakespeare makes him the embodiment of evil. With Iago, as with Richard III, Shakespeare paints a vivid picture of wickedness, a nature twisted by hate and envy. Iago's villainous legacy is accurately reflected in a comment by a federal judge in a 1981 prisoner's rights case, who said the petitioner "resembles a modern-day Iago . . . , sowing mischief wherever he goes."[15]

At least we can give Iago proper credit for, if nothing else, his good lines. His horrible reputation down through the centuries in no way erases the power and eloquence with which Shakespeare endows Iago's speech. To attribute Iago's greatest lines to a buffoon like Polonius is to filch from Iago the little good that is in his name; it is to rob Iago of that one part of his reputation that remains untainted.

WRONGED, SLANDERED, AND UNDONE

Although we tend to think of *Othello* as the Shakespearean play most relevant to slander, damage to reputation is as crucial to *Much Ado about Nothing* as it is to *Othello*. No doubt *Othello* is a greater play, but Kenneth Branagh's spectacular 1993 film of *Much Ado* helped show many viewers that the connecting thread of slander is strong. *Much Ado* virtually turns upon the law of defamation, and it has more than *Othello* to tell us about that legal subject.

Shakespeare leaves no room for doubting the vital role of slander in the play. He repeats the word *slander* incessantly, and it is the key to dramatic action. Count Claudio, a favorite of Prince Don Pedro, has the prince's blessing and encouragement to marry Hero, the maidenly daughter of Leonato. But the prince's evil half-brother, Don John, searching for a way to upset his brother's plans, hatches a nasty scheme to prevent the wedding from taking place. Don John creates the misimpression that virtuous Hero has another lover who visits her the night before her scheduled wedding to Claudio.

Don John falsely tells Don Pedro and Claudio of Hero's alleged infidelity. When the prince and Claudio refuse to believe him, Don John asks them to accompany him that night—the night before the wedding—to observe Hero's window. During the evening, one of Don John's servants comes to Hero's window according to a prearranged plan and, under the watchful eyes of Don Pedro and Claudio, has a lover's conversation with a woman who under cover of darkness appears to be Hero. Unbeknownst to Don Pedro and Claudio, the woman is not Hero, but Hero's maid, Margaret, who is in on Don John's plan.

Don John's charade fools Don Pedro and Claudio. Convinced that Hero is far from the modest maid she seems to be, a furious Claudio decides to shame her at the wedding ceremony the next day. In the Branagh movie, the prearranged tryst with Hero's maid looks like it would have convinced anyone. Yet we are left with the disturbing feeling that Claudio, like Othello, cruelly overreacts based on too little evidence and, like a cad, behaves abominably.

The ceremony starts off well enough until Friar Francis asks the usual question: "If either of you know any inward impediment why / you should not be conjoined, I charge you on your / souls to utter it" (4.1.12–14). Shortly after this statement by the friar, Claudio announces to his stunned and innocent fiancée and her family that he refuses to marry her. "Give not this rotten orange to your friend," Claudio barks at Hero's father, Leonato (4.1.32).

"Would you not swear," Claudio rages on,

> All you that see her, that she were a maid,
> By these exterior shows? But she is none.
> She knows the heat of a luxurious bed.
> Her blush is guiltiness, not modesty.
>
> (4.1.39–42)

Claudio declines to "knit my soul to an approvèd wanton" (4.1.44). To Hero, who has no idea what is going on, Claudio cuttingly says:

> You seem . . .
> As chaste as is the bud ere it be blown.
> But you are more intemperate in your blood
> Than Venus or those pampered animals
> That rage in savage sensuality.
>
> (4.1.57–61)

Prince Don Pedro, silent up to this point, dubs Hero a "common stale" (4.1.65), an Elizabethan phrase for prostitute. And Don John, who knows how false the accusations are, vouches that "these things are true" (4.1.67).

By putting this slander at the heart of *Much Ado*, Shakespeare has given us a superb opportunity and a dramatic setting within which to reconsider, in light of his own artistic use of it, one of the oddest and most mixed-up concepts in the law: defamation per se. This concept, according to modern treatise writers, "is bound to lead to confusion,"[16] and is surrounded by a "crazy quilt of confusion."[17] "No concept in the law of defamation," adds one treatise, "has created more confusion."[18]

In the realm of defamation law, that is saying a lot, for, as *Prosser and Keeton on Torts*, probably the leading legal treatise in the field of torts, points out, "There is a great deal of the law of defamation that makes no sense. It contains anomalies and absurdities for which no legal writer has ever had a kind word."[19]

The charge made against Hero in *Much Ado about Nothing*—that she has not been chaste—occupies a peculiar niche in the law. It is one of the four types of oral accusations known to the law as slander per se. In addition to "imputation of unchastity to a woman," the other three categories of slander per se are: (a) statements that someone committed a crime; (b) statements tending to injure someone in his or her trade, business, profession, office, or calling; and (c) statements that someone has a "loathsome disease," traditionally either venereal disease or leprosy.

To classify an accusation as slander per se brings certain consequences. For the four types of slander in the per se category, no pleading or proof of "special damages," of actual harm to reputation, or of any other damage or financial loss is needed as a prerequisite to recover damages. If a statement qualifies as slander per se, damage is presumed, and that presumption of damage is the hallmark of slander per se. The term "slander per se" starts, therefore, with the nature of the charges made.

Confusion arises from the failure to distinguish slander per se from libel per se. Slander refers to an oral statement, libel to a written one, but that is not the relevant distinction for "per se" purposes. Unlike slander per se, which depends only on whether the defamatory charge falls within one of the four specific slander categories, libel per se requires the writing's defamatory meaning to be apparent from the statement itself. If the defamatory meaning can be understood only by referring to extrinsic facts, it is not libel per se. Libel per se, like slander per se, can support a cause of action without "special damages," that is, actual out-of-pocket losses.

The distinctions between slander per se and libel per se produce results that are often irrational, inconsistent, and hard to explain. For example, since different tests apply, the same statement can be slander per se but not libel per se, and vice versa. One statement may be actionable per se if slander (because it falls within one of the four common law categories) but not actionable per se if libel (because the defamatory meaning is not clear on its face). Another statement may be actionable per se if libel (because the defamatory meaning is clear on its face) but not actionable per se if slander (because it is not within one of the four categories). The reason for such anomalies and inconsistencies is not to be found in logic.

Slander per se has its own illogic. The categories of slander per se are to a great extent arbitrary and out of date. Exactly how the four classes of slander per se achieved their special status is unclear. But that process, murky as it seems to us today, occurred while Shakespeare was living and writing. English defamation law was rapidly changing in Shakespeare's day.

In the sixteenth century the ecclesiastical courts, which had long exercised jurisdiction over defamation, lost power to the common law courts, which began to take defamation cases during the reign of Henry VIII. As the two types of courts competed for jurisdiction, the rule developed that a common law action for slander required proof of "temporal" as opposed to "spiritual" damage. This led to the general rule that someone cannot sue for slander unless actual damage is proved. As a way of extending their jurisdiction, the common law courts carved out exceptions (for the three categories of slander about crime, loathsome disease, and one's trade or business) that would come within the reach of common law courts rather than ecclesiastical courts. By the end of the sixteenth century, when Shakespeare was in his prime, the common law courts had wrested jurisdiction over most of these cases away from the church.[20]

Various theories try to explain the presumption of damages in these three particular categories. One recognizes that by their nature such words are especially likely to cause pecuniary, or "temporal," rather than "spiritual" loss.[21] Another theory is that each category involves circumstances in which it would be difficult to trace specific financial loss.[22] In 1978 a Delaware court stated that "the unifying characteristic of the categories is the tendency of the slander to isolate the object of the defamation from society."[23] Prosser and Keeton say it is unknown whether the categories were adopted for these reasons, or merely to slow the flow of slander suits.[24] Whatever the theory, the categories of slander per se now seem arbitrary.

Part of the rapid legal change in Shakespeare's time concerned how to deal with imputing unchastity to a woman, the slander at issue in *Much Ado*, which was not one of the three original categories of slander per se. On the contrary, the rule was firmly established at common law that a slanderous charge of unchastity was not actionable per se. In Shakespeare's day, English law regarded an accusation of unchastity as purely a "spiritual matter"—that is, a sin—and so it was not actionable without proof of "temporal" damage, such as the loss of a particular marriage.[25] Three leading cases in English law, decided in 1593, 1599, and 1614, all stated this proposition of law while Shakespeare was at the height of his powers.[26]

Presumably, Shakespeare, with all his many legal contacts, was familiar with this rule of law. Might it be too much to suggest that Shakespeare, looking for a topic for a play in the late 1590s, came upon one of those actual cases for the idea for *Much Ado*? For most Shakespeare scholars, it would. Most scholars say the Bard took the best of the play from any number of literary sources. Yet the traditional view may be based on a false premise: the academic notion that the creative writer invariably draws out of the library a batch of books and laboriously patches together a play from these sources.

But it is at least possible that Shakespeare was stimulated, if only in part, by another, unliterary source. After all, the list of novels, stories, and plays inspired by real life events and actual law cases stretches to infinity. Flaubert relied to some extent on a newspaper account for *Madame Bovary*. Theodore Dreiser's *An American Tragedy* drew on a case reported from upstate New York and is set there. Herman Melville's *Moby Dick* had its origin in a press account.[27] If we are honest about the intellectual process—and mystery—of the creative writer, we have to allow for the possibility that Shakespeare picked up the incidents that he wove into *Much Ado about Nothing* from written or oral reports of a contemporary law case.

Always remember Shakespeare's several links with law and lawyers. Perhaps the dramatist overheard some lawyers at the Inns of Court chattering about an important new case. Or perhaps Shakespeare's imagination was stimulated by a written report of a judicial decision. In 1898 Rudyard Kipling suggested that one of Shakespeare's plays, *The Tempest*, grew out of an account of a contemporary shipwreck. The inspiration for *Much Ado about Nothing* may well have come from a real life slander case. With all of the talk and writing about the changes in the law of slander just as Shakespeare was constantly looking for material for a new play, it would have been strange if some of this had not found a reflection in *Much Ado about Nothing*. For Shakespeare's times, such judicial decisions about slander may have been comparable to the impact for our times of Supreme Court decisions on the right to abortion.

Writing *Much Ado* in 1598 or 1599, Shakespeare could well have had in mind the crucial and strikingly parallel case of *Davies v. Gardiner*, which had been decided in 1593.[28] So important was this case that it is still discussed today in widely used legal treatises.[29] The facts sound familiar: a woman engaged to be married is falsely accused of having an illegitimate child and loses her marriage as a result. *Davies v. Gardiner* appears to be the first case of slander for pecuniary damage rather than for the insult.

The court held in *Davies v. Gardiner* that the words do not impute an offense cognizable in the common law courts, but permitted the plaintiff to recover her special damages, that is, the loss of the marriage prevented as a consequence of the scandalous statements. What makes the case so crucial is that it is the decision in which the common law courts resolved to entertain actions where imputation was one of merely spiritual offenses, if special damages were proven. This was a major event, marking the triumph of the common law courts over the church in the realm of defamation.

Another, personal reason exists for thinking Shakespeare had at least a nodding acquaintance with this area of law. In 1613—about fourteen years after Shakespeare wrote *Much Ado about Nothing* and only three years after he wrote *The Winter's Tale*—Shakespeare's elder daughter,

Susanna, a married woman, started a defamation suit because someone had falsely accused her of marital infidelity. For reasons that are unclear, Susanna brought her slander suit in an ecclesiastical court, the Consistory Court at Worcester. She sued John Lawe for spreading rumors that she had "the running of the reins" (gonorrhea) and had been "naught [immoral] with Rafe Smith." Lawe failed to show up in court and was excommunicated. Like Hero in *Much Ado* and Hermione in *The Winter's Tale*, Susanna Shakepeare ultimately won out.

In time, modern statutes and case law created the fourth category of slander per se about female unchastity. England added this category in 1891 with the Slander of Women Act. Most jurisdictions have accomplished the same objective. The New York statute, now embodied in section 77 of the state's civil rights law, originally became law in 1871. It states: "In an action of slander of a woman imputing unchastity to her, it is not necessary to allege or prove special damages." Significantly, many of these changes occurred during the Victorian era, during which society held a special attitude toward woman and sex.

Even though the law of his own day was against him, Shakespeare made a good case in *Much Ado* for presuming damages when a woman's chastity is falsely impugned. Hero as a plaintiff would have met the restrictive legal rule in effect at the end of the sixteenth century. Since Claudio refused to marry her, Hero could even satisfy the legal requirement then in effect under *Davies v. Gardiner*, that she point to the loss of a particular marriage. Hero suffered "temporal" damage. But she suffered more.

So disastrous is the allegation against Hero that those closest to her ostracize her as a result. Her fiancé angrily—if a bit hastily and idiotically—breaks off the engagement. Her father disowns her. "Why, doth not every earthly thing / Cry shame upon her?" Leonato shrieks (4.1.21–22). "Who smirchèd thus and mired in infamy, / I might have said, 'No part of it is mine' " (4.1.134–35). Her cousin Beatrice, while always believing in Hero, assesses the impact in dire phrases. Beatrice attacks Claudio as "a villain, that / hath slandered, scorned, dishonoured my kinswoman" (4.1.302–3). As for Hero, cries Beatrice, "she is wronged, she is slandered, / she is undone" (4.1.312–13).

The effect on Hero is incalculable, and Shakespeare compares it to death. On hearing the charges for the first time at the wedding, she faints. At the suggestion of Friar Lawrence, to "change slander to remorse" (4.1.213), Hero pretends to have died from the slander, and her death from slander becomes a major theme of the play. In a passage of great psychological penetration, the friar describes Hero as "dying . . . upon the instant that she was accused . . . she died upon his words" (4.1.216–25). Another character repeats the same point: "She is dead, slandered to death by villains" (5.1.88). One miscreant echoes: "The / lady is dead upon mine and my master's false / accusations" (5.1.233–35).

The death-from-slander theme continues. Claudio, reading from a scroll, recites:

> Done to death by slanderous tongues
> Was the Hero that here lies . . .
> So the life that died with shame
> Lives in death with glorious fame.
>
> (5.3.3–8)

Her father adds: "She died, my lord, but whiles her slander lived" (5.4.66). And even Hero, on reappearing, states: "One Hero died defiled but I do live, / And surely as I live, I am a maid" (5.4.63–64).

Shakespeare's linking of death to slander shows deep understanding of human nature and experience. Public embarrassment, shame, and humiliation generate strong inward reactions. How many times in our own lives have we heard others say or felt ourselves like saying, "I could have died of embarrassment"? And how many times have we, sadly, heard or read about someone in disgrace who feels driven to something as drastic as suicide? In 1962, recognizing the power of defamation, Pope John XXIII said: "Do not kill! Neither with the sword nor with the word nor with the press." Not just Hero, but all of us are "done to death by slanderous tongues."

Hero's father's reaction is the most intense. Says he to Claudio: "Thy slander hath gone through and through her heart" (5.1.68), adding, "Death is the fairest cover for her shame" (4.1.116). Leonato is completely distraught: "I flow in grief. . . . Hath no man's dagger here a point for me?" (4.1.252, 109). "She is fallen / Into a pit of ink, that the wide sea / Hath drops too few to wash her clean again" (4.1.140–42).

At a loss for what to do, Hero's elderly father challenges Hero's fiancé to a duel. Here we see what happens when the rule of law fails to recognize human needs. Without relief though the courts, self-help becomes the only remedy, and self-help built on revenge is precisely what law seeks to avoid.

But a slander depends to some extent on a victim understanding it. Shakespeare's buffoonish, lunatic constable Dogberry illustrates this point perfectly. Called an "ass" by Don John's henchmen, the ridiculous Dogberry, not knowing what the word means, thinks it a compliment. He is unaware of any harm to his reputation. On the contrary, he is proud of being dubbed an ass. He is slandered and even slanders himself, but does not so much as know it.

As thus drawn by Shakespeare in *Much Ado*, there seems to be at least some basis in reason and experience for presuming damages to flow from

certain slanders. But Shakespeare lived long before the constitutionaliza-
tion of libel law that occurred with the pathbreaking 1964 case of *New
York Times v. Sullivan*[30] and its progeny. Even such an insightful dramatist could not have anticipated the vast changes to be wrought in the law
of libel by a case such as *Sullivan*. Since 1964 the Supreme Court's cases
on defamation have completely unsettled the concept of slander per se.

Like Shakespeare, we too live in an age of rapidly changing defamation
law. The flux and uncertainty in the law today are not the result of a
contest over jurisdiction between ecclesiastical and common law courts,
but of a balancing of the individual's reputational interest and the interest
in freedom of speech. Yet such balancing has in effect led to a new contest
over jurisdiction, this time between federal courts (particularly the Supreme Court) establishing federal constitutional requirements and state
courts deciding state common law issues. The consequence has been no
less complex than at the end of the sixteenth century, and perhaps Shakespeare would have found the jurisdictional clash familiar.

The turning point for slander per se came in 1974 with the Supreme
Court's decision in *Gertz v. Robert Welch, Inc.*[31] There, the Court held,
as a matter of federal constitutional law, that state law "may not permit
recovery for presumed or punitive damages" in a defamation case, unless
the plaintiff proves actual malice—defined in the constitutional sense of
knowing falsity or reckless disregard for the truth. Every plaintiff, even
those alleging defamation per se, must prove actual damage. Characteriz-
ing state laws that allowed recovery of purportedly compensatory damages without actual damage as "an oddity of tort law," the Supreme
Court reasoned that "the states have no substantial interest in securing
for plaintiffs . . . gratuitous awards of money far in excess of any actual
injury." Worried about the chilling effect on free speech, the Court was
concerned that "the doctrine of presumed damages invites juries to punish unpopular opinion rather than to compensate individuals for injury
sustained by the publication of a false fact."[32]

Gertz shook by its roots the common law rule of defamation per se that
allowed for the presumption of damages. Nothing in the text of *Gertz*
limited its holding to media defendants or to public figures. On the contrary, many courts interpreting *Gertz* assumed the Supreme Court meant
its 1974 ruling to be a definitive ruling of general application forbidding
presumed damages to reputation absent actual malice.

Thus did the law appear to be settled, however tentatively, until 1985.
Eleven years after *Gertz*, the Supreme Court in *Dun & Bradstreet v.
Green Moss Builders, Inc.*[33] seemed to modify *Gertz* by holding that in
cases involving a private figure and no matter of public concern, the states
may permit recovery for presumed damages even without a showing of
actual malice. Many states have yet to confront the issue of whether to

retain the post-*Gertz* principle that a private plaintiff must prove actual damage or to return to the pre-1974 rule authorizing recovery for presumed damages. Right now, in most jurisdictions, the issue is an open one. Consequently, the current status of defamation per se is, as a matter of First Amendment constitutional law, in disarray.

Given this disarray, it is impossible to predict what the future holds for slander per se. State courts may or may not, under *Dun & Bradstreet*, allow presumed damages. The Supreme Court may or may not take yet another tack on its zigzag course on this badly charted sea. Shakespeare would perhaps understand our befuddlement.

Another constitutional problem besets the category of slander per se in *Much Ado*. "Imputation of unchastity to a woman," which is the traditional formulation, is obviously not gender neutral. It does not apply to a man. Constitutional requirements about equality of treatment between the sexes undercut this category. To meet this constitutional objection, the American Law Institute in 1977 formulated section 574 of the *Restatement (Second) of Torts* to enlarge the category to embrace an oral imputation of serious sexual misconduct to either a man or woman. How courts will react remains to be seen.

Despite such efforts to modernize the concept, the four categories of slander per se, no matter what their origins, seem arbitrary today. Other slanders are equally if not more grossly defamatory or insulting than the four in the per se category and, therefore, would seem, as a matter of logic and principle, to require no more proof of actual harm. Why should it be slanderous per se to say in the 1980s that a woman has slept with her lover, but not slanderous per se to say that she has AIDS, has the personality of a wet mop, or is incapable of bearing children?

But by now we know the limits of logic in the life of the law. Courts, not knowing precisely how or exactly why the four arbitrary categories of slander per se came into being, have refused to add to them. Judges tend to adhere to the four categories woodenly. Such refusal to change is particularly curious because per se categories of slander were largely a common law creation, designed to permit the law to reflect society's changing attitudes toward reputation. One would have thought that what courts create, courts can change.

A good example of the law's resistance to change in this regard is the category of imputing unchastity to a woman. In the Victorian era, when the law added imputing unchastity to women as a new class of slander per se, such a slander carried certain disgrace. It is more than coincidence that the change occurred during the Victorian age, when most people probably feared that unchastity in women was a bad example, an invitation to anarchy, a wedge in the stones of the temple.

But mores change, and the unchastity category may reflect sensibilities no longer completely relevant to contemporary values. There have been times in the last thirty years of sexual revolution and the women's movement, for example, when it may have been the other way around: to have imputed *chastity* to a woman might have damaged her reputation. A number of feature films in the last two decades have shown young women ridiculed for being virgins. Although sexual attitudes changed, this archaic and outmoded per se category for female unchastity remained.

In Don John, Shakespeare paints a vivid portrait of the mind of a slanderer. There is no complex ambiguity here, no admirable character traits marred by tragic flaws—just simple evil. Don John, the brother of Prince Don Pedro, has lived a disgruntled and envious life in the shadow of his ruling brother. "I am a plain-dealing villain," he says truthfully (1.3.30). "Seek not to alter me" (1.3.34). His slander plan will "prove / food to my displeasure" (1.3.60–61).

To underscore Don John's evil nature, Shakespeare stresses his illegitimacy. Again and again, he is referred to as "the bastard," as if the circumstances of his birth explain his wicked disposition. Shakespeare's linking of illegitimacy and evil is something we will see again in *King Lear* with the character of Edmund.

Don John's twisted mind is far more dangerous than merely a sharp tongue. Beatrice has the sharpest of tongues, which she uses to cut her foil Benedick to ribbons at every turn. At one point, feeling the sting of her verbal lash, Benedick can take no more. But in contrast to Don John, there is something playful not mean, something spunky not sinister, about Beatrice's verbal jousting. The difference is the intent behind the words. Don John is malicious, Beatrice is not.

The law of slander is an effort to control such malice. "If justice cannot tame you," a minor legal functionary warns one of Don John's accomplices, "she / shall ne'er weigh more reasons in her balance" (5.1.201–2).

Much Ado about Nothing stimulates us to think hard about slander, particularly slander per se. Although the legal rules surrounding slander per se have changed much since Shakespeare, they are as illogically byzantine, and in need of overhaul today as they were in 1600. Then, as now, the law of defamation was in great flux. But perhaps comparing slander law uncovers a deeper, happier comparison: Shakespeare's time was marked by constantly changing slander law and by great effervescence of culture; our time certainly has changing defamation law, which may reflect or be a condition of cultural ferment.

One exchange in *Much Ado* sums up both the play's slander theme and the law's response. The line occurs fairly early in the play and serves to foreshadow what is to come. Ironically, the exchange involves Hero, the victim of the play's slander. Hero is talking with her servant Ursula about some good-natured and playful mischief they might work on Hero's cousin Beatrice and her stormy relationship with Benedick.

"And truly, I'll devise some honest slanders / To stain my cousin with," announces Hero (3.1.84–85). "One doth not know / How much an ill word may empoison liking" (3.1.85–86). But *we* know, the law knows, and Hero herself comes to know. That is, perhaps, why Ursula knowingly responds, "O do not do your cousin such a wrong" (3.1.87). And yet Shakespeare was so preoccupied with slander that he wrote even more about it in *The Winter's Tale*.

Chapter Eleven

A JUST AND OPEN TRIAL?

THE WINTER'S TALE

IN *The Winter's Tale*, Hermione, like Desdemona in *Othello* and Hero in *Much Ado*, is wrongly accused of sexual infidelity. When such an accusation is false, it is a slander "whose sting is sharper than the sword's" (2.3.86). In this play, however, Shakespeare builds on the legal theme of slander by creating a suspenseful and emotional trial scene to decide whether the woman is innocent or guilty.

Shakespeare understood what today's publishers are newly discovering about the popularity of legal novels.[1] The Bard knew courtroom trials make for good drama and feed a large public appetite. His most famous trial scene, in *The Merchant of Venice* where Portia rules against Shylock, lives on as a stage triumph. A less famous though highly charged trial scene occupies a central place in *The Winter's Tale*. It is at least as fascinating, and in some ways more so, especially from a legal point of view.

The play opens in Sicily at an unspecified time in the past. Leontes, king of Sicily, has entertained for several months his boyhood friend Polixenes, king of Bohemia. When Polixenes tells his host that it is time to go home, Leontes tries to persuade his old friend to stay, but fails. Where Leontes fails, his good wife, Hermione, almost nine months pregnant with their second child, succeeds. At her request, Polixenes agrees to visit a little longer.

On hearing that his wife accomplished what he could not, Leontes—up to now a calm, gentle, and rational fellow—suddenly becomes insanely jealous. He accuses Hermione of being Polixenes' lover and even goes so far as to claim that Polixenes fathered the baby she carries. In his rage, Leontes orders his courtier Camillo to murder Polixenes, a command that Camillo refuses to carry out, instead warning Polixenes and escaping with him to Bohemia. Amid the tumult Hermione gives birth prematurely, but Leontes, still caught in his fit of jealous frenzy, disowns the baby and declares that the newborn girl is to be set down alone on the countryside, exposed to certain death. He threatens to kill Hermione, but then, pulling back slightly from his own barbarism, has her thrown into prison.

SAVED BY THE ORACLE

Leontes decides to put Hermione on trial, both to resolve the crisis and to show he is not a mad tyrant. "Summon a session," he proclaims,

> that we may arraign
> Our most disloyal lady; for as she hath
> Been publicly accused, so shall she have
> A just and open trial.
>
> (2.3.202–5)

Then, on the day of trial, Leontes reveals his purpose:

> Let us be cleared
> Of being tyrannous since we so openly
> Proceed in justice, which shall have due course
> Even to the guilt or the purgation.
>
> (3.2.4–7)

Given such high-minded goals, the exact trial procedures to be used take on great importance. Who will be the judge? Will there be a jury? What kind of proof will be offered? What quantum of proof will suffice? A trial will prove nothing, neither Hermione's guilt nor Leontes' lack of tyranny, if the trial is merely a sham, a show trial.

As the crucial trial starts, we can hardly know we are about to witness one of the greatest as well as one of the least appreciated courtroom scenes in all literature. The procedures seem strange and lopsided. Leontes appears to be running the courtroom, as if he were judge, prosecutor, jury, and chief witness. He demands that Hermione be produced in court and orders the reading of the indictment.

The false indictment charges Hermione with the capital offense of "high treason" (3.2.14). The alleged treason consists of the defendant's "committing adultery with Polixenes, / King of Bohemia, and conspiring with Camillo to take / away the life of" Leontes (3.2.14–16), whereas in fact it was Leontes who had conspired to murder Polixenes. Specifically, the indictment accuses Hermione of counseling and aiding Camillo and Polixenes "for their better safety, to fly away by night" (3.2.20), such misconduct being "contrary to the faith / and allegiance of a true subject" (3.2.18–19).

Hermione answers these serious charges with a spirited speech in her own defense. She starts by conceding the difficulty of her own position, acknowledging that she will be the only witness for the defense in a hard case.

Since what I am to say must be but that
Which contradicts my accusation, and
The testimony on my part no other
But what comes from myself, it shall scarce boot me
To say "Not guilty." My integrity
Being counted falsehood shall, as I express it,
Be so received.

(3.2.21–27)

But the daunting nature of her courtroom task in no way stops her from trying. "If powers divine," Hermione boldly declares,

Behold our human actions—as they do—
I doubt not then but innocence shall make
False accusation blush, and tyranny
Tremble at patience.

(3.2.28–31)

She then addresses Leontes and reminds him of how well he knows she has been "chaste" and "true" throughout their marriage (3.2.33). Leontes responds with sarcasm, and Hermione goes on to deny the specific charges.

Rather than proceed with witnesses or other proof, as one might expect at a "just and open trial," Leontes and Hermione simply argue with each other, as if they were at a deposition in a modern divorce case. Leontes repeats the charges in homelier language—"You had a bastard by Polixenes" (3.2.83)—and warns that she "shalt feel our justice, in whose easiest passage / Look for no less than death" (3.2.89–90). Such a dark comment hardly foreshadows a fair and unbiased trial before a judge who will suspend judgment until all the evidence is in. Hermione retorts with bravado, "Sir, spare your threats" (3.2.90). Having lost all that gave joy to her life, Hermione claims she has no fear of death, but would like to "free" her "honour" (3.2.109–10).

At this point, we wonder what proof Leontes will put before the court. We know, even if Leontes in his unstable emotional state does not, that Hermione is innocent. "If I shall be condemned / Upon surmises, all proofs sleeping else / But what your jealousies awake," Hermione protests, "I tell you / 'Tis rigour and not law" (3.2.110–13). Are such jealous surmises enough to convict Hermione, as they were to convict Desdemona in Othello's mind?

We never find out. We never learn how the trial would have proceeded in due course. We never know which witnesses would have testified, what they would have testified to, or whether they would have testified truthfully. We never discover exactly what role Leontes would have played in the judicial proceedings in which he was so intimately interested. Shakespeare never tells us any of these things, about which we harbor grave suspicions, because the trial abruptly veers off in a new and unexpected direction.

Hermione dares to try a clever, desperate, and uncertain defense tactic, but one that at least gives her more than a kangaroo court. "Your honours all," Hermione pleads, "I do refer me to the oracle. / Apollo be my judge!" (3.2.113–14). Hermione willingly forgoes whatever procedural safeguards, real or sham, a trial affords her and prepares to accept the judgment of Apollo, the Greek god of truth, through his spokesperson, the oracle at Delphi. In view of Leontes' improper influence with the trial, Hermione made a wise choice.

Such a choice comes as no surprise to those at the trial. "This your request," replies a lord, "is altogether just. / Therefore bring forth, / And in Apollo's name, his oracle" (3.2.115–17). So large a role does Apollo play in the minds of these people, and so accessible is he, that Leontes had previously sent messengers to Delphi to consult with the oracle about Hermione's conduct and to bring back the oracle's sealed written answer. The court grants Hermione's request for trial by Apollo.

Although Hermione's request may not have surprised those at her trial, it strikes us as odd. Does it not represent a throwback to mysticism and irrationality as a means of deciding guilt or innocence, like trial by ordeal or trial by combat? Apart from her justifiable fears of a show trial under Leontes' temporarily evil aegis, why would she give up whatever procedural rights she has and stake all upon her faith in a foreign deity?

The answer may lie in the special role of the Delphic oracle in Greek life and mythology. As the god of truth, Apollo supposedly never uttered a false word. Delphi, the site of Apollo's temple and oracle, was considered the center of the world, to which came many pilgrims from Greece and beyond. Anxious seekers after truth asked questions; answers, often ambiguous and hard to interpret, came from a priestess in a trance. The Delphic oracle provided a direct link between gods and humans, guiding humans to know divine will, so that people believed that through his oracle they came into contact with Apollo. They went away comforted and strengthened.

The Delphic oracle had an important part in Sophocles' *Oedipus Rex*, a play that Shakespeare must have been familiar with and that has some parallels with *The Winter's Tale*. In *Oedipus Rex*, Apollo's oracle warns Laius that his son will kill him. To try to prevent this prophecy from coming true, Laius has his baby son left exposed on a lonely mountain where he was sure to die, just as Leontes does with Hermione's baby daughter.

The Delphic oracle has come down even to the present as a symbol of wise but ambiguous decision making in law. In our own times, the Supreme Court has itself been compared to the Delphic oracle, referring to the Court's exalted status and occasional lack of precision. From a slightly different perspective, the Delphic oracle has been a metaphor to describe legal formalism, which prevailed in America from about the Civil War until World War I and was based on the notion that judges did not make or create law, but merely found or declared, like an oracle, what the preexisting law was.

But to return to Hermione's trial: the messengers swear they have brought back, unopened and unread, the answer from Apollo's priestess. Like a celebrity at the Academy Awards ceremony, an officer then cuts through the seals—and the suspense—by announcing Apollo's judgment:

> Hermione is chaste, Polixenes blameless, Camillo a true subject, Leontes a jealous tyrant, his innocent babe truly begotten, and the king shall live without an heir if that which is lost be not found. (3.2.132–35)

It is, in short, a stunning verdict of acquittal, and a sobering defeat for Leontes.

Leontes, like Oedipus in Sophocles' play, has a hard time accepting the oracle's verdict. "Hast thou read truth?" asks Leontes (3.2.137). "Ay, my lord, even so / As it is here set down," comes the reply (3.2.138). But that is not good enough for the jealousy-ridden Leontes. "There is no truth at all i' th'oracle," objects Leontes (3.2.139). "The sessions shall proceed. This is mere falsehood" (3.2.140).

It now looks as if Leontes, miffed at the oracle's judgment, will force the trial to proceed nonetheless, to an outcome more to Leontes' liking no doubt. That alone makes us skeptical of the fairness of the trial procedures to be followed. It certainly seems as if Leontes is bent on getting the verdict he wants, no matter what. But then tragic events shake Leontes out of his overwrought emotional mood and back to reality.

Two fatal blows make Leontes reasonable again. He first learns that his older child, a son, has died out of anxiety over the queen's fate. Murmurs a humbled Leontes, "Apollo's angry, and the heavens themselves / Do strike at my injustice" (3.2.145–46). Hermione then falls, apparently dying at the news of her son's death. "I have too much believed mine own suspicion" (3.2.150), Leontes admits sadly but accurately.

Wounded so sharply by fate, Leontes returns to his normal, reasonable self. Belatedly, he accepts the judgment of Apollo, complies with the rule of law, realizes how he wronged Hermione, mourns the deaths of wife and son, and wishes to make up with Polixenes and Camillo, whose "piety / Does my deeds make the blacker!" (3.2.170–71).

The trial in *The Winter's Tale* resolves a dramatic crisis, though it also sets the stage for what is to follow in the play. It provides emotional catharsis for the characters in the play, as well as for its viewers. And even if not as fabled as the trial scene in *The Merchant of Venice*, it makes a powerful and lasting impression on the mind, and once again underscores Shakespeare's affinity for things legal.

REASON AND PASSION IN LAW

Queen Hermione's faithfulness to King Leontes is only one of the issues, and not necessarily the most important one, on trial in *The Winter's Tale*. Shakespeare also puts on trial the concept of law itself. In the play he makes reason and emotion, law and passion, compete for dominance. Shakespeare asks a key jurisprudential question: which should control our conduct, reason and law or passion and feeling?

To our great surprise, Shakespeare answers ambiguously. On the one hand, he seems to say the obvious, that law and reason must predominate. But the play, like life itself, is complex, and Shakespeare supplies an alternative, inconsistent answer stressing the need to make reason (law) the servant of feeling. Faced with such unclear and opposite answers, we become confused and uncertain about fundamental legal ideas. We ponder about law and its proper role in society.

On first reading, the play seems to be a warning about the need for law to control emotion, lest disaster result. Leontes, for no cogent reason, loses his mind and without any proof becomes mad with jealousy, a wild emotion that Milton called "the injured lover's hell." Temporarily bereft of reason, the emotionally turbulent Leontes lapses into terrible accusations with serious consequences for all around him. But then law—the trial and the judgment by Apollo—brakes Leontes' careening passions, and after some reinforcement from fate, he resumes his calm, rational life.

The primary dramatic events in the play flow from the root struggle between reason and instinct, from Leontes being swept away by emotion, from his unconscious overwhelming his conscious. They result, as Leontes himself admits, from "being transported by my jealousies / To bloody thoughts and revenge" (3.2.157–58). His terrible accusations are based, in the words of Hermione's friend Paulina, on no more than "weak-hinged fancy" (2.3.119). From an apparently mild-mannered and reasonable ruler, Leontes is transformed into a madman capable of great violence to those—innocent all—whom he loves.

Leontes in his emotionally unstable frenzy stands for the transient triumph of humankind's stubborn subterranean thoughts. So violent, so savage, the submerged stuff of life bubbles up to the surface with baleful consequences. Leontes, like Hamlet, Othello, and Romeo, shows how the primitive impulses and instincts flow in all of us. The Jekyll and Hyde aspects, the dark forces, are always there, kept just beneath the surface by a thin layer of civilization, ready to surge when provoked. These are the internal shadows of civilized people.

To tame and control these dangerous passions is a vital function of law, as shown by *The Winter's Tale*. In this sense, law resembles what Freud talked about in *Civilization and Its Discontents*, where he argued that civilization is impossible without repressing and sublimating primitive instincts like aggression and sex. Law generally serves this repressing function (though in some ways—capital punishment, for example—law itself seems to embody primitive, vengeful instincts). Hermione's trial in *The Winter's Tale*, with its bracing and rehabilitating effect on Leontes, reveals the law's strong tonic of rationality.

The trial in *The Winter's Tale* relies on a potent symbol in Apollo, whose oracle renders the verdict in favor of Hermione and against Leontes. Not only was Apollo the Greek god of truth, but he was also the god of art, painting, sculpture, and epic poetry. He brought fair order and harmony out of confusion, and stood for moderation and sobriety. His motto was "Nothing in excess." As the god of ordered form and logical thought, Apollo represented peace and leisure and repose, esthetic emotion and intellectual contemplation and philosophical calm. Apollo is everything the jealousy-ridden Leontes is not.

Apollo is one thing more: he is considered the maker of laws. Lycurgus, honored as the author of the laws of Sparta, supposedly received those laws from the Delphic oracle. When a Greek colony asked the oracle for advice, it was told to get itself a system of laws. Apollo thus provides divine sanction for law, which was neither the first nor the last time law would be seen as a command from God. In *The Winter's Tale*, Apollo is truth, reason, and law called upon to restrain the out-of-control Leontes.

One would think that such abundant evidence in *The Winter's Tale* amply warrants the inference that the play means emotion must be reined in by law. Yet the critical tradition holds just the opposite. Typical of that literary tradition, Harold Goddard, author of *The Meaning of Shakespeare*, writes that in *The Winter's Tale* Shakespeare plainly shows "that as against his earlier ideal of a balance between instinct and reason ('blood and judgment') he had come to believe that reason should be obedient to imagination."[2] And a few pages later, Goddard adds, "From *Hamlet* on, Shakespeare had been saying, sometimes in poetic and sometimes in religious language, that . . . reason must become the servant of imagination."[3]

Although Goddard's comments about reason obeying imagination accurately reflect the weight of critical authority, they are open to question, or at least to a closer look. First, they ignore the thrust of the trial scene in *The Winter's Tale* and what led up to it, which at a minimum seems to undercut the critical tradition. Second, the reference to *Hamlet* and later plays jars. For all the criticism of Hamlet's delaying rationalizations against taking revenge against his uncle, those delays may actually be what ennobles Hamlet and lifts him, if only for a while, above primal—and lawless—blood instincts. Likewise, *Othello* and *Antony and Cleopatra*, both written after *Hamlet*, demonstrate the tragic consequences of unchecked emotion.

Overlooking these objections, Goddard and others rely heavily for their conclusions on one particular incident in *The Winter's Tale*. After Hermione's baby is left in the open to die, the infant—like Oedipus—is found and saved by a shepherd, who, unaware of her royal blood, raises her as his own child, and names her Perdita, meaning "lost." As she grows up, she becomes beautiful, modest, and poised, and attracts Florizel, the son of Polixenes, king of Bohemia. But Perdita, seemingly a lowborn shepherd lass, is, according to the king, unfit to marry a king's son. So the king gives Prince Florizel a choice between his hope of the throne and the girl he loves.

Florizel, young romantic that he is, chooses love. Responding to a warning from Camillo, now the king's adviser, Florizel objects, "I / Am heir to my affection" (4.4.481–82). "Be advised" (4.4.481), cautions Camillo. "I am, and by my fancy," Florizel answers back:

> If my reason
> Will thereto be obedient, I have reason.
> If not, my senses, better pleased with madness,
> Do bid it welcome.
>
> (4.4.482–85)

"Fancy" here of course means love, but earlier in the play Shakespeare used the same word—"weak-hinged fancy"—to mean the irrational source of Leontes' baseless accusations against Hermione. Florizel, no less than Leontes earlier, has his reason reduced to madness. And Shakespeare—in what Goddard calls "one of the plainest of a number of passages in the later Shakespeare"[4]—seems to champion the abandonment of reason. Substitute law for reason, and the problem is apparent.

The Winter's Tale thus uncovers a basic tension and conflict, of the utmost gravity and importance, regarding the role of law. Within one dramatic work, we see two contradictory interpretations of law's proper function. One interpretation says reason (law) should restrain emotion, the other says reason (law) should obey emotion. These are apparently irreconcilable theories of law, troubling to anyone who thinks seriously about the meaning of law.

Such tension reminds us of something Benjamin Cardozo, a superb literary lawyer and acclaimed judge on the U. S. Supreme Court and New York's highest state court, said in *Paradoxes of Legal Science*. "The reconciliation of the irreconcilable," wrote Judge Cardozo, "the merger of antitheses, the synthesis of opposites, these are the great problems of the law."[5]

In our own country's birth struggles, the founders wrestled with similar questions. A proper legal order, they thought, depends on the relationship between politics and law, on one hand, and psychology, on the other. In *Federalist No. 49*, James Madison admonished that "it is the reason, alone, of the public, that ought to control and regulate the government. The passions ought to be controlled and regulated by government."

In different parts of *The Winter's Tale*, Shakespeare has reason (law) or emotion in the ascendant, much as reason and emotion emerge with varying strength at different moments in each of our individual lives. What if we consider *The Winter's Tale* an early, pre-Freudian, partial map of human psychological processes? In each life there are times when calm reason predominates and other times when unruly emotion controls. The total life, like *The Winter's Tale*, consists of the interplay—sometimes difficult, sometimes smooth—between the two concepts of reason and emotion, with a full and creative life hanging on the outcome.

One way to think about the conflict is to return to the important figure of Apollo in the play. After all, the ambiguity of Shakespeare's response to the tension recalls the cryptic answers emblematic of the Delphic oracle. Apollo, god of reason, calm, and moderation, symbolizes one of two strains. In *The Birth of Tragedy*, written long before his own reason succumbed to madness, Friedrich Nietzsche contrasted this symbol of Apollo with another symbol, Dionysus, the Greek god of wine, the symbol of drunken frenzy, of ultimate abandonment, of passion, chaos, fruitfulness, of joy in action, of ecstatic emotion and inspiration, of instinct and adventure.

Nietzsche's basic thesis in *The Birth of Tragedy* was that passion—the Dionysian power to feel intensely, to awaken the mind under the spell of passion—is necessary but must be balanced to create art. For Nietzsche, the Apollonian and Dionysian strains must merge; the destructive impulses of Dionysus must be harnessed by reason for creative ends, to give birth to tragedy, in Nietzsche's mind the highest form of art.

Nietzsche's analysis in *The Birth of Tragedy* helps us understand the jurisprudential problems raised by *The Winter's Tale*. Just as the birth of art requires a balance between passion and order, between emotion and reason, so too may the birth and creative life of law. For example, in response to the post–Civil War myth of judges as oracles of pure reason, jurists such as Oliver Wendell Holmes and Benjamin Cardozo insisted that we consider the role that human experience, emotion, and passion play in the judicial process.

Developing this theme, Supreme Court Justice William Brennan's 1987 Cardozo Lecture on "Reason, Passion, and 'The Progress of the Law'" argued that the complex "interplay of forces," rational and emotional, conscious and unconscious, "this internal dialogue of reason and passion, does not taint the judicial process, but is in fact central to its vitality."[6] By "passion," Brennan meant "the range of emotional and intuitive responses to a given set of facts or arguments, . . . the passion that puts [people] in touch with the dreams and disappointments of those with whom they deal."[7]

In language reminiscent of Shakespeare in *The Winter's Tale* and Nietzsche in *The Birth of Tragedy*, Brennan brilliantly articulated the quest for balance between the competing forces, the Apollonian and the Dionysian, in the law. Brennan warned of the great threat of "sterile rationality," of "formal reason severed from the insights of passion," and of the need to inject passion "into a system whose abstract rationality had led it astray." Recognizing the need for balance, Brennan added limits: "It is, of course, one thing for a judge to recognize the value that awareness of passion may bring to reason, and quite another to give way altogether to impassioned judgment." His conclusion was clear: "It is only as each generation brings to bear its experience and understanding, its passion and reason, that there is hope for progress in the law."[8]

Justice Brennan's speech, while relatively unknown, may eventually eclipse in importance his many famous judicial opinions. Unlike them, often magnificent and emotional in their own right, Brennan's Cardozo Lecture goes beyond particular issues of constitutional law to the deeper waters of jurisprudential theory. If we listen to Justice Brennan and make passion part of our profession, all of us, judges and lawyers alike, will look at the edifice of the law and feel compelled to ask, as the rehabilitated Leontes does of Hermione's statue in *The Winter's Tale*, "Does not the stone rebuke me / For being more stone than it?" (5.3.37–38).

The Winter's Tale makes clear the function of feeling in life and in the work of the law. Law lies in understanding some part of the dark forces and bringing them under the direction of reason. The deep, universal distrust of law rests on its hostility to what is felt as the pulse of life. Life is warm, hot, glowing; law is cold and dull. Law has apparently nothing to say to the predicament and tragedies of life. Life is immediate and convinces by throbbing in your veins or exploding before your eyes. Law stands on the margin of existence and convinces, if at all, by the roundabout road of argument—words in place of acts. Law the watcher, life the participant.

Whoever checks the sense of life by always proffering ideas and words grows blind to realities. For law to function at its best, a vast amount of material contrary to reason must be examined and understood. Law, with all its shortcomings, can in the end only know life and enhance it if law takes account of feeling. Thought and reason in the law, unless matched by feeling, are empty, delusive things.

LAW AND DISCRETION

Reason and passion in the law—a key theme in *The Winter's Tale*—is also a key theme of legal history and of American legal history in particular. When strict law, "reason's check on pleasure's unruly promptings,"[9] defeats its own purposes by colliding with the supreme welfare of the people, then it triggers a self-correcting mechanism. Equity we call it, and it seems to use discretionary judgment to correct inflexible legal axioms. Equity embodies an emotional component consisting of intention, feeling, empathy, the morality of the heart, to alleviate the rigor of strict law. ("'Tis rigor and not law," complains Hermione.) But equity can deteriorate into whim or pleasure, and this potential for arbitrariness is in turn why reason in the form of strict law is needed. Hence we have the pendulum swing between strict and equitable theories, between reason and emotion, between the double threat of a tyrannically strict construction and an equally tyrannical personal intervention in the law, in short, between law and discretion.

This pendulum helps explain a lot that happens in contemporary American law. The issues raised, for instance, by the 1987 Senate hearings on the failed nomination of Robert Bork to the Supreme Court can be usefully analyzed in terms of the legal tension seen in *The Winter's Tale*. The basic issue of law and discretion, reason and passion in government, began to emerge on Judge Bork's fifth and final day of testimony before the Senate Judiciary Committee. In that unusual Saturday session on September 19, 1987, Judge Bork spent two hours discussing constitutional law with Senator Arlen Specter of Pennsylvania. Displaying sensitivity and understanding of basic principles, both men engaged in debate on a lofty level not often seen in public life, though it is unlikely that either of them knew they were acting out a Shakespearean theme.

After five days of sometimes strident questioning by the entire committee about judicial activism and judicial restraint, unenumerated rights, the meaning of "liberty" in the Fourteenth Amendment, the scope of the "equal protection of the laws" and the doctrine of original intent, the debate reached its intellectual climax with a perceptive comment by the beleaguered Bork.

"Well, Senator," said Bork to Specter at one point, "you are making a very powerful argument for a very strong tradition. I hope—I think what I am saying also comes from a very strong tradition in our constitutional law, going back to Joseph Story and the first Marshall Court." In terms of *The Winter's Tale*, Bork represented reason and strict law, Specter stood for emotion and discretion.

Of all the comments made during the debate on Bork, of all the questions and answers, editorials, advertisements, and media coverage, of all the emotional criticism and defense, this simple, nonconfrontational response by Bork does the most to put what was at stake in true perspective. By explicitly referring to two "very strong traditions," Bork recognized that American constitutional law is the result of competing traditions and ever-present tensions, one of which he symbolized. In many ways, the outcome of Bork's battle would be determined by which one of the two traditions was temporarily in the ascendant. These traditions in constant tension run deeper than superficial labels, as *The Winter's Tale* shows.

CIVIC COURAGE

Every political and legal system develops an attitude toward civic courage, and the legal system of Shakespeare's *Winter's Tale* is no exception. From Antigone's refusal to heed Creon's command to leave her dead brother unburied, to Thoreau's refusal to pay taxes for the Mexican War, from civil rights protestors who refused to obey racially discriminatory laws, to young men who refused to be drafted into the military—in each case a person must decide whether courage or fear should be the basis for political action, which may entail crucial decisions on whether to speak out against government and whether to obey a law he or she views as unjust. In *The Winter's Tale*, Shakespeare makes four characters face such a crisis.

In each of these four legal encounters, Shakespeare—generally thought to be conservative—appears strongly to endorse civic courage. Shakespeare makes this surprising endorsement implicitly in the way he portrays the consequences of the choices for each of the four characters.

The hapless character Antigonus illustrates what happens to even a good man who acts out of fear or misplaced fealty. The first lines spoken by Antigonus, nobleman and adviser of King Leontes, show he is basically an upright fellow. Coming on stage when Leontes has already started to accuse Queen Hermione of infidelity, Antigonus gently and prudently warns Leontes:

> Be certain what you do, sir, lest your justice
> Prove violence, in the which three great ones suffer—
> Yourself, your queen, your son.
>
> (2.1.129–31)

Antigonus's initial words both foreshadow what will occur and attempt a reasonable restraint of misguided power.

The mild curb urged by Antigonus has no effect. Despite Antigonus's ardent defense of Hermione's honor, Leontes ignores his adviser and remains crazed with groundless jealousy. But Antigonus, who sees more clearly, knows better. When Leontes speaks of proving Hermione's guilt and exclaims that "this business / Will raise us all" (2.1.199–200), Antigonus finishes the sentence in an important aside: "To laughter, as I take it, / If the good truth were known" (2.1.200–201).

A hint of a theory of law soon comes from Antigonus. Leontes is upset with Antigonus's failure to stop his wife from nagging the king about Hermione's innocence. Leontes shouts to Antigonus, "Thou art worthy to be hanged / That wilt not stay her tongue" (2.3.109–10). Answers Antigonus, "Hang all the husbands / That cannot do that feat, you'll leave yourself / Hardly one subject" (2.3.110–12). Hence the principle, demonstrated with some humor and also enunciated in *Measure for Measure* (about a ban on nonmarital sex), that law must have public support or else it will be unenforceable.

To punish Antigonus for his wife's incessant pleading, Leontes orders Antigonus "and none but thou" to burn Hermione's newborn baby (2.3.135). Leontes' advisers beg him to change his mind, to which Leontes responds, "What will you adventure / To save this brat's life?" "Anything," replies Antigonus (2.3.162–63). Finally, Leontes directs Antigonus, on pain of torture and death to himself and his wife, to carry the baby "to some remote and desert place, quite out / Of our dominions" and leave it there, "where chance may nurse or end it" (2.3.176–83).

Antigonus, notwithstanding his promise to do "anything" to save the baby's life, neither disagrees nor argues; he obeys meekly, and thereby begins his fall. "I swear to do this," he submits, "though a present death / Had been more merciful" (2.3.184–85). A different Antigonus might have tried to find some way to spare the child, but instead he faithfully carries out Leontes' cruel order.

One view of blind obedience to such an illegal order can be inferred from a dream sequence in the play. Hermione comes to Antigonus in a dream and says: "Good Antigonus, / Since fate, against thy better disposition, / Hath made thy person for the thrower-out / Of my poor babe," you shall be punished (3.3.26–29). "For this ungentle business / Put on thee by my lord," continues Hermione in the dream, "thou ne'er shalt see / Thy wife Paulina more" (3.3.33–35).

What is the result of "good" Antigonus going against his "better disposition" and doing "this ungentle business"? A horrible death: a wild bear rips him apart and eats him. Moreover, the ship on which he traveled, with all its crew, then sinks in a storm. Thus does Shakespearean fate punish those who lack civic courage and carry out unjust laws.

In contrast to Antigonus's sorry end, consider what happens to three other characters in *The Winter's Tale* who, unlike Antigonus, show civic courage and refuse to obey unjust laws. Camillo, like Antigonus one of Leontes' inner circle, reacts differently when commanded to do evil. Shakespeare underlines the contrast to Antigonus by having Camillo exit before Antigonus speaks in the first act. Camillo expresses his general attitude early in the play:

> If ever fearful
> To do a thing where I the issue doubted,
> Whereof the execution did cry out
> Against the non-performance, 'twas a fear
> Which oft infects the wisest.
>
> (1.2.260–64)

Camillo remains true to this credo when he confronts his own personal moral crisis. He vigorously defends Hermione to Leontes, who in turn orders Camillo to poison Polixenes, Hermione's supposed lover. After feigning agreement in the king's presence, Camillo, now alone, weighs what to do.

> I must be the poisoner
> Of good Polixenes, and my ground to do't
> Is the obedience to a master—one
> Who in rebellion with himself, will have
> All that are his so too. To do this deed,
> Promotion follows. If I could find example
> Of thousands that had struck anointed kings
> And flourished after, I'd not do't . . . I must
> Forsake the court.
>
> (1.2.353–63)

Turning his back on certain promotion, Camillo bravely disobeys his ruler. He warns Polixenes, switches allegiance to him, and they both escape safely to Bohemia. There Camillo thrives as Polixenes' chief adviser, returning to his own home at the end of the play when all are reconciled. For disobeying, Camillo ends up triumphant.

A similar triumph awaits Paulina, Antigonus's wife, for challenging Leontes. When Leontes unjustly accuses Hermione, Paulina is outspoken in her honest criticism of Leontes. Like the Old Testament prophet Nathan rebuking King David, Paulina shouts zealous and spirited remonstrances against the injustice done to the queen. She boldly and bravely stands up for truth and loyalty to the queen in the face of the king's dark wrath. She speaks like a crusading lawyer and becomes Hermione's "advocate to th' loud'st" (2.2.42).

In Paulina we recognize a favored figure in American legal and political theory: the citizen-critic of government. At least since a jury acquitted John Peter Zenger in 1735 for his newspaper's criticisms of the colonial governor of New York, democratic theory—if not always practice—in this country has encouraged public criticism of official conduct. James Madison spoke of the "censorial power" being "in the people over the government." Criticism of government is a basic part of our system of free expression and is enshrined in the First Amendment.

Justice Louis Brandeis, who made his legal reputation as the "people's attorney," in his memorable 1927 concurrence in *Whitney v. California* explained why "public discussion is a political duty." He believed that the "final end" of government was to make people "free to develop their faculties" and that the "deliberative forces should prevail over the arbitrary." Brandeis pointed to those who won our independence as believing that "freedom to think as you will and to speak as you think [are] indispensable to the discovery and spread of political truth; that without free speech and assembly discussion would be futile; that with them, discussion affords ordinarily adequate protection against the dissemination of noxious doctrine; that the greatest menace to freedom is an inert people; that public discussion is a political duty; and that this should be a fundamental principle of the American government."[10] This much-quoted passage is one of the high points in American constitutional law, marrying democracy with eloquence.

Another friend of free speech, Justice Hugo Black, reinforced the idea in 1971 in the *Pentagon Papers* case, when the Supreme Court denied the government's attempt to prevent newspapers from publishing the contents of a classified government study about the history of how America became involved in Vietnam. Justice Black, then eighty-five years old, spoke of the press's "essential role in our democracy" of "censur[ing] the government." According to Black, "The press was to serve the governed, not the governors." This means that the press must be "free and unrestrained" so it "can effectively expose deception in government." Calling the publication of the Pentagon Papers "courageous" and "noble," Black said that the newspapers should not be condemned but "should be commended for serving the purpose that the Founding Fathers saw so clearly."[11] Shortly after the *Pentagon Papers* case, Black became terminally ill. His magnificent opinion in that case thus was his valedictory on the Court.

In the landmark 1964 case *New York Times v. Sullivan*, the Supreme Court justified its new constitutional libel test in part as "a privilege for criticism of official conduct." Referring to the "citizen-critic of government," the Court said, "It is as much his duty to criticize as it is the official's duty to administer."[12] And two years later, the Court repeated:

"Criticism of government is at the very center of the constitutionally protected area of free discussion."[13]

The leading citizen-critic of government in The Winter's Tale, Paulina, never actually gets punished by Leontes. He threatens and fulminates, to be sure, but he always holds back from inflicting any true punishment on the outspoken Paulina. Is it possible that even Leontes, mad with jealousy as he is, realizes that criticism is not necessarily disloyalty? That is a lesson both governments and people need to learn.

In the end, Paulina does well. A widow due to Antigonus's death, she ultimately marries Camillo, the play's other brave soul. In the last speech of the play, Leontes describes Paulina, who opposed him every step of his frenzied way, as one "whose worth and honesty / Is richly noted, and here justified" (5.3.145–46).

The fourth character who has courage enough to disobey is Florizel, son of King Polixenes. In love with the apparently lowborn Perdita (unknown as the outcast daughter of King Leontes and Queen Hermione), Florizel disobeys his father's command to give up his girlfriend. Rather than submit to this harsh and irrational parental command, Florizel flees with Perdita (just as the young lovers Hermia and Lysander do in A Midsummer Night's Dream), and in doing so risks his birthright to inherit his father's throne. His courage is rewarded when Perdita's true royal identity comes to light and the two royal families unite in the marriage of Florizel and Perdita.

Everyone except fearful and craven Antigonus comes out well. Shakespeare makes those characters who opposed evil laws—Camillo, Paulina, and Florizel—live long and prosper. Only Antigonus, who knowingly enforced an evil law, finds disaster. Even Leontes, who did evil only while in a temporary fit—while he was not himself—winds up happy and thriving. The basic lesson seems to be that civic courage, whatever its drawbacks, is better than knowingly doing evil.

Shakespeare seems to explain this lesson by stressing the fleeting nature of laws. He opens the fourth act with a Chorus called Time saying that "o'er sixteen years . . . it is in my power / To o'erthrow law, and in one self-born hour / To plant and o'erwhelm custom" (4.1.6–9). Shakespeare's language here strikingly resembles Justice Holmes's passage in his famous 1919 dissent in a free speech case, Abrams v. United States:

If you have no doubt of your premises or your power and want a certain result with all your heart you naturally express your wishes in law and sweep away all opposition. . . . But when men have realized that time has upset many fighting faiths, they may come to believe even more than they believe the very foundations of their own conduct that the ultimate good desired is free trade in ideas.[14]

If time overthrows law and upsets fighting faiths, then civic courage may be less of a threat to the "rule of law," particularly if the refusal to obey flows from a perceived moral duty to a higher, natural, more permanent "law."

The legal dimension of *The Winter's Tale* adds greatly to the play's significance. A piece of dramatic fluff is thus transformed into a multifaceted legal-theatrical experience. Seen from a legal point of view, the play expounds the meaning of a fair trial, the complex interplay of emotion and calm in the law, the roles of law and discretion, and the consequences of civic courage. *The Winter's Tale* is, in short, a highly concentrated and bracing legal brew. In some ways, it anticipates the legal themes of *Richard II.*

Chapter Twelve

TO BREAK OUR COUNTRY'S LAWS

RICHARD II

AT FIRST GLANCE, one would not think *The Winter's Tale* has anything in common with, much less a legal affinity to, *Richard II*. One is a play based on a slander, the other a serious history with a sad ending, and yet the legal affinity is there. In *The Winter's Tale*, civil disobedience of unjust laws seems to be rewarded. In *Richard II*, a character appears to say the opposite: "I am loath to break our country's laws" (2.3.168). In this sense, both plays, so different on the surface, have a common underlying legal theme relating to the rule of law.

Some of Shakespeare's plays have more to say than others about the law. In certain of the plays, the law is either not a factor at all or at most the source of a passing reference. In others, the law dominates the words and action. One of the best examples of a law-dominated history play is *Richard II*.

Richard II is about a real king of England who lost his throne in 1399. The play opens with two of King Richard's noblemen (one of whom is Bolingbroke, the king's cousin) accusing each other of treason. When trial by combat supplies no victor, Richard banishes them both from England. While Bolingbroke is overseas, Richard, dependent on an inner circle of flatterers, governs England poorly, creating economic hardships and waste, and making his subjects unhappy. To fund a war in Ireland, Richard seizes all the property of Bolingbroke's dead father.

Hearing of all these woes in "this scept'red isle," especially the loss of his inheritance, Bolingbroke plans to return to England. It is debatable whether he initially intends simply to recover his inheritance or to topple Richard from the throne. He waits until Richard leaves for Ireland and then successfully leads an invasion. The rebels eventually force Richard to abdicate in favor of Bolingbroke, who thereafter calls himself King Henry IV. In the end, Bolingbroke's henchmen murder Richard in the middle of the night.

RIGHT OF CONFRONTATION

If a thumbnail description of the play's action fails to convey the prominence of legal themes, the play itself stresses them from the very start. The play opens with a trial scene. To weigh the cross-accusations of treason by Bolingbroke and Mowbray, Richard sets himself up as judge and jury. Affording them the right to confrontation—as he himself is afforded later in the play—and relying on the adversary process, Richard says:

> Then call them to our presence. Face to face
> And frowning brow to brow, ourselves will hear
> The accuser and the accusèd freely speak.

(1.1.15–17)

That passage played a key role in a 1988 Supreme Court decision. The issue in *Coy v. Iowa* was whether placing a screen between a defendant and child sexual assault victims during testimony violated the defendant's constitutional right to confront his accusers. In the course of finding a violation, Justice Antonin Scalia wrote for the majority: "Shakespeare was thus describing the root meaning of confrontation when he had Richard the Second say" the line about accuser and accused freely speaking face to face, brow to brow.[1] The dissent, written by Justice Harry Blackmun, thought the majority's reliance on the quotation from *Richard II* was misplaced. According to Justice Blackmun, John Wigmore's famous ten-volume treatise on the law of evidence,[2] a "renowned and accepted authority[,] describes the view of confrontation expressed by the words of Richard II as an 'earlier conception, still current in [Shakespeare's] day' which, by the time the Bill of Rights was ratified, had merged 'with the principle of cross-examination.'"[3]

Which one—Scalia (and the Supreme Court majority) or Blackmun (and the esteemed Wigmore)—is correct is hard to say. It is easy, though, to say that Shakespeare's influence on the law of confrontation has exceeded what one might have thought before looking into the matter. The Bard wrote a history play four hundred years ago, and we turn to it today as authority on the meaning of a constitutional right. Little could Shakespeare have thought that judges and lawyers would wrangle over the legal implications of such lines. Even Shakespeare would be surprised by the power and force of his pen on legal matters.

BIASED JUDGES

Yet there is something fundamentally unfair about Richard sitting in judgment here. His ability to be impartial is in doubt on two grounds. To start with, one of the litigants—Bolingbroke—is the king's first cousin. Second, Bolingbroke accuses Mowbray of plotting the death of the duke of Gloucester, who in fact had been murdered on Richard's orders. Does Richard disqualify himself as judge either on the ground that he will favor his family relation or on the ground of participating in the crime? No. He protests, a bit overmuch perhaps, how "impartial are our eyes and ears"

(1.1.115). But under the circumstances we somehow doubt it, and do not hesitate to think that he should have disqualified himself.

"A fair trial in a fair tribunal is a basic requirement of due process," stated the U.S. Supreme Court in 1955.[4] "Fairness," the Court went on, "of course requires an absence of actual bias in the trial of cases. But our system of law has always endeavored to prevent even the probability of unfairness."[5] To determine exactly what due process requires in this context, our Supreme Court has looked for guidance to English law before the American colonies were settled. Jamestown being the first settlement in 1607, the relevant English law was the law of Shakespeare's England.

On reviewing the law of Shakespeare's time, the Supreme Court ruled in the landmark 1927 case of *Tumey v. Ohio* that it "certainly" violates due process if the judge "has a direct, personal, substantial pecuniary interest in reaching a conclusion."[6] Its canvass of English law, moreover, persuaded the Court to generalize that "every procedure which would offer a possible temptation to the average man as a judge to forget the burden of proof required to convict the defendant, or which might lead him not to hold the balance nice, clear and true between the state and the accused denies the latter due process of law."[7] Winding up its discussion, the Court in *Tumey* pointed out that "a situation in which an officer perforce occupies two practically and seriously inconsistent positions, one partisan and the other judicial, necessarily involves a lack of due process of law."[8]

As the Supreme Court understood, the awful specter of the biased judge is ever present. Just as English law had to deal with that problem in the sixteenth century, so has American law had to cope with it in the twentieth century. Not too many years ago, the day's news was filled with scandal about a New York judge accused by federal prosecutors (but later acquitted) of selling justice to a former beauty queen's boyfriend. There are, unfortunately, other examples. For his part, Shakespeare treats the theme of the crooked judge more than once.

The emphasis on the theme of judicial bias shows up again later in *Richard II*. Bolingbroke's father, John of Gaunt, is one of the king's advisers and takes part in the decision about punishing Bolingbroke. John of Gaunt goes along with a penalty of temporary exile for his son. Afterward, he tells the king that he did so solely to avoid any imputation of partiality.

Similarly in *Measure for Measure*. Angelo is the acting magistrate while the Duke of Vienna pretends to be out of town. Isabella asks Angelo to pardon her brother, who is under a death sentence for sleeping with his fiancée. Angelo agrees to grant the pardon but only if Isabella will sleep with him. Angelo's effort to make justice turn on such a couch payment epitomizes the corrupt judge (not to mention the sexual harasser). Shakespeare strums this theme again at the end of *Measure for Measure*. After Angelo is unmasked, the Duke tells him, "In this I'll be impartial; be you judge / Of your own cause" (5.1 165–66)

No less corrupt is Portia's masquerade as a judge in *The Merchant of Venice*. The conventional view of Portia—with which I disagree—is that she does a wonderful job of tempering law with mercy in judging the lawsuit over Shylock's loan to Antonio. Even so, she had no business in the role of judge. She is interested in the outcome: her husband, Antonio's best friend, was the person for whom the loan was made. She made the case end favorably for her husband's closest friend. Portia's undisclosed bias stripped the blindfold from justice and marred the judgment.

After Portia renders her tainted judgment, her husband, not knowing who she is, tries to bribe her. He sends a servant to give gold to Portia. To her credit, Portia rejects the money. But at that point, a bribe was superfluous. Portia's payment came in other ways; the fix was in from the start.[9]

In *The Winter's Tale*, King Leontes acts as judge and prosecutor in the adultery trial of Queen Hermione. And in *Twelfth Night*, a character is "both the plaintiff and the judge / Of thine own cause" (5.1.351–52).

The descriptions of corrupt judges in Shakespeare say something about the legal ethics of the time. Then, as now, due process of law required judges to be fair and impartial. Then, as now, a biased judge violated basic rights. A judge who had a financial interest in the outcome or was related to the parties was and is rightly deemed incapable of disinterested judgment.

Doubtless Shakespeare was aware of a notable incident involving Sir Thomas More in 1533. When More, lord chancellor for a time under Henry VIII, fell out of favor with his monarch, the first charges brought against him alleged that he took bribes during his term of office. To accuse a judge of taking bribes is a serious business, one calculated to destroy a judicial reputation. If such charges could be proved, More's name among his people would have been blackened. The king's council called More before it to answer the trumped-up charges, and More acquitted himself handily.[10]

More's classic attitude toward bribes shows itself in his famous refusal to accept gifts. A gentleman who had a suit pending in Chancery sent his servant to More with a present of two handsome silver flagons. More, unwilling to accept the gift, skillfully turned it aside. The gentleman, he asked, desired to taste the chancellor's wine? "Go to my cellar," said More. "Fill thy master's ewer with my best wine. Take it home, and let thy master know I do not judge it."

A later lord chancellor, Sir Francis Bacon, had less luck in defending himself against bribery charges. The cultured Bacon was Shakespeare's contemporary and is thought by some to have been the true author of Shakespeare's plays. If so, the portrayals of corrupt judges came from Bacon's firsthand knowledge of judicial bribe taking.

In 1621 Bacon was lord chancellor and at the pinnacle of his public career. But in that year his life fell apart. Parliament drew up twenty-eight articles of impeachment against Bacon for corruption and bribery. There is no doubt Bacon accepted money from litigants (though he sometimes decided against them). At first, Bacon defended himself on the ground of custom—that is, everybody did it. But as more and more proof surfaced, Bacon avoided a trial by resigning and confessing.

Bacon's confession, delivered as a scroll under seal to the House of Lords, was read aloud:

> To the Right Honourable the Lords Spiritual and Temporal, in the High Court of Parliament assembled: The Confession and humble Submission of me, the Lord Chancellor. Upon advised consideration of the charge, descending into my own conscience, and calling my memory to account so far as I am able, I do plainly and ingenuously confess that I am guilty of corruption; and do renounce all defence, and put myself upon the grace and mercy of your Lordships. The particulars I confess and declare to be as followeth.[11]

Bacon then appended the twenty-eight charges.

Francis Bacon's bribe scandal broke five years after Shakespeare's death, so Shakespeare could not have known about it. But the first edition of Bacon's famous *Essays* came out in 1597 and were reissued in 1612, while Shakespeare was very much at work writing plays. Bacon's essays, short discourses on various topics written in the familiar, clean style of the King James Bible, are a pleasure to read even today. As essayists go, Bacon ranks with Montaigne, Addision and Steele, and Macaulay as a master of the art. One of Bacon's essays is, as lawyers like to say, right on point.

In "Of Judicature," Bacon wrote: "The place of Justice is a hallowed place; And therefore, not only the Bench, but the Footpace, and Precincts, and Purprise thereof, ought to be preserved without Scandal and Corruption ... above all things, integrity is their [i.e., judges'] portion and proper virtue."[12]

As this eloquent passage shows, Bacon certainly understood the ground rules and the highest aspirations of justice. His many achievements in fields besides law—his important work in philosophy and natural science—only underscore the magnitude of the distance he fell, as such people as Richard Nixon and Abe Fortas later came to learn. In several ways, though, Bacon was only articulating in his essay what everyone understood. Lord Edward Coke, who sat on a committee of Parliament investigating the charges against Bacon, put it tersely: "A corrupt judge is the grievance of grievances."[13]

This was the setting in which the first folio of Shakespeare's works was published in 1623. Barely two years had passed since Bacon's disgrace. In another two years, a further revised edition of Bacon's *Essays*—including the ironic "Of Judicature"—would be off the presses. And the story of Thomas More's attitude toward bribes was part of the common heritage. Against such a background, Shakespeare's crooked judges must have been readily seen for what they were.

Though much has changed since Shakespeare's day, much abides. One of the values that abides is the abhorrence of the corrupt judge. In all times, in all places, the crooked judge is anathema.

A CONSTITUTIONAL DILEMMA

Beyond these observations, Shakespeare uses *Richard II* to illustrate even larger, ever relevant legal themes. The play is a running commentary on the rule of law. At one point, for instance, the duke of York does not immediately join the rebellious Bolingbroke, saying:

> It may be I will go with you—but yet I'll pause,
> For I am loath to break our country's laws.
>
> (2.3.167–68)

Would that our elected or appointed officials, our Oliver Norths, followed York's example and similarly pause.

Oliver North and the other Iran-Contra figures should read *Richard II.* They would profit by it. Richard's own conduct is a precedent. He finds pretexts for seizing and confiscating the estate of Bolingbroke's father. What kind of law does a lawful king or government represent that resorts to illegal financing for special projects? Or that resorts to means that are technically legal but morally wrong?

In particular, *Richard II* can and should be read as a play about no one—not even the king—being above the law. The play, for example, scorns the feudal doctrine of the divine right of kings. Several times Richard invokes this doctrine as the source of his unchecked power (remember, it was the fourteenth century). He says he is "the deputy elected by the Lord" (3.2.53); if his subjects revolt, "They break their faith to God as well as us" (3.2.97).

The argument takes its starkest form when one of the nobles, Carlisle, objects to Bolingbroke's replacing Richard as king. "Would God," says Carlisle,

> that any in this noble presence
> Were enough noble to be upright judge
> Of noble Richard! . . .

What subject can give sentence on his king? . . .
And shall the figure of God's majesty,
His captain, steward, deputy elect,
Anointed, crownèd, planted many years,
Be judged by subject and inferior breath . . .?

(4.1.108–20)

Carlisle's argument failed, and he was promptly arrested for treason.

Yet essentially the same argument has arisen again and again, even down to our own time. It is impossible to read *Richard II* without thinking of another, more recent Richard who was a leader of a great nation. Inevitably, *Richard II* reminds us of Richard Nixon, a once popular leader who lost his support among the people, who acted as if he were above the law, and who in the end abdicated his position of power. The comparison becomes even eerier when in the last act of Shakespeare's play someone seeks a pardon.

The Supreme Court's 1974 decision in the *Nixon Tapes Case* caught the spirit of *Richard II* when ruling that the presumptive privilege for presidential communications "must be considered in light of our historic commitment to the rule of law."[14] The Court qualified John Marshall's statement as trial judge in the famous 1807 treason case involving Aaron Burr: "In no case of this kind would a court be required to proceed against the president as against an ordinary individual."[15] Wary of the possible implications of such dicta, the Court in *United States v. Nixon* emphasized that "Marshall's statement cannot be read to mean in any sense that a President is above the law."[16]

Richard II contains the very stuff of constitutional law. In this sense, constitutional law does not mean how a particular clause in a particular government document is interpreted but, more broadly conceived, the nature of government itself. A central theme often seen in *Richard II* concerns what happens if a king (or a chief executive) is weak or incompetent. Such a weak chief executive, say some literary critics, creates a power vacuum in society that leads to a de facto power center elsewhere. Enter Bolingbroke, the strong man on a white horse able to seize and hold power.

Somewhere between the divine right of kings, at one extreme, and the man on a white horse, at the other, lies a happier, more moderate form of government. Here is where Shakespeare's political philosophy squints toward constitutional democracy. In one scene, he compares governing to gardening, with a gardener saying, "All must be even in our government" (3.4.37). The intimations of democracy get clearer when he refers to the source of Richard's troubles.

King Richard's troubles arise from his haughty attitude, his failure to

govern with the consent of the governed and his ruinous economic poli-
cies. Says one character:

> The commons hath he pilled [i.e., plundered] with grievous taxes,
> And quite lost their hearts. The nobles hath he fined
> For ancient quarrels, and quite lost their hearts.
>
> (2.1.247–49)

When finally deposed, Richard is forced to sign a confession because
without one "the Commons [i.e., the people] will not then be satisfied"
(4.1.262).

At this point we start to see themes relevant to our own Constitution.
Richard II, with its rejection of authoritarian power, provides some of the
intellectual background of the American Revolution. Written in 1595,
Richard II portrays a people in revolt, a struggle at least in part between
the people's elected representatives and the king over taxes. Such a struggle between king and Parliament was to play itself out in England during
the first half of the seventeenth century. The ideas embodied in such a
struggle were in the air when the English colonized America during the
same century and were a prominent part of Americans' thought patterns
between 1776 and 1787.

THE PARDON POWER

Toward the end of *Richard II*, there is a scene that raises a related constitutional issue. A traitor asks Bolingbroke for a pardon, while another
character warns the new king, "If thou do pardon, whosoever pray, /
More sins for this forgiveness prosper may" (5.3.81–82). On the other
hand, the rigor of the law, as Portia eloquently said in *The Merchant of
Venice*, should be tempered with equity and mercy. Bolingbroke grants
the pardon after hearing the traitor's mother plead:

> An if I were thy nurse, thy tongue to teach,
> "Pardon" should be the first word of thy speech.
> I never longed to hear a word till now.
> Say "Pardon," King. Let pity teach thee how.
> The word is short, but not so short as sweet;
> No word like "Pardon" for kings' mouths so meet.
>
> (5.3.111–16)

Indeed, Bolingbroke adds, "I pardon him as God shall pardon me."

Pause a moment to ponder the subject of pardons and presidents
against a Shakespearean backdrop. *Comedy of Errors* has a character
who says, "I am not partial to infringe our laws. . . . / For we may pity
though not pardon thee" (1.1.4, 97). The power to pardon has on occa-

sion been controversial in recent American history. The U.S. Constitution gives the president sweeping power "to grant reprieves and pardons for offenses against the United States, except in Cases of Impeachment." Although the existence of the pardon power may be unexceptional, its exercise over the last quarter century has raised serious questions that call to mind Shakespeare's comments.

The extent of the president's pardon power, an executive prerogative that has been exercised since the beginnings of America and before, is well settled—up to a point. It does not include authority to pardon in anticipation of offenses, but it may be exercised at any time after an offense is committed, even before indictment. Even though Congress has a concurrent authority to grant a general amnesty, the president can pardon whole classes by a proclamation of amnesty, such as President Jimmy Carter did for all Vietnam-era draft violators. A pardon may be granted absolutely or conditionally and it cannot be changed by Congress. These aspects of the pardon power are unquestioned.

What is questionable is the peculiar use of the pardon power on two modern occasions, once in 1974 and once in 1992. The first episode was President Gerald Ford's post-Watergate pardon of former President Richard Nixon for all crimes the latter may have committed against the United States during his presidency. The second, much more recent episode occurred when President George Bush, after he lost the 1992 election but before his successor had been sworn in, pardoned former Secretary of Defense Caspar Weinberger and five other former high government officials for various offenses in connection with the Iran-Contra scandal. In both cases, the pardons were attacked by many as inappropriate and even improper, though they were never overturned by any court.

The most telling and most common criticism was that those pardons sent the wrong message to the American people. Rather than acts of mercy, they were widely perceived as political payoffs that told the public that, despite pious rhetoric to the contrary, some people were indeed above or beyond the law. What else can ordinary people think when high government officials are allowed to commit crimes without being punished? After each controversial pardon, less famous clients in trouble speak to their criminal lawyers and ask why they (the clients) cannot get the same lenient treatment. No satisfactory answer comes to mind, except that the government, as York says in *Richard II*, should be "loath to break our country's laws" (2.3.168).

This criticism grows when considered from another point of view. In both cases, the president's behavior itself was called into question. Nixon's conduct regarding Watergate, however, was at least known; Bush's role—the pardoner's own role—in the Iran-Contra events remains, at best, only half disclosed but still dubious. Such involvement is not unusual, as Shakespeare realized: "This is his pardon, purchased by such sin / For which the pardoner himself is in" (*Measure for Measure*, 4.2.110–11).

Worse still was President Bush's rationale for the pardons he gave. Bush said of the former officials he pardoned that "their motivation—whether their actions were right or wrong—was patriotism." After claiming not to know the difference between right and wrong, the president went on to dismiss those pardoned actions as "policy differences" that had somehow mysteriously become subject to "criminalization." The offenses with which the pardoned men were charged—lying to Congress—went to the heart of the proper functioning of the constitutionally mandated separation of powers. But Bush quickly went from pardoning individuals for their crimes to denying that their crimes were crimes at all.

Equally unrepentant is the attitude of those receiving such pardons. Rather than contrition or remorse, they crow about vindication and clearing their name. And yet a pardon is by no means a vindication. Unlike an amnesty, which overlooks by entirely wiping out an offense, a pardon merely "remits punishment." A presidential pardon, contrary to the widespread public perception, does not erase the guilty finding. A pardon, wrote Justice Oliver Wendell Holmes in *Burdick v. United States*, "carries an imputation of guilt; acceptance a confession of it."[17] Indeed, when Jimmy Carter was president, no application for a presidential pardon would be passed on by the Justice Department to the White House unless the petitioner formally admitted guilt.

Shakespeare understood all of this, as *Richard II* shows.

TRIAL BY COMBAT

Like *Hamlet* and *The Merchant of Venice*, Shakespeare's *Richard II* supplies us with an important view of at least one aspect of legal history. If *Hamlet* shows the futility of blood revenge as a way to settle wrongs, and if *The Merchant of Venice* shows the need for equity to temper law, then *Richard II* shows the detailed ritual of the dramatic and colorful trial by combat.

Trial by combat, introduced by the Normans to English law, is exactly what it sounds like. In certain criminal cases, the accuser and the accused actually fought each other to determine guilt or innocence, and the fight was to the death. If a defendant was defeated but not killed in the combat, he was immediately hanged on gallows already prepared.

In civil cases, trial by combat was not fought between the parties themselves, but between their respective champions (the first trial lawyers?). In such cases, where the plaintiff had the burden of proof, the adversary won if the stars appeared before the fight ended. Then as now, champions were expensive to hire, so in civil cases trial by combat tended to be limited to lords who could afford the cost, though it was theoretically available to peasants as well.

Trial by combat was part of Richard II's inheritance. He was a Plantagenet, a descendant of William the Conqueror, and the heir of all the changes his Norman ancestors had wrought in English life and law. No more than approximately three hundred years had passed between William's victory at Hastings in 1066 and the birth of Richard II. In *Richard II*, Shakespeare refers to trial by combat not once, not twice, but three times. As early as the first scene of the first act, Shakespeare has Bolingbroke and Mowbray agree to settle their dispute by means of combat. Later in the play, after Bolingbroke has invaded Richard's England with an army in rebellion, Richard challenges his adversary to trial by combat: "Proud Bolingbroke, I come / To change blows with thee for our day of doom" (3.2.184–85). The third reference to trial by combat occurs in act 4, scene 1, when Aumerle and several other noblemen in Bolingbroke's circle throw down gauntlets to each other to resolve various accusations. Trial by combat is thus a repeated and important theme in *Richard II*.

Richard II casts important light on exactly how the process of trial by combat actually worked. As Shakespeare depicts it, the litigants appeared before the king and formally stated their cases. The king would try to reconcile them, but if such alternative dispute resolution failed, a challenge would follow.

For example, Bolingbroke, a nobleman, accuses his fellow nobleman Mowbray of treason and, after doing so, throws his hood or his glove with this challenge:

> If guilty dread have left thee so much strength
> As to take up mine honour's pawn, then stoop.
> By that, and all the rites of knighthood else,
> Will I make good against thee, arm to arm,
> What I have spoke or thou canst worse devise.
>
> (1.1.73–77)

Hence the expression "throw down the gauntlet."
Mowbray accepts the challenge:

> I take it up, and by that sword I swear,
> Which gently laid my knighthood on my shoulder,
> I'll answer thee in any fair degree
> Or chivalrous design of knightly trial;
> And when I mount, alive may I not light
> If I be traitor or unjustly fight!
>
> (1.1.78–83)

Faced with this dispute, and unable to command his two lords to be friends, King Richard sets the date for the trial by combat:

> Be ready, as your lives shall answer it,
> At Coventry upon Saint Lambert's day [i.e., September 17].
> There shall your swords and lances arbitrate
> The swelling difference of your settled hate.
> Since we cannot atone [i.e., reconcile] you, we shall see
> Justice design the victor's chivalry.
>
> (1.1.198–203)

The fight between the two litigants, referred to as "champions," occurs in act 1, scene 3. Shakespeare there depicts some of the protocol at such a trial of arms. Says Richard to his aide:

> Marshal, demand of yonder champion
> The cause of his arrival here in arms.
> Ask him his name and orderly proceed
> To swear him in the justice of his cause."
>
> (1.3.7–10)

Mowbray answers by saying that he comes

> . . . by the grace of God, and this mine arm
> To prove him [i.e., Bolingbroke] in defending of myself,
> A traitor to my God, my king and me.
> And as I truly fight, defend me heaven!
>
> (1.3.22–25)

A similar exchange takes place with Bolingbroke. Richard asks the marshal to inquire of Bolingbroke: "And formally, according to our law, / Depose him in the justice of his cause" (1.3.29–30). Bolingbroke responds that he is

> . . . ready here do stand in arms
> To prove by God's grace, and my body's valour . . .
> That he [i.e., Mowbray] is a traitor foul and dangerous
> To God of heaven, King Richard, and to me.
> And as I truly fight, defend me heaven!
>
> (1.3.36–41)

Just before the fight starts, the litigants and the spectators add a few more words (after all, it is a play). Richard, recognizing his kinship to Bolingbroke but also acknowledging the law, says to Bolingbroke:

> . . . as thy cause is just,
> So be thy fortune in this royal fight.
> Farewell, my blood, which if today thou shed,
> Lament we may, but not revenge thee dead.
>
> (1.3.55–58)

John of Gaunt, Bolingbroke's father, tells his son, "God in thy good cause make thee prosperous!" (1.3.78). Mowbray, feeling the surge of adrenaline, notes how "my dancing soul doth celebrate / This feast of battle with mine adversary" (1.3.91–92).

Preliminary etiquette done with, the trial by combat must proceed. The king turns to his officer and says, "Order the trial, Marshal, and begin" (1.3.99). Announces the marshal, "God defend the right" (1.3.101). The litigants clash, but without result. In their initial pass, neither is killed or even seriously wounded.

Richard then steps in. Exercising his royal prerogative, he calls off the rest of the battle. At least in Shakespeare's version of trial by combat, it is not to the death. To avoid a civil war, King Richard banishes both litigants from England.

Shakespeare's portrayal of trial by combat helps us understand that early and violent method of dispute resolution. Shakespeare wrote *Richard II* in 1595 and the events in the play take place in the late 1300s. Shakespeare was a lot closer in time to trial by combat than we are. Presumably he knew what he was talking about, and what he says is enlightening.

But Shakespeare does not have occasion to explain all of the fascinating aspects of trial by combat. He does not explain, for example, that the champion originally was a witness and bound as a tenant to defend his lord's title. The combat thus was a duel between contradictory witnesses, the outcome of which decided the rights of the parties. In the early days, the champion-witness had to swear that his father, on his deathbed, had informed him that the plaintiff had the right then in dispute and had charged him to maintain that right with all his power. Although this oath (which at one time had been true) was notoriously false by the Middle Ages, Parliament did not then abolish trial by combat, but rather changed the wording of the oath to delete the requirement that a champion also be a witness.

After a while, trial by combat took on some attributes of the modern legal profession. A professional band of champions (i.e., fighters) who undertook business all over the country grew. Courts arranged the dates of battle so that the champions could fit in their engagements conveniently. Some large landowners were so constantly involved in litigation that they maintained their own full-time champions. Sometimes a champion abandoned his client because the other side offered more money.

Trial by combat died hard. It had a curious attraction. In response to unrest in Boston in 1774, for instance, the English government tried to improve the administration of justice in colonial Massachusetts by means of a bill that among other things abolished trial by combat in certain murder cases. This proposal drew opposition in England from those who regarded trial by combat as a great pillar of the Constitution. In the end, the proposal was withdrawn on the grounds that Parliament ought not to restrain the liberties of the colonies. Time passed, and the law, becoming more civilized, finally did away with actual trial by combat in 1819.

Although trial by combat ended, the idea of the champion remained in the person of the advocate who battled, albeit only in a figurative sense, to protect his or her client in court. Courtroom advocacy provides an acceptable substitute for an actual battle between litigants. One important reason for our continued fascination with courtroom advocacy is this residue of trial by combat.

TALK OF WILLS

If there is one line in *Richard II* that summarizes the play, it is in act 4 when Richard says, "Let's choose executors and talk of wills" (3.2.144). For much of the action in *Richard II* involves the law of inheritance and what happens when that legal institution is disturbed. Yet Shakespeare's attitude toward inheritance in *Richard II* is ambivalent.

Richard is king by virtue of the law of inheritance. He often stresses his inherited royal position. But he gets into trouble when he breaches the very law that gives him his regal status. This is but another example of what happens when someone regards himself as above the law and unsettles the delicate equilibrium established by the law.

Like many an anxious heir, Richard wishes for the early death of a wealthy relative (in this case, his uncle, John of Gaunt). "Now put it, God, in his physician's mind," Richard prays,

> To help him [John of Gaunt] to his grave immediately!
> The lining of his coffers shall make coats
> To deck our soldiers for these Irish wars.
>
> (1.4.58–61)

On his uncle's death, he confiscates his property, thereby robbing his cousin Bolingbroke of his inheritance.

After learning what Richard has done, his other uncle, the duke of York, smells trouble. In a passage that previews what is to happen, York voices his misgivings. Did not Gaunt "deserve to have an heir?" asks York. "Is not his heir a well-deserving son?" (2.1.194–95). York sees the irony of Richard's actions: "For how art thou a king / But by fair sequence and succession?" (2.1.199–200).

On top of irony, York detects danger. "If you do wrongfully seize [Bolingbroke's] rights," and revoke the royal letters-patent that enable his attorneys to obtain for him his father's lands, then, says York to the king,

"You pluck a thousand dangers on your head, / You lose a thousand well-disposèd hearts" (2.1.202–7) When Richard fails to heed York's warning, York adds, with dire foreboding, "What will ensue hereof there's none can tell" (2.1.213).

None, that is, except Shakespeare. As York predicts, Richard pays dearly for violating the law of inheritance. Disinherited, Bolingbroke returns to reclaim not only his own inheritance, but also to take away Richard's. Bolingbroke takes back his father's lands and Richard's crown. An inheritance for an inheritance; it is fair enough in a way. Equilibrium is restored, and then some.

All this talk in *Richard II* of inheritance reflects its importance in feudal English life. Stability and status—high values in the fourteenth century—surely follow from inheritance. As a result of inheritance, you knew your place in feudal England: if your father was a tinker, you were a tinker; if your father was a king, you were a king. All so very simple and static.

This is one way to view the role of inheritance in *Richard II*. But it is not the only way.

Part of what attracts us to *Richard II* is a more modern view of inheritance. As Richard and Bolingbroke struggle for the throne, we see modern notions of meritocracy at war with a thin-blooded, weak, and undeserving heir. Bolingbroke represents, at least in part, individual worth and upward mobility triumphant over inherited status and stability. In this respect, Bolingbroke stands for values congenial to the modern mind, and the play becomes a bridge from old to new fundamental social and legal concepts.

The fight between Richard and Bolingbroke reminds us of the following exchange in Carl Sandburg's long poem "The People, Yes":

> "Get off this estate."
> "What for?"
> "Because it's mine."
> "Where did you get it?"
> "From my father."
> "Where did he get it?"
> "From his father."
> "And where did he get it?"
> "He fought for it."
> "Well, I'll fight you for it."

That is exactly what Bolingbroke does with Richard.

Viewed as an attack on the institution of inheritance, *Richard II* fits into the historical movement identified by Henry Sumner Maine in his book *Ancient Law* as the progressive "movement from status to contract." By focusing attention on the individual over his inherited status, Shakespeare's *Richard II* symbolizes one aspect of the idea of progress.

This reading makes sense in light of Shakespeare's milieu. Shakespeare wrote in postfeudal times, in the late 1500s and early 1600s. At the height of the English Renaissance, when many individuals—including himself—were making their way in the world by dint of their own talent and ability, it was only natural for Shakespeare to regard inherited status as a unwarranted brake on a person's potential. The excitement and ferment of the Elizabethan Age were conducive to "progressive" ideas emphasizing individual achievement rather than inherited status.

At the same time, the Elizabethan setting may also explain the ambivalence in Shakespeare's attitude toward inheritance in *Richard II*. England at the end of the sixteenth century was at a transition point in history: no longer in the Middle Ages, but not yet fully in the modern era. Ideas about a number of things, including inheritance, were changing. Shakespeare's contemporaries liked some aspects of inheritance and disliked others. Hence his own mixed feelings, as reflected in *Richard II*.

Important as the law of inheritance is in *Richard II*, it shares the stage with slander and the real or imagined hurt slander can do. On being accused of treason by Bolingbroke, Mowbray says, "I do defy him, and I spit at him, / Call him a slanderous coward and a villain" (1.1.60–61). Even when his king encourages him to ignore the accusation, Mowbray says, "My fair name" can only be saved with "his heart blood / Which breathed this poison" (1.1.167–73). In words reminiscent of Iago's "good name in man or woman" speech, Mowbray adds:

> The purest treasure mortal times afford
> Is spotless reputation;—that away,
> Men are but gilded loam, or painted clay. . . .
> Mine honour is my life. Both grow in one:
> Take honour from me, and my life is done.
>
> (1.1.177–83)

Parts of the play are lessons in civil procedure. The concept of a litigant representing himself without a lawyer finds expression in *Richard II*. "Attorneys are denied me," Bolingbroke complains (2.3.133). "What would you have me do?" (2.3.132). Without aid of counsel, then, "personally I lay my claim / To my inheritance of free descent" (2.3.134–35). Do we discern here the important right to represent oneself?[18]

Shakespeare even comments on the art of advocacy. In act 5, a character says, as I might say of an adversary, "Pleads he in earnest? Look upon his face" (5.3.99). Going on, we learn how to tell the sincere from the false advocate.

His words come from his mouth; ours from our breast.
He prays but faintly, and would be denied;
We pray with heart and soul, and all beside.

(5.3.100–2)

How many times in the courtroom have I said to myself, "His prayers are full of false hypocrisy; / Ours of zeal and deep integrity" (5.3.105–6)?

The play underscores the role of confessions in the law. Bolingbroke's advisers want Richard to admit his wrongdoing before taking away his throne. With language that inevitably reminds us of the Moscow purge trials of the 1930s, Shakespeare has Northumberland answer Richard's question "What more remains?" as follows:

No more, but that you read
These accusations and these grievous crimes
Committed by your person and your followers
Against the state and profit of this land,
That by confessing them, the souls of men
May deem that you are worthily deposed.

(4.1.212–17)

At work here we see psychology and public relations. Confessions always make punishment more fitting.

We could go on and on. We could talk about how the murder of Richard by Henry IV's henchmen closely resembles the assassination of Becket two centuries earlier by Henry II's soldiers; how in both cases the crimes sprang from attempts by subordinates to please superiors who made ill-considered comments; and how the killers learned that leaders have to distance themselves from illegal acts, whether they ordered them or not.

Richard II has modern legal resonances to it. From one perspective, we see the threat of government censorship. When Essex's followers had *Richard II* revived on the eve of their leader's ill-fated rebellion, the performance prompted Queen Elizabeth to make her only known reference to Shakespeare. Worried over the effect of the play being performed, for fear it would encourage rebellion, Elizabeth said, "Know ye not that I am Richard II?" From another perspective we see new legal and social concepts emerging, however tentatively. We see the law moving away from inherited status. We see progress, which hurtles to a climax in *King Lear*'s attitude toward inheritance.

Chapter Thirteen

BREATH OF AN UNFEE'D LAWYER

KING LEAR

EACH OF US has a favorite play by Shakespeare, an individual work that more than any other stimulates, provokes, and unsettles, engaging our mind and then leaving it most intrigued and changed. It may not be the simplest or easiest play to understand; depth and difficulty often add texture and layers of meaning. The comedies may at times seem too frivolous or superficial, although they often hide trenchant insights. A favorite play may in fact be hard to subdue, even to grasp.

For many the culmination of Shakespeare, the best of his plays, his sublime morality play, his greatest dramatic poem is *King Lear*. As A. C. Bradley, the English critic, wrote in 1904, "If we were doomed to lose all [Shakespeare's] dramas except one, probably the majority of those who know and appreciate him best would pronounce for keeping *King Lear*."[1]

The first time I saw *King Lear* I had little idea what was happening. I was a sixteen-year-old high school student who, only having skimmed the play, came nowhere near appreciating what must have been a superb performance by Paul Scofield at New York's Lincoln Center in 1964. But unread as I was, the play's emotional depth and turmoil still pulled me in. The storm scene on the heath, with its utter wildness, made no sense to me then, and hence stuck in my mind as something unresolved. Gloucester's blinding was horrible, yet had to mean more to the story than I then understood. The basic action, the dynamics were too much for a teenager—at least, this teenager—to grasp fully.

About fifteen years passed before I saw my next *King Lear*, and that passage of time made all the difference. By then I had read the play at least twice, albeit still without feeling a command of its essence. But the performance of the Morris Carnovsky as Lear at the American Shakespeare Festival in Stratford, Connecticut, drove home the play's point, his acting clearing up much that was confusing for me. My father's death a few years earlier doubtless intensified my reaction as I watched the play and thought about the relationship between generations. So affected was I that I simply could not talk for hours after that performance.

My most recent *King Lear* was Laurence Olivier's television movie of the play. Olivier was superb, of course, but television just does not do justice to Shakespeare. In spite of great acting in a tragedy of universal significance, the small screen seriously detracts from the audience experience. If a play is to be seen, it is meant to be seen live in a theater, where it can fill up one's entire consciousness for a few hours and the audience can relate to live actors. Even wonderful movies such as Olivier's *Hamlet, Henry V,* and *Richard III,* and Kenneth Branagh's *Henry V* and *Much Ado about Nothing* miss the crucial "live" aspects; but such films at least dominate the mind when seen on the grand silver screen in a darkened movie theater. Watching them on television is far less gripping and fulfilling.

As I see and read and think about *King Lear* again and again, I become more convinced that this play has it all. Rage and passion, cruelty and selfishness, hypocrisy and moral convulsion—all these and more make the play what it is. These qualities are enhanced by their occurring in the context of family, so that each of us can feel them and identify with them personally. Natural affection and the consequences of breaking that bond, genuine love and pretended love, ingratitude of children and their inhumanity to aged parents are part of what goes on. It is a swirling, whirling, overpowering work that stamps itself deeply on the mind.

The underlying theme—the relationship of the generations—expands on the inheritance theme of *Richard II* as it jumps out of the first scene of the first act of the play. *King Lear* opens with the elderly monarch announcing his

> intent
> To shake all cares and business from our age
> Conferring them on younger strengths while we
> Unburdened crawl toward death.
>
> (1.1.38–41)

He plans to give one-third of his kingdom to each of his three daughters, including land, wealth, and power to rule over their domains. Before actually making the transfers, Lear organizes a debasing competition: he asks each daughter to outdo the others in declaring how much she loves him. He suggests that the one who loves him most will get more than the others.

Lear's daughters—Goneril, Regan, and Cordelia—react in two different ways. Goneril and Regan, the two elder, flatter their father with mellifluous words of doting love. Lear responds by giving them their promised thirds. But Cordelia, the youngest and Lear's favorite, cannot bring herself to say publicly her most intimate feelings for her father as a manipulative means of getting something from him. Appalled, Lear mistakes her honesty and modesty as lovelessness and ingratitude. In a fit of anger, he disinherits his best-loved daughter and banishes his trusted adviser Kent, who comes to Cordelia's defense.

From this bizarre event everything else in the play flows. Once Lear has irrevocably given everything he owns to Goneril and Regan, he finds out what monsters they really are. He learns that their pleasing words of filial love were false and hypocritical. Now that they have his property, these two prize daughters bully and abuse their aged father with great cruelty. They strip him of honor and dignity, take away his last remnants of a retinue, and evict him from their homes, sending him out into a stormy night. Realizing "how sharper than a serpent's tooth it is / To have a thankless child" (1.4.268–69), Lear goes mad.

Lear's madness eventually lifts through self-discovery and the love of his faithful daughter, Cordelia. But the price is high. By the end of the play, both Lear and Cordelia are dead, as are the two horrible older daughters, both of whom had fallen in love with the same man. Other characters along the way have been tortured or have died. All in all, *King Lear* is a play about a person's mind and what happens to it as it is buffeted by unanticipated events that dissolve the family.

Unlike *The Merchant of Venice* or *Measure for Measure* or *The Winter's Tale*, *King Lear* is not a play obviously focused on a law trial or ostensibly riddled with legal themes. But this does not mean the play never refers explicitly to law or never pokes light fun at lawyers. On the contrary, in the first act we have the following exchange between Kent and the Fool:

Kent This is nothing, fool.
Fool Then 'tis like the breath of an unfee'd lawyer: you
        gave me nothing for't.

                                                    (1.4.127–30)

In my own practice, I have often heard an updated version of that exchange that goes like this:

Friend or Acquaintance I need some free legal advice.
Lawyer   You get what you pay for.

In this regard, little has changed.

In act 3, when the Fool gives his prophecy of impossible events, he includes, "When every case in law is right" (3.2.87). A little later in the same act, while the great storm rages outside on the heath and inside Lear's brain, Lear imagines his two elder daughters brought to trial. Gripped by his madness, Lear announces that he will arraign them and proceeds to testify against Goneril and Regan, having appointed Edgar and the Fool as judges. Or if we choose to, we could focus on the legal aspects of Edmund's slanders of his brother and father.

By no means is that all the law in *King Lear*. Shakespeare even introduces us to sovereign immunity, the persistent legal doctrine that supposedly puts the king (or modern government) above the law. When Goneril, a ruler by direct descent, is asked if she admits having committed treason, her haughty response is: "Say if I do, the laws are mine, not thine. / Who can arraign me for't?" (5.3.149–50). Based on that dangerous line of Goneril's, which echoes down to our days of Watergate and Iran-Contra, one might write a whole essay on sovereign immunity. Similarly, Goneril also comments on trial by combat. After Edmund loses his duel with the helmeted Edgar, Goneril complains, "By th' law of arms thou wast not bound to answer / An unknown opposite" (5.3.143–44).

But even if not on the surface, deeper and subtler legal themes course through *King Lear*. Seen from a legal vantage point, the play yields several illuminating ideas and allows one to meditate about fundamental legal concepts. For instance, *King Lear* furthers our understanding of why justice is portrayed as blind. The play also is a warning about delegation of authority, a common theme in Shakespeare. Most centrally, *King Lear*'s tension between generations provides a superb occasion to reevaluate the benefits and drawbacks of inheritance and what that legal institution means today. Finally, revealing a long-submerged political correctness, Shakespeare's tragedy explores the effects of discrimination against illegitimates, which invites analysis under the equal protection clause of the Fourteenth Amendment of the Constitution.

THE "INSIGHT" OF BLIND JUSTICE

All its passion, emotion, and moral convulsion make *King Lear* a dramatic machine for rearranging the molecules in our brain so that we view the world differently. As Lear's mind goes through its crucial changes, we identify with that mind and its troubles. We examine ourselves, our closest relationships, and our very lives—and nothing is ever quite the same for us again. *King Lear* virtually compels reexamination of our deepest feelings, our most important values, our very essence. Among the basic values so affected by *King Lear* is the fundamental metaphor of justice.

For centuries the traditional symbol of justice has been a blindfolded woman holding in one hand a balance scale and in the other a sword. Justice wears a blindfold, we are usually told, so she cannot show favoritism or yield to bias or prejudice. Thus, if justice does not see the parties before her, then in weighing the evidence she cannot prefer the strong over the weak, friends over enemies, rich over poor, neighbors over strangers, one race over another, one sex over another. In theory, the law is supposed to treat all equally, without fear or favor, and the blindfold on the symbol of justice is designed to help ensure such equal treatment.

This usual explanation is a good one, as far as it goes. Of course, avoiding biased judgment is a vital attribute of any system of law worthy of the name. And the metaphor of blind justice does convey the basic idea in a meaningful, graceful, and evocative way. Yet for all its symbolic importance, interpreting the blindfold as a means of reducing the role of bias in law is neither the only possible interpretation nor the last word on the subject. *King Lear* provides a new, supplementary, and perhaps even deeper psychological explanation for why the symbol of justice is blindfolded.

Much in *King Lear* turns on the subject of *seeing*. The play is dominated by that single image, the metaphor of darkness and light, blindness and vision. The story of *King Lear* is in many ways the story of how to see more truly. It is, as Goddard demonstrates, the drama of one who at the start has physical eyesight but is morally blind, who over time experiences spiritual lightning that illuminates his lost soul and brings him to the threshold of *in*sight.[2]

King Lear is full of references to eyes and eyesight. Gloucester's unforgettable blinding is obviously one such scene, as is Goneril's earlier cry, "Pluck out his eyes" (3.7.4). But there is much more. When Lear asks Goneril to declare her feelings for him, she replies, "Sir, I love you more than words can wield the matter; / Dearer than eyesight, space, and liberty" (1.1.55–56). Soon after that, when the good counselor Kent tries to intervene on Cordelia's behalf, Lear cries, "Out of my sight!" (1.1.157). Kent replies, "See better, Lear, and let me still remain / The true blank of thine eye" (1.1.158–59). Eventually Lear learns how to "see better."

Large as the number of references is to eyes and eyesight, their significance more than their number is what counts. Of special importance here is a line spoken by the blinded Gloucester on the heath. When Gloucester begs the Old Man who has befriended him to leave him, the Old Man protests, "You cannot see your way." Gloucester replies, "I have no way, and therefore want no eyes. / I stumbled when I saw" (4.1.18–20). That response by the blind Gloucester opens the eyes of our minds, even as the truth opened Gloucester's mind to the characters of his two sons. Before then, people and events in Gloucester's life had swum around him in complicated patterns that he had at best dimly perceived through murky water.

Even the best of us can stumble when we do no more than physically see. Even with physical eyesight, we can be morally and spiritually blind. What we need above all is *in*sight, which is not necessarily related to good physical vision. Lear and Gloucester start to acquire that insight as they experience their lives' traumas. As in the case of Oedipus, the suffering they undergo gives each of them greater understanding and wisdom than mere eyesight ever did—or ever could. They come to feel full of insight; they feel drenched with insight.

Not only is physical eyesight no guaranty of understanding, as *King Lear* shows, but lack of such eyesight may actually enhance other senses and overall awareness and perception. We all are familiar with the psychology of blindness, in which the loss of one sense leads to compensatory development of other senses. By force of necessity, a blind person often has keener senses of hearing, touch, and smell. As Shakespeare points out in *A Midsummer Night's Dream*: "Dark night, that from the eye his function takes, / The ear more quick of apprehension makes" (3.2.178–79). Lear himself tells the blinded Gloucester, "A man may see how this world / goes with no eyes; look with thine ears" (4.5.146–47). Hence the paradox of the blind being more sensitive, seeing better, than the sighted.

Now emerges the *King Lear* explanation for symbolizing justice with a blindfold. Without the blindfold, justice—in addition to showing favor to persons—may "stumble" in a larger, moral sense, as Lear and Gloucester did, and as does the person "that will not see / Because he does not feel" (4.1.62–63). Blindfolded, justice "sees better," sees into the essence of things, sometimes sees more than anyone wants her to. Blind justice compensates by developing the more crucial moral and spiritual sensitivities needed for correctly deciding cases. The desired though perhaps paradoxical result of the blindfold is a justice with greater not lesser, clearer not dimmer, insight.

DELEGATION OF AUTHORITY

One of the more important legal themes vividly shown by *King Lear* concerns the consequences of delegated authority. Lear is the head of state and the source of law. While he reigns, law and order prevail—as far as we know. The text of the play gives no hint of trouble in the realm with Lear on the throne. But his abdication quickly brings in its trail disorder, civil strife, and chaos.

We see this and similar themes frequently in Shakespeare. Delegation of authority is a subset of a larger class of power void. If the lawful authority abdicates, is too weak, or is deposed, moral confusion and often actual fighting take its place. In *Measure for Measure*, the duke pretends to leave Vienna and his hypocritical deputy Angelo makes a mess of enforcing the law. The history plays covering the War of the Roses from *Richard II* through *Richard III* essentially spin from the problems of usurping proper authority. *Julius Caesar* and *Macbeth* offer analogous problems.

The common thread seems to be a contest or tension between law and chaos. Upset the rule of law, these plays seem to say, and you get chaos. Create a power void, and you get civil disorder. Alter the equilibrium of the state and all will not be well until balance is restored. From this perspective, Shakespeare appears to be adopting a conservative line: keep the status quo or else.

But let us consider Shakespeare's point not from the political but from the psychological view, which is not unwarranted given Shakespeare's psychological insight. Suppose we think of the contest as one between human passions being unregulated or mastered. There is plenty of unregulated passion in *King Lear* and much of Shakespeare—and we see the terrible consequences. The lesson seems to be: either master our passions or endure chaos. Might Shakespeare be foreshadowing Freud's thesis in *Civilization and Its Discontents* that civilized society depends on our controlling our passions by partially sublimating our aggressive and sexual drives?

All of a sudden Shakespeare's point about delegation of authority assumes larger meaning. It becomes a deep statement about the role of law. Not only is Shakespeare's theme about law in its most common usage, but it is also a perceptive and prescient comment about what it takes to maintain some control over the dark forces in each of us, a control we call civilization. In this sense, Shakespeare's unhappy description of delegated authority in *King Lear* underscores for us the true role of law in human society.

DIDST THOU GIVE ALL?

The delegation of authority problem in *King Lear*, as in several of the plays, is one aspect of inheritance: succession to power. When the king (the father figure) dies or otherwise yields or loses power, who is the rightful heir to his throne? Succession to power is a large theme in Shakespeare. It figures prominently, for instance, in *Hamlet, Macbeth, Julius Caesar, King John, Richard II, Henry IV* (both parts), *Henry VI* (all three parts), and *Richard III*. But inheritance involves more than succession to power; it also involves succession to property.

Inheritance of property pervades Shakespeare's plays. In addition to the above tragedies and histories, inherited wealth is an issue in *The Merchant of Venice* and *Othello*. In *Merchant*, Shylock tries to disinherit his daughter Jessica, while Portia's judgment undoes Shylock's intent and practically confiscates his estate. Another daughter—Desdemona—is disinherited by her father in *Othello* for her disobedience in marrying the Moor. Inasmuch as inheritance was such a crucial way to transfer wealth in Shakespeare's time, it is no wonder that it occupies center stage in his dramatic works, as it did in his own personal life with the *Lambert* litigation and his own will.

From the widest angle, these issues look like parts of the larger and even more central Shakespearean theme of the relationship of the generations. Whether power, wealth, or status is at stake, what we really are seeing is how the generations relate to one other. Desdemona and Jessica disobey their fathers and choose husbands of their own liking. Portia submits to the casket game for choosing her husband. Hamlet struggles monumentally but finally obeys his father's ghost and seeks blood revenge; Ophelia obeys her father's orders to break off her relationship with Hamlet, and as a result suffers a mental collapse. Romeo and Juliet still see each other despite their parents' feud.

Again and again we see conflicts and tensions between generations. Forces of the past are at work in the present. Action revolves around the authority of the past, usually symbolized by the father, over the present. Will the younger generation seek its freedom, or yield to authority? Such pervasive generational relationships make Shakespeare universal, timeless, and personal. Every audience in every age in every locale must identify with the struggle between the generations.

In *King Lear* that struggle is particularly sharp as the crux of the play. Shakespeare even underscores the inheritance theme in a parallel plot. Not only do we have the searing generational issues of Lear and his daughters, but we also have similar issues with Gloucester and his sons. One of Gloucester's sons—Edmund—is illegitimate, and for that reason has no right, under the law of that time and place, to inherit property. Bitter and full of resentment over his fate, Edmund connives to take his half-brother's inheritance by falsely accusing him of trying to kill their father. "Let me," cries Edmund not so sotto voce, "If not by birth, have lands by wit" (1.2.172). Edmund also informs against his father, which leads to Gloucester's blinding.

With all its tragedy and human sorrow, the doubly stressed inheritance theme in *King Lear* should make us think hard about the legal institution of inheritance. The gratuitous transfer of wealth by will, gift, trust, and otherwise is one of the most basic legal processes, perhaps so basic and so common that we take it too much for granted. *King Lear* makes us reflect on inheritance and consider its positive and negative aspects.

We can sympathize with Lear up to a point. What parent getting on in years has not at least thought about giving his or her property to children so as to see, while alive, the pleasure it can bestow? But look at what happens to Lear when he does exactly that: his daughters Goneril and Regan turn on him as soon as they have their inheritance. *King Lear* is a powerful and compelling argument against inherited wealth.

Lear makes several errors that throw into sharp relief some of the evils of inherited wealth. He uses the prospect of inheritance to manipulate his children. By dangling an inheritance before their eyes, he expects them to act lovingly toward him. Lear, with inheritance as a bribe, tries to control how they will behave. He foolishly sets up the absurd game where each daughter is supposed to say she loves her father more than her sisters do.

But Lear deludes himself. While using the inheritance to manipulate his daughters, he never allows for the possibility of their manipulating him in turn to get the inheritance. Like any father, he wants his children's love—but bribes them for mere *statements* of love. He got what he bought, not what he wanted. Goneril and Regan flatter the manipulative Lear, practicing (like lawyers?) "that glib and oily art" (1.1.224) of saying things they do not mean.

Lear also gives away everything he has while he is still alive. Although we can understand why a rich old man might want to see his children enjoy his gifts, he puts himself totally at their mercy. Lear fails to be psychologically astute about Goneril and Regan. He makes the mistake of believing what they say instead of continuing to hold out the inheritance as an incentive to their continued good behavior. As the Fool reminds Lear:

> Fathers that wear rags
> Do make their children blind;
> But fathers that bear bags
> Shall see their children kind.
>
> (2.2.223–26)

Without property, Lear lost his manipulative leverage, which he craved.

In time Lear realizes his folly. Meeting Edgar, who is disguised as a lunatic, Lear asks, "Didst thou give all to thy two daughters, / And art thou come to this?" (3.4.46–47). After the disguised Edgar mutters crazily about a "foul fiend," Lear asks more questions: "Has his daughters brought him to this pass? / Couldst thou save nothing? Wouldst thou give 'em all?" (3.4.59–60). These questions to Edgar reveal Lear's rueful state of mind.

Lear then falls into the common trap of treating his children unequally. He disinherits one child and divides everything between the other two. Goneril and Regan, who got the inheritance, are still jealous of Cordelia because, as Goneril hisses, "He / always loved our sister most" (1.1.289–90). At least since the biblical story of Joseph and his brothers, we have known the grave risks of a parent too obviously favoring one child over others. When children are treated unequally for inheritance, it often ignites the nastiest fights known to the law.

To be sure, Lear is not the only person ever to make such errors when it comes to inheritance. We all know families—perhaps our own—in which expectations of inheritance control the behavior of members of the family and their relationship to one another. We can certainly empathize with an old man's desire to shuck off economic cares by giving his property to his children in the hope of seeing the happiness it brings.

Inheritance of wealth has, not surprisingly, been a source of controversy for centuries. Experience has taught people, as it taught King Lear, Gloucester, and their families, that inheritance involves the whole range of human emotions: love, hate, jealousy, avarice. When a subject is so charged with emotion, people often have differing views about it, which is precisely what has happened with inherited wealth.

Controversy has produced a continuing debate over the inheritance issues raised by *King Lear*. At least since the late 1800s, when great concentrations of family wealth developed in this country, many Americans have tended to be antagonistic toward inheritance. Opposition to inherited wealth was an important theme of the Progressive and Populist movements in American history. At times, some have even called for the abolition of inheritance, though such proposals have never carried the day. Such popular antagonism, however, led to the enactment of estate and inheritance taxes as a reasonable compromise to reduce the perceived tension between two basic values. One value, liberty, suggests that individuals have the right to do whatever they want with their property. On the other hand, a free society has a strong commitment to the value of equality of opportunity. Balancing these important values is the task of the debate over inheritance, a hard problem for American political theory and American society.

Lear makes one think about the relationship between inheritance and meritocracy. Meritocracy might be even seen as a hidden theme in *King Lear*. Lear's older daughters demonstrate that the recipients of inherited wealth have not earned it, nor does it bear any relationship to their productive abilities or performance. Goneril and Regan are not fit to rule despite their inheritance. When, in the last scene, they taunt each other over their love interest, Edmund, Goneril rebuffs Regan's claims to have made Edmund what he is, saying to her, "In his own grace he doth exalt himself / More than in your addition" (5.3.60–61). Then, after the battle and the duel between Edgar and Edmund, and all has been revealed, Albany proclaims an oath to meritocracy:

> . . . All friends shall taste
> The wages of their virtue, and all foes
> The cup of their deservings.

> (5.3.278–80)

Stressing the significance of this passage is the evocative exclamation, "O, see, see!" which immediately follows. When all this is coupled with the tension in the play between status by birth and status by achievement, one does see the meritocracy leitmotif at work.

This debate over inheritance, kindled again for us by thinking about *King Lear*, may even be creating a new and disturbing paradox. In the past, the basic tension in the inheritance debate has been between meritocracy, equality of opportunity, and upward mobility, on the one hand, and artificial aristocracy, family stability, and freedom to do what one wants with property at death, on the other. Now, as meritocracy has gained in the struggle, it is starting to conflict with another deeply held value, the traditional American sense of social equality. Any triumph of meritocracy makes it harder to resist the invidious conclusion that more economically successful people are in some sense superior people. Hence the paradox that increasing meritocracy might have unpleasant and ominous implications for America.

Aggravating the newly perceived threat to social equality is the role of heredity. As artificial inequalities—e.g., environmental differences and class biases—are lessened, natural inequalities become dominant. Jefferson's "natural aristocracy," in which it is likely that traits of "merit" will be at least in part genetically inherited, may finally rise. But then looms the danger of genetic stratification and a class system. Hence the sad conclusion that greater stratification of society based on merit, which had until recently seemed the most justifiable way to stratify society (assuming society was to be stratified at all), may undermine the traditional American sense of social equality.[3]

The few issues touched on here are by no means all of the issues implicated by Shakespeare's vivid portrayal of inheritance run amok in *King Lear*. But even these few issues show that the institution of inheritance of wealth involves basic value choices related to some of the most fundamental aspects of our society. Yet no one has written a satisfactory history of the relationship of democratic thinking to the institution of inheritance.

STAND UP FOR BASTARDS

Even if all the evils of inherited wealth were somehow abolished, which is unlikely to happen any time soon, there still would remain—as Edmund in *King Lear* demonstrates so well—the problem of inherited status. Edmund, Gloucester's illegitimate son, feels gravely wronged by his outcast status. As an illegitimate, he has no legal right to inherit property. His father has a snickering attitude toward him, calling him "whoreson" (1.1.24) and admitting, "I / have so often blushed to acknowledge him" (1.1.8–9). All of this deprives Edmund of any shred of human dignity.

Nurturing this deep hurt, Edmund feels himself entitled to revenge for the wrong committed against him. He does not feel bound by law and morals, and disregards them whenever it works to his advantage to do so. (Edmund the bastard has the same first name as Edmund Lambert, Shakespeare's antagonist at law in the case involving John Shakespeare's real property. Edmund Lambert was John Shakespeare's brother-in-law, and the case could be described as an attempt by Edmund to steal his brother-in-law's inheritance. Might this have played a role in Shakespeare's choice of name for the bastard in *Lear*?) As he is about to implement his sinister plan to take his legitimate half-brother's inheritance from him, Edmund calls on the heavens: "Now, gods, stand up for bastards!" (1.2.22). Such resentment makes Edmund into, in his own words, "a plain villain," an evil character constantly plotting against and deceiving his own family.

And yet for all his unpleasant qualities, Edmund, thanks to Shakespeare, makes a poignant lament not unlike Shylock's "Hath not a Jew eyes?" speech:

> . . . Why "bastard"? Wherefore "base,"
> When my dimensions are as well compact,
> My mind as generous, and my shape as true
> As honest madam's issue? Why brand they us
> With "base," With "baseness, bastardy—base, base"—
>
> (1.2.6–10)

We read those words, we hear Edmund's haunting cry, and we imagine millions of others bemoaning their outcast fate. Throughout history, the lament has been the same, and for the most part it has gone unanswered.

As long as we distinguish between "legitimate" and "illegitimate" children, the problem will be with us. It is a problem of status, whether or not an estate exists to inherit. For the very categories "legitimate" and "illegitimate" vividly express, as does "bastard," society's age-old response to the status of such children. As Edmund spits out, "As to th' legitimate. Fine word, 'legitimate'" (1.2.18). Lear, angry at Goneril, calls her the worst epithet he can think of: "Degenerate bastard!" (1.4.232). And even today, American law adds to the pain of society's shunning by sometimes throwing up barriers to the exercise of certain rights by illegitimates. In some states, the law restricts illegitimates' rights to sue for a parent's wrongful death, to inherit property, or to claim insurance benefits.

Such discrimination against illegitimates has led to significant developments in American constitutional law. The Fourteenth Amendment to the U.S. Constitution guarantees to all persons "equal protection of the laws." Relying on the equal protection clause, illegitimates have over the last twenty-five years sued, claiming that discrimination against them is unconstitutional. A number of their cases have even reached the Supreme Court, where that tribunal has charted an uneven course. When dealing with illegitimacy-based classifications, the Supreme Court has "properly, if not always consistently or coherently,"[4] scrutinized the laws in question with unusual care.

Shakespeare's Edmund, the nasty bastard in *King Lear*, had something to do with those constitutional developments. In 1968 the first Supreme Court case to strike down as unconstitutional a state statute discriminating against illegitimates relied on and quoted Edmund's moving "Why bastard, wherefore base?" speech. That case, *Levy v. Louisiana*,[5] involved a state law that excluded illegitimates from the class of children entitled to recover for a parent's death. In reviewing that statute, the Court looked closely and found it wanting.

In the majority opinion, written by liberal Justice William O. Douglas, the Court asked a series of daunting rhetorical questions:

> The rights asserted here involve the intimate, familial relationship between a child and his own mother. When the child's claim of damage for loss of his mother is an issue, why, in terms of "equal protection," should the tortfeasors go free merely because the child is illegitimate? Why should the illegitimate child be denied rights merely because of his birth out of wedlock? He certainly is subject to all the responsibilities of a citizen, including the payment of taxes and conscription under the Selective Service Act. How under our constitutional regime can he be denied correlative rights which other citizens enjoy?[6]

Finding no good answers to any of these inquiries, the Court concluded that "it is invidious to discriminate against" illegitimates "when no action, conduct, or demeanor of theirs is possibly relevant to the harm that was done the [deceased parent]."[7]

It was in the opinion's concluding paragraph that Justice Douglas dropped a footnote to *King Lear*. Immediately after the phrase "no action, conduct or demeanor of theirs," Douglas placed footnote six, which started, "We can say with Shakespeare" and then quoted Edmund's moving lament.[8] Placing the footnote in the conclusion gave it special emphasis.

The dissenting opinion in *Levy* took up Justice Douglas's Shakespearean challenge. Rather than allow the quote from *King Lear* to go unanswered, Justice John Harlan's dissent responded in kind. Harlan, superbly educated and with a conservative frame of mind, showed that he too had read and understood *King Lear*. Writing that a grown man may, under the Louisiana statute, sue for the wrongful death of "parents he did not love," Harlan then added in a footnote: "He may even, like Shakespeare's Edmund, have spent his life contriving treachery against his family."[9]

Not content to stop there, Harlan went on to generalize in the footnote: "Supposing that the Bard had any views on the law of legitimacy, they might more easily be discerned from Edmund's character than from the words he utters in defense of the only thing he cares for, himself."[10] Thus did the cultured Harlan hope to pit Edmund's despicable character against his speech. What Edmund is counts more for Harlan than what Edmund says. It is a fascinating and rare treat to see Supreme Court justices, like literary scholars, citing the same Shakespearean play for diametrically opposite propositions.

Justice Douglas's constitutional interpretation of *King Lear* seems to have narrowly won the day, so far, but not by much and, given recent changes in the personnel of the Court, who knows for how long? Decisions after *Levy* have zigged and zagged on discrimination against illegitimates. The Supreme Court has upheld some such laws and overturned others. Along the way, however, the Court has cited both the "fundamental personal rights" endangered by the classification and the invidiousness of discrimination resting on "status of birth."[11] The majority viewpoint of the Court, the result of its tortuous path, says that "the legal status of illegitimacy, however defined, is, like race or national origin, a characteristic determined by causes not within the control of the illegitimate individual, and . . . bears no relation to the individual's ability to participate in and contribute to society."[12]

The illegitimacy cases are part of an evolving constitutional standard. Up until fairly recently, the Supreme Court had devised only two tiers of analysis for dealing with equal protection cases. The first tier, which is practically a constitutional rubber stamp, requires no more than a mere rational basis for the legislative classification. This is the general rule, and it presumes that legislation, especially social and economic legislation, is valid and will be sustained if the classification drawn by the statute is rationally related to a legitimate state interest. Rare is the state law that cannot meet this general rule.

The second tier of equal protection analysis is much more demanding. It calls for "strict scrutiny" of statutes using a "suspect classification," like race or national origin, or impinging on fundamental personal rights protected by the Constitution. Such laws will be sustained only if they are narrowly tailored to serve a compelling state interest. When the Court invokes the "strict scrutiny" test, it almost always means that the statute will be voided.

For years the Supreme Court used this two-tiered equal protection analysis, until it more recently found instances in which it needed a third tier applying an intermediate level of scrutiny. The Court ruled that legislative classifications based on gender, for example, call for a heightened, but not the severest, standard of review. A gender classification fails unless it is substantially related to a sufficiently important governmental interest.[13]

The outcome of a particular case is largely a function of what equal protection test a court applies. The illegitimacy cases since *Levy* have been an effort to expand the suspect classification beyond race and national origin to include illegitimacy too. If illegitimacy were considered a suspect classification, then laws discriminating against illegitimates would have to satisfy the strict scrutiny test. To date, this effort at trying to change constitutional law has been only a partial success.

Although illegitimacy cases moved beyond the minimal rational basis test, they have not yet been elevated to the suspect-classification, strict scrutiny test. Instead, official discrimination based on illegitimacy is, like gender classification, stuck in the intermediate level of somewhat heightened review. The trend in the Court's decisions has been to evaluate discrimination against illegitimates by examining whether a given statute presents an "insurmountable barrier" to equal treatment[14] and whether there is a significant countervailing social interest at stake.[15] Phrased another way, laws discriminating against illegitimates "will survive equal protection scrutiny to the extent they are substantially related to a legitimate state interest."[16]

No doubt Edmund would agree with the view that such discriminatory laws punish illegitimate children for the conduct of their parents. Edmund would probably also agree that only a moral prejudice, unbefitting today's world, could support such discrimination against illegitimate children. Whether constitutional analysis of these issues will change remains to be seen. At a minimum, inequality based exclusively on "status of birth" is hardly a value treasured in our constitutional framework.

One thing we can be sure of is that neither we nor the justices of the Supreme Court should be overhasty in concluding how Shakespeare really felt about illegitimates. Edmund is not a one-dimensional villain. The prejudice and legal disabilities imposed on him because of his birth push him to find some way—legitimate or illegitimate—to make his way in the world and acquire property. We may abhor the means but not the desire for a better material life. He even shows a glimmer, however faint, of a nobler character. After being critically wounded in his duel with Edgar, Edmund is moved by Edgar's account of their father's death. Then, when the dead bodies of Goneril and Regan are brought in, Edmund moans, "I pant for life. Some good I mean to do, / Despite of mine own nature" (5.3.218–19). To realize his promise, he countermands his order to have Cordelia killed, but he is too late.

Edmund is not the only significant illegitimate in Shakespeare's plays. Against Edmund's overwhelmingly evil character must be offset one of the true heroes in all of Shakespeare: Philip (the Bastard) Faulconbridge, the natural king of *King John*. Unlike the treacherous Edmund, Philip the Bastard, as he is called, is truthful, faithful, courageous, direct in speech, humorous, without personal ambition, and utterly loyal to his sovereign and to England. The Bastard completely outshines King John, as if to show what a true meritocracy, a natural aristocracy—with equality of opportunity and careers open to talent rather than birth or inherited status—might produce.

Philip the Bastard thus supplies the right answer to Justice Harlan's point in *Levy v. Louisiana*. The Bastard's character is impeccable. Perhaps if we combine the Bastard's character with Edmund's lament, we will discern the Bard's views of illegitimacy.

The legal aspects of *King Lear* persist in another, unexpected way. In 1992 the book that won the Pulitzer Prize for fiction was an updated and transplanted version of the *King Lear* tale, but with a legal fillip. *A Thousand Acres* by Jane Smiley is a sensitive and insightful novel about an Iowa farmer named Larry (i.e., Lear; note the first initials of all Smiley's main characters) who unexpectedly retires and turns over all his property to his three daughters. The two elder daughters, Ginny (Goneril) and Rose (Regan), believe they deserve the gift. But Caroline (Cordelia), the youngest, thinks it is a bad idea, and in anger her father cuts her out. The family disintegrates.

But what heightens our interest is the large role of law in *A Thousand Acres*. Of all the possible jobs Caroline-Cordelia could have, she is a lawyer. Cordelia is Lear's good daughter, the only one who truly loves him; Caroline is the only daughter in Smiley's novel who sought independence by moving off the farm and earning her own income. She had "talent and energy" and "would prosper well, with enthusiasm and confidence" in any capacity. Is it mere happenstance that Smiley, a professor of English in the Midwest, makes a lawyer out of her Cordelia character?

To top off everything, Smiley's version of the Lear story has a lawsuit and a crucial trial scene. Lawyer Caroline-Cordelia and father Larry-Lear do what any self-respecting aggrieved late twentieth-century Americans would do in their position: they sue the two elder daughters to get back the farm. They turn to the law for help, but the suit has an unfortunate outcome for them, which may symbolize the law's limits. At the end of the trial—a dramatic moment in *A Thousand Acres*—the judge rules against Larry and Caroline, saying, "The law is clear. . . . if you legally sign over your property, it is very hard to change your mind and get it back."[17]

Not only does the judge rule against them, but he imposes sanctions on them for bringing a frivolous suit. Addressing himself to Larry and in particular to Caroline, the judge tells them they "should have bethought themselves before they decided to carry a family fracas this far."[18] For this reason, Larry and Caroline have to pay the other side's fees. We wonder how much law Shakespeare would put in *King Lear* if he were writing it today.

He certainly put a good deal of law into the original. Even as Shakespeare wrote it, *King Lear* is a powerful play about the role of law and its effect on character. No other drama so well illustrates the dangers of inherited wealth. Few other works of literature etch so deeply on the mind the true meaning of blind justice. No less rare is the fictional story, book, poem, or play that so heightens our sensitivity about the disgraceful inequality before the law of illegitimates. It is hard to imagine a more potent dose of dramatic legal medicine than *King Lear*.

Chapter Fourteen

SHAKESPEARE THE SCRIVENER?

SHAKESPEARE'S many legal themes and references have hardly gone unnoticed. Almost from the start, commentators—most of them lawyers with a literary bent—have highlighted Shakespeare's apparent preoccupation with law. Since the 1700s and down to the present, book after book and article after article have discussed, sometimes with the astringent tone of a debate over a hotly contested issue, the legal aspects of Shakespeare's work. This large body of work, built up over centuries, shows signs of growing even larger, which is no doubt a tribute to the endless fascination of Shakespeare generally and the lasting grip he has on the minds of literary lawyers particularly.

To realize, however, that Shakespeare's writings contain a superabundant number of extraordinary allusions to law, lawyers and things legal does not end the inquiry. Nor does simply discovering and starting to explore the wealth of Shakespeare's legal references for some of their current as well as intrinsic meanings, important and stimulating as those meanings may be. Shakespeare's law, with all its dramatic power and dazzling relevance, makes us think and wonder about more than why his legal themes help explain certain of his plays or how those themes might bear on our own lives and times. We read Shakespeare's treatment of law and we consider what else it tells us.

One thing we inevitably think and wonder about is Shakespeare's life. In writing biography, it is common—perhaps crucial—to connect the subject's life with his work, usually in the hope of showing how events in the life give more accurate meaning to particular works. With Shakespeare, because we know relatively little about his life, it is necessary to reverse the usual process and work backward by studying what Shakespeare wrote for whatever light it may shed on his life. We start to contemplate how and why this fellow Shakespeare came to use law the way he did in his work. What might the large amount of law in Shakespeare's writing tell us about the author himself, his life and his background?

The search for the sources of Shakespeare's legal knowledge leads to the wide open spaces of Shakespeare's life. Even the many excellent biographies of Shakespeare concede, as they must when they are honest, that they are re-creating a life from a limited number of known facts, augmenting the facts with speculation or imaginative reconstruction. We are all circumscribed by the gaps in Shakespeare's biography, by the poverty of biographical details.

Aggravating the dearth of biographical information is the interval designated by scholarship as the Lost Years. This is the period from 1584, when Shakespeare was last heard of in Stratford, to 1595, when Shakespeare's presence in London is uncontested. During these Lost Years, the documentary record presents a "virtual blank,"[1] which means that from the age of approximately twenty-one to thirty-one—Shakespeare's major formative period—we have no precise data of what Shakespeare did. The year of his arrival in London is unknown, as are the circumstances that brought him, though there has been much speculation about his reasons for leaving Stratford. But in fact we remain ignorant of what happened.

The voids in Shakespeare's biography, especially the Lost Years, have become wishing wells for certain Shakespearean commentators. Legends about Shakespeare's life have found convenient homes in such biographical black holes, inasmuch as no one can prove the contrary beyond a reasonable doubt. Much could have gone on in those Lost Years, and that gap becomes a way to speculate on what the young Shakespeare did. But of course any speculation must be reasonable and responsible, or else the desires of the commentator will take complete control. In terms of Shakespeare's legal expertise, the biographical gaps in Shakespeare's life have yielded a number of theories, some of them curious.

The presence of so much law in Shakespeare's writings has over the years led some people to think that the author of the plays must have had serious and professional legal training. Their basic reasoning is straightforward. The plays contain a vast number of legal references that are always so apt, precise, and accurate that they could have been written only by someone intimately familiar with the law from long and practical experience. Therefore, when this inference is piled on top of a few other pieces of information thought to be known about Shakespeare's life, the conclusion emerges—to those who may be predisposed to see it that way—that Shakespeare was somehow trained in the law, that he had, as Hamlet says in the gravedigger scene, the "skull of a lawyer." The result has been the "familiar suggestion"[2] that Shakespeare was either a clerk (scrivener, copyist, engrosser, "noverint") to a court in Stratford before going to London, a clerk to a lawyer while in London, or actually a practicing lawyer.

The view of Shakespeare as having been a law clerk or a practicing lawyer is by no means universally held. Asked to believe that Shakespeare was a forerunner of Bartleby the scrivener, many commentators have recoiled and in essence echoed Melville's character's signature response, "I would prefer not to." A fresh look at the arguments and evidence for and against such formal legal training, however, may quiet the debate some-what, or at least make it consider some new ideas.

It is useful at the outset to identify certain emotional, psychological, and professional factors that have in the past played a role in interpreting the evidence. Behind the law clerk/lawyer theory lies a thinly veiled con-ceit of the legal profession. It is no accident that the theory originally sprang from the mind of a lawyer (Edmund Malone, a London barrister in the 1790s) and ever since has been championed most strongly by other lawyers. Such lawyers want Shakespeare to be a lawyer or a law clerk, even if it means disregarding their own training about how to look at evidence without bias. They impose their wishes on the facts, and in so doing, act on their professional self-love in three distinct ways.

The first professional conceit consists of personal projection. Whoever writes about Shakespeare, it is often said, writes about himself or herself. Lawyers writing about Shakespeare who believe in Shakespeare's legal background may fall into the trap of identification. This thesis has led the overwhelming majority of scholars to dismiss most theories of Shake-speare's legal training and attribute other occupations to him.

The second professional conceit is for lawyers to think Shakespeare had to be a lawyer. It is easy enough, of course, to understand why mem-bers of any profession, trade, occupation, or group would like to flatter themselves by thinking that the greatest English writer of all time was one of their own. It enhances the self-esteem of the group. If Shakespeare was a lawyer, then, to the delight of lawyerdom, lawyers can feel a special kinship with his superb writing skills, dramatic sense, and keen under-standing of human nature—in short, his genius. To conclude that Shake-speare was a lawyer is to extol the virtues of being a lawyer.

The third professional conceit is for lawyers to think that no one but a lawyer or one trained in law could write about law. Jealous of their legal learning, and guarding the tricks of their trade from the uninitiated, some lawyers find it hard to believe that nonlawyers can speak their language or write about what they do. Why this should be so—other than snobbery or overprotectiveness—is never spelled out persuasively.

In light of this triple-pronged professional conceit, one becomes wary of the lawyers' arguments. If we know the motivation, the professional complacency that may underlie some of the arguments and attitudes, then we can evaluate what is said more accurately. Wishful thinking has to be discounted when the facts so warrant, or else we will see only what we want to see. When lawyers' insecurities and objective reality clash, it is not reality that must yield. We must, above all, be clear-eyed in looking at the evidence. Mere awareness of lawyers' self-interest in this matter helps us do that.

The skepticism—or at least warning—arising from the professional motives behind the law clerk/lawyer hypothesis supplies a bracing backdrop for considering the evidence itself. But what evidence? That is the essence of the problem. We need a healthy, probing, and questioning cast of mind for a subject encrusted with received wisdom and too much deference to authority. For upon close examination, the evidence in favor of the law clerk/lawyer hypothesis starts to thin, while at the same time evidence and argument against the hypothesis mount. Possibilities persist, but grave doubts remain after all.

Shakespeare's myriad highly technical and correctly used legal expressions have persuaded many that he had a profound knowledge of the law and a "peculiar freedom and exactness in the use of [legal] phraseology."[3] After a while, however, the conventional homage to Shakespeare's legal profundity starts to look like automatic submission to authority. Originating as they do from supposedly expert legal authorities, these pronouncements tend to intimidate and overwhelm lawyer and nonlawyer alike. If leaders of the English bar—including exalted judges—who are presumably better able to evaluate such things, certify that Shakespeare had unusually extensive and preternaturally accurate knowledge of law, who can disagree? This is the argument from authority, often a compelling argument for many people, most of all for lawyers prone by training and mindset to defer to precedent.

By far the most charming example of the argument about a layperson's tendency to make legal mistakes is found in a little-known and even less-cited essay by American humorist Mark Twain. In that essay, titled "Is Shakespeare Dead?" and originally intended to be part of his autobiography, Twain describes an incident from his young adulthood in which he, as a pilot-apprentice, tries to convince a Mississippi riverboat pilot master that Shakespeare could not have learned his law simply by reading books. While on watch, the pilot would read Shakespeare to Twain, who was steering. But the Shakespeare-adoring Mississippi pilot did not read without interruption; "he constantly injected commands" about Twain's steering.[4] The result, according to Twain, was a combination of Shakespearean text and "explosive interlardings" about how to steer a steamboat.

One day, Twain wanted to settle an argument with the pilot over how Shakespeare knew so much about "the laws, and the law-courts, and law-proceedings, and lawyer-talk, and lawyer-ways." So Twain wrote out a passage from Shakespeare "and riddled it with his [i.e., the pilot's] wild steamboatful interlardings." Then he asked the pilot to read it aloud, which the flattered pilot did with gusto. About a week after the dramatic reading, the pilot and Twain argued about whether Shakespeare knew enough law to write the plays attributed to him. As Twain had anticipated from past discussions, the pilot insisted that Shakespeare learned his law from reading books, which allowed Twain to spring his trap. Twain answered that

> a man can't handle glibly and easily and comfortably and successfully the argot of a trade at which he has not personally served. He will make mistakes; he will not, and cannot, get the trade-phrasings precisely and exactly right; and the moment he departs, by even a shade, from a common trade-form, the reader who has sewed that trade will know the writer *hasn't*.

The pilot, for his part, was unconvinced. He said a man could learn the language of any trade by careful reading and studying. As Twain recalled, "But when I got him to read again the passage from Shakespeare with the interlardings, he perceived, himself, that books couldn't teach a student a bewildering multitude of pilot-phrases so thoroughly and perfectly that he could talk them off in book and play or conversation and make no mistake that a pilot would not immediately discover."[5] Twain felt that the episode was a "triumph," and his essay is a serious, though much neglected, contribution to Shakespeare studies, even if somewhat dated and expressed in American vernacular.

As for his own argument that someone must be a lawyer to write about the law without error, Mark Twain himself provides an important and up to now overlooked rebuttal. His novel *Pudd'nhead Wilson* is a noteworthy legal novel about a "nice guy" lawyer in a small town whose lifelong hobby of fingerprinting eventually places him in the legal limelight. Twain's book has trial scenes, involves specialized knowledge, and otherwise displays actual familiarity with legal procedures. *Pudd'nhead Wilson* became a significant model for later American depictions of the legal profession.[6]

Thus, Twain himself seriously undercuts the homespun cleverness of the trick he played on his steamboat pilot master. With *Pudd'nhead Wilson*, Twain showed that a nonlawyer could indeed write knowledgeably and accurately about legal technicalities. In Richard Weisberg's words, Twain writes "exhaustively . . . about law and legal proceedings."[7] To get at reality, we need to look not at what Twain says in his essay on Shakespeare—no matter how beguilingly—but at what he actually does when writing about law. Weisberg has it right when, in another context, he groups Shakespeare and Twain (along with Melville and Dickens) as "brilliant storytellers" who "link their frequent legal themes to the way lawyers talk and write."[8]

Pudd'nhead Wilson reveals deep contradictions in Twain's stance on Shakespeare. Before the actual text of *Pudd'nhead Wilson* starts, Twain offers a brief "Whisper to the Reader" that must startle anyone who has read Twain's essay on Shakespeare. "A person who is ignorant of legal matters," begins Twain's Whisper, "is always liable to make mistakes when he tries to photograph a court scene with his pen." So far, there is no discrepancy between Twain's author's note to his 1894 novel and Twain's position in his 1909 Shakespeare essay. In both pieces—up to this point—Twain says laypersons are bound to make mistakes when writing about legal technicalities.

But then Twain parts company with himself. What he next writes completely subverts his entire argument about Shakespeare's unfamiliarity with law. Continuing his Whisper to the Reader, Twain goes on: "And so I was not willing to let the law chapters in this book go to press without first subjecting them to exhausting revision and correction by a trained barrister." And that is exactly what Twain did, as he tells us: "These chapters are right, now, in every detail, for they were rewritten under the immediate eye of a lawyer," who approved the revisions.

Aye, there's the rub. Why, we might justifiably ask, could not Shakespeare have done the same thing as Twain did, and submit his legal allusions to a lawyer friend from the Inns of Court for vetting and correction? And why did Twain in his 1909 essay deriding Shakespeare's ability to make legal references fail to mention his own simple method, relied upon so successfully and so openly fifteen years earlier with *Pudd'nhead Wilson*, for ensuring the accuracy of a layperson's writing about the intricacies of the law?

Twain's glaring contradiction has, up to now, curiously evaded comment by Shakespeare scholars. The disparity between Twain's essay on Shakespeare and his Whisper to the Reader in *Pudd'nhead Wilson* opens a new line of argument. It may help point the way toward resolving the debate by practical experience.

One way to see if Shakespeare's legal references were unusual in number and aptness is to compare them to those of his contemporaries' references to law. Whether or not they have actually made such a comparison, some commentators—especially American commentators in the nineteenth century—have concluded that "no other dramatist of the time . . . used legal phrases with Shakespeare's readiness and exactness."[9] They have declared with apparent certitude that the legal expressions are more frequent and are used with more precision in Shakespeare's plays than in those of any other playwright of the period.[10]

Measured by any objective test, however, Shakespeare's knowledge of law was far from unusual in the playwrights of his time—Ben Jonson, Christopher Marlowe, Thomas Dekker, Thomas Kyd, and John Webster. Other Elizabethan playwrights often used legal allusions in their plays, and some used them more frequently and more accurately than Shakespeare. According to one respected study done in 1942, Shakespeare "employed about the median number of legalisms, that is to say—about half of his contemporaries used legal terms more frequently than did 'Shake-speare.' "[11] The authors of that study concluded that most of the "more legal" half of the sample used more complicated and complex legal allusions with a degree of accuracy at least equal to Shakespeare's.[12] Another scholar had earlier examined the particular legal references used by Shakespeare and found that each phrase is also used by other contemporary authors.[13]

On the other hand, many of those other contemporary authors were directly connected with the law. Some—John Marston, Francis Beaumont, and possibly John Webster—were members of the legal societies. Some—Thomas Kyd and Thomas Heywood—had connections with law as scriveners or associates of the Inns of Court. For Knight, the "significant fact" is that "Shakespeare, presumed to have no such connection, is as accurate, as rounded, and as concerned about the law . . . as any of these others."[14] This too should be weighed in the balance.

The most common criticism of the law clerk/lawyer theory is that it is speculative and not based on hard evidence. Mark Twain rejected the theory as much too conjectural, and that was the basic theme of his unheralded essay on the subject. He attacked the assumptions made about Shakespeare's life, especially the law clerk theory. For his part, Twain wanted explanations "uncheapened, unwatered by guesses, and surmises, and maybe-so's, and might-have-beens, and could-have-beens, and must-have-beens."[15] (Such a supposedly hardheaded approach led Twain to conclude that the author of Shakespeare's works was a lawyer!)

A good modern example of such conjecture, built on slim and equivocal evidence, is Knight's 1973 book, *Shakespeare's Hidden Life*. Alert to possible criticism that he is indulging in speculation, Knight claims he is merely recreating, not fantasizing, Shakespeare's life. His stated purpose, on the contrary, is "to provide the most complete array of evidence for the case of Shakespeare's legal career, or background in the law" based on "facts which can be legitimately drawn and deduced from existing documents on his life."[16] But even Knight, who does assemble and lay bare what evidence there is, falls victim in the end to surmise. Throughout, Knight does exactly what he seems to eschew, portraying imaginary scenarios as if they actually happened.

The absence of Shakespeare's signature as a witness to legal proceedings and documents is an old and familiar argument against the law clerk/lawyer theory. It assumes that a lawyer or law clerk would in the ordinary course of business have left traces in various legal records, deeds, or wills, for instance, as a witness or otherwise, which would verify his existence. Despite much searching through old documents, no such legal footprints by Shakespeare have been found.

It is understandable that legal allusions and themes—accurate or inaccurate, profound or superficial—should stud Shakespeare's work. Certain cultures, as Richard Weisberg has pointed out in his book *Poethics*, are so dominated by law that the literature of the time abundantly reflects the legal influence.[17] Like ancient Greece and Europe and America in the last two centuries, Elizabethan England was a society enthralled by law. Litigation was common; law was a national preoccupation.

In this setting, many of Shakespeare's expressions, which in modern times are confined to legal usage, were in popular use in Shakespeare's day as clichés and do not imply a special acquaintance with the law. Shakespeare's legal allusions, wrote the persuasive Phillips, "were of that superficial nature which, in a litigious age, would characterize the common speech of the time."[18]

Shakespeare's extraordinary mind explains much about his knowledge of law. Despite a country background without much formal education, he had a great capacity for absorbing and retaining knowledge. His power of acquisition was equaled by his power of close and accurate observation.

With the absorbent kind of mind Shakespeare had, he obviously read in large doses. Accordingly, those who defend Shakespeare's nonprofessional method of learning law often point to reading as the key. As with other self-taught people, reading becomes the easy road to legal knowledge for Shakespeare. And of course he could well have read many law books during and before his time in London. Although people like Mark Twain disparage such a supposition as "only surmise" without evidence,[19] it is hard to believe that an omnivorous reader such as Shakespeare would not, in an era so marked by legal influence, have read some law books on his own even if he never entertained the idea of practicing as a lawyer.

Whatever legal reading Shakespeare did, he lived and worked in an atmosphere permeated by law. The Inns of Court were a central part of his and London's existence. He had friends and acquaintances who were lawyers. No doubt he attended court cases as a spectator. Such a legally charged atmosphere must have had an effect on Shakespeare, thereby enhancing his secondhand knowledge of law.

Shakespeare himself also had considerable firsthand contact with the law. His father, John Shakespeare, was in court sixty-seven times.[20] William was involved in a variety of legal proceedings, in roles ranging from witness to plaintiff, land buyer to moneylender. He employed attorneys; he dealt with them. Such experience would, by itself, go a long way toward giving Shakespeare a working knowledge of the law, something that was far from being a possession of the privileged few. To think that in Shakespeare's day only men of legal training knew anything about the law is wrong. Few of Shakespeare's contemporaries stayed out of court, so it is no surprise that legal terms occur often in Elizabethan literature. Whether or not the dramatists had an Inns of Court audience in mind, it is doubtful that legal allusions were aimed at impressing the elite: they were a natural reflection of everyday life.[21] Shakespeare, moreover, may have interwoven his personal legal experiences into his literary works.

Often overlooked by the law clerk theorists are Shakespeare's sources. Many of Shakespeare's legal and constitutional allusions in the history plays, which some take as evidence of legal training, were derived from the *Chronicles* and other sources. Available to all—and used often by many writers—these allusions from common sources in no way indicate special legal training. They show a craftsman working at his craft: the writing of plays based on historical materials in general circulation at the time. Shakespeare need not have been a law clerk or a lawyer to have gleaned legal expressions from such sources as Holinshead.

Other bits of possible evidence are ambiguous. For example, a passage written by Thomas Nashe, a London writer, and printed in 1590, refers to an unnamed "noverint" (law clerk) turned dramatist. Some say this noverint passage refers to Shakespeare, but it is not at all clear that this is so. Equally ambiguous is Shakespeare's will. If Shakespeare drafted his own will and it reflects specialized and professional training in law, then an inference is possible about Shakespeare's legal facility. Both assumptions, alas, are questionable. Experts have also debated whether Shakespeare's handwriting shows that he learned and wrote in a special legal script—"law hand" or "Chancery hand."

A final piece of evidence is said to be a signature of Shakespeare found in an old law book published in 1568 by William Lambarde, a distinguished English lawyer—the so-called "Lambarde" signature. According to one scholar, the Lambarde signature shows that Shakespeare had close contact with English law and prominent legal figures, that he might have borrowed books on law and other subjects from Lambarde's extensive library. There are limits, however, to what can be inferred from the Lambarde signature.

First there is the question of the signature's authenticity. A debate continues as to whether the signature, as originally thought, is a forgery. Moreover, Shakespeare's name in a law book, even if a genuine signature, does not necessarily mean he actually read it. It could have been a gift from the author. Shakespeare might have acquired it from someone other than the author. In any event, it may well have sat on Shakespeare's shelves unread, just as do many books in many a personal library. To conclude that the Lambarde signature is a vital piece of evidence that Shakespeare was a law clerk is to place too much reliance on a fact that could mean anything or nothing.

An effective way to test a proposition is to see if a counterexample exists. If so, then we know that the proposition is not universally true. Here the specific proposition at issue is whether Shakespeare could have written about the law as he did without legal training. More generally, the proposition to be tested is whether only a lawyer or someone with legal training can write a book about law. If we can find examples of laypersons writing knowledgeably about law, then we have made serious inroads into the argument that Shakespeare had to have legal training.

Of course, many books about law are written by professionally trained and often practicing lawyers. But the number of books about law written by lawyers does not mean that nonlawyers cannot also write about law. Quite the contrary. Twain's *Pudd'nhead Wilson* is a good example. So are Dickens's *Bleak House, The Pickwick Papers, David Copperfield,* and *Great Expectations,* each of which contains extended discussions of law cases, lawyers, the practice of law, or legal subjects. From this century, we can point, as examples, to Tom Wolfe's *Bonfire of the Vanities,* Herman Wouk's *Caine Mutiny,* and Leon Uris's *QB VII.* In the nonfiction realm, two of the finest books about American law—*Simple Justice* by Richard Kluger and *Gideon's Trumpet* by Anthony Lewis—were written by nonlawyers. And a slew of ever popular true crime books, which almost always describe court trials, and legal biographies have come from the pens of nonlawyers.

Such a catalogue, more representative than exhaustive, surely makes it difficult to maintain seriously that only a lawyer or person with legal training could write a book about law. But this should hardly come as a surprise. Tom Clancy, one of our most popular contemporary writers, is a former insurance salesman who has made his best-selling reputation writing spy thriller after spy thriller filled with detailed descriptions of sophisticated naval technology. One need not be a member of the guild to write about it with discernment and understanding. It might even be argued that not being a member provides the distance needed for proper perspective and objectivity.

All things considered, Shakespeare probably used, if he used anything at all, an easy—and by now time-tested—technique for assuring the accuracy of his legal references. It seems highly likely that, if he had any doubts or questions about his legal references, he showed drafts of those legal allusions to lawyer friends who would correct any errors. Such a vetting procedure would be simple, obvious, and convenient, especially with so many lawyers around Shakespeare. It is what Twain did for *Pudd'nhead Wilson* and what other nonlawyer writers have done before and since. Another possibility is that Shakespeare relied on a lawyer friend to show him around the courts so he could soak up atmosphere, just as attorney Eddie Hayes and Judge Burton Roberts showed Tom Wolfe around the courts for his research on *Bonfire of the Vanities.*

These counterexamples show that not only is it possible but indeed fairly common for nonlawyers to write intelligently about the law. This is not based on speculation, surmise, conjecture, or guess, but on simple fact. Others less gifted have done it; therefore Shakespeare could do it.

Based on the evidence, the balance tips toward a verdict against formal legal training. Two fundamental failures of proof hobble the advocates of Shakespeare's formal legal training. First, it is unclear that Shakespeare could not have learned, on his own or with the help of lawyer friends, from reading or life experiences, enough law to equip him to make the legal references in his work. Second, the legal training advocates indulge themselves in an orgy of speculation. What Mark Twain criticizes the law clerk supporters for can just as easily be turned on those who think Shakespeare was a lawyer: absent hard evidence, they are engaging in "guesses, inferences, theories, conjectures."[22] Almost a hundred years ago Bradley warned us that "on all questions relating to Shakespeare, there are plenty of merely lunatic theories."[23] These two flaws, coupled with common sense and the experiences of modern nonlawyer authors writing about law, make it unnecessary that Shakespeare was either a law clerk or a lawyer.

In 1988, sitting on a special law school moot court with Justices Harry Blackmun and John Paul Stevens to decide who wrote Shakespeare's works, Supreme Court Justice William Brennan came to a characteristically reasonable and moderate conclusion: "As for Shakespeare's supposed expertise in the law, Elizabethan legal experts point out that when he uses legal terms in the plays, they are in fact such terms as he himself would have encountered, it seems to me, in his own basic dealings—the deeds and titles to land, and so forth. Or in his sources, because he did consult sources—notably, I guess, Holland Shedd's *Chronicles of England* that was published in 1577."[24] I concur, subject to a motion for reargument based on new evidence.

Such new evidence might always be found. The advocates of Shakespeare's legal training may turn out to be correct. It is certainly possible that he was a law clerk during the Lost Years. I would not want the theory's current unpopularity to stifle further inquiry. Scholarship in this area "should carefully and fearlessly weigh the pros and cons of new documentary evidence." It should not be "timid" or "reluctant," as Knight thinks it has been, "to advance new findings in this area for fear of adding fuel to an old controversy so poorly argued, yet still passionately maintained."[25]

It may be that we can do no better than to throw up our hands and admit, "We do not know." Two scholars who studied the evidence wisely concluded fifty years ago that they could not "dogmatically" say that Shakespeare was not a lawyer, or that he had no legal education. As to that, the scholars were "agnostic: as a matter of biographical fact, we simply do not know." But even such careful scholars could state "categorically" that the evidence is "wholly insufficient to prove such a claim."[26] That tentative, modest, persuasive conclusion has a prudent and intellectually frank ring to it. It appears to represent the truth as we now know it.

Much depends on how we account for the legal knowledge of the author of Shakespeare's works. If we conclude that Shakespeare was either a law clerk or a lawyer or otherwise became sufficiently familiar with legal things, the Shakespeare edifice remains standing undamaged and perhaps even enhanced. But the contrary conclusion—that Shakespeare was not a law clerk or a lawyer and could not otherwise have acquired by himself the legal expertise reflected in the plays—amounts to a powerful cruise missile launched into the midst of Shakespeare scholarship. To answer the question "How did Shakespeare know so much about law?" by saying, "There is no way he could possibly know so much law" is really to conclude that William Shakespeare of Stratford did not write the works of "Shakespeare."

UNACKNOWLEDGED LAWGIVER

Now, even after several of Shakespeare's plays have been examined from a legal vantage point and some controversial aspects of Shakespeare's life considered as they relate to the law and the authorship of the plays themselves, a basic question still drifts unanswered. It is not the familiar query—what does this or that legal allusion in Shakespeare mean?—but something deeper and more elusive: how and why does Shakespeare continue to affect our way of thinking about law and legal problems? The idea of Shakespeare as a dramatist who often referred to the law stops far short of explaining why his work still has such purchase on our legal imagination.

Intellectual candor requires us first to admit the obvious: Shakespeare had no overall theory of law. He wrote plays, not legal treatises.[1] He intended his plays to have audiences and he wanted most of all to please them. That, not jurisprudence, was Shakespeare's primary concern. But even though Shakespeare's intention was to be a dramatist, he still was keenly aware, as we are, of literature's relation to the other forces of society. Shakespeare therefore left, perhaps in spite of himself, a rich legacy to the law.

Such a legacy shows that "law and literature" is a fertile and fruitful interdisciplinary approach to Shakespeare. It uncovers and explains important points of contact between his biography and his writings. It reemphasizes the legal significance of Shakespeare's language. By using the double-barreled law and literature mode of analysis on Shakespeare's plays, we learn more about both the law and the plays. And we get important clues about Shakespeare's continuing leverage on the American legal mind today. Whatever misgivings or doubts Posner may have about law and literature generally, they do not detract from the value of such an approach to Shakespeare.

Shakespeare's legal legacy starts with the links between his life and his work. As often happens in biography, one cannot—and most definitely should not—completely separate the life and the work. Each sheds light on the other, especially with respect to Shakespeare and the law. Events in Shakespeare's life—from his own and his family's experiences with the law, to his contact with lawyers, courts and the Inns of Court—are reflected in the plays. Among his friends, acquaintances, and audiences were many lawyers, for whom he sometimes premiered or revised his plays. And filling in the maddening blank of the Lost Years will one day conclusively resolve whether or not Shakespeare acquired his legal knowledge by working in a law office. Future research by competent and diligent scholars will also, one hopes, eventually lay to rest the debate over whether Shakespeare of Stratford was the author of the plays.

An exquisite aspect of Shakespeare's legacy to the law is his language. Like everyone, all lawyers should read Shakespeare for, if nothing else, the fabled beauty and lasting power of his expression. For lawyers, though, the need is particularly great. In their daily tasks, lawyers depend heavily on words and language; they must be sensitive to nuance and meaning. Yet lawyers are often criticized, and rightly so, for being bad writers. They will become better speakers and writers—and thereby better advocates—for having studied Shakespeare with an eye toward their own profession.[2] The lawyer who understands why Antony's funeral speech succeeds while Brutus's fails understands the value and the core meaning of oral advocacy.

Shakespeare also helps us to better grasp the relationship of law to human nature. His plays, with their splendid representation of character, offer an imaginative portrait of life. They illuminate basic facets of our legal experience. From the need to balance law and discretion, to the relationship of law and morals, from the role of revenge in the law, to what it means to "think like a lawyer," from the impact of defamation on an innocent person's life, to equality before the law, from civil disobedience and civic courage, to the nature of constitutional government—the list of law-related topics in Shakespeare goes on and on, each one pushing us to question our most basic premises of legal understanding. Shakespeare's comments on fair trial procedures, mercy, good lawyers versus bad lawyers, reason and passion in the law, legal interpretation and a host of other legal subjects tumble forth. But unlike the Bard's "poor player / That struts and frets his hour upon the stage, / And then is heard no more" (Macbeth, 5.5.23–25), his remarks on law stay a while in the mind, humming in our ears, reverberating, disturbing, and unsettling.

The profusion of Shakespeare's comments about law is striking. The plays would be a superb teaching tool for law students. A course in "Shakespeare and the Law" could use the plays as a means of getting across many important modern legal concepts. The beauty of it all is that we are not talking about antiquarian legal points of medieval English law, but new-old insights about current legal controversies. What makes Shakespeare so relevant for law is, surprisingly, his timeliness—or, more accurately, his timelessness.

Shakespeare's preoccupation with law tells us something significant about his and his compatriots' attitude toward lawyers. His many cutting remarks about lawyers' tricks culminate in Dick the Butcher's "kill all the lawyers" comment in Henry VI, Part 2. But offsetting this antilawyer strain, this search for easy scapegoats, is Shakespeare's highly favorable description of such honorable lawyers as Humphrey in *Henry VI, Part 2*, and the lord chief justice in both parts of *Henry IV*. Society's ambivalence toward lawyers and the emotional and political nuances of reality as reflected in Shakespeare have continued down to our own times. Whether we admire, loathe, or just enjoy laughing at them, lawyers fascinate Americans, just as they did Shakespeare. Regardless of what Shakespeare actually thought, it is as if his law-filled works really meant to say, "First thing we do, let's *write* about all the lawyers."

It may well be that Shakespeare's writings about law disturbed and unsettled English law. A number of scholars contend that the Bard wrought significant changes in the law of his land. According to their theories, *The Merchant of Venice, Midsummer Night's Dream, Measure for Measure*, and *The Winter's Tale* affected the attitudes of contemporary jurists (who saw the plays) toward law and equity. Going further, these scholars argue that Shakespeare's plays influenced the outcome of the struggle for preeminence between Lord Ellesmere, head of the chancery or equity courts, and Lord Coke, chief justice of the common law courts. Such commentators point to a 1612 decision in which an equity court intervened in a law court's case as a victory for Shakespeare's theory of law. But the truth is we cannot be so sure if Shakespeare's plays, which usually raise questions without giving answers, had anything to do with that result. Maybe they did, maybe they did not.

Whatever his impact on English law, Shakespeare's fingerprints are all over our American legal furniture. Not surprisingly, he has been cited or quoted by American courts more often than any other literary figure. One 1993 study counts nearly 800 judicial opinions in both state and federal courts quoting the Bard, a figure that must have increased since the study was done. These opinions use an amazing 257 different quotations from Shakespeare, ranging from descriptions of black-letter law subjects to ornamental quotations that add a bit of flair, sparkle, and even humor to a judge's work product. Far and away the most frequently cited passage from Shakespeare is "What's in a name? That which we call a rose / By any other word would smell as sweet" (*Romeo and Juliet*, 1.2.8–86). The magnitude of American judicial reliance on Shakespeare is vividly shown by comparing him to the runner-up, John Milton, whose *Paradise Lost* has been cited or quoted a relatively paltry fifty-seven times, and then only to sixteen different passages. The numbers tell the tale.[3]

The 800 cases in which Shakespeare's poetry is quoted do not include another 286 cases invoking Shakespeare as an exemplar or historical figure. If something could happen to Shakespeare, so American judges seem to reason, it could happen to anyone. Thus, in a Supreme Court discussion of the profit motive, Justice Lewis Powell noted that "even Shakespeare may have been motivated by the prospect of pecuniary gain."[4] In arguing against an immigration applicant's homosexuality as a ground for exclusion, Justice William Douglas in dissent objected that "even Shakespeare" might have been homosexual.[5] In the obscenity field, if a law could result in the banning of Shakespeare, then the result—at least to a liberal Justice such as William Brennan—is wrong: "The rationales used could justify the banning from radio of a myriad of literary works, novels, poems, and plays by the likes of Shakespeare."[6]

The sheer number of cases that cite Shakespeare, many of them recent, indicates something significant, something more important than judges' vanity in merely trying to show off their literary learning. It shows, first, how far and wide Shakespeare and his plays have permeated the American legal mind. Second, the many judicial references to Shakespeare reflect the degree to which Shakespeare is still with us in the law. Shakespeare was in step with all the cultural forces of his age and fastened his grip on the future. That Shakespeare's work continues to be frequently cited by judges surrounded by twentieth-century technological changes, that it is still capable of illuminating the future as well as the past and present, is a sign of how alive Shakespeare's work remains, for the law as well as elsewhere.

At least part of Shakespeare's great legal influence flows from the huge scope, the utter expanse, of his work. He wrote so much on so many different topics that one can almost always find in his writings something relevant on which to draw. Shakespeare wrote on so many sides of so many topics that he, like the sprawling mass of legal precedents itself, often yields a quote to support either side of many propositions. Shakespeare's works thus become a legal hope chest: one can find there whatever one wishes for. In their amplitude and range, Shakespeare's works resemble the Bible, and it was Shakespeare's character Antonio in *The Merchant of Venice* who says, "The devil can cite Scripture for his purpose" (1.3.97). Likewise with lawyers citing Shakespeare.

Shakespeare's legal themes also provide insight into our own society. What was once popular in late Elizabethan and early Jacobin England is again popular today in the United States. Just as Shakespeare's plays about law won audiences in London around 1600, so too a rash of legal suspense novels, movies, and television shows about law has been winning vast audiences in America for the past several years. The huge best sellers written by Scott Turow and John Grisham, and feature films based on them, have not slaked the thirst of Americans for stories about lawyers and trials. In their wake, Turow and Grisham wannabes have sent hundreds of book-length manuscripts of legal suspense novels to literary agents who pass the best ones on to publishers.[7]

What does the great current popularity of lawyer novels, movies, and television shows mean? In part it means we have an insatiable appetite for stories about crimes, criminals, trials, and all sorts of juicy crooked lawyer stuff. But so, apparently, did Shakespeare's audiences, and therein lies a clue. An affinity exists between the role of law in Shakespeare's time and in our own time. Law dominated Shakespeare's England and dominates our own America, so that in both societies culture would naturally express itself in terms of law, as has happened in other law-dominated societies. Our society and Shakespearean England have this much in common, and that may intensify our interest in Shakespeare and the law. By studying Shakespeare and the law, we may better understand our own society and our own culture.

The similarities between Shakespeare's England and contemporary America include more than the role of law in society and culture. Both nations were flush with vitality and power: England after its victory over the Spanish Armada in 1588, and America after World War II and, more recently, after the collapse of communism. Both nations were in the midst of great change: England's Tudor dynasty was coming to an end and being replaced by the Stuarts, and America's constant political and social flux was continuing. And through it all the writers write about many sorts of topics, not least of all the law. As our perceptions strengthen, the Shakespearean "moment" reflects our own in law and in other respects.

Beyond these many and important lessons about law and lawyers, beyond the apt quotations and memorable characters, lies another, broader, far more significant yet far more subtle way in which Shakespeare influences our thinking about the law. He speaks to us with an urgency that few writers of our time can muster. We see his long-dead face pressed against the glass of our terrible century, Shakespeare looking in at a time worse than his.

The extent of Shakespeare's reach into the legal subconscious is well illustrated by a short but provocative essay in the *Harvard Law Review* titled "Sonnet LXV and the 'Black Ink' of the Framers' Intention." The article was written during the bicentennial of the Constitution in 1987 by Charles Fried, who was then solicitor general (the official who represents the federal government in the Supreme Court) in the second Reagan administration, and was before and since an estimable law professor at Harvard. Fried intended his essay as a contribution to the still ongoing debate in constitutional law between those who, like him, believe in "original intent" and those who believe in the "living document" approach. But Fried saw the issue even more broadly as whether any legal rule or principle can act as a real constraint on judgment.

To make his point, Fried relies on Shakespeare's Sonnet 65:

> Since brass, nor stone, nor earth, nor boundless sea,
> But sad mortality o'ersways their power,
> How with this rage shall beauty hold a plea,
> Whose action is no stronger than a flower?

> O how shall summer's honey breath hold out
> Against the wrackful seige of battring days
> When rocks impregnable are not so stout,
> Nor gates of steel so strong, but time decays?
> O fearful meditation! Where, alack,
> Shall time's best jewel from time's chest lie hid?
> Or what strong hand can hold his swift foot back?
> Or who his spoil of beauty can forbid?
> O none, unless this miracle have might:
> That in black ink my love may still shine bright.

Fried reads this poem, correctly I think, as showing that the terrible decay of time, described in the first twelve lines, can be overcome by the "miracle" of "black ink" mentioned in the final couplet. The sonnet is about writing, words, and the "miracle that black ink can make even what is most fragile and evanescent shine brightly through time." From that uncontroversial observation, Fried goes on to argue that language and words fix meaning and intent, and through the miracle of black ink we are able to fix and transmit the intentions of framers. "As we can understand Shakespeare's meaning," he says, "so we can understand the Framers' meaning in the Constitution." According to Fried, Sonnet 65 "refutes" the "disturbing" suggestion that "we cannot understand the intention of the framers of laws." He concludes: "It is Shakespeare's miracle of black ink that we, as free persons whose freedom is underwritten by the rule of law, should celebrate."[8]

Whether Fried is right or wrong—or in fact oversimplifies a far more complex problem[9]—the key here is his primary reliance on a Shakespearean sonnet to make an argument in a debate about constitutional interpretation. And there is nothing, for Fried's purpose, unique about Sonnet 65. Others would have served equally well to show the permanence of the written word. Sonnet 18, for instance, contains a similar final couplet: "So long as men can breathe or eyes can see, / So long lives this, and this gives life to thee." Likewise in Sonnet 55:

> Not marble nor the gilded monuments
> Of princes shall outline this powerful rhyme;
> But you shall shine more bright in these contents
> Than unswept stone besmeared with sluttish time.

Fried could have used any one of these three sonnets for his text.

As Fried's essay shows, Shakespeare's true and greatest influence consists of the template he has engraved on our minds. His overlay has affected our thinking about, among other things, law and legal problems. It is not just a matter of well-known lines, but an entire outlook. A culture later than Shakespeare's own strives to locate itself, its own dreams, its own self-image. We often measure, analyze, and consider legal issues against a Shakespearean pattern. If a Supreme Court decision seems to exalt a narrow, literal reading of a statute over real interests of real people, a dissenting justice can later write a law review article invoking *The Merchant of Venice* as support for strict justice yielding to equity.[10] If a court is trying to divine a statute's meaning, a judge can quote *The Tempest* and write, "Legislators' expectations in creating always are best described in Shakespeare's aphorism 'I endow'd thy purposes with words that made them known.' "[11] And these few examples are far from unusual.

In this sense, Shakespeare is the prime example of what Shelley meant when he wrote in *A Defence of Poetry* that "poets are the unacknowledged legislators of the world." It is more than mere chance that Shelley used the word *legislators*. Legislators are lawgivers or lawmakers, and that is an excellent description of Shakespeare. It does not matter that Shakespeare did not anticipate the ultimate effect of his writings upon the law. Nor is it "bardolatry" to recognize the far-reaching extent to which Shakespeare has in fact created a mental framework against which we measure the world of law.

Shakespeare legislated for the future with his plays more than those who draft constitutions, enact statutes, and judge cases. Perhaps, to paraphrase what Justice Holmes once said about thinkers, Shakespeare felt the secret, lonely happiness of the writer who hopes that, hundreds of years after he is dead, people will not only still be reading what he has written but also thinking and acting to the cadence of his thought and language?[12] If he came back today, would he feel a subtle frisson of pleasure at his delayed power? In some ways, he had a prophetic vision of the law more real than Blackstone, more permanent than Coke, more incisive than Marshall, more comprehensive than Holmes. At long last we can acknowledge Shakespeare as one of our greatest lawgivers. And this, the true secret of Shakespeare and the law, explains how we can think of the Bard's mind and, like Hamlet, ask, "Why might not that be the skull of a lawyer?"

NOTES

PROLOGUE

1. Posner, *Law and Literature*, 363.
2. Bradley, *Shakespearean Tragedy*, 20.
3. Not everyone agrees on this point, and an engrossing debate continues between supporters of text and reading, on one hand, and performance and audition, on the other. See Berger, *Imaginary Audition*. See also Hazlitt, *Characters of Shakespear's Plays*, 237, 247–48 (Hazlitt did "not like to see [Shakespeare's] plays acted. . . . Poetry and the stage do not agree well together. . . . the boards of a theatre and the regions of fancy are not the same thing"); Goddard, *The Meaning of Shakespeare*, 1:293 ("The imaginative man will always prefer to read the play rather than to have some obliterating actress come between the text and his heart").
4. Holmes, *Collected Legal Papers*, 252–53.
5. Posner, *Law and Literature*, 13–14.

CHAPTER ONE

1. Grey, *The Wallace Stevens Case*, 1, 35, 39.
2. Posner, "Law and Literature," 1351.
3. Posner, *Law and Literature*, 267, 175, 353, 362, 132, 174, 361, 175.
4. See White, "Book Review," 2032–47.
5. Weisberg, *Poethics*, 3.
6. Grey, *The Wallace Stevens Case*, 67.
7. Posner, *Law and Literature*, 354.
8. White, *The Legal Imagination*, xx.
9. Ferguson, *Law and Letters in American Culture*, 5, 25, 6.
10. Bloom, *Shakespeare's Politics*, 1–2.
11. Posner, *Law and Literature*, 78.
12. Brill, "Watching the Drama of Justice," *American Lawyer*, July–Aug. 1990, 3. See also Walter Goodman, "Television Brings Out a Melodramatic Side of the Legal Process," *New York Times*, 26 July 1990, C15.
13. Knight, *Shakespeare's Hidden Life*, 170–78.
14. These cases as well as the other biographical facts discussed in this section are mentioned in the many standard accounts of Shakespeare's life, as well as in Knight, *Shakespeare's Hidden Life*.
15. Knight, *Shakespeare's Hidden Life*, 284–85.
16. *Browning-Ferris Industries v. Kelco Disposal*, 492 U.S. 257, 290 (1989).
17. Ibid., 265, n.7.
18. Linda Greenhouse, "4 Mysterious Lines (about Fines)," *New York Times*, 30 June 1989, B6.

CHAPTER TWO

1. Spielberg, like Shakespeare, makes more than one anti-lawyer statement in his work. In his film *Jurassic Park*, Spielberg has a dinosaur eat an unlikable lawyer who is hiding in a bathroom sitting on a commode. The audience loved that scene too. Perhaps future critics will write articles and books on Spielberg and the law.

2. Rodell, "Goodbye to Law Reviews," 38, 42.

3. Szatmary, *Shays' Rebellion*, 42; Morris, *Witnesses at the Creation*, 172.

4. These antilawyer comments belie the argument, made by those without knowledge of American history, that comparing Cade's rebellion to Shays' rebellion "is irrelevant because no statements or feelings were expressed about lawyers by Shays or any follower." Lester Forest, "Added Comment on Shakespeare," *New York Law Journal*, 8 Aug. 1988, 2.

5. Szatmary, *Shays' Rebellion*, 42.

6. *Walters v. National Ass'n of Radiation Survivors*, 473 U.S. 305, 371, n.24 (1985) (Stevens, J., dissenting).

7. Lester Forest, "Let's (Not) Kill All the Lawyers," *New York Law Journal*, 19 July 1988, 2 (emphasis added). Many lawyers use false emphatics—such words as *conclusively* or such expressions as "it is clear that"—because "they are afraid they have failed to persuade the reader." Goldstein and Lieberman, *The Lawyer's Guide to Writing Well*, 125.

8. Forest, "Added Comment on Shakespeare," 2.

9. Quoted in Boyarsky, " 'Let's Kill All the Lawyers' " 571, 573.

10. See, e.g., Knight, *Shakespeare's Hidden Life*, 239–40; Goddard, *The Meaning of Shakespeare*, 1:267, 2:11–15.

11. Knight, *Shakespeare's Hidden Life*, 238.

12. Quoted in Savell, "Why Are They Picking on Us?" 72.

13. Mark Galanter and J. T. Knight, "When Bush Sang Praises of Lawyers," *National Law Journal*, 12 Oct. 1992, 13, 13–14.

CHAPTER THREE

1. Posner, *Law and Literature*, 354.

2. *Bowers v. Hardwick* 478 U.S. 186 (1986).

3. Friedman, *American Law*, 161.

4. *Wolfenden Report*, paragraphs 13, 61–62.

5. Devlin, *The Enforcement of Morals*, 17.

6. *Olmstead v. United States*, 277 U.S. 438, 485 (1928) (Brandeis, J., dissenting).

7. Devlin, *The Enforcement of Morals*, 16, 17.

8. Timothy Egan, "Oregon G.O.P. Faces Schism over Agenda of Christian Right," *New York Times*, 14 Nov. 1992, 6.

9. *Bowers*, 478 U.S. at 196.

10. Ibid., 212 (Blackmun, J., dissenting, quoting *Palmore v. Sidoti*, 466 U.S. 429, 433 (1984)).

11. Ibid., 208–12.

12. Ibid., 216 (Stevens, J., dissenting).

13. Holmes, *The Common Law*, 36. This is one of Holmes's more controversial comments. It has been criticized for apparently justifying a tyranny by the majority, perhaps even totalitarianism.

14. Bork, *The Tempting of America*, 246, 258.

15. *Thornburgh v. American College of Obstetricians & Gynecologists*, 476 U.S. 747, 772 (1986).

16. *New York Times*, 18 Mar. 1972, 14.

17. *Bowers*, 478 U.S. at 190, 192–93.

18. Holmes, *The Common Law*, 5.

19. *Bowers*, 478 U.S. at 219 n.11.

20. Ibid., 198, n.2 (Powell, J., concurring).

21. Bickel, *The Least Dangerous Branch*, 148, 152, although the books are full of dead-letter statutes that make good comic filler in newspapers and magazines. See also Calabresi, *A Common Law for the Age of Statutes*.

22. *Reitman v. Mulkey*, 387 U.S. 369 (1967).

23. The title of the book is *Shakespeare vor der foruni der Jurisprudenz*, and is discussed in Phillips, *Shakespeare and the Lawyers*, at 59.

24. *Trop v. Dulles*, 356 U.S. 86, 100–101 (1958).

25. *Furman v. Georgia*, 408 U.S. 238 (1972).

26. *McGautha v. California*, 402 U.S. 183, 198 (1971).

27. *Woodson v. North Carolina*, 428 U.S. 280, 304 (1976).

28. *United States v. Apfelbaum*, 445 U.S. 115, 131, n.13 (1980).

29. Denvir, "William Shakespeare and the Jurisprudence of Comedy," 825, 834–35.

30. Frye, *Northrop Frye on Shakespeare*, 142.

31. Posner, *Law and Literature*, 104.

32. Ibid., 243.

33. Ibid., 107–9.

34. *Bowers*, 478 U.S. at 191.

35. Knight, *Shakespeare's Hidden Life*, 228–35.

36. These cases are discussed in William Schmidt, "Adultery as a Crime: Old Laws Dusted Off in a Wisconsin Case," *New York Times*, 30 Apr. 1990, A1; 8 May 1990, A12; Elizabeth Kolbert, "Using Blue Laws to Keep Spouses from Scarlet Life," *New York Times*, 21 Sept. 1990, B1; Andrea Sachs, "Handing Out Scarlet Letters," *Time*, 1 Oct. 1990, 98.

Chapter Four

1. Moody, *Shakespeare: "The Merchant of Venice,"* 61.

2. See, e.g., Danson, *The Harmonies of the Merchant of Venice*; Gross, *Shylock*; Bronstein, "Shakespeare, the Jews and *The Merchant of Venice*," 10; Hecht, "*The Merchant of Venice*," 140–229; Stoll, *Shakespeare Studies*, 255–336.

3. See, e.g., Moody, *Shakespeare: "The Merchant of Venice"*; Charleton, *Shakespearean Comedy*, 123–60; Murry, "Shakespeare's Method," 153–73; Koffler, "Terror and Mutilation in the Golden Age," 116–34.

4. See, e.g., von Jhering, *Der Kampf um's Recht*; Eagleton, *William Shakespeare*, 36–37; Weisberg, *Poethics*, 99–100.

5. Hecht, "*The Merchant of Venice*," 186–87.

6. See, e.g., Keeton, *Shakespeare's Legal and Political Background*, 10–21.

7. For a recapitulation of legal descriptions of the bond, see Phillips, *Shakespeare and the Lawyers*, 102–16; on the automatic nature of the forfeiture, see Keeton, *Shakespeare's Legal and Political Background*, 136.

8. See Weisberg, *Poethics*, 95.

9. Andrews, *Law versus Equity in "The Merchant of Venice."*

10. Posner, *Law and Literature*, 97.

11. Himmelfarb, "Victorian Values/Jewish Values," 23, 28–29.

12. See Saxe, "Shylock, Portia and a Case of Literary Oppression," 115–24; Noonan, *Bribes*, 323–25.

13. Hazlitt, *Characters of Shakespear's Plays*, 322.

14. Weisberg, *Poethics*, 100.

15. Ibid. To be absolutely fair to Weisberg, I may be misreading him. When Weisberg describes Portia as an "exquisite heroine," I interpret that to mean he finds her character (including her legal role) attractive. But he may in fact be distinguishing between her dramatic role and her legal role.

16. See also the comment in *Timon of Athens*: "Crack the lawyer's voice, that he may never more false title plead, Nor sound his quillets shrilly" (4.3.172–74).

17. Alscher, "Staging Directions for a Balanced Resolution to the Merchant of Venice Trial Scene," 1–34.

18. Stevens, "The Shakespeare Canon of Statutory Construction," 1373, 1387. For those who have not yet had the pleasure of reading Mortimer's Rumpole books, Rumpole always refers, in interior monologues, to his imperious wife as She Who Must Be Obeyed.

19. Weisberg, *Poethics*, 93–104.

20. See, e.g., Stoll, *Shakespeare Studies*, 331–36.

21. Harold Bloom, "Operation Roth," *New York Review of Books*, 22 Apr. 1993, 45, 48.

22. See, e.g., *Redgrave v. Boston Symphony Orchestra*, 855 F.2d 888 (1st Cir. 1988).

23. See, e.g., Editorial, "Dirty Minds, or Little Minds," *New York Times*, 25 Aug. 1990, 22; Gross, "Enter Politics, Stage Left," *New York Times*, 26 Aug. 1990, sec. 1, 26.

24. Posner, *Law and Literature*, 33.

25. Knight, *Shakespeare's Hidden Life*, 178–90, 280–86.

26. Emery, in Andrews, *Law versus Equity in "The Merchant of Venice,"* ix.

Chapter Five

1. Olivier, *On Acting*, 76, 89, 79, 83.

2. See Jones, *Hamlet and Oedipus*.

3. Posner, *Law and Literature*, 26, 263.

4. *United States v. Watson*, 423 U.S. 411, 438 (1976) (Marshall, J., dissenting).

5. Bradley, *Shakespearean Tragedy*, 102.

6. Holmes, *The Common Law*, 6.

7. "An Angelo for Claudio, death for death! Haste still pays haste, and leisure

answers leisure, like doth quit like, and Measure still for Measure" (*Measure for Measure*, 5.1 405–7).

8. Bacon, "Of Revenge," in *Essays*, 18.

9. Holmes, *The Common Law*, 33.

10. Quoted in ibid., 36.

11. Posner, *Law and Literature*, 59, 70.

12. Holmes, *The Common Law*, 35–36.

13. Bacon, "Of Studies," in *Essays*, 204.

14. *Ecclesiastes*, 12:12.

15. Weisberg, *The Failure of the Word*, 8–9. Posner criticizes Weisberg—wrongly, I think—for describing Hamlet this way. See Posner, *Law and Literature*, 64–66.

16. Bradley, *Shakespearean Tragedy*, 115.

17. *Farmers Reservoir and Irrigation Co. v. McComb*, 337 U.S. 755, 772 (1949) (Frankfurter, J., concurring).

18. See Brackley, "Shakespeare and the Almighty Dollar," *Justinian* (May 1990): 24.

19. White, *The Legal Imagination*, 859.

20. St. Johns, *Final Verdict*, 63–64.

21. Posner criticizes any effort to connect the multiplying interpretations of *Hamlet* with the multiplying interpretations of the Constitution. One cannot argue, he says, "the inscrutability of the Constitution from *Hamlet*." Posner, *Law and Literature*, 265–68. Fair enough.

22. Olivier, *On Acting*, 85.

CHAPTER SIX

1. Rich, "Some Romans and Countrymen Conspire Anew to Murder Caesar," *New York Times*, 23 March 1988, C17.

2. Posner, *Law and Literature*, 278–81, 359–60. My discussion of the funeral speeches draws heavily on Posner's.

3. *Lakeside v. Oregon*, 435 U.S. 333, 345–346 (1978).

4. McGinniss, *Fatal Vision*, 503–10.

5. Posner, *Law and Literature*, 360.

6. Pocock, *The Machiavellian Moment*, 505.

7. Schlesinger, *Imperial Presidency*, 442, n.28, ix, 377, 388. See also Ely, *War and Responsibility*.

8. "Brutus" (17 Jan. 1788), in Ketcham, *The Anti-Federalist Papers*, at 287–88.

9. Quoted in Schlesinger, *Imperial Presidency*, 35.

10. *Youngstown Sheet & Tube Co. v. Sawyer*, 343 U.S. 579, 654 (1952) (Jackson, J., concurring).

11. Schlesinger, *Imperial Presidency*, 418.

12. Ibid., 418.

13. Ibid., 324.

14. Quoted in ibid., 24–25.

15. Quoted in ibid., 59.

16. Quoted in Gilbert, *Winston S. Churchill: Finest Hour, 1939–1941*, 106.
17. *Ex Parte Milligan*, 71 U.S. (4 Wall.) 281, 295, 297 (1866).
18. *Youngstown*, 343 U.S. at 646 (Jackson, J., concurring).
19. Sowell, *A Conflict of Visions*, 172–203.

CHAPTER SEVEN

1. Quoted in Goddard, *The Meaning of Shakespeare*, 1:77.
2. Gilmore, *The Ages of American Law*, 111.
3. For authors' intent theory, applied to law, see generally Meese, "Address Before the D.C. Chapter of the Federalist Society Lawyers Division," in Levinson and Mailloux, *Interpreting Law and Literature*, 25–33; Bork, *The Tempting of America*.
4. Although virtually unknown to most lawyers, the term *hermeneutics* is beginning to appear more frequently in legal literature, albeit only tentatively and without all of its implications recognized or explored. Much more work needs to be done in this area. Fully analyzing the implications of hermeneutics in the law is as worthwhile as comprehension of textual meaning and development of interpretive skill.
5. *Scott v. Sandford*, 19 How. 393, 426 (1857).
6. White, *The Legal Imagination*, 758.
7. See Goddard, *The Meaning of Shakespeare*, 1:79.
8. Hazlitt, *Characters of Shakespear's Plays*, 244.
9. Quoted in Padover, ed., *Thomas Jefferson on Democracy*, 155.
10. Goddard, *The Meaning of Shakespeare*, 1:80.

CHAPTER EIGHT

1. Wilson, *The Fortunes of Falstaff*, 17.
2. Keeton, *Shakespeare's Legal and Political Background*, 155–62.
3. Knight, *Shakespeare's Hidden Life*, 169.

CHAPTER NINE

1. Kendall, *Richard the Third*, 393.
2. Williamson, *The Mystery of the Princes*, 193.
3. Costain, *The Last Plantagenets*, 426.
4. Drewett and Redhead, *The Trial of Richard III*, ix.
5. Kendall, *Richard the Third*, 434.
6. Williamson, *The Mystery of the Princes*, 193 (emphasis in original).
7. Rossiter, "Angel with Horns," in Bloom, ed., *William Shakespeare: Histories & Poems*, 170.
8. Kendall, *Richard the Third*, 418.
9. Costain, *The Last Plantagenets*, 406.
10. *Meerpool v. Nizer*, 560 F.2d 1061, 1065 (2d Cir. 1977), *cert. denied*, 434 U.S. 1013 (1978) (referring to a book about the Rosenberg spy trial).
11. *Welch v. Penguin Books USA, Inc.* (Sup. Ct. Kings Co.), *New York Law Journal*, 12 Apr. 1991, 25.

12. Gora, "Introduction: Literature, Life, and the Law," *Brooklyn Law Review* 51 (1985): 225.

13. *Geisler v. Petrocelli*, 616 F.2d 636, 639 (2d Cir. 1980). I represented the plaintiff, Melanie Geisler.

14. *Welch v. Penguin Books USA*, 25.

15. Ibid., quoting Note, "'Clear and Convincing' Libel: Fiction and the Law of Defamation," *Yale Law Journal* 92 (1983): 538–41.

16. For cases upholding such suits, see, e.g., *Bindrim v. Mitchell*, 92 Cal. App. 3d 61, 155 Cal. Rptr. 29 (Ct. App. 1979) (affirming verdict of libel against writer and publisher of "novel"); *Geisler v. Petrocelli*, 616 F.2d 636 (2d Cir. 1980) (reversing dismissal of libel and false light privacy claim against author and publisher of "novel").

For cases throwing out such suits, see, e.g., *Springer v. Viking Press*, 90 A.D.2d 315, 457 N.Y.S.2d 246 (1st Dep't 1982), *aff'd*, 60 N.Y.2d 916, 470 N.Y.S.2d 579, 458 N.E.2d 1256 (1983) (affirming dismissal of libel claim arising out of "novel"); *Welch v. Penguin Books USA, Inc.*, 25 (dismissing libel-in-fiction complaint).

17. Quoted in Aaron, "What Can You Learn from a Historical Novel?" *American Heritage* 43 (Oct. 1992): 55.

18. Michiko Kakutani, "Fiction and Reality: Blurring the Edges," *New York Times*, 25 Sept. 1992, C1, C31.

19. John Bayley, Foreword to Bradley, *Shakespearean Tragedy*, 11.

20. "It is one of the proudest boasts of imaginative authors . . . that they are conveying truth through their work." Gay, *Style in History*, 190. "Imaginative writers normally claim that their fictions penetrate to truths of a high and general kind. . . . But these free-floating truths emerge from a context of untruths." Ibid., 193.

21. One is struck by the number of discussions about this subject in recent years.

22. Janet Maslin, "Facts Don't Always Give the True Story," *New York Times*, 8 Nov. 1987, sec. 5, 25.

23. Gay, *Style in History*, 188–207. See also Himmelfarb, "The Abyss Revisited," 337, 346–47 (criticizing historians favoring "freedom from fact" over "fact fetishism").

24. Carr, *What Is History?* 12.

25. *Masson v. The New Yorker Magazine*, 881 F.2d 1452 (9th Cir. 1989), *rev'd*, 111 S. Ct. 2419 (1991).

26. Albert Scardino, "Ethics, Reporters and the New Yorker," *New York Times*, 21 Mar. 1989, C20.

27. John Taylor, "Holier than Thou," *New York Magazine*, 27 Mar. 1989, 35.

28. *Masson*, 881 F.2d at 1477–78 (dissenting opinion).

29. Because the jury disagreed on the amount of damages the trial judge later threw out the whole verdict and ordered a new trial on all issues (except that the *New Yorker* was dismissed from the case).

30. *Masson*, 1485.

31. Quoted in Taylor, "Holier than Thou," 35.

32. John O'Connor, "The Line between Drama and Lies," *New York Times*, 31 Dec. 1992, C11.

33. *Masson*, 881 F.2d at 1485.

34. In this sense McGinniss was criticized for the virtue of full disclosure. Given McGinniss's disclosures, it is hard to understand how a critic could write that "one of the pivotal problems with Mr. McGinniss's book" is that it does "not even announce" itself as a work "of fiction, but instead masquerade[s] as the truth." Michiko Kakutani, "Is It Fiction? Is It Nonfiction? And Why Doesn't Anyone Care?" *New York Times*, 29 July 1993, C13.(In the spirit of full disclosure, I was McGinniss's lawyer in the suit against him by Jeffrey MacDonald, the convicted murderer in McGinniss's book *Fatal Vision*.)

35. An excellent discussion of this debate can be found in Kakutani, "Fiction and Reality," C1; and Michiko Kakutani, "When History Is a Casualty," *New York Times*, 30 Apr. 1993, C1. Kakutani concludes her first essay by saying that it is "dangerous to mistake fictional representations for the real thing" because, among other things, it "means living in a dimly lighted world of shadows, mirrors and self-delusions, content with approximations and soothing misrepresentations, instead of continuing to try to discern the truth."

CHAPTER TEN

1. Bloom, *Shakespeare's Politics*, 47.

2. *Rosenblatt v. Baer*, 383 U.S. 75, 86 (1966).

3. Ibid., 92 (Stewart, J., concurring).

4. For a thoroughly engaging mock appeals court decision following a fictional murder trial of Othello, see Nagle, "Commonwealth v. Othello," 104–9.

5. Hazlitt, *Characters of Shakespear's Plays*, 200.

6. Kott, *Shakespeare Our Contemporary*, 118–19.

7. *Watt v. Longsdon*, 1 K.B. 130 (1930).

8. *Milkovich v. Lorain Journal Co.*, 497 U.S. 1, 12.

9. *Onassis v. Christian Dior*, 122 Misc. 2d 603, 610, 472 N.Y.2d 254, 260 (Sup. Ct. N.Y. Co. 1984), aff'd, 110 A.D.2d 1095, 488 N.Y.2d 943 (1st Dep't 1985).

10. *People v. Rosenberg*, 45 N.Y.2d 251, 264 408 N.Y.S.2d 368, (1978). In a 1979 case from Hawaii about the right of parents to give their child any surname they wish, a federal court quoted Iago's passage in full as support for the proposition that "one's name becomes a symbol of one's self." *Jech v. Burch*, 466 F. Supp. 714, 719 (D. Haw. 1979).

11. *Katz v. Superior Court*, 141 Cal. Rptr. 234 (Ct. App. 1977).

12. *United States Gypsum Co. v. Schiavo Bros., Inc.*, 450 F. Supp. 1291, 1294 (E.D. Pa. 1978).

13. *Penasquitos Village, Inc. v. NLRB*, 565 F.2d 1074, 1085 (9th Cir. 1977); *Abatti Farms, Inc. v. Agricultural Labor Relations Board*, 165 Cal. Rptr. 887, 107 Cal. 3d 317 (Ct. App. 1980).

14. *Lindros v. Torrance Unified School District*, 108 Cal. Rptr. 185, 570 P.2d 361, 9 Cal. 3d 524 (1973).

15. *Green v. Arnold*, 512 F. Supp. 650, 651 (W.D. Tex. 1981).

16. Sack, *Libel, Slander and Related Problems*, 100.

17. Smolla, *Law of Defamation*, sec. 7.05[1], p. 7–6.

18. Sack, *Libel, Slander and Related Problems*, 94.

19. *Prosser and Keeton on Torts*, 771.

20. See Keeton et al., *Prosser and Keeton on Torts*, 772; *Restatement (Second) Torts*, sec. 568, Comment b.

21. Holdsworth, "Defamation in the Sixteenth and Seventeenth Centuries," 302, 397–401.

22. *Restatement (Second) Torts*, sec. 575, Comment b.

23. *Spence v. Funk*, 396 A.2d 967, 970 (Del. 1978).

24. *Prosser and Keeton on Torts*, 788.

25. Ibid., 793.

26. *Davies v. Gardiner*, Popham 36, 79 Eng. Rep. 1155 (1593); *Oxford v. Cross*, 4 Co. Rep. 18, 76 Eng. Rep. 902 (1599); *Matthew v. Crass*, Cro. Jac. 323, 79 Eng. Rep. 276 (1614).

27. See Oliver Stone, "Fiction's Claim on Fact," *New York Times*, 27 July 1992, A17.

28. *Davies*, Popham 36, 79 Eng. Rep. 1155 (1593).

29. See, e.g., *Prosser and Keeton on Torts*, 793; Plucknett, *A Concise History of the Common Law*, 494.

30. *New York Times v. Sullivan*, 376 U.S. 254 (1964).

31. *Gertz v. Robert Welch, Inc.*, 418 U.S. 323 (1974).

32. Ibid., 349.

33. *Dun & Bradstreet v. Green Moss Builders, Inc.*, 472 U.S. 749 (1985).

CHAPTER ELEVEN

1. Fein, "Forget Those Legal Briefs: Novels by Lawyers Pay Off," *New York Times*, 20 July 1991, D6.

2. Goddard, *The Meaning of Shakespeare*, 2:269.

3. Ibid., 273.

4. Ibid., 269.

5. Cardozo, *Paradoxes of Legal Science*, 254.

6. Brennan, "Reason, Passion, and 'The Progress of the Law,'" *Record of the Association of the Bar of the City of New York* 42 (Dec. 1987): 948.

7. Ibid., 958, 970.

8. Ibid., 961, 962.

9. Grey, *The Wallace Stevens Case*, 87.

10. *Whitney v. California*, 274 U.S. 357, 375 (1927) (Brandeis, J., concurring).

11. *New York Times Co. v. United States*, 403 U.S. 713, 714–20.

12. *New York Times v. Sullivan*, 376 U.S. at 282.

13. *Rosenblatt v. Baer*, 383 U.S. 75, 85 (1966).

14. *Abrams v. United States*, 250 U.S. 616, 630 (1919).

CHAPTER TWELVE

1. *Coy v. Iowa*, 487 U.S. 1012, 1016 (1988).

2. Wigmore, *Evidence*, 5:153, n.2.

3. *Coy*, 487 U.S. at 1029, n.3 (Blackmun, J., dissenting).

4. *In re Murchison*, 349 U.S. 133 (1955).

5. Ibid.

6. *Tumey v. Ohio*, 273 U.S. 510, 524 (1927).

7. Ibid., 532.

8. Ibid., 534.

9. For criticism of Portia's judicial ethics, see Noonan, *Bribes*, 323–25; Saxe, "Shylock, Portia and a Case of Literary Oppression," 115–24.

10. Marius, *Thomas More*, 453.

11. For an imaginative account of Bacon's impeachment, see Bowen, *Francis Bacon*, 177–204.

12. Bacon, *Essays*, 222.

13. Bowen, *Francis Bacon*, 189.

14. *United States v. Nixon*, 418 U.S. 683, 708 (1974).

15. *United States v. Burr*, 25 Fed. Cas. 187, 192 (No. 14,694) (CC Va. 1807).

16. *Nixon*, 418 U.S. at 715.

17. *Burdick v. United States*, 236 U.S. 79, 90–91 (1915).

18. In *Faretta v. California*, 422 U.S. 806 (1975), the Supreme Court held that the Sixth Amendment guarantees the right to represent oneself.

CHAPTER THIRTEEN

1. Bradley, *Shakespearean Tragedy*, 225.

2. Goddard, *The Meaning of Shakespeare*, 2:143–47.

3. Kaus, *The End of Equality*, 25–57.

4. Tribe, *American Constitutional Law*, 1553, secs. 16–24.

5. *Levy v. Louisiana*, 391 U.S. 68, 71 (1968).

6. Ibid., 71.

7. Ibid., 72.

8. Ibid., 72, n.6.

9. Ibid., 78, n.3.

10. Ibid.

11. *Weber v. Aetna Casualty & Surety Co.*, 406 U.S.164, 172, 176 (1972).

12. *Matthews v. Lucas*, 427 U.S. 495, 505 (1976).

13. For a description of current three-tiered equal protection analysis, see *City of Cleburne, Texas v. Cleburne Living Center*, 473 U.S. 432, 439–41 (1985).

14. *Labine v. Vincent*, 401 U.S. 532 (1971).

15. *Weber v. Aetna Casualty & Surety Co.*, 406 U.S. 164 (1972).

16. *Mills v. Hablvetzel*, 456 U.S. 91, 99 (1982).

17. Smiley, *A Thousand Acres*, 325.

18. Ibid., 326.

CHAPTER FOURTEEN

1. Schoenbaum, *Compact Documentary Life*, 95. See also Knight, *Shakespeare's Hidden Life*, 1–25.

2. Jaszi, Appellant's Briefs, in "In Re Shakespeare," 645, 675.

3. White, "William Shakespeare, Attorney at Law and Solicitor in Chancery," 84.

4. Twain, "Is Shakespeare Dead?" 138, 139. Knight's only reference to this essay is as a passing citation included in someone else's work. See Knight, *Shakespeare's Hidden Life*, 108, n.2. This yields the reasonable inference that even Knight, our best-informed scholar on the subject, has not read Twain's essay.

5. Twain, "Is Shakespeare Dead?" 141–42.

6. Weisberg, *Poethics*, 56. The legal aspects of *Pudd'nhead Wilson* are so marked that the book can be found in John Wigmore, "A List of One Hundred Legal Novels," *Illinois Law Review* 17 (1922): 26.

7. Weisberg, *Poethics*, 202. See also D. M. McKeithan, *Court Trials in Mark Twain*, passim.

8. Weisberg, *Poethics*, 223.

9. White, "William Shakespeare, Attorney at Law and Solicitor in Chancery," 84.

10. Heard, *Shakespeare as a Lawyer*, 48.

11. Boyle, Appellee's Briefs, in "In Re Shakespeare," 757, referring to Clarkson and Warren, *The Law of Property in Shakespeare and the Elizabethan Drama*. "Other Elizabethan playwrights frequently employed legal maxims in their plays, usually in a more direct form than Shakespeare." Phillips, *Shakespeare and the Lawyers*, 177. See also ibid., 191.

12. Phillips, *Shakespeare and the Lawyers*, 177. See also Keeton, *Shakespeare's Legal and Political Background* ("The legal and political ideas which he incidentally expresses were part of the intellectual equipment of all educated men of his time, and his touch was sensitive").

13. Robertson, *The Baconian Heresy*, 38–177.

14. Knight, *Shakespeare's Hidden Life*, 106.

15. Twain, "Is Shakespeare Dead?" 172.

16. Knight, *Shakespeare's Hidden Life*, 25.

17. Weisberg, *Poethics*, x.

18. Phillips, *Shakespeare and the Lawyers*, 189.

19. Twain, "Is Shakespeare Dead?" 152.

20. Robertson, *The Baconian Heresy*, 145–46.

21. Boyle, Appellee's Briefs, in "In Re Shakespeare," 757.

22. Twain, "Is Shakespeare Dead?" 149.

23. Bradley, *Shakespearean Tragedy*, 96.

24. Opinions of the Justices, in "In Re Shakespeare," 820 (Brennan, J.).

25. Knight, *Shakespeare's Hidden Life*, 123–24.

26. Clarkson and Warren, *The Law of Property in Shakespeare and the Elizabethan Drama*, 285–86.

Epilogue

1. Denvir, "William Shakespeare and the Jurisprudence of Comedy," 825.

2. It is no coincidence that one of the founders of the law and literature movement has written a valuable book for improving lawyers' writing. In *When Lawyers Write*, Richard Weisberg stresses the importance of reading good literature.

3. Domnarski, "Shakespeare in the Law," 317, 319.

4. *Central Hudson Gas & Electric Corp. v. Public Service Commission of New York,* 447 U.S. 557, 579 (1980).

5. *Boutilier v. INS,* 387 U.S. 118, 130 (1967) (Douglas, J., dissenting).

6. *FCC v. Pacifica Foundation,* 438 U.S. 726, 770 (1978) (Brennan, J., dissenting).

7. See John Grisham, "The Rise of the Legal Thriller: Why Lawyers Are Throwing Books at Us," *New York Times Book Review,* 18 Oct. 1992, 33.

8. Fried, "Sonnet LXV and the 'Black Ink' of the Framers' Intention," 751, 758. Several of Shakespeare's sonnets contain legal allusions.

9. Posner also "take[s] exception to Charles Fried's effort to infer the intelligibility of the Constitution from the intelligibility of Shakespeare's Sonnet LXV." Posner thinks Fried's effort is part of "the misguided quest for literary analogies to problems of legal interpretation." Posner, *Law and Literature,* 266–67.

10. Stevens, "The Shakespeare Canon of Statutory Construction," 1373, 1386–7.

11. *Pompano v. Michael Schiavone & Sons, Inc.,* 680 F.2d 911 (2d Cir. 1982), quoting *The Tempest,* 1.2.437–38.

12. See Holmes's speech "The Profession of the Law," in Posner, ed., *The Essential Holmes,* 220.

WORKS CITED

Note: All quotations from Shakespeare are taken from the *Oxford Shakespeare.* Edited by Stanley Wells and Gary Taylor. Oxford: Clarendon Press, 1988.

Aaron, Daniel. "What Can You Learn from a Historical Novel?" *American Heritage* 43 (Oct. 1992): 55.

Alscher, Peter J. "Staging Directions for a Balanced Resolution to 'The Merchant of Venice' Trial Scene." *Cardozo Studies in Law and Literature* 5 (1993): 1–34.

Andrews, Mark Edwin. *Law versus Equity in "The Merchant of Venice."* Boulder: University of Colorado Press, 1965.

Bacon, Francis. *Essays.* London: Oxford University Press, 1975.

Berger, Harry, Jr. *Imaginary Audition: Shakespeare on Stage and Page.* Berkeley: University of California Press, 1989.

Bickel, Alexander M. *The Least Dangerous Branch.* Indianapolis: Bobbs-Merrill 1962.

Bloom, Allan (with Harry J. Jaffa). *Shakespeare's Politics.* New York: Basic Books, 1964.

Bloom, Harold. "Operation Roth." *New York Review of Books,* 22 Apr. 1993, 45–48.

Bork, Robert H. *The Tempting of America: The Political Seduction of the Law.* New York: Free Press, 1990.

Bowen, Catherine Drinker. *Francis Bacon: The Temper of a Man.* Boston: Little, Brown, 1963.

Boyarsky, Saul. "'Let's Kill All the Lawyers': What Did Shakespeare Mean?" *Journal of Legal Medicine* 12 (1991): 571–74.

Boyle, James D. A. Appellee's Briefs. In "In Re Shakespeare: The Question of Authorship." *American University Law Review* 37 (1988): 725–98, 809–18.

Brackley, P. J. "Shakespeare and the Almighty Dollar." *Justinian* (May 1990): 24.

Bradley, A. C. *Shakespearean Tragedy.* London: Macmillan, 1904. Reprint. London: Penguin, 1991.

Brennan, William J., Jr. "Reason, Passion, and 'The Progress of the Law.'" *Record of the Association of the Bar of the City of New York* 42 (Dec. 1987): 948–77.

Brill, Steven. "Watching the Drama of Justice." *American Lawyer* July–Aug. 1990, 3.

Bronstein, Herbert. "Shakespeare, the Jews and *The Merchant of Venice.*" *Shakespeare Quarterly* 20 (1969): 10.

Calabresi, Guido. *A Common Law for the Age of Statutes.* Cambridge, Mass.: Harvard University Press, 1982.

Cardozo, Benjamin N. *The Paradoxes of Legal Science.* In *Selected Writings of Benjamin Nathan Cardozo.* Edited by Margaret E. Hall. New York: Matthew Bender, 1975.

Carr, E. H. *What Is History?* Harmondsworth, England: Penguin Books, 1964.

Charleton, H. B. *Shakespearean Comedy.* New York: Macmillan, 1938.

Clarkson, P., and C. Warren. *The Law of Property in Shakespeare and the Elizabethan Drama.* Baltimore: Johns Hopkins University Press, 1942.

Committee on Homosexual Offenses and Prostitution, *Wolfenden Report.* London, 1957.

Costain, Thomas B. *The Last Plantagenets.* New York: Popular Library, 1962.

Danson, Lawrence. *The Harmonies of the Merchant of Venice.* New Haven: Yale University Press, 1978.

Denvir, John. "William Shakespeare and the Jurisprudence of Comedy." *Stanford Law Review* 39 (1987): 825–49.

Devlin, Patrick. *The Enforcement of Morals.* Oxford: Oxford University Press, 1979.

Domnarski, William. "Shakespeare in the Law." *Connecticut Bar Journal* 67 (1993): 317–51.

Drewett, Richard, and Mark Redhead. *The Trial of Richard III.* Gloucester: Alan Sutton, 1985.

Eagleton, Terry. *William Shakespeare.* New York: B. Blackwell, 1986.

Ely, John Hart. *War and Responsibility.* Princeton, N.J.: Princeton University Press, 1993.

Ferguson, Robert. *Law and Letters in American Culture.* Cambridge, Mass.: Harvard University Press, 1984.

Fried, Charles. "Sonnet LXV and the 'Black Ink' of the Framers' Intention." *Harvard Law Review* 100 (1987): 751–60.

Friedman, Lawrence M. *American Law: An Introduction.* New York: W. W. Norton, 1984.

Frye, Northrop. *Northrop Frye on Shakespeare.* Edited by Robert Sandler. New Haven: Yale University Press, 1986.

Gay, Peter. *Style in History.* New York: W. W. Norton, 1989.

Gilbert, Martin. *Winston S. Churchill: Finest Hour, 1939–1941.* Boston: Houghton Mifflin, 1983.

Gilmore, Grant. *The Ages of American Law.* New Haven: Yale University Press, 1977.

Goddard, Harold C. *The Meaning of Shakespeare.* 2 vols. Chicago: University of Chicago Press, 1951.

Goldstein, Tom, and Jethro K. Lieberman. *The Lawyer's Guide to Writing Well.* Berkeley: University of California Press, 1991.

Gora, Joel M. "Introduction: Literature, Life, and the Law." *Brooklyn Law Review* 51 (1985): 225–31.

Grey, Thomas C. *The Wallace Stevens Case: Law and the Practice of Poetry.* Cambridge, Mass.: Harvard University Press, 1991.

Gross, John. *Shylock: A Legend and Its Legacy.* New York: Simon & Schuster, 1993.

Hazlitt, William. *Characters of Shakespear's Plays.* Everyman's Library. New York: Dutton, 1969.

Heard, Franklin F. *Shakespeare as a Lawyer.* Boston: Little, Brown, 1883.

Hecht, Anthony. "The Merchant of Venice: A Venture in Hermeneutics." In *Obligati: Essays in Criticism.* New York: Atheneum, 1986.

Himmelfarb, Gertrude. "Victorian Values/Jewish Values." *Commentary* (Feb. 1990): 23–31.

———. "The Abyss Revisited." *The American Scholar* 61 (Summer 1992): 337–49.

Holdsworth, William. "Defamation in the Sixteenth and Seventeenth Centuries." *Law Quarterly Review* 40 (1924): 302, 397–401.

Holmes, Oliver Wendell. *The Common Law.* Boston: Little, Brown, 1881. Reprint. Edited by Mark DeWolfe Howe. Boston: Little, Brown, 1963.

———. *Collected Legal Papers.* New York: Harcourt, Brace and Howe, 1920.

Jaszi, Peter. Appellant's Briefs. In "In Re Shakespeare: The Question of Authorship." *American University Law Review* 37 (1988): 645–724, 799–808.

Jhering, Rudolf von. *Der Kampf um's Recht.* Vienna, 1886. Translated in H. H. Furness, ed. *The Merchant of Venice: A New Variorum Edition of Shakespeare.* 1888. Reprint. New York: Dover, 1964.

Jones, Ernest. *Hamlet and Oedipus.* New York: W. W. Norton, 1949.

Kaus, Mickey. *The End of Equality.* New York: Basic Books, 1992.

Keeton, G. W. *Shakespeare's Legal and Political Background.* New York: Barnes & Noble, 1967.

Keeton, W. Page, Dan B. Dobbs, Robert E. Keeton, and David G. Owen. *Prosser and Keeton on the Law of Torts.* 5th ed. St. Paul, Minn.: West Publishing Co., 1984.

Kendall, Paul Murray. *Richard the Third.* London: Allen & Unwin, 1955.

———, ed. *Richard III: The Great Debate.* New York and London: W. W. Norton, 1965.

Ketcham, Ralph, ed. *The Anti-Federalist Papers.* New York: New American Library, 1986.

Knight, W. Nicholas. *Shakespeare's Hidden Life: Shakespeare at the Law, 1585–1595.* New York: Mason & Lipscomb, 1973.

———. "Patrimony and Shakespeare's Daughters." *Hartford Studies in Literature* 9 (1977): 175–86.

———. "Shakespeare's Court Case." *Law and Critique* 2 (1991): 103–12.

Koffler, Judith. "Terror and Mutilation in the Golden Age." *Human Rights Quarterly* 5 (May 1983): 116–34.

Kott, Jan. *Shakespeare Our Contemporary.* Translated by Bolesaw Teborski. New York: W. W. Norton, 1966.

Levinson, Sanford, and Stephen Mailloux, eds. *Interpreting Law and Literature: A Hermeneutic Reader.* Evanston, Ill.: Northwestern University Press, 1988.

McGinniss, Joe. *Fatal Vision.* New York: Putnam, 1983.

McKeithan, D. M. *Court Trials in Mark Twain and Other Essays.* New York: Nijhoff, 1958.

Marius, Richard. *Thomas More.* New York: Vintage Books, 1985.

Moody, A. D. *Shakespeare: The Merchant of Venice.* London: Edward Arnold, 1964.

Morris, Richard B. *Witnesses at the Creation.* New York: New American Library, 1985.

Murry, J. M. "Shakespeare's Method: The Merchant of Venice." In *Shakespeare.* New York: Harcourt Brace, 1936.

Nagle, P. Michael. "Commonwealth v. Othello." *University of Maryland Law Forum* 7 (1977): 104–9.

Noonan, John. *Bribes.* Berkeley: University of California Press, 1984.

Olivier, Laurence. *On Acting.* New York: Simon & Schuster, 1986.

Opinions of the Justices. In "In Re Shakespeare: The Question of Authorship." *American University Law Review* 37 (1988): 819–76.

Padover, Saul K., ed. *Thomas Jefferson on Democracy.* New York: New American Library, 1939.

Phillips, O. Hood. *Shakespeare and the Lawyers.* London: Methuen, 1972.

Plucknett, Theodore F. T. *A Concise History of the Common Law.* 5th ed. Boston: Little, Brown, 1956.

Pocock, J.G.A. *The Machiavellian Moment.* Princeton: Princeton University Press, 1975.

Posner, Richard. "Law and Literature: A Relation Reargued." *Virginia Law Review* 72 (1986): 1351–92.

———. *Law and Literature: A Misunderstood Relation.* Cambridge, Mass.: Harvard University Press, 1988.

———, ed. *The Essential Holmes.* Chicago: University of Chicago Press, 1992.

Robertson, J. M. *The Baconian Heresy.* London: Herbert Jenkins, 1913.

Rodell, Fred. "Goodbye to Law Reviews." *Virginia Law Review* 23 (1936): 38–45.

Rossiter, A. P. "Angel with Horns: The Unity of Richard III." In Harold Bloom, ed. *William Shakespeare: Histories & Poems,* 170. New York: Chelsea House Publishers, 1986.

Sack, Robert D. *Libel, Slander and Related Problems.* New York: Practicing Law Institute, 1980.

St. Johns, Adela Rogers. *Final Verdict.* Garden City, N.Y.: Doubleday, 1962.

Savell, Lawrence. "Why Are They Picking on Us?" *American Bar Association Journal* (Nov. 1992): 72–75.

Saxe, David B. "Shylock, Portia and a Case of Literary Oppression." *Cardozo Studies in Law and Literature* 5 (1993): 115–24.

Schlesinger, Arthur M., Jr. *The Imperial Presidency.* Boston: Houghton Mifflin, 1973.

Schoenbaum, Samuel. *William Shakespeare: A Compact Documentary Life.* Rev. ed. Oxford: Oxford University Press, 1987.

Smiley, Jane. *A Thousand Acres.* New York: Alfred A. Knopf, 1992.

Smolla, Rodney A. *Law of Defamation.* New York: Clark Boardman Callaghan, 1992.

Sowell, Thomas. *A Conflict of Visions.* New York: William Morrow, 1987.

Stevens, John Paul. "The Shakespeare Canon of Statutory Construction." *University of Pennsylvania Law Review* 140 (1992): 1373–87.

Stoll, Edgar Elmer. *Shakespeare Studies.* New York: Macmillan, 1927.

Szatmary, David P. *Shays' Rebellion.* Amherst: University of Massachusetts Press, 1980.

Tey, Josephine. *The Daughter of Time.* New York: Macmillan, 1951.

Tribe, Laurence H. *American Constitutional Law.* 2d ed. Mineola, N.Y.: Foundation Press, 1988.

Twain, Mark. "Is Shakespeare Dead?" In *The Outrageous Mark Twain*, edited by Charles Neider, 137–89. New York: Doubleday, 1987.

Weisberg, Richard H. *The Failure of the Word: The Protagonist as Lawyer in Modern Fiction*. New Haven: Yale University Press, 1984.

———. *Poethics: And Other Strategies of Law and Literature*. New York: Columbia University Press, 1992.

———. *When Lawyers Write*. Boston: Little, Brown, 1987.

White, James B. *The Legal Imagination: Studies in the Nature of Legal Thought and Expression*. Boston: Little, Brown, 1973.

———. "Book Review: What Can a Lawyer Learn from Literature?" *Harvard Law Review* 102 (1989): 2032–47.

White, Richard Grant. "William Shakespeare, Attorney at Law and Solicitor in Chancery." *Atlantic Monthly* 4 (July 1859): 84.

Wigmore, John. *Evidence*. Vol. 5. Revised by James H. Chadbourn. Boston: Little, Brown, 1974.

———. "A List of One Hundred Legal Novels." *Illinois Law Review* 17 (1922): 26–41.

Williamson, Aubrey. *The Mystery of the Princes*. Gloucester: Alan Sutton, 1981.

Wilson, John Dover. *The Fortunes of Falstaff*. Cambridge: Cambridge University Press, 1943.

INDEX

Abrams v. United States, 191
Addenbrooke, John, 18
Addison, Joseph, 118
adultery. *See* infidelity
Adventures of Huckleberry Finn, The (Twain), 86
advocacy: oral, 108–13, 208–9, 240
Ages of American Law, The (Gilmore), 128
Alien Statute, 76, 79–81, 84, 85
Alscher, Peter, 80, 81
amateurism, xiii–xiv
American Bar Association, 34
American Law Institute, 173
American Revolution, 118–19, 200
American Shakespeare Festival (Stratford, Conn.), 210
American Tragedy, An (Dreiser), 169
amnesty, 201, 202
Ancient Law (Maine), 68, 207–8
Angelo (character), 45–46, 55–59, 65
Anti-Federalists, 118
antifornication laws, 43–44, 49. *See also* infidelity
anti-Semitism. *See* prejudice
Antigone (Sophocles), 128, 187
Antigonus (character), 187–89, 191
Antony, Marc (character), 107, 110–13, 115
Antony and Cleopatra (Shakespeare), 183
Apollo, 179, 182, 184. *See also* Delphic oracle
appearances, as misleading: in *The Merchant of Venice*, 66, 77–79, 85; in *A Midsummer Night's Dream*, 126
Aristotle, 13, 152
asses, 133–34, 171
Association of the Bar of the City of New York, 10
audiences: in *A Midsummer Night's Dream*, 125–26, 129–31; and orators, 113; Shakespeare's, 13–15, 30–31, 235
Audley, John, 16
authority. *See* ends and means; power

Bacon, Francis (Sir): as alleged writer of Shakespeare's plays, xiii, 197; essays by,

94, 97, 197–98; as Inns of Court member, 14; as lord chancellor, 196–97
Beard, Charles, 116
Beaumont, Francis, 233
Becker, Carl, 151
Becket, Thomas à, 209
bedroom tricks, 42–43, 53, 56, 86
Bellott, Stephen, 18
Belott v. Mountjoy, 18–19
"benefit of clergy," 30
Bible, 11, 97, 242
Bickel, Alexander, 47–48
Biddle, Francis, 55
Bierce, Ambrose, 23
Billy Budd (Melville), 10
Birth of Tragedy, The (Nietzsche), 184, 185
Black, Hugo (Justice), 161, 190
Blackfriar Gate-house, 19
Blackmun, Harry (Justice), 21, 40–41, 43, 194, 237
Blackstone, William (Sir), 245
Bleak House (Dickens), 7, 236
blindness. *See* justice: blindness of
Bloom, Harold, 85
Bonfire of the Vanities (Wolfe), 236
Bork, Robert, 41–42, 44, 186–87
Bottom the Weaver (character), 126, 132–34
Bowers v. Hardwick, 36–37, 39–40, 43–49, 62
Bradley, A. C., xiv, 92–93, 98, 151, 210, 237
Branagh, Kenneth, 165, 211
Brandeis, Louis (Justice), 39, 98, 190
Brennan, William (Justice), 185, 237, 242
bribery, 196–98
Brill, Steven, 12
British Broadcasting Company, 145, 149
Brock, David, 56
Browning-Ferris Industries v. Kelco Disposal, 20
Brutus (character), 107, 109–15, 121
Brutus Seeing the Bodies of His Sons (David), 114
Bryant, William Cullen, 10
Burdick v. United States, 202

Burke, Edmund, 101
Burr, Aaron, 199
Bush, George, 23, 33, 34, 201–2
Butler, Lady Eleanor (character), 147

Cade, Jack (character), 25–33
Caesar (character), 121
Caesar and Cleopatra (Shaw), 94
Caine Mutiny (Wouk), 8, 236
cameras: in courtrooms, 12–13
Camillo (character), 189
Campbell, John (Lord), xvi
Camus, Albert, 7
capital punishment: for disobedient daugh-
    ters, 126–27; exemptions from, 30; for
    infidelity, 36, 49–51, 127; in United
    States, 95; for usury, 85, 127–28; and
    vengeance, 182. See also executions
Capote, Truman, 144, 152
Cardozo, Benjamin (Justice), 183–84
Cardozo Law School, 6
Cardozo Studies in Law and Literature, 7,
    10
Carnovsky, Morris, 210
Carr, E. H., 153
Carter, Jimmy, 201, 202
Castro, Fidel, 29
Cato (Addison), 118
censorship: in Elizabethan England, 31–32,
    209; of The Merchant of Venice, 85–86
chancery courts (England), 66, 73, 89, 241
Choate, Rufus, 11
Chronicles of England, Scotlande, and Ire-
    lande (Holinshed), 29, 235, 237
Churchill, Winston, 123
Cicero, 109, 113
civic courage. See civil disobedience
civil disobedience: in A Midsummer Night's
    Dream, 125, 128; in The Winter's Tale,
    187–92, 193
Civilization and Its Discontents (Freud), 95,
    182, 216
civil rights movement, 74
Clancy, Tom, 236
classics, 66–67. See also reading
class revolt: in Henry VI, Part 2, 26–31
Clement's Inn (London), 139
clergy, 30
Coke, Edward (Lord), 89, 197, 241
Comedy of Errors, The (Shakespeare), 14,
    127, 140, 200
commercial law. See contract law

Common Law, The (Holmes), 41, 93
common law courts (England), 66, 73, 89,
    167–68, 169, 241
communism, 31
compensatory damages, 94
compromise, 140–41
Conflict of Visions, A (Sowell), 124
confrontation: right of, 193–94
Connecticut, 47, 63, 209, 210
Conroy, Frank, 144
Constitutional Convention, 120
constitutional law. See Founding Fathers;
    interpretation; republicanism; U.S. Con-
    stitution
Continental Army, 118
contract law: in Belott v. Mountjoy, 18–19;
    John Shakespeare's involvement with,
    16–17; in Measure for Measure, 42–43;
    in The Merchant of Venice, 65, 67, 68–
    74, 83–84, 131; in Richard III's case,
    146–47
Cooper, James Fenimore, 10
Coriolanus (Shakespeare), 31
Costain, Thomas B., 149
Coy v. Iowa, 194
Crime and Punishment (Dostoyevsky), 104
criminal law: and morality, 37, 39, 48; and
    revenge, 94, 95

Dana, Richard Henry, Jr., 10
Danton, Georges-Jacques, 29
Daughter of Time, The (Tey), 145
Daumier, Honoré, 23, 34
David, Jacques-Louis, 114
David Copperfield (Dickens), 236
Davies v. Gardiner, 169, 170
dead-letter statutes, 46–49, 63
death: from slander, 170–71
death penalty. See capital punishment
deductive logic, 101
defamation: in Much Ado about Nothing,
    165–75; in New Yorker magazine case,
    153; in Othello, 156–65; question of
    Shakespeare's, against Richard III, 148–
    51, 154–55; in Richard II, 208; Susanna
    Shakespeare's suit alleging, 19, 169–70
defamation per se, 166–68, 172, 173, 174
Defense of Poetry, A (Shelley), 245
Dekker, Thomas, 232
Delacorte Theatre (New York City), xi, 157
DeLillo, Don, 155
Delphic oracle, 177–80, 182, 184

democracy, 199. *See also* republicanism
Demosthenes, 113
desuetude, 46–49, 63
Devil's Dictionary (Bierce), 23
Devlin, Patrick, 38–39, 40, 42, 43
Dickens, Charles, 23, 231, 236
Dick the Butcher (character), 25–26, 27, 29–33, 135, 138, 240
Dionysus, 184, 185
Discourses and Histories (Machiavelli), 115
discretion. *See* judges: discretion of
discrimination. *See* equal protection; prejudice
divine right of kings, 198, 199
docudrama, 143–44, 148, 150, 154
Dogberry (character), 171
Donne, John, 14
Dostoyevsky, Feodor, 7, 104
Douglas, William (Justice), 161, 222–23, 242
dowries, 18
Dred Scott decision, 131
Dreiser, Theodore, 169
due process, 84, 85, 195, 196
Dun & Bradstreet v. Green Moss Builders, Inc., 172–73

ecclesiastical courts, 167–68, 170
Economic Interpretation of the Constitution, An (Beard), 116
Edmund (character), 174, 217
Edward, prince of Wales (character), 145, 146–48
Edward IV (character), 146
Elizabeth I, 209
Elizabethan England. *See* censorship; Inns of Court; law: in Elizabethan England; Renaissance
Ellesmore, Lord, 89, 241
ends and means: in *Julius Caesar*, 121–24; in *Richard III*, 142, 143–55
"Enforcement of Morals, The" (lecture), 38
English law. *See* law: in Elizabethan England
equal protection, 79–82, 84, 85, 213, 221–23
equity, 60, 62–65, 73, 82–83, 89, 131, 186, 202
Executioner's Song (Mailer), 152
executions: public, 13
executive privilege, 199. *See also* government; sovereign immunity

Ex Parte Milligan, 123
"eye for an eye," 93–94
eyesight: in *King Lear*, 214–15

Failure of the Word, The (Weisberg), 7, 98
fair trials, 195. *See also* judges; trial scenes
false emphatics, 248n.7
Falstaff (character), 135, 136–37
family. *See* generations: relations between; inheritance
Fang, Master (character), 139
Fatal Vision (McGinniss), 111
Federalist Papers, 184
feminism, 9; in *The Merchant of Venice*, 81–82
Ferguson, Robert, 10
Few Good Men, A (movie), 105
Feynman, Richard, xiv
fiction vs. history, 143–55
Final Verdict (St. Johns), 105
Firm, The (Grisham), 8
Fitzwater, Marlin, 33
Flaubert, Gustave, 7, 11, 169
Florizel (character), 191
Fogel, Judge, 164
Folger Shakespeare Library (Washington, D.C.), xiv–xv, 20
Ford, Gerald, 201
Fortas, Abe (Justice), 197
Fortinbras (character), 91, 94
Fortunes of Falstaff, The (Wilson), 136
Founding Fathers (U.S.), 59, 116, 117, 131. *See also* republicanism; U.S. Constitution
Frankfurter, Felix (Justice), 98–99
fraud: in *The Merchant of Venice*, 72
freedom of speech. *See* censorship; defamation; U.S. Constitution: First Amendment
Freud, Sigmund, 90, 95, 126, 182, 216
Fried, Charles, 243–44
Frye, Northrop, 57
Furman v. Georgia, 50–51

gambling contract, 72
Garrison, Jim, 148
Geisler v. Petrocelli, 150–51
gender classification, 223–24
generations: relations between, 210–11, 213, 217–19
Georgia. See *Bowers v. Hardwick*; *Furman v. Georgia*
Gerry, Elbridge, 120
Gertz v. Robert Welch, Inc., 172

Gideon's Trumpet (Lewis), 236
Gilmore, Grant, 128
Glanville v. Courtney, 89
Globe Theatre (London), 14
Gloucester. *See* Humphrey, duke of
   Gloucester
Goddard, Harold C., 132, 182–83, 214
good faith: and contract law, 67
government: public criticism of, 190–91.
   See also civil disobedience; law: public re-
   spect for
Gray's Inn (London), 14, 139–40
Great Expectations (Dickens), 236
Greene, John, 139
Greenfield, Edward (Judge), 163
Greer, Judge, 162
Grisham, John, 8, 242
guilt: and pardons, 202

habeas corpus, 122–23
Hamilton, Alexander, 119, 133
Hamlet (Shakespeare), xv, 90–106; Ham-
   let's delay in, 91–92, 94–98, 183; Ham-
   let's lawyerly character in, 97–106; inher-
   itance in, 17, 216; "law's delay" in, 18,
   26, 92; movies of, 211; reason vs. passion
   in, 182–83; revenge in, 88, 90–106, 202,
   217; "to be, or not to be" speech in, 92
Hardwick, Michael, 36, 49
Harlan, John (Justice), 222–23, 225
Hart, H. L. A., 40
Harvard Law Review, 243
Hathaway, Anne, 42
Hayes, Eddie, 236
Hazlitt, William, 77, 132, 160
Helms, Jesse, 86
Henry, Patrick, 117
Henry IV (character), 135–36
Henry IV (Shakespeare): as allegory about
   law, 135–42, 143, 216; illegal authority
   in, 96; lord chief justice in, 135–38, 142,
   143, 241
Henry V (character), 137–39
Henry V (Shakespeare), 211
Henry VI, Part 2 (Shakespeare): "kill all the
   lawyers" reference in, 10, 15, 18, 22, 24–
   34, 100, 135, 138, 143, 240–41; succes-
   sion in, 216
Henry VII (character), 144, 145, 147, 148
hermeneutics, 130, 252n.4
Heywood, Thomas, 233
Hill, Anita, 56–57, 156–57

*Historic Doubts on the Life and Reign
   of King Richard the Third* (Walpole),
   145
history vs. fiction, 143–55
Hoffman, Dustin, 66
Hoffman, François-Benoît, 103
Holinshed, Raphael, 29, 235, 237
Holmes, Oliver Wendell, Jr. (Justice), 27,
   45, 184, 245; on free speech, 191; on law
   and morality, 41; on law and vengeance,
   93, 95, 96; on pardons, 202; on reading,
   xv
homosexuality, 36–40, 43–44, 45, 242
Hook (movie), 23–24, 34
Horneby, Thomas, 18
Hotspur (character), 135–36, 141
Humphrey, duke of Gloucester (character),
   32–33

Iago (character): "good name" speech by,
   163–64, 208
illegitimacy, 146–47, 174, 213, 217, 220–
   26
imagination, 129–32
Imperial Presidency, The (Schlesinger), 117,
   119
In Brief Authority (Biddle), 55
In Cold Blood (Capote), 152
inductive logic, 102
infidelity, 44–45, 170; charges of, in United
   States, 63; in *Measure for Measure*, 36; in
   Much Ado about Nothing, 165–75; as
   Shakespearean theme, 8; in *The Winter's
   Tale*, 176–81
inheritance: in *King Lear*, 211, 216–26; in
   Richard II, 206–9, 211; Shakespeare's,
   17, 19, 217
Inns of Court (London), 13–15, 29, 30,
   139–40, 233, 234, 235
insanity defense, 106, 160
interpretation: constitutional, 8, 20, 33, 75–
   76, 78, 130–31, 243–44; Jefferson on,
   122–23; in law and literature, 8–9, 20–
   21; in *Measure for Measure*, 58–61, 65;
   in *The Merchant of Venice*, 65, 68–70,
   74–75, 77–79; in *A Midsummer Night's
   Dream*, 129–32
Iran-Contra affair, 124, 198, 201, 213
Irving, John, 154
Irving, Washington, 10
Isabella (characer), 57–58, 65
"Is Shakespeare Dead?" (Twain), 230–34

Jackson, Andrew, 119
Jackson, Robert (Justice), 119, 123
James I (King of England), 15, 62–63, 88
jealousy, 160
Jefferson, Thomas, 122, 123, 132, 133, 220
Jeffries, Judge, 77
Jewish law: on *lex talionis*, 93–94
Jews. See *Merchant of Venice, The*
JFK (movie), 143, 148
John XXIII (Pope), 171
Johnson, Lyndon, 96
Johnson, Samuel, 11
Jonson, Ben, 232
judges: corrupt, 56, 194–98; in *The Merchant of Venice*, 77–79, 84, 85, 196; discretion of, 73–75, 186–87; good, 61–62. *See also* equity; judicial restraint; justice
judicial restraint, 98–99
Julia, Raul, 157
Julius Caesar (Shakespeare), 31; authority in, 216; as docudrama, 143; as high school text, xv, 108; legal themes in, 107–124; revenge in, 88, 107–8
Jurassic Park (movie), 248n.1
justice, 65; blindness of, 77, 79, 213–15, 226; in *Julius Caesar*, 107. *See also* equity; judges

Kafka, Franz, 11
Kakutani, Michiko, 254n.35
Kendall, Paul Murray, 145, 148
Kennedy, John F., 143, 148
Kennedy, Ted, 154
King John (Shakespeare), 216, 225
King Lear (Shakespeare), xv; illegitimacy in, 174, 213, 217, 220–26; inheritance in, 17, 211; legal issues in, 210–26; power void in, 55, 96
kings: divine right of, 198, 199
Kipling, Rudyard, 169
Kluger, Richard, 236
Knight, W. Nicholas, 31, 89, 233, 237, 257n.4
Kohler, Josef, 49
Kott, Jan, 160
Kozinski, Alex, 154
Kronman, Anthony, 117
Kyd, Thomas, 232, 233

"Lady or the Tiger, The" (Stockton), 28–29
Laertes (character), 91, 94, 106
Lakeside v. Oregon, 110–11

Lambarde, William, 235
Lambert, Edmund, 16–17, 217, 221
Lane, John, 19
language: importance of, to lawyers, 7, 97–98, 141–42, 240, 248n.7; Shakespeare's, 239. *See also* reading; writing
Laski, Harold, 27
Last Brother, The (McGinniss), 154
law: in Elizabethan England, 13–15, 66, 72, 73, 89, 103–4, 167–70, 195, 234–35, 241–43; evolution of, 90–106; and human behavior, 58–60, 90–106, 128, 240; as humanism, 5, 6–7; and literature, xi–xvii, 4–21, 239; multidisciplinary studies in, xi–xvii, 9, 239; passion vs. reason in, 181–87; perverted, 32–34, 187–92, 193; and public policy, 68, 70–71, 84–85; public respect for, 44–46, 188, 200–202; Roman, 72; as science, 5–6; Shakespeare's knowledge of, xi–xvi, 11–20, 168–70, 217, 227–40; strict adherence to, 65–73; teaching of, through Shakespeare's plays, xii, 240. *See also* criminal law; dead-letter statutes; lawyer(s); U.S. Supreme Court; *specific legal issues and cases*
—letter vs. spirit of: in *Measure for Measure*, 58–61, 65; in *The Merchant of Venice*, 65–73; in *A Midsummer Night's Dream*, 126, 127–28, 131; in *The Winter's Tale*, 176–87
Law and Humanities Institute, 6–7, 10
Law and Letters in American Culture (Ferguson), 10
Law and Literature (Posner), xvii, 5–6, 95–96
Lawe, John, 170
"law revels," 14
lawyer(s): benefits of literature to, 6, 7, 240; famous creators among, 10–11, 103; Hamlet as, 97–103; ideal of, 117; interest of, in Shakespeare, xv–xvi; oral advocacy by, 108–13, 208–9, 240; in Shakespeare's audiences, 13–15, 30–31, 235; Shakespeare's complimentary portrait of, 135–38, 142, 143, 241; Shakespeare's reference to killing all, 10, 15, 18, 22–34, 100, 135, 138, 143, 240–41; thinking like, 101–3; and trial by combat, 205–6. *See also* language; law; "literary lawyers"; U.S. Supreme Court; *names of specific lawyers, judges, and justices*

Least Dangerous Branch, The (Bickel), 47
Lee, Harper, 8
Legal Imagination, The (White), 9–10, 131
legislature, 117–21
"lender liability doctrine," 71
Levy v. Louisiana, 222–25
Lewis, Anthony, 236
lex talionis, 93–94
liability, 144
libel. *See* defamation
libel per se, 167. *See also* defamation per se
Lincoln, Abraham, 11, 122, 123, 133
lion similes, 46
"literary lawyers," 6, 95, 183
literature: reader's response to vs. author's
    intent in, 130; use of history in, 143–55;
    use of legal structures in, 4–5, 8, 102;
    value of, 6–7, 240. *See also* law: and liter-
    ature
litigation psychosis, 88
London: law as theater in, 13. *See also* Inns
    of Court
lord chief justice (character), 135–38, 142,
    143, 241
Lost Lawyer, The (Kronman),117

Macbeth (Shakespeare), xv, 96, 216
Macbird (Garson), 96
MacDonald, Jeffrey, 111–12
McGinniss, Joe, 111, 154
Machiavelli, Niccolò, 115
Machiavellian Moment, The (Pocock), 115–
    16
Madame Bovary (Flaubert), 11, 169
Madison, James, 184, 190
"Madisonian dilemma," 42
madness, 183. *See also* insanity defense
Mailer, Norman, 152
Maine, Henry Sumner, 68, 207–8
Malcolm, Janet, 153–54
Malone, Edmund, 229
Manningham, John, 14–15, 140
Margolick, David, 162–63, 164
Marlowe, Christopher, 232
marriage contracts, 18–19, 42–43
Marshall, John (Justice), 186, 199, 245
Marshall, Thurgood (Justice), 91
Marston, John, 233
Matisse, Henri, 103
Meaning of Shakespeare, The (Goddard),
    182
Measure for Measure (Shakespeare): cor-

rupt judges in, 195–96; infidelity in, 8,
    127; legal impact of, 241; legal themes in,
    11, 35–64, 65, 75, 80, 93, 143, 188; at
    New York Shakespeare Festival, xi–xii;
    power void in, 55–56, 96, 215
Meese, Edwin, 129
Melville, Herman, 10, 169, 231
Merchant of Venice, The (Shakespeare), xv;
    corrupt judge in, 77–79, 84, 85, 196; in-
    heritance in, 216; legal impact of, 241; as
    legal parable, xii, 3–4, 7, 11, 17, 35, 64–
    89, 127–28, 131, 143, 202, 245; legal
    programs on, 10; mercy in, 52, 54;
    sources for, 17; trial scene in, 176, 181,
    200. *See also* Portia; Shylock
mercy, 52–54, 65, 201; Portia's speech on,
    75, 76–77, 79, 200
meritocracy: vs. inheritance, 207–8, 219–
    20, 225
Middle Temple (London), 14, 29, 140
Midsummer Night's Dream, A (Shake-
    speare), 125–35, 191, 215, 241
Milkovich v. Lorain Journal Co., 163
Milton, John, 11, 122, 181, 241
minorities. *See* outsiders
miscegenation, 41
Misérables, Les (musical), 45
Moby Dick (Melville), 169
moderation: in application of law, 58, 62
morality: legal enforcement of, 35, 37–43,
    63. *See also* privacy
More, Thomas (Sir), 148, 196, 198
Morris, Robert and Gouverneur, 119
Mortimer, John, 81
Morton, John, 148
Moscow trials, 209
Mountjoy, Mary, 18
Much Ado about Nothing (Shakespeare):
    defamation in, 165–75; infidelity in, 19;
    movie of, 165, 211; sources for, 168–70
Mystery of the Princes, The (Williamson),
    148

name. *See* reputation
Nashe, Thomas, 235
National Endowment for the Arts, 86
National Enquirer, 153
New York County Lawyers' Association,
    10
New Yorker magazine, 153–54
New York Shakespeare Festival (New York
    City), xi, xvii, 157

New York Times, 108, 162
New York Times v. Sullivan, 172, 190
Nicholson, Jack, 105
Nietzsche, Friedrich, 184, 185
Nixon, Richard M., 119, 120, 197, 199, 201. *See also* Watergate incident
Nixon Tapes case, 199
nonenforcement of laws. *See* dead-letter statutes
nonfiction novels, 144, 152
North, Oliver, 124, 198

obscenity, 86. *See also* censorship
O'Connor, Sandra Day, xv, 20, 81
Oedipal complex, 90, 95
Oedipus Rex (Sophocles), 179, 180
"Of Judicature" (Bacon), 197–98
"Of Revenge" (Bacon), 94
Olivier, Laurence, 90, 106, 210–11
On Acting (Olivier), 90
Onassis, Jacqueline Kennedy, 163
oracle. *See* Delphic oracle
oral advocacy, 108–13, 208–9, 240
Othello (Shakespeare), 86, 183; defamation in, 156–65; infidelity in, 19; inheritance in, 216–17
outsiders: and strict adherence to law, 65, 74, 79–82

Papp, Joseph, xi, 107–8
Paradise Lost (Milton), 122, 241
Paradoxes of Legal Science (Cardozo), 183–84
pardons, 199, 200–202
passion: crimes of, 160, 183; vs. reason in law, 181–87. See also *Civilization and Its Discontents*
Paulina (character), 189–90, 191
Pentagon Papers case, 47, 123, 190
"People, Yes, The" (Sandburg), 207
Pepys, Samuel, 125, 126
Pericles, 113
Philadelphia Convention, 119
Phillips, O. Hood, 234
Pickwick Papers, The (Dickens), 236
poaching, 16
Pocock, J. G. A., 116
Poethics and Other Strategies of Law and Literature (Weisberg), 7, 82, 234
Polonius (character), 91, 106, 163, 164, 165
Populist movement, 219

Portia (character): appeal of, 83–85; morality of, 76–79, 81–82, 86, 196; ruling by, 66, 68–73, 131, 200; similarities between Isabella and, 65
Posner, Richard, 10, 35; on *Hamlet*, 90, 95–96, 251nn. 15 and 21; on *Julius Caesar*, 109, 112; on law and literature, xiv, xvii, 5–9, 11, 58, 239, 251n.21, 258n.9; on law in biased system, 74; on *Measure for Measure*, 60–61; on power, 59; on trial scenes, 12; on vengeance and law, 88
Powell, Lewis (Justice), 47, 49, 241
power: abuse of, 54–57; contest for, in *Julius Caesar*, 117–21; delegation of, 55–56, 213, 215–16; illegal, in Shakespeare's plays, 55, 96, 215; lack of, in *Henry VI, Part 2*, 25; lack of, in *King Lear*, 55, 96, 215–16; lack of, in *Richard II*, 55, 119, 199; succession to, 216–20. *See also* ends and means; sexual harassment
prejudice: in *The Merchant of Venice*, 66, 71, 76–77, 79–84, 85–86
presidency, 117–21. *See also* executive privilege; sovereign immunity
Presumed Innocent (Turow), 8
privacy, 36–37, 43–44, 149
professionalism, xiv
Progressive movement, 219
Prosser and Keeton on Torts, 166, 168
public policy, 68, 70–71, 84–85
Pudd'nhead Wilson (Twain), 231–32, 236
punishment: cruel and unusual, 49–51
Pyramus and Thisbe (from *A Midsummer Night's Dream*), 125, 126, 129

QB VII (Uris), 236
Quiney, Richard, 19

racism: in *The Merchant of Venice*, 76. *See also* miscegenation
reading: importance of, 11–12, 30
Real Anita Hill, The (Brock), 56
reason: vs. passion in law, 181–87
"Reason, Passion, and 'The Progress of the Law' " (Brennan), 185
Rehnquist, William (Justice), 54, 163
Reid, Alistair, 153
Reitman v. Mulkey, 48
Renaissance: and republicanism, 115; similarities between contemporary United States and, 242–43. *See also* law: in Elizabethan England

Report of the Committee on Homosexual Offenses and Prostitution (Wolfenden Report), 38, 40, 43, 48
representation: in court, 208
republicanism: in *Julius Caesar*, 108, 113–17; in *A Midsummer Night's Dream*, 132–34; in United States, 118, 119–21. *See also* democracy
Republican National Convention (1992), 23, 39
reputation, 143, 144; as theme of *Othello*, 156–65; and "what's in a name?" 241. *See also* defamation
Restatement (Second) of Torts, 173
revenge. *See* vengeance
revenge plays, 86–87
revolution: and lawyers in *Henry VI, Part 2*, 26–33. *See also* American Revolution
Rich, Frank, 108
Richard, duke of York (character), 145, 146–48
Richard II (character), 141
Richard II (Shakespeare), 135; legal themes in, 193–209; power void in, 55, 119; succession in, 216
Richard III (character): imaginary civil lawsuit against Shakespeare by, 149–51, 154–55; Shakespeare's portrayal of, 144–48, 154–55, 156, 165
Richard III (Shakespeare), 86; as docudrama, 143–55; illegal authority in, 96; movie of, 211; succession in, 216
robbery, 162–63
Roberts, Burton (Judge), 236
Robespierre, Maximilien-François-Marie-Isidore de, 29
Roe v. Wade, 39
Rogers, Earl, 105–6
Rogers, Philip, 17–18
Roman law, 72
Romeo and Juliet (Shakespeare), xv, 20, 217, 241
Roosevelt, Franklin D., 120
Rossiter, A. P., 148
Rousseau, Jean-Jacques, 128

St. Johns, Adela Rogers, 105
Sandburg, Carl, 207
Scalia, Antonin (Justice), 194
Schama, Simon, 155
Schlesinger, Arthur, 117, 119, 121
Schumann, Robert, 103

Scofield, Paul, 210
Scott, Walter, 11
Scottish law, 62–63
Scrutton, Judge, 162
searches: illegal, 123
se defendendo, 103–4
self-deprecation, 111
settlement, 140–41
sexual conduct. *See* homosexuality; infidelity; morality; privacy
sexual harassment, 156; in *Measure for Measure*, 56–57, 195
sexual repression, 57–58
Shakespeare, John, 16–17, 221, 234
Shakespeare, Judith, 19
Shakespeare, Susanna, 19, 169–70
Shakespeare, William: audiences of, 13–15, 30–31, 235; on civil disobedience, 191; inheritance of, 17; judicial citations of works by, 20–21, 54, 99, 110–11, 163, 194, 222, 241–42, 244–45; on lawyers, 11, 15, 18, 22–34, 100, 135–38, 142–43, 240–41; legal knowledge of, xi–xvi, 11–20, 168–70, 217, 227–40; legal legacy of, 20, 89, 239–45; as legal reformer, 31; "lost years" of, xiii, 228, 237, 240; marriage of, 42; modern relevance of, xvi–xvii, 12, 240, 242; popularization of works of, xv; on vengeance, 88; will of, 19, 217, 235; as writer of "Shakespeare's" works, 238, 240. *See also* law: in Elizabethan England; law: and literature; *names of plays and characters of*
"Shakespeare, the Animated Tales," xv
Shakespearean Tragedy (Bradley), 151
Shakespeare Our Contemporary (Kott), 160
Shakespeare's Hidden Life (Knight), 233
Shakespeare v. Lambert, 16–17, 217, 221
Shallow, Justice (character), 139, 140
Shaw, George Bernard, 94
Shawn, William, 154
Shays' Rebellion, 27
Shelley, Percy Bysshe, 245
Sherman, Roger, 120
Shylock (character), 65, 66, 79, 82–83, 85–86, 127–28, 221
Silence, Justice (character), 139
Simple Justice (Kluger), 236
Simpson, Alan, 156–57, 159, 163
slander. *See* defamation
Slander of Women Act, 170

slander per se, 167, 172, 173, 174. *See also* defamation per se
Smiley, Jane, 225–26
Smith, Rafe, 170
Snare, Master (character), 139
Socrates, 128
sodomy, 36–37, 39–40, 43–45, 49, 62
"Sonnet LXV and the 'Black Ink' of the Framers' Intention" (Fried), 243–44
sonnets (Shakespeare's): legal references, 14, 258n.8; reputation in, 156
Sophocles, 128, 179, 180
sovereign immunity, 213. *See also* executive privilege; government; law: public respect for
Sowell, Thomas, 124
Specter, Arlen, 186–87
Spielberg, Steven, 23, 34, 248n.1
Star, 153
Steel Seizure case, 119, 123
Stephen, James (Sir), 95
Stevens, John Paul (Justice), 28, 40–41, 47, 48, 111, 237
Stevenson, Robert Louis, 11
Stewart, Potter (Justice), 159
Stockton, Frank, 29
Stone, Harlan F. (Justice), 89
Souter, David, 12
Stone, Oliver, 31, 143, 148
Story, Joseph (Justice), 119, 186
"Stratford tithes," 18
Stravinsky, Igor, 103
"strict scrutiny," 223–24. *See also* equal protection
Supreme Court. *See* U.S. Supreme Court
synergy, 4

Taming of the Shrew, The (Shakespeare), 14
Taney, Roger (Justice), 131
taxes: estate and inheritance, 219
television: in courtroom, 12–13; mock trial of Richard III on, 145, 149; Shakespeare's plays on, 210–11
Tempest, The (Shakespeare), 169, 245
Tempting of America, The (Bork), 41
testimony: questionable, 144
Tey, Josephine, 145
Thackeray, William Makepeace, 11
Thomas, Clarence, 56–57, 156–57, 159
Thoreau, Henry David, 187
Thousand Acres, A (Smiley), 225–26
To Kill a Mockingbird (Lee), 8

totalitarianism, 28
Tower of London, 145, 146, 147
trial by combat, 202–6, 213
trial lawyers. *See* lawyer(s)
trial scenes: as dramatic literary technique, 8, 12–13, 102; *Hamlet*'s play-within-a-play likened to, 105–6; in *The Merchant of Venice*, 3–4, 65–73, 176, 181; number of, in Shakespeare's plays, xii, 13; in plays by Shakespeare's contemporaries, 15; in *Richard II*, 193–94; in *A Thousand Acres*, 225–26; in *The Winter's Tale*, 176–81. *See also* advocacy; fair trials
Troilus and Cressida (Shakespeare), 31
Truman, Harry S., 123
Tudor dynasty, 144–48, 155
Tumey v. Ohio, 195
Turow, Scott, 8, 242
Twain, Mark, 230–32, 233, 236, 237
Twelfth Night (Shakespeare), xv, 14–15, 140, 196

U.S. Constitution: Eighth Amendment to, 49–50; First Amendment to, 150, 158, 161, 163; Fourteenth Amendment to, 81, 213, 221; interpretation of, 8, 20, 33, 75–76, 78, 130–31, 243–44; lawyers as upholders of, 34; on presidential pardons, 201. *See also* Constitutional Convention; Founding Fathers; interpretation; republicanism; U.S. Supreme Court
U.S. Senate: and Bork, 44, 186; and Thomas, 156–57
U.S. Supreme Court: on capital punishment, 50–51; on defamation, 172–73; on desuetude, 48; on executive privilege, 199; on fair trials, 195; on free press, 190–91; on illegitimacy, 221–24; likened to Delphic oracle, 18; on privacy, 43–44; on reputation, 159; Shakespearean citations by, 20–21, 54, 99, 110–11, 163, 194, 222, 241–42, 244–45; on slavery, 131; on suspension of habeas corpus, 123
United States v. Nixon, 199
Uris, Leon, 236
usury law, 16–17, 71, 85

vanity, 136, 138, 139
vengeance: in *Hamlet*, 90–106, 202; and law, 171, 182; in *The Merchant of Venice*, 66, 86–88
Vidal, Gore, 155

Vienna: medieval law in, 36, 79–81. *See also* Alien Statute
"void as against public policy" doctrine. *See* law: and public policy

Walford, John, 16
Walken, Christopher, 157
Wall Street (movie), 31
Walpole, Horace, 145
Washington, George, 118
Watergate incident, 121, 201, 213
Watt v. Longsdon, 161–62
Webster, Daniel, 11, 141
Webster, John, 232, 233
Weinberger, Caspar, 201
Weisberg, Richard, 10; on *Hamlet*, 98, 251n.15; on law and literature, 6–8, 11, 234, 257n.2; on *The Merchant of Venice*, 77, 82–83; on Twain, 231
Westminster Hall (London), 13
When Lawyers Write (Weisberg), 7, 257n.2
White, James Boyd, 9–10, 11, 102, 131
Whitney v. California, 190
Wigmore, John, 194, 257n.6

Williams, William Carlos, xii
Williamson, Aubrey, 148
wills: in *Richard II*, 206–9; Shakespeare's, 19, 217, 235
Wilson, John Dover, 136
Winter's Tale, The (Shakespeare), 169–70, 241; defamation in, 175, 176–92; infidelity in, 19
Wisconsin, 63
Wolfe, Tom, 144, 236
Wolfenden Report, 38, 40, 43, 48
Woodville, Elizabeth, 146–47
wordplay. *See* language
Wordsworth, William, 11
World According to Garp, The (Irving), 154
Wouk, Herman, 8, 236
writing: reading literature of benefit to, 7, 240, 257n.2

Yale Journal of Law and Humanities, 10
Yale Law Journal, 116

Zenger, John Peter, 190

CPSIA information can be obtained
at www.ICGtesting.com
Printed in the USA
LVHW011630091222
734911LV00005B/511